The Effects of Early Adversity on Neurobehavioral Development

The Minnesota Symposia on Child Psychology

Volume 31

The Effects of Early Adversity on Neurobehavioral Development

The Minnesota Symposia on Child Psychology

Volume 31

Edited by

Charles A. Nelson
The University of Minnesota

2000

LAWRENCE ERLBAUM ASSOCIATES, PUBLISHERS
Mahwah, New Jersey   London

Lawrence Erlbaum Associates, Inc., Publishers
10 Industrial Avenue
Mahwah, New Jersey 07430

Cover design by Kathryn Houghtaling Lacey

Library of Congress Cataloging-in-Publication Data

The effects of early adversity on neurobehavioral development / edited by Charles A. Nelson.
    p. cm. – (Minnesota symposia on child psychology ; v. 31)
  Includes bibliographical references and index.
  ISBN 0-8058-3406-0 (cloth : alk. Paper)
    1.   Child psychopathology—Etiology. 2. Pediatric neuropsychiatry. 3. Prenatal
Influences. 4. Stress in children. I. Nelson, Charles A. (Charles Alexander) II. Minnesota
Symposia on child psychology (Series) ; v. 31.

  RJ499 .E34 2000
  618.92'89071—dc21

                                         00-041100

Printed in the United States of America
10   9   8   7   6   5   4   3   2   1

Contents

Preface

The present volume represents the 31st in our long, established series of the Minnesota Symposium on Child Psychology.

The Minnesota Symposium has been around long enough to have witnessed rather substantial changes in its 31 years. Not surprisingly, these changes are reflected in the field of developmental psychology as a whole. Early in its history, for example, the symposium provided a survey of child psychology, broadly defined; thus, we would have represented on our stage experts in cognitive development, social development, perceptual development, and so forth. As the many specialties within our discipline began to form and take hold, the Symposium was transformed to represent the latest and most cutting edge research within a given domain; for example, there are volumes specifically dedicated to cognitive development, social development, and perceptual development. The next metamorphosis, not surprisingly, was for our specialties to become specialized. Unfortunately, with this superspecialization came the potential for insularity. In response to this trend, we have begun to see movement toward integration within and across specialties and disciplines. I believe this trend captures where we currently are in the evolution of developmental psychology (perhaps psychology as a whole); it is exemplified in several recent symposium volumes on, for example, *Dynamical Systems* (edited by Megan Gunnar) and *Cultural Processes in Child Development* (edited by Ann Masten).

Volume 31 of the Minnesota Symposium series continues this trend, and then some. As is becoming increasingly obvious, there has been a burgeoning of interest in the relation between biological development, particularly brain development, and behavioral development. I, for one, welcome this shift in focus, as it does a better job of reflecting the whole child, and all of development. Not surprisingly, many of the individuals who are concerned with the theoretical side of brain-behavior (or biology and behavior) relations are also concerned with the more practical side. Thus, one might ask how a particular insult, be it biological or psychological, affects development in particular domains. The chapters that comprise the current volume collectively capture this subtle dance between biological development and behavioral development in the service of examining the effects of early adversity on neurobehavioral development. Individuals interested in this volume will likely represent the disciplines of developmental psychology and psychopathology, child psychiatry, toxicology, developmental and behavioral pediatrics, behavioral neurology, and special education.

The first three chapters in this volume represent traditional approaches to early childhood risk: specifically, the effects of nutritional deprivation on neurobehavioral development; the sequelae of early pre- or perinatal injury; and the effects of early teratogenic exposure. In the first chapter, for example, Raghavendra Rao and Michael Georgieff, of the University of Minnesota, provide an excellent tutorial on the effects of early nutrition on brain and behavioral development. Drs. Georgieff and Rao are neonatologists, and Dr. Georgieff directs the University's Neonatal Intensive Care Unit Follow Up program. An international authority on nutrition, Dr. Georgieff draws on his research on iron deficiency to illustrate the effects of early nutrition on neurobehavioral development. In chapter 2, Susan Rose of the Albert Einstein College of Medicine (along with her coauthor, Judith Feldman), describes her ground-breaking cross-sectional and longitudinal studies on the effects of pre- or perinatal risk factors on early cognitive development, with a particular emphasis on the effects of prematurity. And, in chapter 3, Sandra and Joseph Jacobson from Wayne State University (both pioneers in examining the effects of teratogen exposure) discuss their work on the effects of alcohol, lead, and PCB exposure on cognitive development. As is the case with the Rose and Feldman chapter, the Jacobsons describe both the short-term and long-term effects of such exposure on development.

The next two chapters in the volume are concerned with the effects of deleterious postnatal environments on neurobehavioral development. In chapter 4, for example, Dana Johnson, from the University of Minnesota, reviews the work to date on the effects of institutionalization on child development broadly construed. A neonatologist by training, Dr. Johnson is Director of the University's International Adoption Clinic. He is the foremost expert on the pediatric sequelae of institutionalized adoption, and this expertise is clearly illustrated in his contribution to this book. Importantly, this work is complemented by the following chapter, also written by a colleague at the University of Minnesota, Dr. Megan Gunnar. Dr. Gunnar is perhaps the leading expert on the effects of early stress on human psychobiological development. She has done landmark studies on stress reactivity in infants, and more recently, on children who have experienced institutionalized adoption. The story she tells in her chapter is fascinating, and goes a long way in accounting for how early stressful experiences affect biobehavioral development.

The theme of the effects of early exposure to stressful events continues into chapter 6, by Mary Schneider and Colleen Moore, of the University of Wisconsin. These authors are interested in a phenomenon that is exceedingly difficult to study in the human: the effects of prenatal stress on development. The reason this is difficult to study, of course, is because of the myriad of factors that cannot be controlled or regulated or in some cases even measured in the human child. As a result, Dr. Schneider has performed some elegant studies in the monkey, where one can more precisely examine how maternal stress affects the developing monkey.

The three chapters on pre- and postnatal exposure to stressful environments do a wonderful job of describing the behavioral and psychobiological sequelae of early stressful experiences. The next chapter in the volume brings with it a change in gears to consider the risk to children that are exposed to maternal psychopathology. In chapter 7 we hear from Geraldine Dawson and her colleague Sharon Ashman. Dr. Dawson is a pioneer in approaching developmental psychopathology from a neuropsychological perspective. She has done groundbreaking work on autism and, more recently, has been studying the effects of maternal depression on infants' neurobehavioral development. Dawson and Ashman share the results of their longitudinal study of this issue and, more generally, examine the importance of early maternal experience on later development

The final chapter is concerned with the genetic mechanisms that may underlie maladaptation and compromised developmental trajectories. Here we learn from Kathleen Merikangas, of Yale University, a leading expert in genetic epidemiology. Merikangas focuses attention on two things. First, how can we use genetic information in guiding our theories and research on developmental psychopathology, and second, what is known about the role of genes in influencing internalizing and externalizing disorders in children?

This is the final volume in this series that I will oversee, and is perhaps the one of which I am most proud. Although the work described in these chapters was presented in the 20th century, the integrative approach to development represents what I envision our science will be like in the 21st century. I hope that the ensuing years will prove my prediction prescient and not naïve.

Charles A. Nelson

The Effects of Early Adversity
on Neurobehavioral Development

The Minnesota Symposia
on Child Psychology

Volume 31

1

▼▼▼▼▼▼▼▼▼

Early Nutrition and Brain Development

Raghavendra Rao
Michael K. Georgieff
Division of Neonatology, Department of Pediatrics (RR and MKG)
and Institute of Child Development (MKG), University of Minnesota

Nutrients and growth factors regulate brain development during prenatal and postnatal life. Animal studies have demonstrated that brief periods of dietary manipulation, either deficiency (absolute and relative) or supplementation, during a vulnerable period of brain development could have long-lasting effects on the structure and function of the brain (Dobbing, 1990; Lucas, 1994). Although such a programming effect has not been conclusively demonstrated in humans, epidemiological studies suggest that early nutrition may influence neurodevelopment in humans as well (Lucas, 1998). However, due to its plasticity, a developing brain may also be more amenable to repair following such nutritional perturbations (Dobbing, 1990; Morris, Halliwell, & Bowery, 1989). Furthermore, due to the prioritization of nutrient delivery to the brain and the filtering effect of the blood-brain barrier, the developing brain may be spared the adverse effect of nutrient perturbations. Despite such structural brain sparing, nutritional deficiencies may still exert an adverse effect on the functional outcome of neurodevelopment (Georgieff, 1998). For the same regulatory reasons, nutrient overabundance may produce positive, negative, or no effects on the brain. In this chapter, the association between nutrients and early neurodevelopment are discussed. The general principles of research on the interaction between early nutrition and neurodevelopment are discussed initially, followed by a brief discussion on the role of individual nutrients on neurodevelopment. Because of their global significance, two conditions—chronic energy malnutrition and iron deficiency—are reviewed. Finally, the role of nutrient supplementation on neurodevelopment is discussed.

GENERAL PRINCIPLES OF NUTRITION

All nutrients are essential for normal neuronal cell growth and development. The timing of delivery of the specific nutrient is important in determining its effect on brain development. For example, in rats, iron deficiency during the perinatal period results in a small brain size (Rao et al., 1999), decreased oxidative metabolism in cognitively important areas of the brain (de Ungria et al., 1999), and permanent adverse effects on learning and behavior (Felt & Lozoff, 1996), while iron deficiency in postweanling rats has minimal, if any, effect on brain size (Chen, Conner, & Beard, 1995) and no effect on oxidative metabolism (Mackler, Person, Miller, Inamdar, & Finch, 1978). Furthermore, brain iron deficits in such situations appear to be amenable to iron rehabilitation (Youdim & Ben-Shachar, 1987). Epidemiological studies have suggested that such an effect of timing might also be operational in humans. Although early nutritional restriction during the intrauterine period (e.g., due to placental vascular insufficiency) results in a smaller brain size in infants, late onset intrauterine growth retardation (IUGR) due to pregnancy-induced hypertension in the mother has a brain-sparing effect (Greene, 1991). Similarly, while the adverse cognitive effects associated with early iron deficiency appear to be irreversible (Lozoff, 1990), those present in iron-deficient older infants and children probably could be reversed by iron therapy (Bruner, Joffe, Duggan, Casella, & Brandt, 1996).

A nutrient that promotes normal brain development at one time may be toxic at another. For example, while iron is essential for normal brain development during infancy, abnormal iron homeostasis with demonstrable iron deposition has been postulated in the pathogenesis of such neurodegenerative disorders as Parkinson's disease (Kienzl et al., 1995) and Alzheimer's disease in adults (Cornett, Markesbery, & Ehmann, 1998). In addition, a nutrient that promotes normal brain development at a particular concentration may be toxic at another, as seen by the development of microcephaly and mental retardation with exposure to high levels of vitamin A during early pregnancy (Willhite, Hill, & Irving, 1986). Many nutrients are regulated within a narrow therapeutic range.

Individual nutrients can affect brain development through their effect on neuroanatomy, neurochemistry, or both. The structural effects are due to the effect of nutrients on cell division and growth. Such an effect on neurons would affect the size of the developing brain, while the effect on supporting structures (e.g., oligodendrocytes) could affect myelination and nerve conduction. Neurochemical effects of nutrients are mediated through neurotransmitter–receptor synthesis and regulation. While malnutrition (deficiency or overabundance) of any of the nutrient categories could adversely affect brain development, certain nutrients appear to exert a more profound effect than others. Depending upon the nutrient and the timing of its malnutrition, these adverse effects could be reversible or permanent. Table 1.1 provides a list of the nutrients and their putative effect on the developing brain.

Just as nutrient deficiencies can have an adverse effect, supplementation of certain nutrients may have a beneficial effect on neurodevelopment. Supplementation of infant formula with certain long-chain polyunsaturated fatty acids (LCPUFAs,

TABLE 1.1

Effect and the Putative Mechanism of Individual Nutrients on Neurodevelopment

Nutrient	Clinical Effect	Putative Mechanism	Reference
Protein-Energy	Reduced IQ, verbal ability and spatial ability	Decreased cell DNA and RNA, altered synaptogenesis, neurotransmission and myelination, and decreased growth factor concentration and activity	Bass et al., 1970; Chanez et al., 1985; Cragg, 1972; Jones & Dyson, 1976; Winnick & Rosso, 1969
Iron	Reduced DQ, learning and memory tasks, behavioral abnormalities (affect and interpersonal interactions)	Hypomyelination and impaired lipid metabolism, altered neurotransmission, energy failure and decreased DNA synthesis	Dallman, 1985; Georgieff et al., 1992; Guiang et al., 1997; Larkin & Rao, 1990; Tanaka et al., 1995; Yehuda, 1987, 1990
Iodine	Reduced IQ	Being a major constituent of thyroid hormones, affects gene expression of other hormones and growth factors	Kretchmer et al., 1996; Russel, 1998; Vulsma & Kooistra, 1995
Zinc	Impaired learning and response to stimulus, reduced activity and attention	Altered DNA and protein synthesis	Golub et al., 1995; Wasansuit, 1997
Vitamin A	Blindness, respiratory, and genitourinary infections	Altered retinal function, maintenance of cell metabolism, cellular integrity	Greer, 1997
Vitamin B6	Seizures and irritability	Altered N-methyl-D-aspartate receptors in the CNS	Eastman & Guilarte, 1992; Guilarte, 1993
Folic Acid	Deficiency has been postulated in neural tube defects	Altered methionine-homocysteine metabolism	Lewis, 1998; MCR Vitamin Study Research Group, 1991
Long-chain polyunsaturated fatty acids	No definable syndrome of deficiency in humans, supplementation is thought to enhance visual function and cognition in at-risk infants	Constituent of biological membranes, substrate for lipid-derived mediators of cell-to-cell communication and signal transduction	Carlson, 1997; Lucas, 1997
Nucleotides and ribonucleotides	No known deficiency states; has been supplemented to enhance growth in those with intestinal cell injury due to intrauterine growth retardation	Precursor of DNA and RNA	Cosgrove et al., 1996; Yu, 1998

3

discussed later) such as docosahexaenoic acid (DHA) and arachidonic acid (AA) (Carlson, 1997; Innis, 1997; Woltil, van Beusekom, Schaafsma, Muskiet, & Okken, 1998) or nucleotides (Axelsson et al., 1997; Woltil et al., 1995; Yu, 1998), as well as general fortification of preterm breast milk (Gordon, 1997; Lucas, 1998) may confer beneficial neurodevelopmental effects. While studies are essential to evaluate the effect of a particular nutrient on brain development in a controlled manner, it must be remembered that nutrients rarely act in isolation (Lozoff, 1990). The influence of an individual nutrient on brain development depends upon its interaction with other nutrients, the amenability of the developing brain to nutritional intervention, and environmental stimulation (Dobbing, 1990).

Fundamental Questions on the Relationship of Early Nutrition to Neurodevelopment

The importance of early nutrition on neurodevelopment has been the focus of research since the turn of the 20th century (Haiti, 1904) and has gained renewed interest recently (Dobbing, 1990). Initial studies focused on the outcome of children affected by early malnutrition from developing countries and were confounded by other environmental factors, such as lack of stimulation and poor socioeconomic status (Cravioto, de Licardie, & Birch, 1966). More recently, experimental nutritional interventions with strict randomization of groups and adequate follow-up have provided more compelling data that early nutrition affects brain development in humans (Gorman, 1995; Morley, 1996).

Any research on the interaction between early nutrition and brain development should:

1. Assess whether nutrient-induced structural alterations also result in functional alterations in the developing brain (e.g., behavior). An effect on brain structure without associated adverse functional outcome may not be of clinical significance (Dobbing, 1990).
2. Establish the closeness of the linkage between structural and functional outcome.
3. If the two are not closely linked, then explore the reasons for the variations in the functional (i.e., behavioral) outcome of nutritionally based alterations in brain development. If confounding covariables appear responsible for the variations in the functional outcome, the possible usefulness of these covariables in designing remedial measures that would reverse or minimize the adverse effects of malnutrition on neurodevelopment need to be evaluated.

Experimental Approach: Clinical Trials in Humans

To answer these fundamental questions, appropriate experimental methodology is necessary. One approach has been to conduct clinical studies in representative populations. By and large, these have been epidemiological studies of specific nutrient deficiency (with or without subsequent supplementation) in a population at risk (e.g., effect of iron deficiency on learning and behavior by Deinard, Gilbert, Dodds, & Egeland, 1981; Lozoff, Wolf, Urrutia, & Viteri, 1985; Walter, 1994). Epidemiological studies need not be on deficiency states alone. The effects of nutrient supplementation on neurodevelopment have also been studied by this method (Waber et al., 1981). While providing valuable information about the population at risk, the confounding variables that are also present in the populations studied can often result in indirect implications of the role of the nutrient in outcome measures in such studies.

One way to overcome the effect of confounding variables is to conduct randomized clinical trials of individual nutrients. For ethical reasons, these have been mostly supplementation studies, although short-term deprivation studies have also been conducted (Walter, De Andraca, Chadud, & Perales, 1989). Examples of such studies include protein-energy supplementation of infants and children (reviewed by Gorman, 1995), DHA supplementation on cognitive development and visual acuity of preterm infants (Carlson, 1997), and folate supplementation during periconception and postconception to prevent neural tube defects (MRC Vitamin Study Research Group, 1991). To overcome the effect of confounding variables, as well as to avoid inferences due to chance alone (beta error), large sample sizes are necessary. Despite having a sufficiently large number of enrollees, a clinical trial may still run the risk of assigning cause and effect to an epiphenomenon (i.e., both factors are true, but unrelated by cause and effect). Also, the data may be specific for the population from which the sample has been drawn and hence cannot be generalized. Finally, clinical studies usually do not provide any information about the mechanism of the interaction between the nutrient in question and neurodevelopment. They are useful to postulate questions about cause and effect, and therefore the putative mechanism. These postulations frequently lead to mechanistically based experimental designs in humans and in animal models.

Small-scale clinical trials have been conducted to evaluate the putative mechanism through which a specific nutrient exerts its effect on neurodevelopment. An example of such a trial is the use of visual evoked response (VER) for assessing the effect of DHA supplementation in human infants (Birch, Hoffman, & Uauy, 1992). VER could be considered appropriate in this instance since it provides a measure of myelination of visual neural tracts, the putative mechanism through which DHA is hypothesized to be beneficial (Neuringer, Connor, & Lin, 1986). Such clinical trials have some shortcomings. The putative mechanism of interaction with neurodevelopment is generally obtained from animal models and may not be extrapolated to humans. Since the human trials evaluate the putative mechanism, there is a danger of assigning a false role (positive or negative) to the nutrient in question. A structural, metabolic, or both types of change in the brain may not imply or predict a related behavioral change in humans and animal models (Dobbing, 1990). Furthermore, the conventional tests used to evaluate the functional outcome in humans may not measure the motivational aspect and the capacity to perform. Finally, the small-scale clinical trials may not have any clinical relevance to the population at large.

In order to link nutrient status to neurodevelopment, large- and small-scale randomized clinical trials in humans must meet a certain standard to constitute a biologic proof of cause and effect. Typically, in nutrient-neurodevelopment research, psychological tests are used as outcome measures. According to Singer (1997), in planning a prospective clinical study, the psychologic assessment must: (a) be standardized (i.e., have a uniform set of procedures for administration and scoring); (b) be reliable (i.e., measure a cohesive construct in a similar fashion across time); and (c) be valid (i.e., measure the construct it purports to). Given the increasing knowledge of cognitive neuroscience [functional MRI (fMRI) and real time event related potentials (ERP)], a fourth criterion must now be considered; that is, the psychological assessment must be matched to the pathophysiology of the biologic event (Georgieff, 1998).

In matching the psychological assessment to the underlying central nervous system (CNS) pathology, most researchers rely on clinical or animal models. Evaluating for signs of spasticity in the lower extremities as an outcome measure of periventricular leukomalacia in preterm infants is an example of such a model. Lower extremities are preferentially affected in that condition due to involvement of the descending motor tracts that subserve the lower extremities (Volpe, 1998). While such *motor* models appear to be specific and sensitive to the underlying pathology, cognitive models are more difficult to create because of the diffuse nature of cognitive circuitry (Nelson, 1995). Applicability of such models in the evaluation of the cognitive system depends upon the insult and the brain structure vulnerable to injury in such insult. For example, since the hippocampus is targeted in iron deficiency (de Ungria et al., 1999; Erikson, Pinero, Connor, & Beard, 1997), evaluation of recognition memory could be considered a specific test for assessing the effect of iron deficiency on cognitive development. A more generalized test, such as the Bayley Scales of Infant Development, in such a situation probably has less predictive value (Walter, 1990). Conversely, Bayley Scales appear to be more useful for evaluation of the effect of protein-energy malnutrition, which has a more global effect on cognitive systems (Pollitt & Gorman, 1994). Other more complex behaviors (e.g., anxiety) recruit neural generators from across the CNS, and may be very difficult to assess with respect to nutrient involvement.

Experimental Approach: Animal Models

Research has relied heavily on animal models to understand the mechanisms of interaction between nutrition and brain development. Such models allow isolation of individual nutritional variables while controlling for genetic–environmental variables. With careful choice of the species (homology to human brain vis-à-vis structure, timing and nutrient homeostasis) and standardized tests (generally based on the specificity for the anatomic site), models can be created to test various hypotheses of interaction between nutrient(s) and brain development. Examples of such models include use of rats for evaluating the effect of iron deficiency on hippocampal metabolism (de Ungria et al., 1999) and function (Felt & Lozoff, 1996), and the use of rhesus monkeys to evaluate the effect of fatty acid deficiency on visual function (Neuringer et al., 1986). The weakness of any animal model is its relevance to the human, both structurally and functionally (Dobbing, 1990). Hence, the information obtained from animal models may not always be applicable to humans.

Model Building: An Integrated Approach

An integrated approach that combines all three experimental aspects will provide maximum information about the interaction between nutrition and neurodevelopment, and is thus ideal for research in this field. In observational (e.g., epidemiological) studies, the nutritional status and neurodevelopmental measurements are obtained at one time point to demonstrate an association between the two. A prevalence rate is calculated using the data. A randomized, double-blind, placebo, controlled trial then tests the hypothesis that the two conditions are interconnected in a cause-and-effect manner by matching non-nutritional confounding factors, such as socioeconomic status, parental education and involvement, in the experimental and control groups. An appropriate animal model will then evaluate the mechanism(s) involved in the interaction between the nutrient and brain structure, metabolism and function, and ways to correct the adverse effects, if any. The data from animal studies can then be used to fashion corrective and preventive measures in humans (initially as short clinical studies, and later applied to the whole population at risk). Thus, an integrated approach from field-to-bench-to-field, with each experimental approach complementing others, would provide the most comprehensive biological proof for the interaction between the nutrient and neurodevelopment.

SPECIFIC NUTRITIONAL CONDITIONS AFFECTING BRAIN DEVELOPMENT: PROTEIN-ENERGY MALNUTRITION

Protein-energy malnutrition (PEM) is the most common and extensively studied nutritional disorder in humans. Chronic energy deficiency, rather than protein deficiency, appears to be the significant underlying pathology in this condition (Pollitt & Gorman, 1994). Clinical conditions of PEM during the vulnerable period of brain development include starvation during early childhood (almost exclusively seen in developing countries) (Kretchmer, Beard, & Carlson, 1996), IUGR (Crouse & Cassady, 1994), and conditions that either prohibit adequate feeding (prematurity–acute illnesses during the neonatal period) or result in increased need (chronic illnesses: renal, gastrointestinal, cardiorespiratory, and infectious diseases) (Wahlig & Georgieff, 1995).

Clinical studies of postnatal PEM are confounded by the fact that it is rarely a pure clinical condition, often being associated with other nutrient deficiencies and environmental stressors (Cravioto et al., 1966; Pollitt & Gorman, 1994). In developing countries, chronic energy malnutrition is generally associated with poor parental nutritional status, education, or both, which could independently affect maternal–infant interactions (Dobbing, 1990). Even a relatively pure condition of PEM due to IUGR is associated with conditions known to affect postnatal mother–infant interactions, such as poor prenatal care, maternal smoking, teenage pregnancies and poor socioeconomic status (Crouse & Cassady, 1994).

Antenatal Chronic Protein-Energy Restriction

IUGR due to placental insufficiency is a good model for evaluating the effect of protein-energy restriction during the antenatal period on brain growth and development. Due to its rapid growth spurt, the brain is likely to be vulnerable to the effect of nutrient restriction during the intrauterine period. Studies have demonstrated decreased brain cell DNA (Chanez, Privat, Flexor, & Drian, 1985), decreased RNA content (Bass, Netsky, & Young, 1970; Winnick & Rosso, 1969), ultrastructural changes in synapses (Cragg, 1972; Jones & Dyson, 1976), decreased neurotransmitter production (Wiggins, Fuller, & Enna, 1984), altered myelination (McMorris & Dubois-Dalcq, 1988; Saneto, Low, Melnor, & de Vellis, 1988), and reduced growth factor concentrations and activity (Fellows, 1987; Nishijima, 1986) in growth restriction due to intrauterine PEM.

Long-term neurodevelopmental abnormalities have been demonstrated in small-for-gestational-age (SGA) infants affected by IUGR (Winer & Tejani, 1994). Up to 15% of asymptomatic infants born after a pregnancy complicated by maternal hypertension have mild neurodevelopmental abnormalities (Spinello et al., 1993). Cognitive rather than motor abnormalities appear to be the prevalent impairments (Gottleib, Biasini, & Bray, 1988).

Traditionally, infants and children affected by IUGR have been evaluated for cognitive impairments well after the infancy period (Winer & Tejani, 1994). Findings at this age are potentially confounded by environmental factors that could have a positive or negative influence on cognitive development. Cognitive evaluation during the neonatal period is probably the best chance to determine the effect of malnutrition on neurocognitive development in these infants as this is the time when postnatal environmental confounders have minimal influence. However, it should be noted that confounding environmental and genetic factors could still exert some influence on cognitive development at this age, since maternal nutritional status, socioeconomic status, education, smoking and chemical abuse, and poor prenatal care affect the fetus (Crouse & Cassady, 1994).

In this respect, a recent study by Strauss and Dietz (1998) is worthy of discussion. The study population consisted of approximately 45,000 infants followed in the National Collaborative Perinatal Project during the years 1959–76. The 2,719 SGA infants in this cohort were compared with 43,104 appropriate-for-gestational-age

(AGA) infants at 7 years of age. In addition, 220 of these SGA infants were compared with a subsequent AGA sibling and also with the 43,000 nonrelated AGA infants. Outcome variables were the Wechsler Intelligence Scale for Children (WISC) to assess intelligence and the Bender–Gestalt Test (BGT) to assess visual–motor development.

Children with IUGR had lower IQ (90.6 vs. 96.8) and BGT scores (57.3 vs. 62.3) in comparison to the AGA population cohort. However, in comparison to their AGA siblings, their IQ (91.0 vs. 92.4; $p = 0.19$) and BGT scores (58.9 vs. 60.3; $p = 0.18$) were not different. Only those SGA children who had a head circumference below 2 SD scored lower in both cohorts. The authors concluded that IUGR had little impact on intelligence and motor development except when associated with large deficits in head circumference (Strauss & Dietz, 1998).

However, such a conclusion may not be completely valid. While not significant at the 0.05 level ($p = 0.18$ and $p = 0.19$, for IQ and BGT scores, respectively; see aforementioned), SGA children did have a trend for lower IQ and BGT scores when compared with their AGA siblings, thus suggesting the possibility of a beta error in the study. Furthermore, the broad-based developmental tests used in the study might not have adequately assessed the neurodevelopmental impairments associated with mild (head sparing) IUGR. While they are good screening tools that provide a summary of overall developmental abilities, they lack sufficient specificity and sensitivity to identify any subtle effects on items such as spatial working memory, recognition memory, or memory strategy (Georgieff, 1998). Thus, more sensitive and specific electrophysiological and psychological tests could have discerned subtle neurodevelopmental abnormalities in this group of children.

Based on the evidence currently available, it can be concluded that: (a) chronic fetal PEM can reduce head size at birth—this reduced head size likely representing decreased number and size of the neurons, decreased myelination, and synaptogenesis; (b) the behavioral effects of such an interaction include reduced cognitive and spatial ability; and (c) head sparing during fetal PEM may or may not constitute a significant neurobehavioral risk.

Postnatal Protein-Energy Malnutrition

Prematurity. Preterm infants have significantly decreased nutrient stores and growth delays. Maternal–fetal nutrient delivery is maximal during the third trimester; being born early, preterm infants are denied this source of nutrients. The American Academy of Pediatrics Committee on Nutrition (1985) recommends the optimal diet for premature infants is one that supports growth at intrauterine rates, without imposing stress on the infants' immature metabolic or excretory functions. Due to the physiologic immaturity of the gastrointestinal and excretory systems, it may not be possible to emulate intrauterine growth rates in premature infants. Physical illnesses during their stay in the neonatal intensive care unit (NICU) also affect the nutritional requirements of these infants (Wahlig & Georgieff, 1995). Finally, health care providers may not be adept in providing optimal nutrition to these infants. As a result, 23% of infants with a birth weight < 1,500 gm become microcephalic (head circumference < 5th percentile) during their NICU stay (Hack et al., 1991). Furthermore, even with optimum nutrition, catch-up head growth to original percentiles may take many months in these infants (Georgieff et al., 1985). In light of the data from infants with smaller head size due to prenatal growth restriction, it is probable that delayed postnatal head growth could be associated with the impaired developmental outcome.

Hack et al. (1991) showed that small head size at 8 months is related to poor neurodevelopmental outcome at 8 years. Thus, postnatal head growth, which summarizes the adverse effects of many perinatal and postnatal risk factors, is a strong predictor of early development (Gross et al., 1983). Although multiple potential conditions could affect the head growth in preterm infants (e.g., hypoxia, intracranial hemorrhage), malnutrition appears to be an important one.

Infants who are AGA at birth and are malnourished < 4 weeks show rapid catch-up growth by the time of discharge from the NICU, reach the 50th percentile for head circumference by 12 months postconceptional age, and have average Mental Developmental Index (MDI) (99) and Performance Developmental Index (PDI) (95) scores (Georgieff, Hoffman, Periera, Bernbaum, & Hoffman-Williamson, 1985). The longer the duration of postnatal malnutrition (up to 4 weeks), the greater the velocity of catch-up head growth. In contrast, infants who are AGA at birth and are malnourished > 4 weeks show no catch-up head growth, reaching only the 20th percentile for head circumference at 12 months, with lower MDI (95) and PDI (86) scores. SGA infants demonstrate more profound head growth and developmental deficits even with a shorter duration of postnatal malnutrition. They do not experience catch-up head growth if the duration of postnatal malnutrition is longer than 2 weeks, as if the duration of postnatal malnutrition is an extension of the prenatal malnutrition already present.

Chronic Dietary Energy Deficiency. There is a low but significant association between measures of chronic mild to moderate energy malnutrition and suboptimal cognitive development in infants and children. Anthropometric measures of chronic energy malnutrition correlate with cognitive performance, visual motor integration, and measures of academic achievement (Wachs, 1995). However, a definite cause-and-effect relationship has yet to be established. Although biosocial factors and simultaneous deficiency of other nutrients might have confounded this association, supplementation studies argue for adequate energy nutrition for normal neurodevelopment (Gorman, 1995). Supplementation appears to have a beneficial effect on broad measures of cognitive development in preschool children (Gorman, 1995), particularly if supplementation encompasses both prenatal and postnatal periods of life (Waber et al., 1981). The beneficial effect appears to be less in younger infants. Long-term follow-up studies of the supplemented infants have demonstrated beneficial effects on scholastic achievement skills (Pollitt & Gorman, 1994), even though measures of IQ and of basic cognitive processes appear to be unaffected (Gorman, 1995).

It appears that there are critical windows for head growth in the young child. Once missed, rates of catch-up growth are reduced. Chronic energy deficit, either prenatal or postnatal, severe enough to affect catch-up head growth appears to result in significant developmental deficits. Nutritional interventions that aim to achieve optimum protein-energy nutrition are warranted during this period.

IRON DEFICIENCY

Iron deficiency is the second most common nutritional deficiency (after protein-energy), and the most common single nutrient deficiency in the world (Levin, Pollitt, Galloway, & McGuire, 1993). Infants are particularly prone to iron deficiency between the ages of 6 and 24 months (Lozoff, 1990), an age during which important developmental processes are occurring in the brain (Dobbing, 1990). Since iron is essential for oxidative phosphorylation, myelination, cell division and neurotransmission (Guiang & Georgieff, 1997), iron deficiency during this period appears to result in permanent cognitive impairments in spite of successful iron rehabilitation (Lozoff, 1990; Walter, 1994). Multiple theories have been postulated to explain the deleterious effect of iron deficiency on neurodevelopment; more than one mechanism probably is operative simultaneously.

Hypomyelination and Altered Lipid Metabolism

Iron is essential for lipid metabolism in the developing nervous system. The iron-containing multienzyme complex, Δ 9-desaturase, is involved in the production of monoenoic fatty acids essential for normal myelination (Larkin & Rao, 1990). Iron restriction during rapid brain growth spurt in rats results in reduction of myelin-specific lipids, such as 24:1w9, total lipids and total brain cholesterol (Larkin, Jarratt, & Rao, 1986), and is associated with decreased myelin (Larkin & Rao, 1990). Since myelination is regarded as a "once and for all" process that occurs only during early development, disruption of this process due to iron restriction could result in irreversible neurodevelopmental impairments (Larkin & Rao, 1990).

Decreased membrane fluidity index has been demonstrated in the plasma membranes of the hippocampus, striatum and cerebral cortex in iron deficiency because of a significant increase in the amount of cholesterol (Yehuda, 1987). It has been postulated that neuronal conduction is altered in states of decreased membrane fluidity index, which might contribute to the learning impairment seen in states of iron deficiency (Roncagliolo, Garrido, Walter, Periano, & Lozoff, 1998; Yehuda, 1990a).

Altered Neurotransmission

It has been hypothesized that the effects of iron deficiency on behavior are mediated by a decrease in the functional activity of dopamine-D2 receptors (Yehuda, 1990b). In states of iron deficiency, dopamine receptor-mediated behaviors have been found to be modified, resulting in reduced learning ability in perinatal rats (Yehuda, 1990b). Altered dopamine receptor, function, or both are potential central neurotransmitter mechanisms responsible for behavioral impairments present in iron deficiency (Felt & Lozoff, 1990).

Altered Neuronal Proliferation

Iron is an essential cofactor for ribonucleotide reductase, the rate-limiting step in DNA synthesis (Reinard & Ehrenberg, 1983). Brain regions that contain mitotically active neurons after birth (hippocampus and cerebellum) could thus be preferentially affected by early iron deficiency, resulting in decreased neuronal density and subsequently affecting neurodevelopment (Connor, 1994).

Altered Cellular Energy Metabolism

Iron in the form of cytochromes is a required component of cellular oxidative metabolism in the brain (Dallman, 1985). Decreased cytochrome c concentrations and cytochrome c oxidase activity have been demonstrated in early iron deficiency in animals (Dallman, 1985; Georgieff, Schmidt, Mills, Radmer, & Widness, 1992; Guiang, Georgieff, Lambert, Schmidt, & Widness, 1997; Tanaka et al., 1995), and in regions of the brain that are important for certain cognitive operations (e.g., memory) (de Ungria et al., 1999). As in nonbrain organs such as the heart, skeletal muscle, and the liver (Blayney, Royston, Jacobs, Henderson, & Muir, 1976; Mackler, Grace, & Finch, 1984; Masini et al., 1994), severe brain-iron deficiency could adversely affect cellular energy production and organ performance.

More than one mechanism is likely operating in the etiology of the cognitive abnormalities present in states of iron deficiency. Furthermore, a particular mechanism may be more specific at a given cognitive region than the others. For example, while the effect on DNA synthesis is likely to be more pervasive, as evidenced by the small brain size seen in animal models (Connor, 1994; Rao et al., 1999), the effect on energy metabolism appears to be nonuniform, with certain cognitively important areas being preferentially affected more than others (de Ungria et al., 1999). Similarly, the effect on the dopamine-D2 receptor will be operative only in areas that are rich in such receptors, while the effect on myelination will be maximum in the cognitive tracts in the brain and spinal cord (Larkin & Rao, 1990).

Determining the Likely Biologic Effect of Iron Deficiency

Behavioral assessments that are specific to the biologic effect of iron deficiency can be designed in humans and animal models. In the past, it was argued that the available investigative modalities would not be able to find a strong cause-and-effect association between the anatomic–biochemical derangement and the behavioral outcome in iron deficiency, especially during early development, because of the lack of specificity of the outcome measures (Dobbing, 1990). However, with the advent of electrophysiological [e.g., brain stem auditory evoked response (BAER) and ERP] and neuroimaging evaluations [fMRI, magnetic resonance spectroscopy (MRS)], more accurate evaluation is now a greater possibility (Nelson, 1997; Roncagliolo et al., 1998).

Clinical Syndromes of Iron Deficiency: Scope of the Problem

According to the third National Health and Nutrition Examination Survey (NHANES III, 1988–1994), in the United States, 9% (approximately 700,000) of toddlers aged 1 to 2 years are iron deficient, in spite of improved dietary iron intake (Looker, Dallman, Carroll, Gunter, & Johnson, 1997). Poor dietary intake of iron and gastrointestinal blood loss, either due to cow's milk intolerance or due to intestinal parasitosis, are the most common etiologies for iron deficiency during infancy and early childhood (Pearson, 1990).

Another group at risk for iron deficiency is teenage girls. NHANES III data suggest that 9% to 11% of adolescent girls and women of childbearing age (approximately 7.8 million women) are affected by iron deficiency (Looker et al., 1997). Iron deficiency in this group is due to excessive menstrual blood loss as well as to a diet poor in bioavailable iron. Pregnancy during teenage and early adulthood also puts this group at risk for iron deficiency (Groner, Holtzman, Charney, & Millitts, 1986).

Research from our laboratory over the last 10 years has identified a third group at risk for iron deficiency. Significant brain-iron deficiency has been demonstrated during the prenatal and perinatal periods in infants born after gestations complicated by conditions such as maternal diabetes mellitus, IUGR due to maternal hypertension (Chockalingam, Murphy, Ophoven, Weisdorf, & Georgieff, 1987; Georgieff et al., 1990; Georgieff, Petry, Wobken, & Oyer, 1996; Petry et al., 1992), or severe maternal iron deficiency (Rusia, Madan, Agarwal, Sikka, & Sood, 1995).

Severe maternal iron deficiency (Hgb < 8.5 gm/dL) occurs in < 1% of pregnancies in the United States. However, in developing countries, this appears to be the most common risk factor for perinatal iron deficiency (B. Lozoff, personal communication, 1999). IUGR due to maternal hypertension affects approximately 5% of all pregnancies. Decreased iron stores (serum ferritin levels) are found in approximately 50% of infants born after such pregnancies (Chockalingam et al., 1987). Based on the 1992 census, close to 75,000 infants with IUGR are born with low iron stores in the United States annually. Five to ten percent of gestations are complicated by maternal diabetes mellitus. Up to 65% of the infants born after such a pregnancy [infants of diabetic mothers (IDM)] have low body iron stores (approximately 150,000 infants annually; Georgieff et al., 1990). Hence, close to 225,000 infants are affected by prenatal and perinatal iron deficiency in the United States annually. It is estimated that close to one-fourth (75,000) of these infants are at risk for significant brain-iron deficiency (Georgieff et al., 1990).

Assessing Cognitive Effects Due to Iron Deficiency in Human Populations

Cognitive effects due to iron deficiency can be assessed at each of these age groups. Each age group poses advantages as well as disadvantages of such an evaluation to establish the link between iron and development.

Evaluation In Infants And Children. In humans, iron deficiency is most prevalent among 6- to 24-month-old infants, coinciding with the latter part of the brain growth spurt with active myelination and synaptogenesis in progress (Lozoff, 1990; Walter, 1994). Since deficiency of other nutrients is relatively uncommon during this period, especially in developed countries, the cognitive impairments uncovered in this age group could be attributed solely to iron deficiency. The disadvantages of studying this age group are that, for ethical reasons, no randomization is possible and it is not possible to eliminate confounding social variables (such as family background, maternal depression, neonatal factors, and blood lead levels) that could affect cognitive development in these infants and children (Lozoff, 1990; Lozoff et al., 1998). Nevertheless, most of our current knowledge on the interaction between iron and human neurodevelopment is derived from the extensive research in this age group.

Iron-deficiency anemia in 6- to 24-month-old infants has been associated with lower mental and motor capacities when compared with nonanemic infants (Lozoff, Brittenham, Viteri, Wolf, & Urrutia, 1982; Walter, Kowalskys, & Stekel, 1983). Their mental developmental score on the Bayley Scales on average is 10 to 12 points lower than the nonanemic controls, with particularly poor performance in verbal items (Lozoff, 1990). The poor performance in mental test scores could in part be related to behavioral disturbances (particularly in affect) that have been described in these infants (Lozoff et al., 1998). The general observation is that the more severe and chronic the iron-deficiency anemia the more pronounced the adverse effect on developmental test scores appears to be (Lozoff et al., 1987; Walter et al., 1989), being generally negligible in the absence of anemia (Lozoff, 1990; Nokes, van den Bosch, & Bundy, 1998). It is possible that refinements in the psychological assessment tests, the recent advances in neurocognitive investigative tools (fMRI, ERP and MRS), or both, could uncover subtle deleterious effects with less severe iron deficiency.

To establish conclusively a cause-and-effect relation between iron deficiency and developmental impairments, researchers have included a therapeutic trial of iron in their study designs. Improved cognitive abilities with iron treatment would provide convincing evidence that behavioral changes observed in iron-deficient infants are indeed due to iron deficiency and not due to an associated factor. By and large, iron supplementation has failed to reverse impaired cognitive abnormalities in iron-deficient infants and children despite correcting their hematological abnormalities (Lozoff, 1990; Lozoff et al., 1982; Walter et al., 1989). Two potential interpretations of the data exist. While failure of iron rehabilitation to reverse the cognitive impairments could be due to associated nutrient deficiencies and environmental factors, it could also suggest that the adverse effects of iron deficiency during infancy and early childhood are permanent and irreversible (Lozoff, 1990). Thus, conclusive biologic proof of a deleterious effect of iron deficiency on behavior remains lacking. Nevertheless, prevention of iron deficiency appears to be of utmost importance in infants and young children.

Evaluation Of Teenage Girls. By evaluating the cognitive effects of iron deficiency in teenage girls, one could potentially differentiate between the adverse effects of iron deficiency on neuroanatomy versus neurochemistry. Brain growth is relatively complete at this age; thus, iron deficiency is more likely to affect cognitive function through an effect on neurochemistry, rather than on neuroanatomy. However, as with infants and children, this study population cannot be randomized for ethical reasons. Deficiencies of other nutrients (e.g., zinc) that could also affect cognitive function are common in teenage girls (Golub, Keen, Greshwin, & Hendricks, 1995).

A limited number of studies have been conducted on the effect of iron deficiency on cognitive function in teenage girls. In a group of 13- to 18-year-old, nonanemic, iron-deficient adolescent girls, Bruner et al. (1996) demonstrated differential improvement on cognitive function after iron therapy. While learning and memory tests improved with 8 weeks of iron supplementation, tests for attention did not. Similarly, supplementation of iron during pregnancy in 18- to 24-year-old women improved the cognitive performance of the mother (Groner et al., 1986). Hence, iron-deficient adolescent girls appear to perform suboptimally. Unlike infants and younger children, iron rehabilitation appears to reverse these effects. The reversibility suggests that the adverse behavioral effects of iron deficiency in this group of children is probably mediated through neurochemical (e.g., dopamine receptor), neurophysiologic (e.g., oxidative phosphorylation) mechanisms, or both, and not by irreversible structural changes (e.g., myelination, cell division) in the brain.

Evaluation Of Cognitive Effects Of Fetal–Neonatal Iron Deficiency. The fetal–neonatal period offers an excellent opportunity to evaluate the cognitive effects of iron deficiency. Animal studies have demonstrated that specific cognitive structures, such as the hippocampus, appear to be particularly vulnerable to its effects (de Ungria et al., 1999; Felt & Lozoff, 1996). Hence, evaluation of hippocampally based cognitive function could potentially demonstrate the effects of iron deficiency during this age. However, infants who are at risk for iron deficiency during the perinatal period (IDM and IUGR) are also exposed to multiple neurological risk factors during the fetal–neonatal period. These risk factors (hypoxia, hypoglycemia, and polycythemia) could also target the hippocampus (Walsh & Emerich, 1988) and confound the results. Compared to the general population, these infants have poorer long-term cognitive outcomes (Rizzo et al., 1995; Winer & Tejani, 1994). Electrophysiological studies from our laboratories have suggested impairments in hippocampally based auditory and visual recognition memory tasks during the newborn period and at 6 months, respectively, in IDMs (Nelson et al., 1999). As these infants are exposed to multiple neurologic risk factors during the fetal and perinatal periods that could have targeted their hippocampus, it is possible that their perinatal iron deficiency could have played a primary or potentiating role in these cognitive impairments. Future studies are needed to provide more definite cause-and-effect evidence.

Strategies to Demonstrate a Biologic Effect of Iron Deficiency on Developing Brain in Animal Models

In lieu of assessing human newborn infants after induction of iron deficiency, animal models are a reliable substitute to demonstrate the effect of perinatal iron deficiency on cognitive structures and tracts, provided the limitations of cross-species relevance is accepted. Rats, by virtue of their homology to humans with respect to neurodevelopment (Dobbing, 1990) and brain-iron homeostasis (Connor, 1994; Hill & Switzer, 1984), have been traditionally used in studies of this nature (Dobbing, 1990; Felt & Lozoff, 1996). By dietary manipulation during gestation, we have been able to induce a brain-iron deficiency of a magnitude seen in IDM and IUGR infants (40% decrease) in this model.

In such a model, we evaluated the effect of perinatal iron deficiency on the regional metabolic activity of brain structures hypothesized to be involved in memory in 10-day-old rats (de Ungria et al., 1999). Neurodevelopmentally, 7- to 10-day-old rats are equivalent to full-term human newborn infants (Dobbing, 1990). Cytochrome oxidase (CytOx) activity was measured in 21 cognitive and noncognitive brain structures as a measure of regional metabolic activity. CytOx is the terminal, iron-containing enzyme essential for oxidative phosphorylation, and its level within the neurons is a reflection of antecedent in vivo metabolic activity (Wong-Riley, 1989). Because perinatal iron-deficient rats demonstrate abnormalities in recognition memory tasks (Felt & Lozoff, 1996), we hypothesized that CytOx activity will be decreased in brain structures associated with recognition memory.

Brain-iron staining was homogeneously reduced by a mean of 86% (range: 75–100%) and CytOx activity was decreased by a mean of 23% (range: 0–42%) in the iron-deficient group ($p < 0.001$). However, despite the homogeneous loss of iron staining, CytOx activity loss was selective. Five of the seven brain struc-

TABLE 1.2

Loss of Iron Staining and cytochrome Oxidase Activity in Brain Structures of Iron-Deficient Rats

Structures With Greatest CytOx Loss			Structures With Least CytOx Loss		
Structure	CytOx Loss	Iron Loss	Structure	CytOx Loss	Iron Loss
Hippocampus CAI	42%*	97%*	Entorhinal cortex	0%	85%*
Cingulum	41%*	83%*	Anterior thalamus	0%	93%*
Orbital cortex	37%*	88%*	Caudate-putamen	6%	93%*
Substantia nigra-compacta	37%*	85%*	Amygdala-central	6%	94%*
Hippocampus CA3a,b	34%*	100%*	Amygdala-lateral	10%	77%*
Hippocampus CA3c	33%*	90%*	Medial habenula	16%	94%*
Hippocampus dentate gyrus	32%*	93%*	Piriform cortex	17%*	84%*

*denotes significant loss compared to controls, $p < 0.01$.

tures with greatest CytOx activity loss were structures associated with recognition memory (Table 1.2). In contrast, structures involved in emotional–affective memory circuits and implicit memory circuits were among the least affected. Therefore, despite a similar degree of reduction in regional iron staining, perinatal iron deficiency appears to affect the neuronal metabolic activity of brain structures that are associated with memory processing.

In a second study (Rao et al., 1999), we evaluated whether perinatal iron deficiency increases the vulnerability of the hippocampus to hypoxia–ischemia, a common perinatal insult in IDM and IUGR infants. In 7-day-old iron-deficient and iron-sufficient rats, right-sided hypoxic–ischemic (HI) injury was induced by the immature Levine model (Rice et al., 1981).[1] The degree of right-sided hippocampal injury (in comparison to the unligated left side) was evaluated by CytOx activity loss on day 8 (acute injury) and loss of Nissl staining on day 14 (long-term injury).

Iron-deficient rats sustained a greater degree of right-sided hippocampal injury than iron-sufficient rats. More hippocampal subareas in this group were affected both on day 8 and on day 14 (Fig. 1.1). The severity of injury in individual hippocampal subareas also was greater when compared with the iron-sufficient rats (Table 1.3).

Thus, perinatal iron deficiency appears to: (a) adversely affect the metabolic activity of cognitively important brain structures in a selective manner; and (b) increase the vulnerability of certain subareas of the hippocampus to HI injury. These effects explain the persisting cognitive abnormalities demonstrated in this animal model (Felt & Lozoff, 1996). Despite the caveat about cross-species extrapolation, these findings may also have implications to human infants at risk for perinatal brain-iron deficiency (IDM and IUGR infants).

Biological Role for Iron Deficiency in Cognitive Impairments: Summary

A strong association appears to have been established between iron deficiency during early infancy and suboptimal cognitive function. Since this age group coincides with the latter part of rapid brain development, a case could be made that iron deficiency has a detrimental effect on neurodevelopment. However, a definite cause-and-effect relationship has not yet been established since: (a) despite adequate iron rehabilitation, it has not been possible to reverse the cognitive impairments in iron-deficient infants and children; and (b) the possible role of as-

---

[1]In the immature Levine model (Rice et al., 1981), unilateral common carotid artery is permanently ligated in a 7-day-old rat and the animal is exposed to 8% oxygen for $2^{1}/2$ hours. Both ischemia and hypoxia are necessary for neuronal injury to occur. Hence, only the hippocampus ipsilateral to the ligated side sustains injury in this model. The unligated side remains uninjured and provides an internal control to the ligated side in each animal.

Hippocampal Subarea Involvement 24 Hours Post Hypoxic-Ischemic Injury

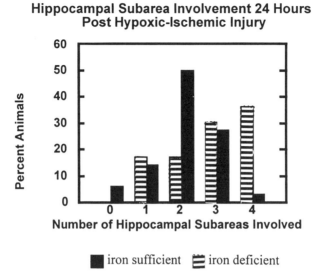

Number of Hippocampal Subareas Involved

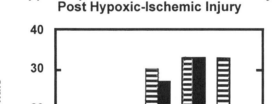

■ iron sufficient   ▤ iron deficient

Hippocampal Subarea Involvement 7 Days Post Hypoxic-Ischemic Injury

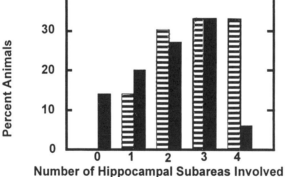

Number of Hippocampal Subareas Involved

FIG. 1.1.   Hippocampal subarea involvement in iron-deficient and iron-sufficient rats significantly different by Mantel-Haenszel Chi-Square test, both at 24 hours ($p = 0.038$) and at 7 days ($p = 0.014$).

sociated confounders (biosocial factors and other nutrient deficiencies) has not been ruled out with certainty in the affected population. Thus, iron deficiency could be a condition coexisting in a population that is at risk for cognitive impairments due to an as yet determined cause, and may not be the etiology of these impairments per se. On the other hand, failure of iron rehabilitation to reverse cognitive impairments in iron-deficient infants suggests that iron deficiency dur-

TABLE 1.3
Loss of Cytochrome c Oxidase (CytOx) Activity (top) and Nissl Staining (Bottom) in the Right
Hippocampal Subareas in Iron-Deficient and Iron-Sufficient Rats Following a Hypoxic-Ischemic
(HI) Insult on Postnatal Day 7[1]

Loss of CytOx Activity 24 Hours After the HI Insult

Hippocampal Sub area	Iron-Deficient Animals	Iron-Sufficient Animals
CA1	6 ± 12*	4 ± 5*
CA3a,b	2 ± 9	0 ± 7
CA3c	8 ± 8*	1 ± 7
Dentate gyrus	8 ± 7*	2 ± 6

Loss of Nissl Staining 7 Days After the HI Insult

Hippocampal Subarea	Iron-Deficient Animals	Iron-Sufficient Animals
CA1	10 ± 8*	6 ± 6*
CA3a,b	11 ± 7*	0 ± 13
CA3c	$0 + 11$	1 ± 10
Dentate gyrus	6 ± 6*	2 ± 6

Note. Data are presented as percentage loss of intensity of staining on ligated right side when
compared with the staining of the corresponding hippocampal subarea on the unligated (internal
control) left side in each group.
[1]$N = 30$ per group for CytOx activity; $N = 15$ per group for Nissl staining.
*$p < 0.02$ (left vs. right in individual group of animals).

ing the vulnerable period of brain development could have an irreversible adverse
effect on neurodevelopment. Until a more definitive role of iron deficiency in
cognitive impairment has been established and an optimum method of iron rehabilitation has been designed (or both), it appears prudent to prevent this condition
during early development to promote optimum neurodevelopment.

NUTRIENT SUPPLEMENTATION STUDIES

One or more nutrients have been supplemented with a goal to enhance normal
neurodevelopment. These practices may or may not be supported by sufficient
long-term data. Duration of supplementation spans the periconceptional period
through pregnancy and infancy in most instances. In areas where nutritional deficiencies are endemic, supplementation of protein energy (Gorman, 1995) and
iodine (Kretchmer et al., 1996) during pregnancy and early childhood appears to

have a beneficial effect on neurodevelopment of infants. On the other hand, excessive supplementation of certain other nutrients (e.g., hypervitaminosis A) appears to have a detrimental effect. Similarly, the desire to supplement a nutrient after birth should be tempered with the caution about toxicity due to its use. Nutrient supplementation of infant formula during early infancy has tried to emulate the intake of a breastfed full-term infant. The goal is to offset nutrient deficiencies due to preterm birth and illnesses during the immediate neonatal period. As with supplementation during gestation, some supplementation could be beneficial (e.g., energy supplementation; Georgieff et al., 1985) or detrimental (e.g., iron-induced hemolytic anemia in states of vitamin E deficiency; Melhorn, & Gross, 1971). Following is a brief description of certain nutrient supplementations that may affect early neurodevelopment.

Arachidonic Acid and Decosahexaenoic Acid Supplementation

LCPUFA supplementation in infant formulas to promote cognitive development has been a major research focus in infant nutrition. LCPUFAs, including DHA (22:6n-3) and AA (20:4n-6), are present in human breast milk. The improved psychomotor development index (Bayley Scales) at 18 months of preterm infants fed breast milk (Lucas, 1997, 1998) suggests the presence of a cognitively beneficial nutrient factor in breast milk, although it could also be due to non-nutritional factors (Richards et al., 1998). LCPUFA has been considered such a nutrient and has been supplemented in infant formulas.

Both AA and DHA are major constituents of the nervous system, with DHA particularly being abundant in the retina. They are essential components of all biological membranes, including neurons, and also probably are involved in cell-to-cell communication and in signal transduction (Carlson, 1997). Animal studies have demonstrated reduced DHA content in retina and brain, associated with impairment in retinal function and alterations in behavior in dietary DHA deficiency (Lucas, 1997). However, because of the complexity of human cognitive function and the interspecies differences in the timing of brain growth spurt, extrapolation of the animal data to humans may not be possible.

Human milk contains AA and DHA; the average content of each of these fatty acids depends on maternal diet, with higher levels being found with diets rich in marine mammals and fish, and lower levels in vegan vegetarians (Innis, 1997). Studies have demonstrated reduced plasma and red cell membrane AA and DHA levels in infants fed formulas unsupplemented with LCPUFAs (Jorgensen et al., 1996). Similarly, autopsy studies have demonstrated reduced brain DHA content in formula-fed infants (Makrides, Neumann, Byard, Simmer, & Gibson, 1994). The functional significance of both of these findings is controversial (Lucas, 1997).

Randomized trials to evaluate the effect of LCPUFA supplementation in formulas have been conducted in full-term and preterm infants. It has been suggested that preterm infants have a special need for LCPUFAs because of: (a) their rapid brain growth; (b) concern about the maturity of their biosynthetic pathways of LCPUFAs; and (c) their frequent state of negative energy metabolism that might result in LCPUFAs and their precursors being used as energy sources. In preterm infants fed a formula containing a sufficient amount of alpha-linolenic acid (LNA), erythrocyte DHA levels continue to decline. Although enzymatically capable, unlike animals and full-term human infants, preterm infants may not be able to produce quantitatively sufficient amounts of DHA from its precursor LNA (Carlson, 1997). Thus, DHA appears to be a conditionally essential nutrient in preterm infants. Since most of the transplacental transfer of DHA occurs between 26 and 40 weeks of pregnancy (Clandinin et al., 1980), preterm infants depend almost exclusively on a dietary source for their DHA requirement.

LCPUFA Supplementation Trials In Preterm Infants. Randomized double-blind trials have compared the efficacy of LCPUFA supplementation in preterm formulas. At least 1.35% of the energy was provided as alpha linolenic acid (range: 1.35–2.5%). Visual acuity, early cognitive function (visual recognition memory, Bayley mental developmental index) were periodically evaluated until 12 months of age (Carlson, 1997). Visual acuity and preferential looking grating acuity were found to be higher in n-3 LCPUFA-supplemented infants. However, this beneficial effect was transient, lasting only up to 2 months after the supplementation was discontinued. The supplemented infants also were found to perform better on tests of visual recognition memory, and to have a significantly higher Bayley mental developmental index (109.2 vs. 96.2) at 12-months corrected age (Birch et al., 1992; Carlson, 1997).

As summarized by Lucas (1997), data from such studies do not provide uniform evidence of benefit from LCPUFA supplementation in preterm infants. While there is evidence of early improvement in visual acuity and performance, this appears to be transient. The effect on cognitive development appears to be inconsistent, with a combination of AA and DHA probably having a beneficial effect on the mental developmental index and information processing. The studies are affected by small sample size, significant drop-out of study subjects and relatively short-term follow-up. Some deleterious effects on physical growth and head circumference were present in the LCPUFA-supplemented group. A higher incidence of infection (thereby suggesting impaired immunity) and prolonged bleeding time also were seen in supplemented infants. Until these safety issues are addressed by long-term studies, routine LCPUFA supplementation of formula-fed preterm infants cannot be made.

LCPUFA Supplementation Trials In Full-term Infants. Studies of dietary n-3 fatty acid supplementation in formula-fed full-term infants have not consistently provided any beneficial role of supplementation on visual function and neurodevelopment (Innis, 1997; Lucas, 1997). Visual acuity was not improved, except transiently at 2 months, in supplemented infants. However, there was biochemical evidence that DHA and AA levels were lower in unsupplemented, formula-fed infants (Innis, 1997). Unlike preterm infants, no deleterious effect on physical growth was seen with supplementation in full-term infants. As with the preterm studies, duration of follow-up in these studies has been short (< 2 years) and sample sizes have been small (Lucas, 1997). Therefore, with the current data, routine supplementation of LCPUFAs in formula-fed, full-term infants does not appear to be warranted.

Nucleotide Supplementation

Nucleotides, constituent units of RNA and DNA, are naturally present in human milk (Thorell, Sjoberg, & Hernell, 1996). They and their metabolites (nucleosides and nucleic acids) are presumed to play a significant role in many biological processes, including neurodevelopment (Carver & Walker, 1995). In preterm newborn infants and IUGR infants, a dietary source of nucleotides is considered conditionally essential for synthesis of RNA and DNA because of the limited de novo synthesis in these infants (Yu, 1998). Since bovine milk-based formulas lack adequate quantities of nucleotides, especially cytidine and adenosine, there appears to be a need for nucleotide supplementation of these formulas (Yu, 1998). The role of nucleotide supplementation in full-term infants is unclear. However, SGA infants receiving nucleotide supplementation have demonstrated significantly better physical and head growth (Cosgrove, Davies, & Jenkins, 1996). Nucleotide supplementation of infant formula appears to have a beneficial effect on infants at risk of generalized nutritional deficiencies. Furthermore, since nucleotide supplementation also appears to have a beneficial effect on immune function (Pickering et al., 1998), deleterious effects of intercurrent infection (e.g., meningitis) on neurodevelopment could be reduced.

SUMMARY AND CONCLUSIONS

There is little question that optimal nutrient support is important for brain growth and development. Although small variations in nutrient delivery are not likely to cause substantial changes in neurodevelopment, larger or prolonged deficits of particularly key nutrients such as protein–energy and iron are more problematic for the developing brain. The key time periods during which nutrient deficiencies or supplements have their greatest long-term impact on neurodevelopment need to be defined, although it appears that the fetal and neonatal brain is particularly vulnerable because of its rapid growth. Since different areas of the brain mature at different times, nutrient deficiencies such as protein–energy or iron which potentially affect all cells in the brain would have a greater effect on those areas that are maturing at the time of the deficiency. Furthermore, establishing linkages between nutrient deficiencies and neurodevelopment (and subsequently neurobehavioral outcome) must account for the specificity of the nutrient for certain brain structures or processes. Thus, the assessment of fatty acid deficiency in the first

2 years of life must include either anatomic or electrophysiologic documentation of hypomyelination since 0–2 years represents the critical period for that process. Neurobehaviorally, this deficiency might express as reduced speed of processing, although the particular system that demonstrates this effect would likely depend on the timing of the insult within those first 2 years.

This matching of the neurobehavioral outcome to the proposed pathophysiology of the nutrient deficiency can only be accomplished through generating a composite picture via multiple investigational strategies including animal models and direct human assessment. Global outcome measures that assess nutrient deficiencies are helpful when deficits are demonstrable, but are not useful as a way of demonstrating a lack of an effect, since these tests lack specificity for the predicted pathology. In the long run, strategies to identify nutrients important for normal brain development will rely on epidemiological studies in humans to detect candidate nutrients, backed by more specific, pathophysiologically oriented, in-depth (but often indirect) assessments of small cohorts of humans. Given the multivariate nature of human experimentation, highly controlled animal (especially knock-out models) or cell culture experiments must be used to unequivocally establish the effect of a given nutrient on neuronal growth, function, or both.

ACKNOWLEDGEMENTS

The authors would like to thank Marissa de Ungria, MD, for constructive suggestions, Ginny Lyson for editorial assistance, and the National Institutes of Health (NICHD) (1-R29HD292421) for their support.

REFERENCES

American Academy of Pediatrics Committee on Nutrition. (1985). Nutritional needs of low-birth-weight infants. *Pediatrics, 75*, 976–986.

Axelsson, I., Flodmark, C. E., Raiha, N., Tacconi, M., Visentin, M., Minoli, I., Moro, G., & Warm, A. (1997). The influence of dietary nucleotides on erythrocyte membrane fatty acids and plasma lipids in preterm infants. *Acta Paediatrica, 86*, 539–544.

Bass, N. H., Netsky, M. G., & Young, E. (1970). Effect of neonatal malnutrition on the developing cerebrum. *Archives in Neurology, 23*, 289–302.

Birch, E. E., Birch, D. G., Hoffman, D. R., & Uauy, R. (1992). Dietary essential fatty acid supply and visual acuity development. *Investigative Ophthalmology and Visual Science, 33*, 3242–3253.

Blayney, L., Royston, B.-W., Jacobs, A., Henderson, A., & Muir, J. (1976). The effects of iron deficiency on the respiratory function and cytochrome content of rat heart mitochondria. *Circulatory Research, 39*, 744–748.

Bruner, A. B., Joffe, A., Duggan, A. K., Casella, J. F., & Brandt, J. (1996). Randomized study of cognitive effects of iron supplementation in non-anemic iron-deficient adolescent girls. *Lancet, 348*, 992–996.

Carlson, S. E. (1997). Long-chain polyunsaturated fatty acid supplementation of preterm infants. In J. Dobbing (Ed.), *Developing brain and behaviour: The role of lipids in infant formula* (pp. 41–102). San Diego: Academic Press.

Carver, J. D., & Walker, W. A. (1995). The role of nucleotides in human nutrition. *Journal of Nutritional Biochemistry, 6*, 58–72.

Chanez, C., Privat, A., Flexor, M. A., & Drian, M. J. (1985). Effect of intrauterine growth retardation on developmental changes in DNA and [14C]thymidine metabolism in different regions of rat brain: histological and biochemical correlations. *Brain Research, 353*, 283–292.

Chen, Q., Connor, J. R., & Beard, J. L. (1995). Brain iron, transferrin and ferritin concentrations are altered in developing iron-deficient rats. *Journal of Nutrition, 125*, 1529–1535.

Chockalingam, U. M., Murphy, E., Ophoven, J. C., Weisdorf, S. A., & Georgieff, M. K. (1987). Cord transferrin values in newborn infants at risk for prenatal uteroplacental insufficiency and chronic hypoxia. *Journal of Pediatrics, 111*, 283–286.

Clandinin, M. T., Chappel, J. E., Leong, S., Heim, T., Swyer, P. R., & Chance, G. W. (1980). Intrauterine fatty acid accretion rates in human brain: Implications for fatty acid requirements. *Early Human Development, 4*, 121–129.

Connor, J. R. (1994). Iron acquisition and expression of iron regulatory proteins in the developing brain: Manipulation by ethanol exposure, iron deprivation and cellular dysfunction. *Developmental Neuroscience, 16*, 233–247.

Cornett, C. R., Markesbery, W. R., & Ehmann, W. D. (1998). Imbalances of trace elements related to oxidative damage in Alzheimer's disease brain. *Neurotoxicology, 19*(3), 339–345.

Cosgrove, M., Davies, D. P., & Jenkins, H. R. (1996). Nucleotide supplementation and the growth of term small for gestational age infants. *Archives of Diseases in Childhood, 74*(2), F122–125.

Cragg, B. G. (1972). The development of cortical synapses during starvation in the rat. *Brain, 95*, 143–150.

Cravioto, J., de Licardie, E. R., & Birch, H. G. (1966). Nutrition, growth and neurointegrative development: an experimental and ecologic study. *Pediatrics, 38*, 319–372.

Crouse, D. T., & Cassady, G. (1994). The small for gestational age infant. In G. Avery, M. A. Fletcher, & M. G. MacDonald (Eds.), *Neonatology: Pathophysiology and management of the newborn* (4th ed., pp. 369–398). Philadelphia: Lippincott.

Dallman, P. R. (1985). Biochemical basis for the manifestations of iron deficiency. *Annual Review of Nutrition, 6*, 13–40.

de Ungria, M., Rao, R., Wobken, J., Luciana, M., Nelson, C. A., & Georgieff, M. K. (1999). Selective loss of cytochrome oxidase (CytOx) activity occurs in neonatal rat brain following perinatal iron deficiency. Manuscript submitted for publication.

Deinard, A. S., Gilbert, A., Dodds, M., & Egeland, B. (1981). Iron deficiency and behavioral deficits. *Pediatrics, 68*, 828–833.

Dobbing, J. (1990). Vulnerable periods in developing brain. In J. Dobbing (Ed.), *Brain, behaviour, and iron in the infant diet* (pp. 1–25). London: Springer-Verlag.

Eastman, C. L., & Guilarte, T. R. (1992). Vitamin B6, kynurenines and central nervous system function: Developmental aspects. *Journal of Nutritional Biochemistry, 3*, 618–632.

Erikson, K. M., Pinero, D. J., Connor, J. R., & Beard, J. L. (1997). Regional brain iron, ferritin and transferrin concentrations during iron deficiency and iron repletion in developing rats. *Journal of Nutrition, 127*, 2030–2038.

Fellows, R. (1987). IGF-1 supports survival and differentiation of fetal rat brain neurons in serum-free hormone-free defined medium. *Society for Neuroscience Abstracts, 13*, 1615.

Felt, B. T., & Lozoff, B. (1990). Neurochemical basis of behavioural effects of brain iron deficiency in animals. In J. Dobbing (Ed.), *Brain, behaviour, and iron in the infant diet* (pp. 63–81). London: Springer-Verlag.

Felt, B. T., & Lozoff, B. (1996). Brain iron and behavior of rats are not normalized by treatment of iron deficiency anemia during early development. *Journal of Nutrition, 126*, 693–701.

Georgieff, M. K. (1998). Intrauterine growth retardation and subsequent somatic growth and neurodevelopment. *Journal of Pediatrics, 133*, 3–5.

Georgieff, M. K., Hoffman, J. S., Periera, G. R., Bernbaum, J., & Hoffman-Williamson, M. (1985). Effect of neonatal caloric deprivation on head growth and 1-year developmental status in preterm infants. *Journal of Pediatrics, 107*, 581–587.

Georgieff, M. K., Landon, M. B., Mills, M. M., Hedlund, B. E., Faassen, A. E., Schmidt, R. L., Ophoven, J. J., & Widness, J. A. (1990). Abnormal iron distribution in infants of diabetic mothers: spectrum and maternal antecedents. *Journal of Pediatrics, 117*, 455–461.

Georgieff, M. K., Petry, C. D., Wobken, J. D., & Oyer, C. E. (1996). Liver and brain iron deficiency in newborn infants with bilateral renal agenesis (Potter's syndrome). *Pediatric Pathology, 16,* 509–519.

Georgieff, M. K., Schmidt, R. L., Mills, M., Radmer, W. J., & Widness, J. A. (1992). Fetal iron and cytochrome c status after intrauterine hypoxemia and erythropoietin administration. *American Journal of Physiology, 262*, R485–R491.

Golub, M. S., Keen, C. L., Greshwin, M. E., & Hendricks, G. (1995). Developmental zinc deficiency and behavior. *Journal of Nutrition, 125*, 2263S–2271S.

Gordon, N. (1997). Nutrition and cognitive function. *Brain and Development, 19*, 165–170.

Gorman, K. S. (1995). Malnutrition and cognitive development: evidence from experimental/quasi-experimental studies among the mild-to-moderately malnourished. *Journal of Nutrition, 125,* 2239S–2244S.

Gottleib, D. J., Biasini, F. J., & Bray, N. W. (1988). Visual recognition memory in IUGR and normal birthweight infants. *Infant Behavior and Development, 11*, 223–228.

Greene, M. F. (1991). Fetal assessment. In J. P. Cloherty & A. R. Stark (Eds.), *Manual of neonatal care* (3rd ed., pp. 34–46). Boston: Little, Brown.

Greer, F. R. (1997). Special needs and dangers of fat-soluble vitamins A, E and K. In R. C. Tsang, S. H. Zlotkin, B. L. Nichols, & J. W. Hansen (Eds.), *Nutrition during infancy: principles and practice* (2nd ed., pp. 285–312). Cincinnati, OH: Digital Educational Publishing Inc.

Groner, J. A., Holtzman, N. A., Charney, E., & Millitts, E. (1986). A randomized trial of oral iron on tests of short-term memory and attention span in young pregnant women. *Journal of Adolescent Health Care, 7*, 44–48.

Gross, S. J., Oehler, J. M., & Echerman, C. O. (1983). Head growth and developmental outcome in very low birthweight infants. *Pediatrics, 71*, 70–75.

Guiang, S. F., III, & Georgieff, M. K. (1997). Fetal and neonatal iron metabolism. In W. W. Fox & R. A. Polin (Eds.), *Fetal and neonatal physiology* (2nd ed., pp. 401–410). Philadelphia: Saunders.

Guiang, S. F., III, Georgieff, M. K., Lambert, D. J., Schmidt, R. L., & Widness, J. A. (1997). Intravenous iron supplementation effect on tissue iron and hemoproteins in chronically phlebotomized lambs. *American Journal of Physiology, 273*, R2124–R2131.

Guilarte, T. R. (1993). Vitamin B_6 and cognitive development: Recent research findings from human and animal studies. *Nutrition Reviews, 51*, 193–198.

Hack, M., Breslau, N., Weissman, B., Aram, D., Klein, N., & Borawski, E. (1991). Effect of very low birth weight and subnormal head size on cognitive abilities at school age. *New England Journal of Medicine, 325*, 231–237.

Haiti, S. (1904). The effect of partial starvation on the brain of the white rat. *American Journal of Physiology, 12*, 116–127.

Hill, J. M., & Switzer, R. C. (1984). The regional distribution and cellular localization of iron in the rat brain. *Neuroscience, 11,* 595–603.

Innis, S. M. (1997). Polyunsaturated fatty acid nutrition in infants born at term. In J. Dobbing (Ed.), *Developing brain and behaviour: the role of lipids in infant formula* (pp. 103–167). San Diego, CA: Academic Press.

Jones, D. B., & Dyson, S. E. (1976). Synaptic junction in undernourished rat brain. An ultrastructural investigation. *Experimental Neurology, 51*, 529–535.

Jorgensen, M. H., Hernell, O., Lund, P., Holmer, G., & Michaelsen, K. F. (1996). Visual acuity and erythrocyte docosahexaenoic acid status in breast-fed and formula-fed term infants during the first four months of life. *Lipids, 31,* 99–105.

Kienzl, E., Puchinger, L., Jellinger, K., Linert, W., Stachelberger, H., & Jameson, R. F. (1995). The role of transition metals in the pathogenesis of Parkinson's disease. *Journal of Neurological Science, 134* (Suppl.), 69–78.

Kretchmer, N., Beard, J. L., & Carlson, S. (1996). The role of nutrition in the development of normal cognition. *American Journal of Clinical Nutrition, 63*, 997S–1001S.

Larkin, E. C., Jarratt, B. A., & Rao, G. A. (1986). Reduction of relative levels of nervonic to lignoceric acid in the brain of rat pups due to iron deficiency. *Nutrition Research Review, 6*, 309–317.

Larkin, E. C., & Rao, G. A. (1990). Importance of fetal and neonatal iron: Adequacy for normal development of central nervous system. In J. Dobbing (Ed.), *Brain, behaviour, and iron in the infant diet* (pp. 43–62). London: Springer-Verlag.

Levin, H. M., Pollitt, E., Galloway, R., & McGuire, J. (1993). Micronutrient deficiency disorders. In D. T. Jamison, W. H. Mosley, A. R. Measham, & J. L. Bobadilla (Eds.), *Disease control priorities in developing countries* (pp. 421–451). New York: Oxford University Press.

Lewis, D. P., Van Dyke, D. C., Stumbo, P. J., & Berg, M. J. (1998). Drug and environmental factors associated with adverse pregnancy outcomes. Part III: Folic acid: Pharmacology, therapeutic recommendations, economics. *Annals of Pharmacotherapy, 32*, 1087–1095.

Locksmith, G. J., & Duff, P. (1998). Preventing neural tube defects: The importance of periconceptional folic acid supplements. *Obstetrics & Gynecology, 91*, 1027–1034.

Looker, A. C., Dallman, P. R., Carroll, M. D., Gunter, E. W., & Johnson, C. L. (1997). Prevalence of iron deficiency in the United States. *Journal of the American Medical Association, 277*(12), 973–976.

Lozoff, B. (1990). Has iron deficiency been shown to cause altered behavior in infants? In J. Dobbing (Ed.), *Brain, behaviour, and iron in the infant diet* (pp. 107–131). London: Springer-Verlag.

Lozoff, B., Brittenham, G. M., Viteri, F. E., Wolf, A. W., & Urrutia, J. J. (1982). The effects of short-term oral iron therapy on developmental deficits in iron-deficient anemic infants. *Journal of Pediatrics, 100*, 351–357.

Lozoff, B., Brittenham, G. M., Wolf, A. W., McClish, D. K., Kuhnert, P. M., Jimenez, E., Jimenez, R., Mora, L. A., Gomez, I., & Kranskoph, O. (1987). Iron-deficiency anemia and iron therapy: Effects on infant developmental test performance. *Pediatrics, 79*, 981–995.

Lozoff, B., Klein, N. K., Nelson, E. C., McClish, D. K., Manuel, M., & Chacon, M. E. (1998). Behavior of infants with iron-deficiency anemia. *Child Development, 69*, 24–36.

Lozoff, B., Wolf, A. W., Urrutia, J. J., & Viteri, F. E. (1985). Abnormal behavior and low developmental test scores in iron-deficient anemic infants. *Journal of Developmental and Behavioral Pediatrics, 6*, 69–75.

Lucas, A. (1994). Role of nutritional programming in determining adult morbidity. *Archives of Diseases in Childhood, 71*, 288–290.

Lucas, A. (1997). Long-chain polyunsaturated fatty acids, infant feeding and cognitive development. In J. Dobbing (Ed.), *Developing brain and behaviour: The role of lipids in infant formula* (pp. 3–39). San Diego, CA: Academic Press.

Lucas, A. (1998). Programming by early nutrition: An experimental approach. *Journal of Nutrition, 128*, 401S–406S.

Mackler, B., Grace, R., & Finch, C. A. (1984). Iron deficiency in the rat: Effects on oxidative metabolism in distinct types of skeletal muscle. *Pediatric Research, 18*, 499–505.

Mackler, B., Person, R., Miller, L. R., Inamdar, A. R., & Finch, C. A. (1978). Iron deficiency in the rat: Biochemical studies of brain metabolism. *Pediatric Research, 12*, 217–220.

Makrides, M., Neumann, M. A., Byard, R. W., Simmer, K., & Gibson, R. A. (1994). Fatty acid composition of brain, retina, and erythrocytes in breast- and formula-fed infants. *American Journal of Clinical Nutrition, 60*, 189–194.

Masini, A., Salvioli, G., Cremonesi, P., Butti, B., Gallisi, D., & Ceccarelli, D. (1994). Dietary iron deficiency in the rat. I. Abnormalities in energy metabolism of the hepatic tissue. *Biochimica Et Biophysica Acta, 1188*, 46–52.

McMorris, F. A., & Dubois-Dalcq, M. (1988). Insulin-like growth factor I promotes cell proliferation and oligodendroglial committment in rat glial progenitor cells in cells developing *in vitro*. *Journal of Neuroscience Research, 21*, 199–209.

Melhorn, D. K., & Gross, S. (1971). Vitamin E-dependent anemia in the premature infant. I. Effects of large doses of medicinal iron. *Journal of Pediatrics, 79,* 569–580.

Morley, R. (1996). The influence of early diet on later development. *Journal of Biosocial Science, 28,* 481–487.

Morris, R. G. M., Halliwell, R. F., & Bowery, N. (1989). Synaptic plasticity and learning. II. Do different kinds of plasticity underlie different kinds of learning? *Neuropsychologia, 27,* 41–59.

MRC Vitamin Study Research Group. (1991). Prevention of neural tube defects: Results of the Medical Research Council Vitamin Study. *Lancet, 338*(8760), 131–137.

Nelson, C. A. (1995). The ontogeny of human memory. *Developmental Psychology, 31,* 723–738.

Nelson, C. A. (1997). Electrophysiological correlates of early memory development. In H. W. Reese & M. D. Franzen (Eds.), *Thirteenth West Virginia University Conference on Life Span Development in Psychology: Biological and neuropsychological mechanisms* (pp. 95–131). Hillsdale, NJ: Lawrence Erlbaum Associates.

Nelson, C. A., Wewerka, S., Thomas, K. M., Tribby-Walbridge, S., deRegnier, R.-A., & Georgieff, M. (1999). Neurocognitive sequelae of infants of diabetic mothers. Manuscript under review.

Neuringer, M., Connor, W. E., & Lin, D. S. (1986). Biochemical and functional effects of prenatal and postnatal s-3 fatty acid deficiency on retina and brain in rhesus monkeys. *Proceedings of the National Academy of Sciences of the United States of America, 83,* 4021–4025.

Nishijima, M. (1986). Somatomedin-C as a fetal growth promoting factor in amino acid composition of cord blood in Japanese neonates. *Journal of Perinatal Medicine, 14,* 163–169.

Nokes, C., van den Bosch, C., & Bundy, D. A. P. (1998). Infants and young children (6-24 months). In *A report of the International Nutritional Anemia Consultative Group: The effects of iron deficiency and anemia on mental and motor performance, educational achievement, and behavior in children. An annotated bibliography* (pp. 7–22). Washington, DC: .

Pearson, H. A. (1990). Prevention of iron-deficiency anemia: Iron fortification of infant foods. In J. Dobbing (Ed.), *Brain, behaviour, and iron in the infant diet* (pp. 177–190). London: Springer-Verlag.

Petry, C. D., Eaton, M., Wobken, J., Mills, M., Johnson, D. E., & Georgieff, M. K. (1992). Iron deficiency of liver, heart and brain in newborn infants of diabetic mothers. *Journal of Pediatrics, 121,* 109–114.

Pickering, L. K., Granoff, D. M., Erickson, J. R., Masor, M. L., Cordle, C. T., Schaller, J. P., Winship, T. R., Paule, C. L., & Hilty, M. D. (1998). Modulation of the immune system by human milk and infant formula containing nucleotides. *Pediatrics, 101,* 242–249.

Pollitt, E., & Gorman, K. S. (1994). Nutritional deficiencies as developmental risk factors. In C. A. Nelson (Ed.), *Threats to optimal development: Integrating biological, psychological, and social risk factors. The Minnesota symposia on child psychology* (Vol. 27, pp. 121–144). Hillsdale, NJ: Lawrence Erlbaum Associates.

Rao, R., de Ungria, M., Sullivan, D., Wu, P., Wobken, J., Nelson, C. A., & Georgieff, M. K. (1999). Perinatal brain iron deficiency increases the vulnerability of the rat hippocampus to hypoxic-ischemic injury. *Journal of Nutrition, 129,* 199–206.

Reinard, P., & Ehrenberg, A. (1983). Ribonucleotide reductase—a radical enzyme. *Science, 221,* 514.

Rice, J. E., III, Vannucci, R. C., & Brierley, J. B. (1981). The influence of immaturity on hypoxic-ischemic brain damage in the rat. *Annals of Neurology, 9,* 131–141.

Richards, M., Wadsworth, M., Rahimi-Foroushani, A., Hardy, R., Kuh, D., & Paul, A. (1998). Infant nutrition and cognitive development in the first offspring of a national UK birth cohort. *Developmental Medicine and Child Neurology, 40,* 163–167.

Rizzo, T. A., Dooley, S. L., Metzger, B. E., Cho, N. H., Ogata, E. S., & Silverman, B. L. (1995). Prenatal and perinatal influences on long-term psychomotor development in offspring of diabetic mothers. *American Journal of Obstetrics & Gynecology, 173,* 1753–1758.

Roncagliolo, M., Garrido, M., Walter, T., Peirano, P., & Lozoff, B. (1998). Evidence of altered central nervous system development in infants with iron deficiency anemia at 6 mo: Delayed maturation of auditory brainstem responses. *American Journal of Clinical Nutrition, 68*(3), 683–690.

Rusia, U., Madan, N., Agarwal, N., Sikka, M., & Sood, S. K. (1995). Effect of maternal iron deficiency anaemia on foetal outcome. *Indian Journal of Pathology & Microbiology, 38,* 273–279.

Russel, W. E. (1998). Endocrine and other factors affecting growth. In W. W. Fox & R. A. Polin (Eds.), *Fetal and neonatal physiology* (2nd ed., pp. 295–305). Philadelphia: Saunders.

Saneto, R. P., Low, K. G., Melnor, M. H., & de Vellis, J. (1988). Insulin/insulin-like growth factor I and other epigenetic modulators of myelin basic protein expression in isolated oligodendrocyte progenitor cells. *Journal of Neuroscience Research, 21,* 210–219.

Singer, L. T. (1997). Methodological considerations in longitudinal studies of infant risk. In J. Dobbing (Ed.), *Developing brain and behaviour: The role of lipids in infant formula* (pp. 209–251). San Diego, CA: Academic Press.

Spinello, A., Stronati, M., Ometto, A., Fazzi, E., Lanzi, G., & Guaschino, S. (1993). Infant neurodevelopmental outcome in pregnancies complicated by gestational hypertension and intra-uterine growth retardation. *Journal of Perinatal Medicine, 21,* 195–203.

Strauss, R. S., & Dietz, W. H. (1998). Growth and development of term children born with low birth weight: Effects of genetic and environmental factors. *Journal of Pediatrics, 133,* 67–72.

Tanaka, M., Kariya, K., Kaihatsu, K., Nakamura, K., Asakura, T., Kuroda, Y., & Ohira, Y. (1995). Effects of chronic iron deficiency anemia on brain metabolism. *Japanese Journal of Physiology, 45,* 257–263.

Thorell, L., Sjoberg, L.-B., & Hernell, O. (1996). Nucleotides in human milk: Sources and metabolism by the newborn infant. *Pediatric Research, 40,* 845–852.

Volpe, J. J. (1998). Brain injury in the premature infant. Neuropathology, clinical aspects, pathogenesis and prevention. *Clinical Perinatology, 24,* 56–71.

Vulsma, T., & Kooistra, L. (1995). Motor and cognitive development in children with congenital hypothyroidism (reply to letter). *Journal of Pediatrics, 126,* 673–674.

Waber, D. P., Vuori-Christiansen, L., Ortiz, N., Clement, J. R., Christiansen, N. E., Mora, J. O., Reed, R. B., & Herrara, M. G. (1981). Nutritional supplementation, maternal education, and cognitive development of infants at risk of malnutrition. *American Journal of Clinical Nutrition, 34,* 807–813.

Wachs, T. D. (1995). Relation of mild-to-moderate malnutrition to human development: Correlation studies. *Journal of Nutrition, 125,* 2245S–2254S.

Wahlig, T. A., & Georgieff, M. K. (1995). The effects of illness on neonatal metabolism and nutritional management. *Clinical Perinatology, 22,* 77–96.

Walsh, T. J., & Emerich, D. F. (1988). The hippocampus as a common target of neurotoxic agents. *Toxicology, 49,* 137–140.

Walter, T. (1990). Has iron deficiency been shown to cause altered behavior in infants? In J. Dobbing (Ed.), *Brain, behaviour, and iron in the infant diet* (pp. 107–131). London: Springer-Verlag.

Walter, T. (1994). Effect of iron-deficiency anaemia on cognitive skills in infancy and childhood. *Baillieres Clinical Haematology, 7,* 815–827.

Walter, T., De Andraca, I., Chadud, P., & Perales, C. G. (1989). Iron deficiency anemia: Adverse effects on infant psychomotor development. *Pediatrics, 84,* 7–17.

Walter, T., Kowalskys, J., & Stekel, A. (1983). Effect of mild iron deficiency on infant mental developmental scores. *Journal of Pediatrics, 102,* 519–522.

Wasantwisut, E. (1996). Nutrition and development: Other micronutrients' effect on growth and cognition. *Southeast Asian Journal of Tropical Medicine and Public Health, 28*(Suppl. 2), 78–82.

Wiggins, R. C., Fuller, G., & Enna, S. J. (1984). Undernutrition and the development of the brain neurotransmitter systems. *Life Science, 35,* 2085–2094.

Willhite, C. C., Hill, R. M., & Irving, D. W. (1986). Isotretinoin-induced craniofacial malformations in humans and hamsters. *Journal of Craniofacial Genetics & Developmental Biology* (Suppl. 2), 193–209.

Winer, E. K., & Tejani, N. (1994). Four-to-seven-year evaluation in two groups of small-for-gestational-age infants. In N. Tejani (Ed.), *Obstetrical events and developmental sequelae* (2nd ed., pp. 77–94). Boca Raton, FL: CRC Press.

Winnick, M., & Rosso, P. (1969). The effect of severe early malnutrition on cellular growth of the human brain. *Pediatric Research, 3,* 181–184.

Woltil, H. A., van Beusekom, C. M., Schaafsma, A., Muskiet, F. A., & Okken, A. (1998). Long-chain polyunsaturated fatty acid status and early growth of low birth weight infants. *European Journal of Pediatrics, 157,* 146–152.

Woltil, H. A., van Beusekom, C. M., Siemensma, A. D., Polman, H. A., Muskiet, F. A., & Okken, A. (1995). Erythrocyte and plasma cholesterol ester long-chain polyunsaturated fatty acids of low-birth-weight babies fed preterm formula with or without ribonucleotides: Comparison with human milk. *American Journal of Clinical Nutrition, 62,* 943–949.

Wong-Riley, M. T. T. (1989). Cytochrome oxidase: An endogenous metabolic marker for neuronal activity. *Topics in Neuroscience, 12,* 94–101.

Yehuda, S. (1987). Nutrients, brain biochemistry and behavior: A possible role for the neuronal membrane. *International Journal of Neuroscience, 35,* 21–36.

Yehuda, S. (1990a). Importance of fetal and neonatal iron: Adequacy for normal development of central nervous system. In J. Dobbing (Ed.), *Brain, behaviour, and iron in the infant diet* (pp. 43–62). London: Springer-Verlag.

Yehuda, S. (1990b). Neurochemical basis of behavioural effects of brain iron deficiency in animals. In J. Dobbing (Ed.), *Brain, behaviour, and iron in the infant diet* (pp. 63–81). London: Springer-Verlag.

Youdim, M. B. H., & Ben-Shachar, D. (1987). Minimal brain damage induced by early iron deficiency: Modified dopaminergic neurotransmission. *Israel Journal of Medical Sciences, 23,* 19–25.

Yu, V. Y. H. (1998). The role of dietary nucleotides in neonatal and infant nutrition. *Singapore Medical Journal, 39,* 145–150.

2

▼▼▼▼▼▼▼▼

The Relation of Very Low Birthweight to Basic Cognitive Skills in Infancy and Childhood

Susan A. Rose
Judith F. Feldman
Albert Einstein College of Medicine

Over the past several years, we have been studying the development of cognitive abilities in infants, differences between preterms and full-terms on these infant abilities, and the relation of infant abilities to later outcome. In the course of this work, we have also probed the specificity of the later cognitive deficits associated with prematurity. In the present chapter, we review some of our findings, focusing on: (a) cognitive differences between preterms and full-terms in infancy, (b) cognitive differences between them in later childhood, (c) the relation of infant to childhood abilities, (d) the role of memory and processing speed, two specific abilities, in explaining preterm deficits on more global measures of cognition, and finally, (e) the relation of Respiratory Distress Syndrome (RDS), a medical risk factor prevalent in preterms, to memory impairments in infancy and later childhood.

BACKGROUND

Since 1989 advances in the care of preterm infants have led to dramatic increases in survival rates of those born at very low birthweight. As smaller and younger infants survive, concerns about their subsequent outcome and development have increased. The evidence suggests that, as a group, these infants are at considerable risk for cognitive and behavioral difficulties. Studies of outcomes in early and middle childhood have shown repeatedly that preterms perform more poorly

than control subjects on tests of intelligence, language, and academic achievement (Eilers, Desai, Wilson, & Cunningham, 1986; Hunt, Cooper, & Tooley,
1988; Klebanov, Brooks-Gunn, & McCormick, 1994; Klein, Hack, & Breslau,
1989; McCormick, 1989; Saigal, Rosenbaum, Szatmari, & Dugal, 1991; Scottish
Low Birthweight Study Group, 1992; for reviews see Alyward, Pfeiffer, Wright,
& Verhulst, 1989; Escobar, Littenberg, & Petitti, 1991; Hoy, Bill, & Sykes, 1988).

The results of recent studies are particularly revealing because they generally
include important design features that were often absent in earlier studies. The
most notable improvements are in (a) sample size, which has been larger and
more representative than before, (b) the length of follow-up, which now often extends well into middle childhood and even into adolescence, and (c) the inclusion
of normal birthweight controls, a rarity in earlier studies. In fact, in a metanaly-
sis of 80 studies of low birth weight infants, less than a third included a full-term
control or comparison group (Alyward et al., 1989). Control groups are essential
in order to avoid confounding regional differences in socioeconomic and environmental factors with the effects of prematurity. Moreover, scores on standardized tests tend to shift over time making comparison with control groups all the
more important. For example, consider the highly popular Bayley Scales of Infant
Development, the major instrument used to evaluate infants through 2 years of
age. This test was recently restandardized, resulting in about a 10-point downward
shift in the mean. Thus, recent studies that relied exclusively on the old norms
may well have underestimated the deficits associated with prematurity.

Of the recent follow-up studies, three are useful for illustrating the nature of
the cognitive difficulties that are often associated with prematurity (Hack et al.,
1992; Rickards et al., 1993; Ross, Lipper, & Auld, 1991). Each used a fairly large,
representative sample, included appropriate control groups, and focused on the 8-
year outcome of children born at very low birth weight (< 1500g). All three found
that the mean IQ, though generally in the normal range for both groups, averaged
as much as 10 points lower for preterms than for their normal birthweight controls; moreover, 6%–8% of the preterms had scores indicating mental deficiency
(IQ < 70), whereas only 2.3% of the population at large have scores this low. The
preterms also scored lower in all areas of academic achievement, including reading, arithmetic, and spelling. Even among those with normal intelligence, about
20% displayed learning disabilities. In all three studies, preterms continued to
perform more poorly than full-terms even when differences due to socioeconomic status (SES), neurological impairment, and neonatal health were controlled.

The vast majority of these follow-up studies using school-aged children have focused almost exclusively on the more global aspects of cognition. Aside from the inclusion of assessments of language development, studies of specific cognitive abilities have been rare. Such assessments are important because deficits in the more
specific or elementary abilities may provide the key to understanding the basis or
substrate of the more complex, global deficits and provide clues as to the nature of
some of the learning disabilities with elevated prevalence in low birth weight popu-

lations. Memory and processing speed are two elementary processes thought to be particularly important underpinnings of individual differences in more molar cognitive abilities (e.g., Detterman, 1987a,b; 1990; Hale, 1990; Kail, 1986, 1988). Although data are sparse, a few recent studies of school-age children have included a brief memory task in their batteries. All report poorer memory among preterms than among their age-matched full-term peers. This was true for visual sequential memory (the bead memory test from the Stanford-Binet, Rickards et al., 1993; the test of visual sequential memory from the Illinois Test of Psycholinguistic Abilities [ITPA], Rose et al., 1992); auditory memory (Ross et al., 1991), and memory tasks using visual and auditory selective reminding (Hack et al., 1992). Although these studies constitute a promising beginning in the study of specific abilities, most of the contrasts have involved but a single measure rather than the multiplicity of measures necessary to define a construct. Because any given measure is influenced by the specific methods and materials used, single measures are, of necessity, only indirect and limited indicators of a construct. The use of two or more converging measures not only avoids confounding the assessment of a construct with its specific operationalization but also, by broadening the range of overlapping abilities assessed, increases the replicability of the results (see Salthouse, 1996).

COGNITION IN INFANCY

Until recently, studies of infant development—in normal as well as at-risk samples—have also relied almost exclusively on global measures, such as the Bayley Scales of Infant Development (Bayley, 1969). These tests are useful as descriptive instruments, providing normative data on various aspects of current functioning and development, and allowing for the identification of certain sensorimotor deficits. However, scores on the infant tests have proven largely unrelated to scores on intelligence tests in later childhood, even for risk groups. The classic longitudinal studies of mental development found little stability in performance from infancy to later childhood (e.g., Bayley, 1958), a finding confirmed repeatedly in subsequent research (Kopp & McCall, 1982). For a long time, this lack of stability was thought to result largely from profound developmental changes in the nature of intelligence, as early sensorimotor developments were superseded by the qualitatively different achievements that characterize abstract, verbal, and symbolic reasoning. Recently, investigators have begun to examine the possibility that the discontinuity may have more to do with the nature of infant and child tests than with any inherent discontinuities in the nature of cognition. Whereas the infant tests are weighted heavily with items assessing imitation, sensorimotor maturity, and emotional expressiveness, the childhood tests are weighted heavily with items assessing memory, speed of processing, verbal ability, and spatial abilities. Given the nature of the differences in content of infant and childhood tests of general ability, it is hardly surprising that the relation between the two has been so poor.

However, the past two decades (1980s and 1990s) have witnessed a virtual explosion of new approaches to the study of infant cognition. Paradigms have been developed that tap aspects of mental functioning that are ostensibly more akin to the cognitive processes assessed in later childhood. In particular, investigators have begun to study individual and group differences, and developmental growth, in specific abilities such as processing speed, memory, learning, and categorization.

Much of this newer work takes as its point of departure an infant's proclivity to attend more to novel than to familiar stimuli. By focusing on the distribution and changes in the allocation of attention as a new stimulus is introduced, assimilated, and becomes, in turn, familiar, it is possible to examine how infants acquire, store, and retrieve information. For example, varying the time allotted for assimilation provides information about processing speed; manipulating the dimensions on which novel and familiar stimuli differ provides information about the nature of what is encoded; varying the time elapsed before testing for recognition provides information about duration of storage; and finally, varying such elements as contextual cues provides information about the factors influencing retrieval. The work in this area has relied largely on two paradigms: habituation and the paired comparison. Given the prominence of both in infant research, it is worth describing them in some detail and being aware of their differences.

In habituation, an infant is repeatedly presented with a target stimulus until attention wanes (habituates). In the most popular variant, infant-controlled habituation (see Bornstein & Benasich, 1986; Colombo & Mitchell, 1990; Horowitz, Paden, Bhana, & Self, 1972), the number of trials is not preset; rather, testing continues until the duration of the infant's looks declines by a certain proportion (generally 50%) of initial duration. Speed of habituation is generally defined in terms of the total time or number of trials taken to reach criterion. It is thought that the infant forms a mental schema of the stimulus during habituation (Sokolov, 1969). Often, a novel stimulus is introduced after criterion is reached and the amount of looking to this new stimulus is compared to the amount of looking on the final trials with the original one. Recovery of attention to the new stimulus is taken as evidence that the decrement is not due to fatigue; it also provides evidence that the infant can discriminate the novel from the habituation stimulus.

In the paired comparison paradigm, infants are first given a brief period of familiarization, during which they are shown a single target or two identical targets (see Fantz, 1964; Fantz, Fagan, & Miranda, 1975). Unlike habituation, this initial familiarization is relatively brief and preset in duration so no waning of attention to the stimulus need occur. During testing, the familiar target is paired with a new one and attention to both is monitored. Recognition memory is assessed by differential responsiveness to the two. Since infants typically spend more time looking at the novel member of the pair, the primary index of performance is a novelty preference, defined as the percentage of looking during the test that is directed to the novel target (e.g., Fagan, 1974; Rose & Feldman, 1990). Often, the novelty scores from several different problems are averaged to yield an overall score.

The preference for novelty found in the paired-comparison paradigm is considered an index of recognition memory. This preference is thought to arise because the infant, having completed assimilation of the information in the familiar stimulus, turns his or her attention to encoding the information in the new target. As in habituation, it is presumed that the infant forms a mental schema of the stimulus during familiarization. During the test, this schema is reactivated and used as the basis for discriminating the novel target from the familiar one. While preferences for the familiar stimulus occasionally emerge during the early stages of stimulus processing, these tend to be supplanted by novelty responses when processing is complete (e.g., Rose, Gottfried, Melloy-Carminar, & Bridger, 1982; Wagner & Sakovits, 1986). No conclusions can be drawn from a lack of preference, as this could indicate either failure to recognize the original stimulus or a developmental transition from familiarity to novelty preference.

There are three distinctions between the paradigms for habituation and visual recognition memory that are worth noting. First, in habituation, infants tend to have much longer exposure to the initial stimulus than in the paired-comparison paradigm. Indeed, the paired-comparison paradigm gained popularity when it became clear that infants often distinguish novel from familiar stimuli before they have habituated to the familiar one. In using the paired-comparison paradigm to probe for individual differences, familiarization times are selected that approach the minimum needed for a group of infants of a given age to exhibit a mean novelty score significantly above chance (50%). Second, the preset familiarization times will necessarily be too brief for all infants to have completed processing. Given the limited familiarization time, only those who process quickly, efficiently retain information from familiarization to test, and discriminate the new stimulus from the old one will show high novelty scores. Third, as a consequence, novelty scores have a different meaning in the habituation and paired-comparison procedures. In habituation, they are unlikely to discriminate between individuals because all infants have presumably processed the initial stimulus completely. Therefore, all infants are likely to respond preferentially to the novel stimulus (i.e., dishabituate). In visual recognition, by contrast, novelty scores have greater variation in that only those infants who have processed the stimulus in the limited time allotted are expected to show a novelty preference. Furthermore, the actual magnitude of the novelty score is important and may reflect the strength rather than the mere presence or absence of recognition. In a 1989 paper, Rose et al. found that the magnitude of novelty percentages, when averaged over a series of problems, related to later cognitive performance over and above a simple count of the number of problems on which the scores exceeded a cutpoint designated as indicating a novelty response. Thus, novelty scores may discriminate among infants precisely because they capture differences in how thoroughly infants have processed the initial stimulus, in how well they have retained it over the interval that separates familiarization and test, or both.

In our own lab, we have been using the paired-comparison paradigm to assess visual recognition memory, cross-modal transfer, and tactual recognition memory, each of which is thought to reflect processes that are central to infant mental functioning. We used these techniques (along with object permanence) in a number of cross-sectional studies exploring preterm–full-term differences in infant cognition and in a more recent longitudinal study in which the children were followed from 7 months to 11 years. The general findings of these studies are described in the next several sections.

Visual Recognition Memory

Recognition memory is assessed in our laboratory using the paired comparison paradigm described previously. Most frequently, we have used abstract patterns, faces, and three-dimensional geometric shapes as stimuli. In all studies using preterms, testing was done at the infant's corrected age, that is, age from the expected date or birth, so that performance differences are not confounded with biological maturity.

In the first study (Rose, 1980), 6-month-olds were tested for recognition of abstract patterns and faces. Initially, when familiarization times were quite brief (5 to 20 seconds, depending on the problem) the preterms failed to differentiate between novel and familiar test stimuli on any of three problems, whereas the full-terms showed significant novelty preferences on two of them. That is, the scores for the group of preterms hovered around chance whereas those for the full-terms were significantly greater than chance. The poor performance of preterms was replicated in a second group of infants given the same problems with the same familiarization (or study) times. However, the preterms' performance improved dramatically when familiarization times were increased. Their success when given more time to study the original stimulus makes it clear that they could encode, store, and retrieve information about the familiar target, as well as discriminate between the test stimuli. It also indicates that they are decidedly slower at encoding the information than were their full-term counterparts.

These findings were reinforced and extended in a second study where the slower processing speed of preterms was found to persist throughout the entire first year of life (Rose, 1983). Here, 6- and 12-month olds were tested for recognition of three-dimensional shapes after familiarization times of 10, 15, 20, and 30 seconds. At both ages, preterms required longer familiarization times than full-terms before they exhibited reliable novelty preferences. At 6 months, full-terms achieved significant scores with only 15 seconds of familiarization, whereas preterms needed 30 seconds. At 12 months, full-terms achieved significant scores with as little as 10 seconds of familiarization (the briefest interval used), whereas preterms required 20 seconds. Thus, while both groups encoded the stimuli faster as they got older, preterms continued to require longer familiarization than full-terms. These results suggest that there are persistent differences between preterms and full-terms throughout at least the first year of life in this very fundamental aspect of cognition.

Cross-modal Transfer

Our research on cross-modal transfer has dealt primarily with infant's recognition of an object in the face of a change in sensory modality. More specifically, we have studied infants' recognition by sight of an object previously only felt or only explored orally. This ability to recognize that an object or event experienced in one modality is the same or equivalent to an object or event experienced in a different modality is referred to as cross-modal transfer. The nature and base for cross-modal abilities has remained a matter of considerable research and philosophical speculation since Aristotle first postulated the existence of a common sense (see Marks, 1978). Nonetheless, there is no doubt that, despite the very different sense impressions involved in seeing and feeling, adults represent objects in memory in a unified way. In other words, they perceive a single object despite the different modalities in which they encounter it.

We adapted the paired-comparison paradigm to study cross-modal transfer in infancy. In doing this, the stimuli are presented either tactually or orally during familiarization and visually during the test phase. When the stimuli are presented in different modalities during familiarization and testing, the occurrence of recognition memory demonstrates cross-modal transfer. For tactual (manual) familiarization, an object is placed in one of the infant's hands; the experimenter then cups her hands around the infant's to shield the object from the infant's view. Most infants tended to actively explore the object; if they do not palpate spontaneously, the experimenter gives the object a half- or quarter-turn every 10–15 seconds. For oral familiarization, the object is attached to a thin transparent filament (one end of which is held firmly by the experimenter) and then placed in the infants' mouth; the experimenter cups her hand over the infant's upper lip to shield the object from the infant's view and touch.

Using this paradigm, we have found evidence of cross-modal transfer in full-terms at 6 months of age, although performance is more robust at 12 months (e.g., Gottfried, Rose, & Bridger, 1977; Rose, Gottfried, & Bridger, 1981). At the older age, middle-class full-terms visually recognized simple shapes after 30 seconds of tactual or oral familiarization (although neither lower-class full-terms nor preterms showed such transfer, see Rose, Gottfried, & Bridger, 1978). The success of middle-class full-terms on tactual–visual cross-modal problems has been replicated in other studies from our lab (Rose, Gottfried, & Bridger, 1983; Rose & Orlian, 1991).

Tactual Recognition Memory

To determine whether young infants can recognize objects solely on the basis of tactual information, we developed a procedure in which testing took place in total darkness and was videotaped under infrared light. During familiarization, infants are presented a tray containing four identical geometric objects that they are free to manipulate for a period of 1 minute. During the test, four replicas of a novel shape are added to the tray for a 2-minute test period. In our initial studies, we found that 12-month-olds had significant novelty scores, that is, they spent more time manipulating novel than familiar stimuli in the dark (Gottfried & Rose, 1980; see also Rose & Orlian, 1991). Although cross-modal abilities are clearly dependent on intramodal abilities, there is evidence that cross-modal abilities are not reducible to intramodal ones, since infants who show adequate visual and tactual recognition do not necessarily succeed in cross-modal problems (Rose & Orlian, 1991).

Object Permanence

Object permanence, like visual recognition memory and cross-modal transfer, is thought to tap aspects of mental representation. Whereas visual recognition and cross-modal transfer both assume that current visual input is compared to a stored representation of previous input, object permanence is concerned with how the stored representations map on to reality, namely, with whether infants understand that their representations refer to objects that continue to exist in the real world even when out of sight. Piaget (1954) believed that object permanence constitutes one of the major cognitive achievements of infancy. By observing changes in the pattern of errors infants made in searching for hidden objects, he concluded that infants only slowly come to realize that an object's existence in space and time is maintained even when it is out of view.

Piaget's inital work has spawned a veritable cottage industry as investigators attempt to understand the course of object permanence. The principal tasks used to assess object permanence generally have the infant watch while an attractive toy is hidden and then observe if, where, and how she or he sets about to retrieve it. Often, infants who readily reach for an object that is placed in front of them will not do so if it is covered. Even when they readily remove the cover, they often do not respond appropriately when the hiding place is changed. Despite having watched closely while the change takes place, they ignore the new location and search in the original hiding place. The need to remember the new location, and to inhibit the tendency to search in a previously correct location, hampers performance.

In our own work, we have used the Einstein Scale of Object Permanence (Corman & Escalona, 1969) to assess object permanence in 12-month-old preterms and full-terms (Rose & Wallace, 1985b). In this scale, the infant is called upon to retrieve objects over an increasingly complex series of visible and invisible displacements. Self-corrections are permitted and the infant's final responses are categorized by stages, beginning with Stage 3 (Piaget's stages 1 and 2 are applicable only at younger ages); Stage 3—recovers an object that has been partially but not fully hidden; Stage 4—recovers a completely hidden object, but errs on succeeding trials when the location of the object is changed; Stage 5—correctly retrieves hidden objects, but only if their displacement had been visible (e.g., if the object is hidden in the experimenter's hand and then moved to its hiding place, the infant errs by only searching for it in the experimenter's hand); and Stage 6—correctly retrieves objects even after invisible displacements. The infant's score is the highest stage achieved.

Overall, performance of full-terms was considerably better than that of the preterms. Although none of the infants in either group completed Stage 6, 85% of the full-terms had completed Stage 5 (and the remaining 15% had completed Stage 4). By contrast, only 42.5% of the preterms had completed Stage 5 (another 42.5% had completed Stage 4, whereas the remaining 14% had only completed Stage 3).

LONGITUDINAL STUDY OF VERY LOW BIRTH WEIGHT CHILDREN FROM INFANCY TO 11 YEARS OF AGE

The preterm–full-term differences discussed previously can be taken as an indication of the concurrent validity of the infant tasks as measures of early cognitive ability. These findings, along with some early evidence that these infant measures were predictive of later cognitive ability (Rose & Wallace, 1985a, 1985b), set the stage for our most recent longitudinal study, in which preterms and full-terms were followed from infancy to 11 years of age. While the primary focus of this work was on cognitive continuity from infancy, a secondary focus was on the comparability of performance of preterms and full-terms at each age of follow-up.

The two groups followed from infancy to 11 years of age consisted of a cohort of very low birth weight (< 1500 g) children and their group-matched full-term controls. In infancy, the principal measures were assessments of visual recognition memory, cross-modal transfer, tactual recognition memory, and object permanence at 7 and 12 months. At the outset of this project, our primary aim was to determine whether and to what extent these relatively new measures of infant cognition related to later cognitive competence. This being the case, we selected outcome measures at 2–11 years of age that were largely global in nature, and which had stong reliability and validity, primarily developmental quotients, and IQ scores.

As the study progressed, we became increasingly interested in the nature of the infant abilities themselves and the basis for their relation to later general cognition. To begin to address these issues, we incorporated more specific measures into the later follow-ups, particularly in the final assessment at 11 years of age. Here we included measures of the four specific abilities that DeFries and Plomin had identified as principal components of intelligence: memory, speed, and verbal and spatial ability (DeFries & Plomin, 1985). Two of these, namely, memory and speed, have been widely considered as likely components of the infancy measures; both have also been found to be deficient in preterms relative to full-terms (Escobar et al., 1991; Hack et al., 1992).

Sample

In the longitudinal sample, there were 109 children (63 preterms and 46 full-terms). Children from the two groups were similar in demographic factors: birth order (approximately half were first born), maternal age (mean of about 23 years), maternal education (65% high school graduates), ethnicity (predominately African American and Hispanic) and SES (nearly 60% of the families were classified as unskilled or semiskilled, according to the Hollingshead Four-factor Index, 1975). The only demographic difference that approached significance was a higher proportion of females in the preterm sample compared to the full-term group (61.9% vs. 41.3%). Details are presented in Rose, Feldman, Wallace, and McCarton (1989, 1991).

Preterms had originally been selected as a prototypic risk group. All were born weighing < 1500g. The birth weight of those included in the present study averaged 1154 g and their gestational age averaged 31.2 weeks; 44% were born small-for-gestational-age (SGA) and 74% had suffered RDS. (Information concerning intraventricular hemorrhage is limited since ultrasonography was not routinely available at the time these children were born.) Seven of the children had major neurological sequelae; six had cerebral palsy and one had hypotonia. All children were ambulatory without braces, although one child had required braces before surgery. None of the analyses were affected by excluding these children.

Full-terms all had normal births and uneventful prenatal and perinatal courses. Given the low SES of both cohorts, the full-terms could be considered to be socially at risk while the preterms could be considered to have double hazard, that is, to be at risk both biologically and socially (Escalona, 1982).

Specific Cognitive Abilities in Infancy

Infants in this sample were tested on the same four tasks described previously: visual recognition memory was assessed at 7 months and 1 year, and cross-modal transfer, tactual recognition memory, and object permanence were assessed at 1 year.

The assessment of visual recognition memory at 7 months included nine problems using as stimuli abstract patterns, photographs of faces, and three-dimensional geometric forms (three problems of each type). Familiarization times were 5 seconds for patterns, and 20 seconds each for faces and geometric forms. At 1 year, infants were given three problems of visual recognition memory and four problems of cross-modal transfer; the stimuli for both were three-dimensional geometric forms. Familiarization time was 15 seconds for each visual problem and 25 seconds for each cross-modal problem. Infants also received two problems of tactual recognition memory, each consisting of a 60-second period of tactual familiarization followed by a 2-minute test. Object permanence was tested using the Einstein Scale (Corman & Escalona, 1969). For greater detail on the procedures used at 7 months and 1 year see Rose, Feldman, Wallace, and McCarton, 1989, 1991.

As can be seen in Table 2.1, differences between preterms and full-terms in this longitudinal sample largely replicate those of the cross-sectional studies discussed previously. The performance of preterms was poorer than that of full-terms on visual recognition memory (significantly so at 7 months, marginally so at 1 year), tactual recognition memory, and object permanence. Cross-modal scores were similar and at chance for both groups, replicating the findings presented earlier for infants from predominately lower-class (but not middle-class) backgrounds.

In this study, we also examined several ancillary measures from the familiarization phase of visual recognition memory at 7 months. These included the duration of individual looks (a measure prominent in habituation studies), the duration of pauses, the percentage of looks on which the infant shifted attention between the paired targets, and exposure time, or the time taken to accrue a given amount of familiarization. The results indicated that preterms had longer pauses between successive looks and required lengthier exposure time. These longer pauses indicate that, once lost, the preterms' attention was not as readily regained as the full-terms. On those problems in which there were paired targets during familiarization, preterms tended to have lengthier looks (a style associated with less efficient processing) and were less likely to shift attention back and forth and actively compare the two stimuli. Overall, in addition to having lower novelty scores on test, preterms were less able to recruit, sustain, and shift attention during familiarization (for a fuller discussion of results see Rose, Feldman, McCarton, & Wolfson, 1988).

TABLE 2.1
Specific Cognitive Abilities in Infancy by Birth Status

Measures	Full-terms			Preterms			
	N	M	SD	N	M	SD	t
7 Months							
Visual recognition memory	45	55.0[a]	14.2	46	51.6	8.5	2.19**
12 Months							
Visual recognition memory	46	56.0[a]	5.9	59	53.6[a]	7.7	1.70*
Cross-modal transfer	46	50.2	6.9	58	49.5	6.0	0.59
Tactual recognition memory	39	63.3[a]	22.3	32	51.4	25.8	2.09**
Object permanence	42	4.6	0.7	33	4.2	0.8	2.35**
N (%) completing each stage							
Stage 3	4 (10%)			7 (21%)			
Stage 4	10 (24%)			13 (39%)			
Stage 5	28 (67%)			13 (39%)			

[a]Novelty scores are significantly different from chance expectation of 50% ($p < .01$).
*$p \leq .05$. **$p \leq .01$, two-tailed.

Specific Cognitive Abilities in Childhood

The children were seen semiannually from 7 months to 3 years, annually from 4–6 years, and, for a final assessment, at 11 years of age. As noted earlier, although global measures were used at every age, at 11 years we also included systematic assessments of four specific abilities that have figured prominently in cognitive research, namely, memory, speed-of-processing, verbal ability, and spatial ability. Our measure of these abilities were drawn from two batteries. The first, the Specific Cognitive Abilities Test (SCA: DeFries & Plomin, 1985; see also Thompson, Detterman, & Plomin, 1991), is a paper-and-pencil battery that includes two tests of each of the four abilities. Researchers initially identified these four distinct but intercorrelated abilities in factor analytic studies of tests of adult cognition; they then developed age-appropriate versions for childhood.

The other battery, the Cognitive Abilities Test (CAT: Detterman, 1988, 1990) is a computerized series of tasks assessing speed of information processing, memory, and attention. All stimuli are patterns created by lighting different numbers and arrangements of squares from four-by-four arrays. For each task, trials begin with the child touching a *home bar* on the touch-sensitive screen; responses are made by moving the finger from the home bar to a response box. For most tasks, speed is measured as decision time (DT), the time from onset of the test phase of each trial to the initiation of a response (i.e., latency to release the home bar). For some tasks, however, speed is measured by reaction time, the time from test onset to response completion. Attention is measured by the standard deviation of decision time (SDDT) or reaction time (SDRT). Memory is measured by accuracy on tasks involving recognition or recall. Feedback is provided on each trial by a beep (correct) or a buzz (incorrect). We used 7 of the 12 CAT tasks; a substantial subset that took approximately 1½ hours to administer.

Preterm–full-term differences in each domain are presented in Tables 2.2–2.5. Although most of data presented in these tables is drawn from the 11-year assessment, where there is data from earlier ages tapping the same theoretical constructs, those data are given as well.

Memory

SCA At 11 Years.   There were two tasks: picture recognition and name-face association. Both had an immediate and delayed component, with higher scores on each reflecting better memory. Picture recognition involved the child's picking out of an array of 40 drawings the 20 that he or she had been allowed to view for 1 minute. Name-face association involved recalling the simple names associated with each of eight photographs of adults' faces. The immediate and delayed components of each were standardized separately, using the full sample, and then averaged.

As can be seen in Table 2.2, preterms performed more poorly than full-terms on both components.

TABLE 2.2
Memory in Childhood by Birth Status

Measures	Full-terms		Preterms		Standardized Difference (β)
	M	SE	M	SE	
SCA (11 year)	(n = 40)		(n = 50)		
Composite	.3	.1	-.2	.1	.37**
Immediate	.3	.1	-.2	.1	.33*
Delayed	.2	.1	-.2	.1	.28*
CAT (11 year)	(n = 40)		(n = 50)		
Learning	44.6	1.8	36.0	1.6	.40**
Probe recall	43.1	1.2	38.2	1.0	.36**
Sternberg memory search	93.6	1.5	87.5	1.3	.35**
Recognition memory	79.8	1.8	71.8	1.6	.37**
Measures from 6 years	(n = 44)		(n = 47)		
WISC-R digit span	9.5	.4	6.9	.4	.42**
ITPA visual sequential	35.7	.9	31.3	.9	.34**

Note 1. The SCA is the test of Specific Cognitive Abilities. Component scores (pictures and name-face associations) were standardized within the sample as a whole and averaged to form the immediate, delayed, and composite scores; all values thus are standard scores (z-scores). The CAT is the Cognitive Abilities Test; scores are percent correct. The WISC-R digit span and the visual sequential subtest from the ITPA (Illinois Test of Psycholinguistic Abilities) are standardized scores with means of 10 ($SD = 3$) and 36 ($SD = 6$), respectively. (ITPA scores are missing for one preterm and one full-term.)
Note 2. All 11-year scores are adjusted for gender and age.
*$p \leq .05$. **$p \leq .01$, two tailed.

CAT At 11 Years. Memory was assessed with four tasks: learning, probe recall, Sternberg memory search, and recognition memory. Learning involved memorization of the spatial position of each stimulus in a horizontally displayed array; successive sets increased in size. Probe recall again assessed memory for spatial position of a stimulus in a horizontally displayed array; here, however, the array length remained invariant (six stimuli) and the target and distractor stimuli changed on each trial. Sternberg memory search assessed efficiency in searching for items held in working memory. This was done by having the child indicate whether a probe was or was not a member of a previously memorized set; sets varied in size from one to four stimuli. Recognition memory assessed incidental memory for stimuli seen in previous tasks. Again, the child indicates whether a probe had or had not been seen previously.

As seen in Table 2.2, preterms also erred more than full-terms on these tasks.

Measures From Earlier Ages (6 Years). Memory was assessed at 6 years, with the digit span subtest from the Wechsler Intelligence Scale for Children-Revised (WISC-R) and with the test of visual sequential memory from the ITPA

TABLE 2.3
Processing Speed in Childhood by Birth Status

Measures	Full-terms		Preterms		Standardized Difference (β)
	M	SE	M	SE	
SCA (11 year)	(n = 40)		(n = 50)		
Composite	.4	.1	-.3	.1	.36**
Perceptual speed	22.8	1.0	18.0	.9	.40**
Finding A	30.3	1.6	25.6	1.4	.24*
CAT (11 year)	(n = 40)		(n = 50)		
Reaction time ((ms)	547	22	539	19	See Note 2
Sternberg memory search (ms)	912	41	1012	36	-.22†
Tachistoscopic threshold (ms)	131	19	198	16	-.31*
WISC-R (6 year)	(n = 44)		(n = 47)		
Coding	10.7	.4	9.6	.4	.18†

Note 1. Component scores of the SCA reflect the number of items completed in the time allowed; components were standardized within the sample and then averaged to form the composite. Except for tachistoscopic threshold, which is the median threshold, scores on the CAT are mean decision times. The WISC-R coding is a standardized score with a mean of 10 (SD = 3).

Note 2. For the CAT reaction time measure, although the adjusted means did not differ between groups, there was a significant interaction such that the preterms were faster than the full-terms when faced with only one choice of response (simple reaction time), but slower than the full-terms when faced with eight choices (choice reaction time).

Note 3. All 11-year scores are adjusted for gender and age.
† ≤ .10. *p ≤ .05. **p ≤ .01, two tailed.

(Kirk, McCarthy, & Kirk, 1968). Digit span reflects the number of digits the child is able to repeat forwards and backwards. Scores are standardized to a mean of 10 and a standard deviation of 3. Visual sequential memory requires the reproduction of increasingly lengthy sequences of complex abstract figures from memory. Scores are standardized to a mean of 36 and a standard deviation of 6.

Full-terms scored close to the norm on both tasks whereas preterms' scores averaged about one standard deviation below the norm (Table 2.2).

Speed

SCA At 11 Years. There were two tasks: perceptual speed and find *A*. The first is a match-to-sample task, in which the child indicates as quickly as possible which of four alternatives in each row matches the target on the left; the second task involves pointing out, from a list of words, those which contained the letter *A*. In each case the score is the number of correct responses within a 2-minute period.

As shown in Table 2.3, preterms were significantly slower than full-terms on both tasks.

CAT At 11 Years. The three tasks from the CAT on which the preterms performed more slowly were reaction time, Sternberg memory search, and tachistoscopic threshold. In the Reaction time task, the child touches as quickly as possible the stimulus box that lights up in a set of 1, 2, 4, 6, or 8 boxes. The time taken to decide among the alternative (decision time) was measured in milliseconds. While the overall mean decision time of preterms and full-terms did not differ, a significant interaction indicated that preterms were faster than full-terms when there was only one position in which the stimulus could appear (simple reaction times) but slower than full-terms when the stimulus could appear in any of eight positions (choice reaction time). For the Sternberg task, described previously, preterms took longer than full-terms to decide whether a probe was or was not a member of the memory set (decision time scored only for correct responses). The tachistoscopic threshold task used the method of ascending limits to determine the shortest time needed to correctly determine whether or not two stimuli are identical. The measure shown in Table 2.3, the median threshold over 20 series, indicates that thresholds are higher for preterms, indeed, they were nearly half again as long.[1]

Measures From Earlier Ages (6 Years). There was only one measure of speed from an earlier age, namely, the coding subtest of the WISC-R at 6 years of age. Here the child places distinctive marks in different forms according to the model on top of the page (e.g., a single vertical line inside a star); a child's score depends on the number of items correctly completed in a limited time (120 seconds maximum). The performance of preterms was marginally worse than that of the full-terms.

Verbal Ability

SCA At 11 Years. Receptive vocabulary is assessed with the Peabody Picture Vocabulary Test (PPVT: Dunn & Dunn, 1981), and verbal fluency with the Educational Testing Service (ETS) test of verbal fluency. In the PPVT, the child must select from four panels the one depicting the meaning of a word; scores are standardized to a mean of 100 ($SD = 15$). In the ETS test of verbal fluency, the child names as many animals as possible in 1 minute; then does the same for round things and things that begin with the letter *S*.

As can be seen in Table 2.4, preterms provided significantly fewer examples on the fluency test and performed marginally worse on the PPVT.

Measures From Earlier Ages (3, 4, and 6 Years). At 3 and 4 years of age, measures of comprehension and expression were obtained using the Reynell Scales of language development (Reynell, 1969); scores are standardized to a mean of 0 ($SD = 1$). At 6 years, analogous measures were obtained using the listening and

---

[1]There were four additional tasks from the CAT that yielded measures of response speed: learning, probe recall, recognition memory, and stimulus discrimination. With these tasks, preterms had slower reaction times but differences were not significant.

TABLE 2.4
Verbal Ability in Childhood by Birth Status

Measures	Full-terms		Preterms		Standardized Difference (β)
	M	SE	M	SE	
SCA (11 year)	(n = 40)		(n = 50)		
Composite	.3	.1	-.2	.1	.33**
Receptive Vocabulary (PPVT)	93.5	3.4	85.8	2.9	.21
Fluency	36.8	1.5	31.3	1.3	.33*
Measures from 3 years	(n = 33)		(n = 31)		
Reynell comprehension	-.8	.1	-1.0	.1	.14
Reynell expression	-1.1	.2	-.8	.2	-.21
Measures from 4 years	(n = 36)		(n = 33)		
Reynell comprehension	-.1	.2	-1.4	.2	.52**
Reynell expression	-.7	.2	-.8	.2	-.04
Measures from 6 years	(n = 44)		(n = 47)		
TOLD comprehension	93.5	2.1	83.7	2.0	.34**
TOLD expression	91.1	2.0	80.8	2.0	.36**

Note 1. The PPVT (Peabody Picture Vocabulary Test) is standardized to a mean of 100 (*SD* = 15). The score for verbal fluency is the total number of responses given over the 3 minutes. These components of the SCA were standardized within the sample and then averaged to form the composite. The Reynell is a standardized test with a mean of zero (*SD* = 1); only cases having scores on both Reynell subtests and the concurrent IQ test were included. The TOLD (Test of Language Development) is a standardized test with a mean of 100 (*SD* = 15).
Note 2. All 11-year scores are adjusted for gender and age.
*$p \le .05$. **$p \le .01$, two tailed.

speaking quotients of the Test of Language Development-Primary (TOLD-P; New-comer & Hammill, 1982); these scores are standardized to a mean of 36 (*SD* = 6).

As can be seen in Table 2.4, at all three ages, both groups performed somewhat below test norms; however, preterms performed significantly worse than full-terms on receptive language at 4 years and on both aspects of language at 6 years.

Spatial Ability

SCA At 11 Years. This was the only age at which spatial ability was assessed. Again there were two tasks. The first was a hidden figures test in which the child was to select, from many line drawings, those containing the embedded target. The second was a spatial relations test, in which the child selects, from sets of four pictures, the one that, when mentally rotated would complete a pictured square.

As can be seen in Table 2.5, preterms did worse than full-terms on both subtests and on the composite.

TABLE 2.5
Spatial Ability in Childhood by Birth Status

Measures	Full-terms		Preterms		Standardized Difference (β)
	M	*SE*	*M*	*SE*	
SCA (11 year)	($n = 40$)		($n = 50$)		
Composite	.3	.2	-.2	.1	.30*
Hidden figures	47.4	3.6	34.7	3.2	.30*
Spatial relations	8.8	1.5	4.5	1.3	.24*

Note 1. Component scores reflect the number of items completed in the time allowed; components were standardized within the sample and then averaged to form the composite.
Note 2. Scores are adjusted for gender and age.
*$p \leq .05$, two tailed.

General Cognitive Ability in Infancy and Childhood

Children in the longitudinal sample also received repeated developmental exams throughout the follow-up period. General cognitive performance was measured using the Mental Developmental Index (MDI) of the Bayley Scales of Infant Development (Bayley, 1969) at 12, 18, and 24 months; the Stanford-Binet Intelligence Scale, Form L-M (Terman & Merrill, 1973) at 3 and 4 years; the Wechsler Preschool and Primary Scale of Intelligence (WPPSI; Wechsler, 1967) at 5 years; and the Wechsler Intelligence Scales for Children-Revised at 6 and 11 years (WISC-R; Wechsler, 1974).

Scores for preterms from our longitudinal study and their full-terms counterparts are provided in Table 2.6. (Sample sizes vary somewhat from year to year because some children dropped out and others missed one or another visit.) Two aspects of these data are notable. First, at each age, preterms had significantly lower scores than the full-terms. Generally, the means for the preterms were about 10 points lower than those for the full-terms, with scores for the preterms in the 80s and those for the full-terms in the 90s. Notably, this difference stayed constant across the years.

Second, the results of a trend analysis support the visual impression that, for both groups, scores increased from 7 months to 1 year, declined steeply at 1.5 to 2 years, continued somewhat lower at 3 years, and then rose gradually until 6 years. The steep decline at 2 years of age has been reported previously for low SES full-terms (Golden & Birns, 1983) and preterms (Escalona, 1982). We are not sure whether this decline is spurious, due to inflation of 12-month Bayley scores (Liaw & Brooks, 1993) or real, due to the negative impact of poor environment that often begins to exert an influence on development around this age. The increase in IQ scores after age 3 may be related to the changes in testing instrument, although Escalona (1982) observed a similar upturn without a change

TABLE 2.6
General Cognitive Ability From Infancy Through Childhood by Birth Status

	Full-terms			Preterms			
Measures	N	M	SD	N	M	SD	t
Bayley MDI (7 mos)	44	96.7	14.2	46	82.5	13.8	4.81**
Bayley MDI (1 year)	46	101.3	8.9	59	90.8	16.3	4.20**
Bayley MDI (1.5 year)	42	103.4	12.3	42	82.9	14.9	6.86**
Bayley MDI (2 year)	44	91.5	12.1	56	81.8	14.5	3.58**
Stanford-Binet IQ (3 year)	39	87.8	11.8	50	81.0	13.3	2.53*
StanfordBinet IQ (4 year)	41	92.2	10.1	45	82.9	10.7	4.15**
WPPPSI IQ (5 year)	40	95.4	13.0	49	86.9	11.1	3.32**
WISC-R IQ (6 year)	44	97.5	11.8	47	87.8	13.5	3.62**
WISC-R IQ (11 year)	40	98.9	11.9	50	89.6	11.3	3.79**

*$p \leq .05$. **$p \leq .01$, two tailed.

in test. However, the upturn may well be due to the participation of many of the children from both groups in preschool programs, which we informally noted often began around 3 years.

Relation Between Infant and Childhood Abilities

Although this chapter is concerned principally with differences between preterms and full-terms, it is worth noting that the infant measures were significantly related to a number of the later measures. Moreover, the cross-age relations were similar for both groups—preterms and full-terms, a finding of particular interest given the failure of standardized infant developmental tests to relate to later cognition (for related work see Colombo, 1993; DiLalla et al., 1990; Fagan, 1984; McCall & Carriger, 1993; Sigman, Cohen, Beckwith, Asarnow, & Parmelee, 1991; Sigman, Cohen, Beckwith, & Parmelee, 1986; Thompson, Fagan, & Fulker, 1991).

Of the four infant measures discussed earlier, three were found to predict childhood IQ, a global measure of cognition. Visual recognition memory (especially from 7 months) predicted IQ at virtually all the follow-up assessments through 11 years (rs ranged from .37 to .65). Cross-modal transfer (from 12 months) predicted the same outcomes (rs ranged from .25 to .51) and object permanence (also from 12 months) predicted IQ through 6 years (rs ranged from .28 to .47). For details of these findings see Rose and Feldman, 1995; Rose, Feldman, and Wallace, 1992; Rose, Feldman, Wallace, and McCarton, 1989, 1991.

In addition, a number of the infant measures were related to the specific abilities that we measured in later childhood. The 7-month measure of visual recognition memory was most broadly related, correlating with nearly all the measures at 11 years (perceptual speed, memory, verbal ability, and spatial ability), as well as with earlier measurements of these abilities (Rose & Feldman, 1995, 1997; Rose, Feldman, & Wallace, 1988, 1992; Rose, Feldman, Wallace, & Cohen, 1991). Infant measures of cross-modal transfer and object permanence also showed relations with the measures of more specific abilities from later childhood, although these relations were more differentiated. The relations of infancy measures to later outcomes, spanning 10 or more years, support the notion that individual differences in cognition (i.e., the maintenance in rank) are continuous and that the cognitive differences between preterms and full-terms have their origins in infancy.

Overall, the infant measures were most consistently related to later speed and memory, a finding compatible with theoretical notions that these two basic processes underlie the infant measures. These speculations are reinforced by two additional findings. First, in a canonical correlation between the major infant abilities and the four SCA composites, a single canonical factor emerged. This factor was most parsimoniously interpreted as reflecting speed (Rose & Feldman, 1995). Second, the infancy-IQ relations were substantially reduced after statistically controlling for composites of speed and memory (created by combining measures from the CAT and SCA); in addition, structural equation modeling indicated that there were significant paths between 7-month visual recognition memory and 11-year IQ going through speed and memory (Rose & Feldman, 1997).

Speed and Memory Account for Preterm–Full-term Differences

In the previous sections, the four specific abilities were placed on an equal footing, with each considered to be a major component of cognition. Some investigators, however, would consider verbal and spatial abilities as more molar than speed and memory. For example, individual differences in speed and memory have frequently been singled out as forming the cornerstones of cognition (Deary, 1988; Hale, 1990; Jensen, 1987; Kail, 1986, 1988; Vernon, 1987). This hypothesized role in cognition, coupled with the pervasive difficulties shown by preterms on both abilities, raises the possibility that individual differences in speed and memory may account for the IQ differences found between the two groups.

To evaluate this possibility, we examined the relation between birth status and IQ both before and after controlling for memory and speed (Rose & Feldman, 1996). In the first of a series of multiple regressions predicting IQ, only gender and age were entered along with birth status. In successive equations, composites of memory and speed were entered alone and in combination. The results indicated that, taken together, memory and processing speed accounted for much of the 10-point difference in IQ. These data are shown in Table 2.7, where we have combined measures of speed and memory from the CAT and SCA. Here the difference in IQ between preterms and full-terms is given by the unstandardized re-

TABLE 2.7

Results of Hierarchical Multiple Regressions Examining Preterm–Full-term Differences in IQ, Verbal Ability, and Spatial Ability Controlling for speed and Memory

Variables	Differences Between Preterms and Full-terms		Variance Uniquely Accounted for by Birth Status	Significance	
	B	SE	sr^2	t	p
Full scale IQ					
None[a]	10.31	3.04	.11	3.38	.001
Speed	6.32	2.87	.04	2.20	.030
Memory	4.66	3.01	.02	1.55	.125
Memory and speed	4.21	2.92	.02	1.44	.153
Verbal ability from the SCA					
None[a]	.53	.21	.07	2.56	.012
Speed	.31	.20	.02	1.53	.130
Memory	.15	.21	.00	.73	.468
Memory and Speed	.13	.21	.00	.62	.540
Spatial ability from the SCA					
None[a]	.54	.22	.06	2.48	.015
Speed	.25	.21	.01	1.20	.232
Memory	.11	.22	.00	.51	.614
Memory and speed	.07	.21	.00	.32	.753

[a] None signifies no control for memory or speed; gender and age are controlled in all regressions. Preterm-full-term difference is represented by a variable coded dichotomously as 1 = preterm and 2 = full-term.

gression coefficients (B) from each equation; the percent variance in IQ uniquely accounted for by birth status is given by the squared semipartial coefficients.

As seen in Table 2.7, with only age and gender controlled, the mean difference between preterms and full-terms amounted to 10.3 IQ points, and about 11% of the variance in IQ was attributable to birth status. The difference between groups was reduced to about 4.2 IQ points when controlling for speed and memory—a difference that was not statistically significant—and left only 2% of the variance in IQ uniquely attributable to birth status.

If verbal and spatial abilities are really more molar constructs, it is possible that differences in speed and memory would account for preterms' difficulties in these domains as well. And indeed, as can be seen from the regressions shown in the bottom panels of Table 2.7, this appears to be the case. For verbal and spatial ability alike, with gender and age controlled, the mean difference between preterms and full-terms amounted to about ½ a standard deviation. In other words, controlling only for gender and age, 6% to 7% of the variance in these abilities was attributable to birth status. However, the difference between groups was reduced to about ¹/₁₀ of a standard deviation when controlling for speed and memory, with no variance attributable to birth status remaining.

Thus, the differences between preterms and full-terms in verbal and spatial ability, as well as in IQ, were wiped out when speed and memory were controlled. These results suggest that a substantial part of the cognitive difficulties associated with very low birth weight reflects difficulties in memory and processing speed.

Relation of Medical Risk to Memory in Preterms

In an effort to further pinpoint the source of the preterms' relatively poor performance, we examined the relationship between medical risk factors and the various measures of cognition from infancy and later childhood. Risk factors included the Obstetrical and Postnatal Complications Scales of Littman and Parmelee (1978), as well as a number of more specific factors, including total days of postnatal hospitalization, birth weight, gestational age, SGA status, Apgar scores, and several indices of respiratory distress.

Whereas most medical risk factors were generally unrelated to infant and later outcomes, there were interesting relations between RDS and memory both in infancy and at 11 years. As noted earlier, a fairly large percentage of our preterm sample (76%) had been diagnosed with RDS. This diagnosis required both the presence of clinical evidence of respiratory distress in the first hours of life and characteristic thoracic roentgenograms (Harrod, L'Heureux, Wanengstein, & Hunt, 1974).

Of the preterms with RDS, most required mechanical ventilation. Ordinal scales indexing the severity of RDS were formed based on the presence of the diagnosis and the number of days of mechanical ventilation required: no RDS, mild

RDS (no days on respirator), moderate RDS (1 to 3 days on respirator), and severe RDS (more than 3 days on respirator).[2] Children with more severe RDS showed poorer memory in infancy, as well as at 6 and 11 years. Severity was negatively correlated with 7-month visual recognition memory ($r = -.27$, $n = 36$, and $p < .05$), the 6-year measure of digit span ($r = -.32$, $n = 38$, and $p < .05$), and with two 11-year memory measures from the CAT—Sternberg memory search and recognition memory ($r = -.31$ and $-.33$, respectively, $n = 40$, and $p < .05$). Other indices of respiratory problems, namely, days on a respirator, days receiving oxygen, and days of continuous positive airway pressure, were similarly related to these memory measures, with rs ranging from $-.20$ to $-.51$.

Mechanisms Underlying Preterm Deficits in Speed and Memory

Memory. While our understanding of the neurophysiological mechanisms of infant performance is still fairly rudimentary, one possible mechanism underlying memory deficits in preterms is suggested by the association of poor memory performance with RDS in our sample. Despite treatment to maintain adequate oxygenation, infants with RDS are likely to suffer hypoxic-ischemic episodes, disturbances in cerebral perfusion, or both (Cooke, Rolfe, & Howe, 1979). This type of injury, which deprives the brain of oxygen, has long been known to be a major perinatal cause of neurological morbidity in infants, particularly in preterms; moreover, neurons of the hippocampus, an area of the brain involved in short-term memory, are especially vulnerable to such injury (Volpe, 1995). Animal models have demonstrated quantifiable neuropathological changes in response to controlled degrees of cerebral ischemia, with particularly severe pathological changes in the CA1 region of the hippocampus (Davis, Tribuna, Pulsinelli, & Volpe, 1986; Pulsinelli, Brierley, & Plum, 1982). Such hypoxic-ischemic brain injury has been shown to result in memory deficits in nonhuman primates (Hyman, Parker, Berman, & Berman, 1970; Sechzer, 1969).

Many of the memory tasks we used at 6 and 11 years assessed what is commonly called *declarative or explicit* memory. This type of memory involves the conscious (i.e., explicit) recollection of facts or events (Squire, 1992; see also Nelson, 1995), and is dependent on the hippocampus and associated structures. Declarative memory is impaired in patients with histologically confirmed lesions of the hippocampus (and associated medial temporal lobe structures, or both). Not only are the tasks we used at the older ages dependent on these brain structures, but two lines of evidence indicate that the task of visual recognition memory used in infancy is too. First, McKee and Squire (1993) found that adult patients who were suffering from bilateral damage to the hippocampal formation or diencephalic regions failed to

---

[2]Initially, the RDS scale had only 3 points (infants with mild RDS were excluded), and it is this version that was used in examining relations between RDS and 7-month measures; the entire 4-point scale was used in all correlations with performance at older ages.

show significant novelty response when delays of only 2 minutes were interposed between familiarization and test (see also, Reed & Squire, 1997). Second, Bachevalier and her coworkers showed that bilateral removal of the amygdala, hippocampus, and surrounding cortex in infant monkeys impaired their performance on paired comparison tasks given in infancy; moreover, when the lesioned monkeys reached adulthood, their performance was also impaired on delayed-nonmatch-to-sample, the benchmark task used to assess explicit memory in adult monkeys (Bachevalier, Brickson, & Hagger, 1993; Bachevalier, Brickson, Hagger, & Mishkin, 1990; Malkova, Mishkin, & Bachevalier, 1995; see also Monk, Gunderson, Webster, & Mechling, 1996). Such findings led Nelson (1995) to characterize infant performance on the paired comparison task as representing at least a rudimentary form of explicit, or pre-explicit, memory.

Speed.   Speed of processing is both less well-defined than memory and its basis less well understood. At a psychological level, speed can mean anything from speed of encoding to speed of retrieval, and even then, it is unclear whether differences in processing speed are caused by differences in the ability to process quickly, maintain an engaged state, disengage attention, redeploy attention efficiently, or whether such differences are secondary to the motor responses generally used to index speed.

Detailed neurophysiological information on brain mechanisms underlying processing speed is not available. However, it is thought that hypoxic-ischemic injury may impair or delay the development of myelin, a major factor in conduction velocity in associative nerve tracts (i.e., tracts linking different brain structures), and thus impair the speed with which signals pass from one area of the brain to another. Hypoxic-ischemic injury, a very important problem in the perinatal period, is often accompanied by intraventricular hemorrhage, periventricuar leukomacia, or both in the preterm. One of the consistent neuropathological consequences of (IVH) is destruction of germinal matrix with its glial precursor cells (Volpe, 1995). Destruction of glial precursor cells in the germinal matrix would result either in loss of the oligodendroglial progenitors of myelin or in the disruption of their migration. Aside from the ill effects on nerve conduction velocity, the hypoxic-ischemic episodes could possibly impair transmission because of impairment to synaptic densities. Although myelination has most often been studied in relation to motor speed, its relation to cognitive processing is suggested by findings that patients with demyelinating diseases, such as multiple sclerosis have deficits on tests of processing speed (Rao, 1985). Additionally, otherwise healthy elderly adults who demonstrate marked white matter abnormalities (seen as lucencies on CT scans and as hyperintensities on MRI scans) show cognitive deficits on tasks involving speed of encoding (Ylikoski et al., 1993). However, there is a paucity of work in the area and a lack of detailed and systematic information about the size and location of white matter lesions typically found in very low birth weight preterms, and their relation to functionally specialized brain regions.

SUMMARY AND CONCLUSIONS

Overall, our findings point to information processing deficits in preterms that are detectable at least by 6 months of age, and perhaps earlier (see Sigman et al., 1986, 1991; Wallace, Rose, McCarton, Kurtzberg, & Vaughan, 1995), persist throughout the first year, and may forecast cognitive deficits in later childhood. The childhood deficits are global, as reflected in IQ scores, a measure of general cognitive ability (preterms scored about 10 points lower than full-terms), and specific, as reflected in lower scores on measures of several specific cognitive abilities. Deficits in two of the specific abilities, namely, memory and processing speed, accounted for much of the 10-point difference in IQ between preterms and full-terms. Finally, there was some evidence linking RDS to memory deficits in preterms. These findings support and extend earlier findings in ways that have important implications for understanding the extent, nature, and course of cognitive delays in preterms.

First, they support recent findings (see introduction) that preterms score lower than full-terms on general measures of cognition. More importantly, they extend these findings in a fundamental way by indicating that speed of processing and memory may provide the basis for the observed deficits in more general cognitive ability. Memory and processing speed, the two specific abilities that accounted for the IQ differences between preterms and full-terms in the present study, have long been linked theoretically to cognition. Age-related increases in speed of processing tend to be ubiquitous and to follow similar developmental trajectories across domains (Kail, 1986, 1988). The global nature of this trend, and the striking similarity of age differences across tasks, led Kail (1991) to suggest that age-related increases in speed of processing are due to a central limiting factor that increases with age. Moreover, although age-related changes in working memory have long been thought to be critical to many cognitive abilities (e.g., Baddeley, 1986; Carpenter, Just, & Shell, 1990), recent evidence indicates that the age-related changes in speed of processing may underlie this relation. For example, Fry and Hale (1996) observed a developmental cascade between 7 and 9 years in which information processing becomes faster, leading to improvements in memory, which in turn led to increases in fluid intelligence (e.g., Raven's progressive matrices). Thus, deficits in speed and memory have broad implications for deficits in the more molar measures of cognition, such as IQ, academic achievement, and learning disabilities.

Second, given the continuity found between infant and childhood abilities, the infant measures hold promise for aiding in the early detection of mental retardation and the evaluation of medical and obstetric interventions. However, since the cross-age correlations are only modest, and the reliability of the infant measures relatively poor, the extent to which any of the infant measures are currently useful for more than global screening is unclear (but see Fagan, Singer, Montie, & Shepherd, 1986; Fagan & Vasen, 1997). Nonetheless, the findings of cognitive continuity do suggest that the roots of later cognitive difficulties can be found in infancy and that deficits may be detectable much earlier than previously thought. The clinical importance of infant information processing measures would be reinforced if they proved useful as outcomes in clinical trials. Although some effort is underway to use them in this fashion, the results are not yet available. Ultimately, the extent to which cognitive difficulties might be ameliorated will depend on a better understanding of the nature of early cognitive difficulties and on a better delineation of the factors that place the infant at risk for such deficits.

Third, the fact that memory impairments in preterms were related to the severity of RDS raises the possibility that the hypoxic-ischemic injury associated with this condition may account for some of the memory deficits seen in infancy and later childhood. As noted earlier, hypoxic-ischemic injury is known to be a major perinatal cause of morbidity (Volpe, 1995) and has been shown to cause memory impairment in nonhuman primates (e.g., Sechzer, 1969). Moreover, neurons of the hippocampus, an area of the brain thought to underlie performance on tasks of declarative memory, is known to be particularly vulnerable to hypoxic-ischemic insult.

Finally, it should be kept in mind that our samples are not severely compromised. We exclude infants with major sensori-neural impairment (deaf, blind, and congenital abnormalities) and most children scored within 1 standard deviation of the test mean. Considering their fragile beginnings, the majority were developing normally and the deficits we detect might be considered subtle. Nonetheless, it should be noted that even a 10-point difference between groups can signal major consequences, and indeed the literature suggests that these infants are overrepresented among the learning disabled. Thus, the impairments detected in infancy and throughout childhood, even if subtle, may have major consequences for the well-being of the child.

REFERENCES

Aylward, G. P., Pfeiffer, S. I., Wright, A., & Verhulst, S. J. (1989). Outcome studies of low birth weight infants published in the last decade: A meta-analysis. *Journal of Pediatrics, 115*, 515–520.

Bachevalier, J., Brickson, M., & Hagger, C. (1993). Limbic-dependent recognition memory in monkeys develops early in infancy. *NeuroReport, 4*, 77–80.

Bachevalier, J., Brickson, M., Hagger, C., & Mishkin, M. (1990). Age and sex differences in the effects of selective temporal lesion on the formation of visual discrimination habits in rhesus monkeys (*Macaca mulatta*). *Behavioral Neuroscience, 104*, 885–899.

Baddeley, A. D. (1986). *Working memory*. Oxford, England: Clarendon Press.

Bayley, N. (1958). Value and limitations of infant testing. *Children, 5*, 129–133.

Bayley, N. (1969). *Bayley Scales of Infant Development*. San Antonio, Texas: Psychological Corporation.

Bornstein, M. H., & Benasich, A. A. (1986). Infant habituation: Assessments of individual differences and short-term reliability at five months. *Child Development, 57*, 87–99.

Carpenter, P. A., Just, M. A., & Shell, P. (1990). What one intelligence test measures: A theoretical account of the processing in the Raven Progressive Matrices Test. *Psychological Review, 97*, 404–431.

Cooke, R. W. I., Rolfe, P., & Howe, P. (1979). Apparent cerebral blood-flow in newborns with respiratory disease. *Developmental Medicine and Child Neurology, 21*, 154–160.

Colombo, J. (1993). *Infant cognition: Predicting later intellectual functioning*. Newbury Park, CA: Sage.

Colombo, J., & Mitchell, D. W. (1990). Individual differences in early visual attention: Fixation time and information processing. In J. Colombo & J. Fagen (Eds.), *Individual Differences in Infancy: Reliability, Stability, Prediction* (pp. 193–228). Hillsdale, NJ: Lawrence Erlbaum Associates.

Corman, H. H., & Escalona, S. K. (1969). Stages of sensorimotor development: A replication study. *Merrill Palmer Quarterly, 15*, 351–361.

Davis, H. P., Tribuna, J., Pulsinelli, W. A., & Volpe, R. T. (1986). Reference and working memory of rats following hippocampal damage induced by transient forebrain ischemia. *Physiology and Behavior, 37*, 387–392.

Deary, I. J. (1988). Intelligence and encoding speed in infants, adults and children. *Cahier de Psychologie Cognitive/European Bulletin of Cognitive Psychology, 8*, 462–468.

DeFries, J. C., & Plomin, R. (1985). *Origins of individual differences in infancy: The Colorado Adoption Project*. Orlando, FL: Academic Press.

Detterman, D. K. (1987a). Theoretical notions of intelligence and mental retardation. *American Journal of Mental Deficiency, 92*, 2–11.

Detterman, D. K. (1987b). What does reaction time tell us about intelligence? In P. A. Vernon (Ed.), *Speed of information processing and intelligence* (pp. 177–199). Norwood, NJ: Ablex.

Detterman, D. K. (1988). *CAT: Cognitive Abilities Test*. Unpublished test, Case Western Reserve University (Available from Douglas K. Detterman, Department of Psychology, Case Western Reserve University, Cleveland, Ohio, 44106).

Detterman, D. K. (1990). CAT: Computerized abilities test for research and teaching. *MicroPsych Network, 4*, 51–62.

DiLalla, L. F., Thompson, L. A., Plomin, R., Phillips, K., Fagan, J. F., Haith, M. M., Cyphers, L. H., & Fulker, D. W. (1990). Infant predictors of preschool and adult IQ: A study of infant twins and their parents. *Developmental Psychology, 26*, 759–769.

Eilers, B. L., Desai, N. S., Wilson, M. A., & Cunningham, M. D. (1986). Classroom performance and social factors of children with birth weights of 1,250 grams or less: Follow up at 5 to 8 years of age. *Pediatrics, 77*, 203–208.

Escalona, S. (1982). Babies at double hazard: Early development of infants at biological and social risk. *Pediatrics, 70*, 670–676.

Escobar, G. J., Littenberg, B., & Petitti, D. B. (1991). Outcome among surviving very low birthweight infants: A meta-analysis. *Archives of Diseases of Childhood, 66*, 204–211.

Fagan, J. F. (1974). Infant's recognition memory: The effects of length of familiarization and type of discrimination task. *Child Development, 45*, 351–356.

Fagan, J. F. (1984). The relationship of novelty preference during infancy to later intelligence and later recognition memory. *Intelligence, 8*, 339–346.

Fagan, J. F., Singer, L. T., Montie, J. E., & Shepherd, P. A. (1986). Selective screening device for the early detection of normal or delayed cognitive development in infants at risk for later mental retardation. *Pediatrics, 78*, 1021–1026.

Fagan, J. F., & Vasen, J. H. (1997). Selective attention to novelty as a measure of information processing. In J. A. Burack & J. T. Enns (Eds.), *Attention, Development, and Psychopathology*. New York: Guilford.

Fantz, R. L. (1964). Visual experience in infants: Decreased attention to familiar patterns relative to novel ones. *Science, 146*, 668–670.

Fantz, R. L., Fagan, J. F., & Miranda, S. B. (1975). Early visual selectivity. In L. Cohen & P. Salapatek (Eds.), *Infant perception: From sensation to cognition* (Vol. 1, pp. 249–346). New York: Academic Press.

Fry, A. F., & Hale, S. (1996). Processing speed, working memory, and fluid intelligence: Evidence for a developmental cascade. *Psychological Science*, in press.

Golden, M., & Birns, B. (1983). Social class and infant intelligence. In M. Lewis (Ed.), *Origins of intelligence* (2nd ed., pp. 347–398). New York: Plenum.

Gottfried, A. W., & Rose, S. A. (1980). Tactile recognition memory in infants. *Child Development, 51*, 69–74.

Gottfried, A. W., Rose, S. A., & Bridger, W. H. (1977). Cross-modal transfer in human infants. *Child Development, 48*, 118–123.

Hack, M. B., et al. (1992). The effect of very low birth weight and social risk on neurocognitive abilities at school age. *Journal of Developmental and Behaviorial Pediatrics, 13*, 412–420.

Hale, S. (1990). A global developmental trend in cognitive processing speed. *Child Development, 61*, 653–663.

Harrod, J. R., L' Heureux, P., Wanengstein, O. D., & Hunt, C. E. (1974). Long-term follow-up of severe respiratory distress syndrome tested with IPPB. *Pediatrics, 84*, 277–286.

Hollingshead, A. B. (1975). *The four-factor index of social status*. Unpublished manuscript, Yale University at New Haven, CT.

Horowitz, F. D., Paden, L. Y., Bhana, K., & Self, P. A. (1972). An infant control procedure for the study of infant visual fixations. *Developmental Psychology, 7*, 90.

Hoy, E. A., Bill, J. M., & Sykes, D. H. (1988). Very low birthweight: A long-term developmental impairment? *International Journal of Behaviorial Development, 11*, 37–67.

Hunt, J. V., Cooper, B. A. B., & Tooley, W. H. (1988). Very low birth weight infants at 8 and 11 years of age: Role of neonatal illness and family status. *Pediatrics, 82*, 596–603.

Hyman, A., Parker, B., Berman, D., & Berman, A. J. (1970). Delayed response deficits in neonatally asphyxiated rhesus monkeys. *Experimental Neurology, 28*, 4420–425.

Jensen, A. R. (1987). Individual differences in the Hick paradigm. In P. A. Vernon (Ed.), *Speed of information-processing and intelligence*. Norwood, NJ: Ablex.

Kail, R. (1986). Sources of age differences in speed of processing. *Child Development, 57*, 969–987.

Kail, R. (1988). Developmental functions for speeds of cognitive processing. *Journal of Experimental Child Psychology, 45*, 339–364.

Kail, R. (1991). Developmental change in speed of processing during childhood and adolescence. *Psychological Bulletin, 109*, 490–501.

Kirk, S. A., McCarthy, J. J., & Kirk, W. (1968). *Illinois Test of Psycholinguistic Abilities (Rev. ed.)*. Urbana: University of Illinois.

Klebanov, P. K., Brooks-Gunn, J., & McCormick, M. C. (1994). School achievement and failure in very low birth weight children. *Developmental and Behavioral Pediatrics, 15*, 248–256.

Klein, N. K., Hack, M., & Breslau, N. (1989). Children who were very low birth weight: Development and academic achievement at nine years of age. *Journal of Developmental and Behavioral Pediatrics, 10*, 32–37.

Kopp, C. B., & McCall, R. B. (1982). Predicting later mental performance for normal, at-risk, and handicapped infants. In P. B. Bates & O. G. Brim (Eds.), *Life span development and behavior* (Vol. 4, pp. 33–61). New York: Academic Press.

Liaw, F. R., & Brooks-Gunn, J. (1993). Patterns of low-birth-weight children's cognitive development. *Developmental Psychology, 29*, 1024–1035.

Littman, B., & Parmelee, A. H. (1978). Medical correlates of infant development. *Pediatrics, 61*, 470–474.

Malkova, L., Mishkin, M., & Bachevalier, J. (1995). Long-term effects of selective neonatal temporal lobe lesions on learning and memory in monkeys. *Behavioral Neuroscience, 109*, 397–404.

Marks, L. E. (1978). *The unity of the senses: Interrelations among the modalities*. New York: Academic Press.

McCall, R. B., & Carriger, M. S. (1993). A meta-analysis of infant habituation and recognition memory performance as predictors of later IQ. *Child Development, 64*, 57–79.

McCormick, M. C. (1989). Long-term follow up of NICU graduates. *Journal of the American Medical Association, 261*, 1767–1772.

McKee, R. D., & Squire, L. R. (1993). On the development of declarative memory. *Journal of Experimental Psychology: Learning, Memory, and Cognition, 19*, 397–404.

Monk, C. S., Gunderson, V. M., Grant, K. S., & Mechling, J. L. (1996). A demonstration of the memory savings effect in infant monkeys. *Developmental Psychology, 32*, 1051–1055.

Nelson, C. A. (1995). The ontogeny of human memory: A cognitive neuroscience perspective. *Developmental Psychology, 31*, 723–738.

Newcomer, P. L., & Hammill, D. D. (1982). *Test of Language Development-Primary*. Austin, Tx: Pro-ed.

Piaget, J. (1954). *The construction of reality in the child*. New York: Basic Books.

Pulsinelli, W. A., Brierley, J. B., & Plum, F. (1982). Temporal profile of neuronal damage in a model of transient forebrain ischemia. *Annals of Neurology, 11*, 491–498.

Rao, S. M. (1995). Neuropsychology of multiple sclerosis. *Current Opinion in Neurology, 8*, 216–220.

Reed, J. M., & Squire, L. R. (1997). Impaired recognition memory in patients with lesions limited to the hippocampal formation. *Behavioral Neuroscience, 111*, 667–675.

Reynell, J. (1969). *Reynell developmental language scales*. Windsor, England: NFER.

Rickards, A. L., Kitchen, W. H., Doyle, L. W., Ford, G. W., Kelly, E. A., & Callanan, C. (1993). Cognition, school performance, and behavior in very low birth weight and normal weight children at 8 years of age: A longitudinal study. *Developmental and Behavioral Pediatrics, 14*, 363–368.

Rose, S. A. (1980). Enhancing visual recognition memory in preterm infants. *Developmental Psychology, 16*, 85–92.

Rose, S. A. (1983). Differential rates of visual information processing in fullterm and preterm infants. *Child Development, 54*, 1189–1198.

Rose, S. A., & Feldman, J. F. (1990). Infant cognition: Individual differences and developmental continuities. In J. Colombo & J. W. Fagen (Eds.), *Individual differences in infancy*. Hillsdale, NJ: Lawrence Erlbaum Associates.

Rose, S. A., & Feldman, J. F. (1995). Prediction of IQ and specific cognitive abilities at 11 years from infancy measures. *Developmental Psychology, 31*, 685–696.

Rose, S. A., & Feldman, J. F. (1996). Memory and processing speed in preterm children at eleven years: A comparison with full-terms. *Child Development, 67*, 2005–2021.

Rose, S. A., & Feldman, J. F. (1997). Memory and speed: Their role in the relation of infant information processing to later IQ. *Child Development, 68*, 630–641.

Rose, S. A., Feldman, J. F., McCarton, C. M., & Wolfson, J. (1988). Information processing in seven-month-old infants as a function of risk status. *Child Development, 59*, 589–603.

Rose, S. A., Feldman, J. F., & Wallace, I. F. (1988). Individual differences in infant information processing: Reliability, stability, and prediction. *Child Development, 59*, 1177–1197.

Rose, S. A., Feldman, J. F., & Wallace, I. F. (1992). Infant information processing in relation to six-year cognitive outcomes. *Child Development, 63*, 1126–1141.

Rose, S. A., Feldman, J. F., Wallace, I. F., & Cohen, P. (1991). Language: A partial link between infant attention and later intelligence. *Developmental Psychology, 27*, 798–805.

Rose, S. A., Feldman, J. F., Wallace, I. F., & McCarton, C. (1989). Infant visual attention: Relation to birth status and developmental outcome during the first 5 years. *Developmental Psychology, 25*, 560–575.

Rose, S. A., Feldman, J. F., Wallace, I. F., & McCarton, C. (1991). Information processing at 1 year: Relation to birth status and developmental outcome during the first five years. *Developmental Psychology, 27*, 723–737.

Rose, S. A., Gottfried, A. W., & Bridger, W. H. (1978). Cross-modal transfer in infants: Relationship to prematurity and socio-economic background. *Developmental Psychology, 14*, 643–652.

Rose, S. A., Gottfried, A. W., & Bridger, W. H. (1981). Cross-modal transfer in 6-month-old infants. *Developmental Psychology, 17*, 661–669.

Rose, S. A., Gottfried, A. W., & Bridger, W. H. (1983). Infant's cross-modal transfer from solid objects to their graphic representations. *Child Development, 54*, 686–694.

Rose, S. A., Gottfried, A. W., Melloy-Carminar, P. M., & Bridger, W. H. (1982). Familiarity and novelty preferences in infant recognition memory: Implications for information processing. *Developmental Psychology, 18*, 704–713.

Rose, S. A., & Orlian, E. K. (1991). Asymmetries in cross-modal transfer. *Child Development, 62*, 706–718.

Rose, S. A., & Wallace, I. F. (1985a). Cross-modal and intra-modal transfer as predictors of mental development in fullterm and preterm infants. *Developmental Psychology, 21*, 949–962.

Rose, S. A., & Wallace, I. F. (1985b). Visual recognition memory: A predictor of later cognitive functioning in preterms. *Child Development, 56*, 843–852.

Ross, G., Lipper, E. G., & Auld, P. A. M. (1991). Educational status and school-related abilities of very low birth weight premature children. *Pediatrics, 88*, 339–346.

Saigal, S., Rosenbaum, P., Szatmari, P., & Campbell, D. (1991). Learning disabilities and school problems in a regional cohort of extremely low birth weight (< 1000 g) children: A comparison with term controls. *Journal of Developmental and Behavioral Pediatrics, 12*, 294–300.

Salthouse, T. A. (1996). The processing-speed theory of adult age differences in cognition. *Psychological Review, 103*, 403–428.

Scottish Low Birthweight Study Group (1992). The Scottish low birthweight study: 11. Language attainment, cognitive status, and behavioural problems. *Archives of Disease in Childhood, 67*, 682–686.

Sigman, M., Cohen, S. E., Beckwith, L., Asarnow, R., & Parmelee, A. H. (1991). Continuity in cognitive abilities from infancy to 12 years of age. *Cognitive Development, 6*, 47–57.

Sigman, M., Cohen, S. E., Beckwith, L., & Parmelee, A. H. (1986). Infant attention in relation to intellectual abilities in childhood. *Developmental Psychology, 22*, 788–792.

Sechzer, J. A. (1969). Memory deficit in monkeys brain damaged by asphyxia neonatorum. *Experimental Neurology, 24*, 497–507.

Sokolov, E. N. (1969). The modelling properties of the nervous system. In M. Cole & I. Maltzman (Eds.), *A handbook of contemporary Soviet psychology*. New York: Basic Books.

Squire, L. R. (1992). Memory and the hippocampus: A synthesis from findings with rats, monkeys, and humans. *Psychological Review, 99*, 195–231.

Terman, L. M., & Merrill, M. A. (1973). *Stanford-Binet Intelligence Scale, Form L-M*. Boston: Houghton Mifflin.

Thompson, L. A., Detterman, D. K., & Plomin, R. (1991). Associations between cognitive abilities and scholastic achievement: Genetic overlap but environmental differences. *Psychological Science, 2*, 158–165.

Thompson, L. A., Fagan, J. F., & Fulker, D. W. (1991). Longitudinal prediction of specific cognitive abilities from infant novelty preference. *Child Development, 67*, 530–538.

Vernon, P. A. (Ed.). (1987). *Speed of Processing and Intelligence*. Norwood, NJ: Ablex.

Volpe, J. J. (1995). *Neurology of the Newborn* (3rd ed.). Philadelphia: Saunders.

Wagner, S. H., & Sakovits, L. J. (1986). A process analysis of infant visual and cross-modal recognition memory: Implications for an amodal code. In L. P. Lipsitt & C. K. Rovee-Collier (Eds.), *Advances in Infancy Research* (Vol. 4, pp. 195–217). Norwood, NJ: Ablex.

Wallace, I. F., Rose, S. A., McCarton, C. M., Kurtzberg, D., & Vaughan, H. G. (1995). Relations between infant neurobehavioral performance and cognitive outcome in very low birth weight preterm infants. *Developmental and Behavioral Pediatrics, 16*, 309–317.

Wechsler, D. (1967). *Manual for the Wechsler Preschool and Primary Scale of Intelligence*. New York: Psychological Corporation.

Wechsler, D. (1974). *Intelligence Scale for Children-Revised*. New York: Psychological Corporation.

Ylikoski, R., Ylikoski, A., Erkinjuntti, T., Sulkava, R., Raininko, R., & Tilvis, R. (1993). White matter changes in healthy elderly persons correlate with attention and speed of mental processing. *Archives of Neurology, 50*, 818–824.

3

▼▼▼▼▼▼▼▼▼

Teratogenic Insult and Neurobehavioral Function in Infancy and Childhood

Sandra W. Jacobson
Department of Psychiatry and Behavioral Neurosciences
Wayne State University School of Medicine

Joseph L. Jacobson
Department of Psychology
Wayne State University

Neurobehavioral assessment has become an important tool for evaluating the consequences of intrauterine exposure to chemical agents routinely encountered in the environment as well as substances, including alcohol and drugs, used by the mother during pregnancy (Riley & Vorhees, 1986). At first, it was assumed that the placenta acts as an effective barrier preventing toxic substances in the maternal blood stream from reaching the fetus. It is now understood that most toxic substances cross the placenta, the exceptions being those that are nonlipid soluble, ionize at tissue pH, or have a molecular weight greater than 600 (Coyle, Wayner, & Singer, 1976). Early experimental research revealed the role of irradiation, viral and bacterial infection, and malnutrition in producing fetal malformations previously thought to be genetically caused (Hutchings, 1978). The thalidomide tragedy (Tuchmann-Duplessis, 1975) and the identification of fetal alcohol syndrome (Jones & Smith, 1973) attracted greater attention to the field and made clear that a variety of chemical agents could be harmful to humans. More recently, man-made environmental substances have come under scientific scrutiny to determine their potential teratogenicity and whether they are harmful at dosages ordinarily ingested or absorbed by humans. Findings such as these have stimulated a new research area concerned with the impact of toxic substances on human development and functioning.

Initially, the field of teratology dealt with the study of environmentally induced abnormalities associated with exposure to toxic agents during the prenatal period, including morphological, physiological, and biochemical deficits or abnormalities (Coyle et al., 1976; Wilson, 1977). Studies were primarily conducted in animal laboratories, so that random assignment could be used, and timing and varying dosages of exposure could readily be examined. Attention focused on the period of organogenesis, at which time the embryo is most sensitive to gross structural malformation. Other less obvious abnormalities, such as growth retardation, dermatoglyphic changes, and minor structural abnormalities that are not externally visible (e.g., abnormalities of the vertebrae and ribs), have also been associated with embryonic exposure to various drugs (Coyle et al., 1976). However, studies of vitamin A administered later in the early fetal period revealed nonlethal brain damage and led to the investigation of behavioral effects, including disturbances of arousal or state regulation, specific learning disabilities, impaired motor coordination, and mental retardation (Hutchings, 1978). This and other evidence broadened the scope of teratology to include exposure to toxic substances in the postembryonic period and the functional deficits resulting from this exposure. A basic premise emerging from studies on hypervitaminosis A (Butcher, 1976), salicylates (Butcher, Vorhees, & Kimmel, 1972), and methylmercury (Weiss & Spyker, 1974) is that behavioral changes, some fairly subtle, can be produced at dosage levels below those producing gross physical abnormalities.

This premise is illustrated by the hypothetical dose-response curves shown in Fig. 3.1 (Vorhees, 1986). Embryolethal effects are seen at the highest doses; functional effects, at the lowest. A fourth curve representing growth has been suggested, but it is not yet clear whether it belongs between the functional and malformation curves. Animal research has succeeded in identifying what some teratologists call pure behavioral teratogens, such as propoxyphene, which produce behavioral abnormalities without affecting growth or physical development (Vorhees, Brunner, & Butcher, 1979). Various drugs, such as tranquilizers, stimulants, and analgesics, do not selectively destroy embryonic cells and are, therefore, not technically teratogens. But these drugs produce functional effects, including growth retardation and behavioral deficits, by interfering with neurochemical mechanisms in the fetal brain (Hutchings, 1978).

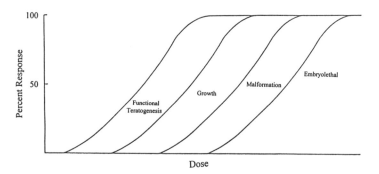

FIG. 3.1. Idealized dose-response curves showing the relation between the four primary manifestations of teratogenesis.

The term *behavioral teratology*, first used by Werboff and Gottlieb (1963), is defined as the "identification of agents which cause abnormal behavior in offspring, and the assessment of functional consequences of an insult during prenatal development" (Jensh, 1983, p. 171). Vorhees et al. (1979), Hutchings (1978), and Spyker (1975) each suggested some working principles for this new specialty of teratological research. The following summarizes the major principles generated by the research findings reported to date.

1. Particularly at low or subteratogenic levels agents may cause subtle behavioral changes in the absence of gross functional or morphological defects.
2. Agents that produce gross central nervous system (CNS) malformations at higher doses are more likely to cause congenital behavioral anomalies.
3. The pattern of behavioral effects is dependent on the stage at which exposure occurs and the type of substance to which the organism is exposed.
4. There is no *safe period* during gestation, since the period of fetal susceptibility to behavioral effects extends beyond the period when the CNS is resistant to gross malformations.
5. The genotype interacts with the agent in determining behavioral effects.
6. The extent of the behavioral effect appears to be dose dependent.

In the case of alcohol exposure, the discovery of a link between heavy maternal drinking during pregnancy and mental retardation (i.e., fetal alcohol syndrome) was facilitated by the distinctive craniofacial dysmorphology that serves as a marker of prenatal exposure in the most severely affected children. Since that discovery (Jones & Smith, 1973), several studies have demonstrated that less severe cognitive deficits are found in children born to women who drink at lower levels during pregnancy (e.g., Goldschmidt et al., 1996; J. Jacobson et al., 1993; S. Jacobson, Jacobson, Sokol, Martier, & Ager, 1993; Streissguth, Bookstein, Sampson, & Barr, 1993). A recent National Academy of Sciences Institute of Medicine report (Stratton, Howe, & Battaglia, 1996) has suggested a new term for CNS impairment in nonsyndromal children—alcohol-related neurodevelopmental disorder (ARND). Although the deficits associated with full fetal alcohol syndrome (FAS) are more devastating for the individual child, the subtler developmental problems associated with ARND are far more prevalent (J. Jacobson, Jacobson, Sokol, & Ager, 1998). Because children with ARND lack distinctive dysmorphic features, however, it is more difficult to study the relation of prenatal alcohol exposure to their cognitive and behavioral deficits and to identify individuals affected at lower levels of exposure, particularly if the mother either denies or has forgotten how much alcohol she consumed during the pregnancy.

Although some apical tests, such as, IQ or the Bayley Scales of Infant Development (Bayley, 1969), appear to be sensitive to exposure to a broad range of neurotoxicants, in principle one would expect different brain regions and substrates to vary in their sensitivity to different chemical agents. This differential vulnerability would, in turn, be expected to lead to different patterns of neurobehavioral impairment. ARND is currently defined as any "complex pattern of behavior or cognitive abnormalities that . . . cannot be explained by family background or environment alone," which has been linked in "clinical or animal research . . . [to] alcohol ingestion" in a child exposed during pregnancy (Stratton et al., 1996, pp. 19–20). If a distinctive alcohol-related neurobehavioral profile could be identified, the ARND diagnosis could be limited to children exhibiting that profile, and the link between their alcohol exposure and the observed deficits could be made with greater confidence. An alcohol-related behavioral profile would also be invaluable in designing educational interventions specifically targeted to affected children. In addition, if deficits are found in domains of cognitive function that have been found in human and animal lesion and neuroimaging studies to be mediated by specific brain regions and neural pathways, these deficits may provide important clues regarding the neurochemical and neuroanatomical processes through which prenatal alcohol exposure impacts on CNS development.

Does prenatal exposure to a range of toxicants generally affect the same developmental outcomes, or does exposure to each substance lead to a unique neurobehavioral profile? The search for a behavioral profile has also been undertaken by researchers studying effects of prenatal exposure to other toxic agents on neurobehavioral development. An attempt to identify a *behavioral signature* for lead exposure has still proven inconclusive (Alber & Strupp, 1996; Bellinger, 1995; Bellinger, Stiles, & Needleman, 1992; Garavan, Morgan, Levitsky, Hermer-Vazquez, & Strupp, in press; Hilson & Strupp, 1997; Strupp et al., in press). However, failure to detect differences in behavioral profile may, in part, be an artifact of the global intelligence or developmental tests and measures that have been used to assess outcome.

At the same time, there has been an advance in infant assessment research in recent years with the development of new, more specific, narrow band infant tests, which have proven to be more predictive of later intelligence than the global tests, such as, the Bayley Scales of Infant Development (Colombo, 1993; Fagan, 1984; Fagan & McGrath, 1981; McCall & Carriger, 1993; Rose & Feldman, 1995, 1997; Rose, Feldman, Futterweit, & Jankowski, 1997). Much attention has recently been paid to understanding the nature of the underlying components of infant cognition that may help explain this continuity. A critical question is whether these infant measures reflect a unitary process, a general factor, as measured by IQ, or different, relatively independent underlying components of cognitive functioning. A goal of our research has been to see whether these information-processing tests are more sensitive to subtle prenatal exposure, whether different toxins impact differentially on these measures (thereby suggesting different underlying components are affected), or whether infants exposed to diverse substances perform more poorly as a group on these infant tests. Our basic hypothesis is that difficulty detecting a behavioral profile is due in part to the use of more global measures of development and intelligence. In addition, detection of a behavioral profile will be facilitated by deconstruction of these global measures and assessment of the association of differential exposure or risk factors to their component parts.

Both issues will be addressed using data from three different cohorts we have studied: (a) a Detroit African American cohort of 480 mothers and children exposed prenatally to alcohol and cocaine; (b) a Michigan cohort of 313 mothers and children prenatally exposed to an environmental contaminant, polychlorinated biphenyls (PCBs); and (c) a small cohort of Taiwanese infants whose mothers were accidentally exposed to high levels of PCBs from contaminated rice oil. Cognitive effects of prenatal exposure to alcohol, cocaine, and PCBs, are examined to determine whether exposure to each substance results in a common or different pattern of impairment on a set of narrow-band infant and school-aged child assessments.

Our findings from these studies suggest that processing speed and memory–attention constitute relatively independent underlying components of cognitive function, which are differentially affected by different teratogens and lead to distinct long-term neurobehavioral patterns of effects. We will present three kinds of data in support of this position: one entails an examination of the interrelations among the infant measures in a factor analysis; another examines the predictive validity of the processing speed and memory–attention components; and the third suggests how teratological data can be used to better understand the underlying structure of infant cognition. Although teratological data are usually used to assess specific adverse health and cognitive deficits related to prenatal exposure, the findings presented here demonstrate their relevance in addressing basic developmental issues. Lastly, we will review our most current findings on the adverse effects of PCBs at 11 years and alcohol at 7.5 years postpartum and some of the clinical implications of these findings for affected children.

FETAL ALCOHOL EXPOSURE

FAS is now recognized as the leading known cause of mental retardation in the United States, surpassing Down syndrome and spina bifida. About 1 child of 100 born to heavy drinking mothers ($\geq$ 1oz absolute alcohol/day (AA/day) or more during pregnancy, which is the equivalent of about 2 drinks/day) shows the full FAS. The link between maternal alcohol abuse during pregnancy and intellectual impairment in childhood was first documented in the United States by Jones and Smith (1973) in their discovery of FAS.

The standard criteria for diagnosing FAS are: (a) intrauterine, and/or postnatal growth retardation; (b) CNS impairment; and (c) a distinctive pattern of facial characteristics, including short palpebral fissures, an elongated midface, a long and flattened philtrum, thin upper lip, and flattened maxilla (Sokol & Clarren, 1989; Stratton et al., 1996). Figure 3.2 shows a South African infant and young girl, who have both been diagnosed as having FAS.

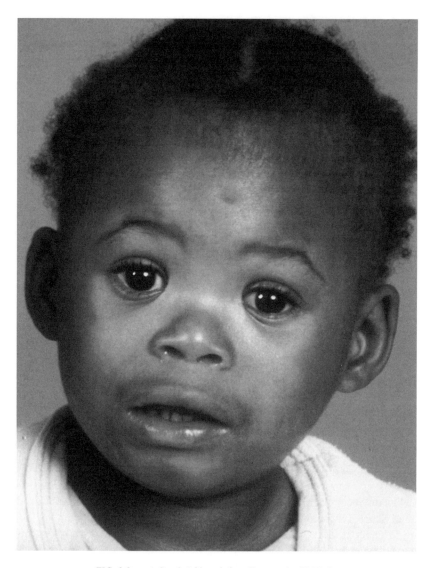

FIG. 3.2a.   A South African infant diagnosed with FAS.

Intellectual and behavioral impairment is the most disabling feature of FAS. About half of FAS patients are mentally retarded (IQ < 70), and virtually all exhibit serious attentional and behavioral problems (Streissguth et al., 1991). Recent findings from studies of children and adolescents with FAS suggest a specific pattern of neurodevelopmental impairment including arithmetic deficiency, extreme difficulty with abstract reasoning, complex attention, goal-directed behavior, and executive function, despite apparent competence in communication

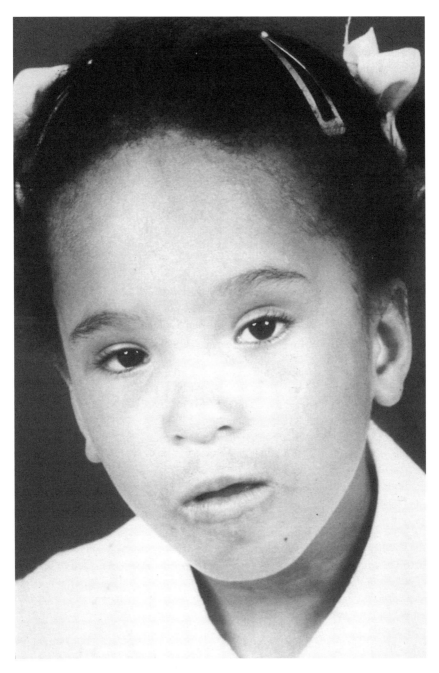

FIG. 3.2b.   A South African girl diagnosed with FAS.

skills. Maladaptive behaviors, including poor judgment and difficulty perceiving social cues, are also common in individuals with FAS. Findings from longitudinal follow-up studies of adolescents and adults with FAS in the United States, Germany, and France indicate that, while some of the facial anomalies diminish with age (Aase, 1994; Lemoine & Lemoine, 1992; Spohr, Willms, & Steinhausen, 1993) and there is catch-up growth for weight during adolescence, particularly among girls, microcephaly (Lemoine & Lemoine, 1992; Spohr et al., 1993; Streissguth et al., 1991) and intellectual problems persist and behavioral, emotional, and social problems become more pronounced, even when the home environment changes for the better (Lemoine & Lemoine, 1992; Streissguth et al., 1991). Meanwhile, findings from several large, well-controlled, prospective, longitudinal studies have since shown similar but less severe developmental deficits in children born to mothers who drank during pregnancy at lower levels, indicating that FAS represents the severe end of a continuum of ARND in children (e.g., Coles et al., 1997; Jacobson & Jacobson, 1994; Streissguth et al., 1994).

The identification of a pattern of neurobehavioral deficits in nonsyndromal alcohol-exposed children is important because some children lacking the full facial dysmorphology, in fact, appear to be as affected as full syndromal children (Mattson, Riley, & Jernigan, 1994); while others who are alcohol exposed exhibit comparable though less severe deficits. It has been assumed that the characteristic facial features are indicative of more severe CNS impairment, but recently it has been suggested that timing of exposure may be responsible for the dysmorphic features. And that some infants whose mothers did not drink heavily at precisely the right window of exposure will not *have the face* but may still suffer many of the same neurobehavioral problems associated with later maternal heavy drinking.

When we began our research in Detroit in 1986, it was not clear to what extent moderate levels of alcohol exposure produce neurobehavioral and growth deficits similar to FAS; whether these occur in a dose-dependent fashion, or whether there is a threshold below which the exposed infant is not affected. We were interested to see whether some of the newer infant information-processing assessments from developmental psychology might indicate specific domains of cognitive functioning affected by prenatal exposure. These questions led us to use what we thought might be the most sensitive infant tests with better predictive validity than more traditional sensorimotor assessments, such as, the Bayley Scales of Infant Development (Bayley, 1969), which have been used in virtually all studies on effects of exposure. We hoped to be able to detect prenatal effects very early in development rather than waiting until the child was older. This approach has at least two advantages: from a clinical perspective, detection of effects in infancy may allow for earlier interventions and, from a scientific standpoint, many environmental factors influence the child's performance and subtle prenatal effects can be more difficult to detect as the child gets older. We also expected that the newer infant information-processing skills would be affected by fewer socioenvironmental factors than those assessed on the traditional, apical Bayley Scales.

Detroit Cohort

Our Detroit cohort is comprised of economically disadvantaged African-American mothers and their children, who were born between 1986 and 1989 (J. Jacobson et al., 1993; S. Jacobson et al., 1993). The 480 mothers in the sample are predominantly lower class, poorly educated, unmarried, and on welfare (Table 3.1). Women were recruited prenatally on the basis of their alcohol and drug use. All

TABLE 3.1
Sample Characteristics

	N	Mean	SD	Range
Maternal characteristics				
SES[a]	383	19.8	8.5	8.0–63.0
Age	480	26.4	6.0	14.1–43.9
Marital status (% married)	480	10.8	--	--
Education (year)	480	11.7	1.6	6.0–18.0
Welfare recipients (%)	404	81.3	--	--
Gestational age at initial screening (week)	480	23.3	7.9	6.0–40.0
Number of prenatal visits	480	5.3	3.2	1.0–14.0
Parity	480	2.4	1.5	1.0–11.0
Verbal IQ (PPVT-R)	387	73.1	13.3	40.0–115.0
HOME Inventory	397	30.9	4.7	15.0–43.0
Beck Depression Inventory	388	10.9	7.3	0.0–38.0
Infant characteristics				
Birth weight (gm)	480	3090.7	541.9	1560.0–4536.0
Birth length (cm)	471	48.7	2.9	38.0–55.0
Head circumference (cm)	469	33.9	1.7	24.0–37.5
Gestational age at birth (week)	480	39.3	1.6	32.5–43.0
Sex of infant (% male)	480	57.3	--	--
Alcohol (oz AA/day)[b]				
At conception	384	1.0	2.0	0.0–24.8
During pregnancy	400	0.3	0.6	0.0– 6.5
At 7.5 years	242	1.3	2.3	0.0–14.0
Cocaine (days/month)[b]				
During pregnancy	150	3.8	3.7	0.1–20.0
At 7.5 years	28	8.4	9.2	0.0–30.0
Marijuana (days/month)[b]				
During pregnancy	147	3.0	3.3	0.1–19.2
At 7.5 years	108	6.6	8.6	0.1–30.0
Smoking (cigarettes/day)[b]				
During pregnancy	300	14.4	10.8	1.0–60.0
At 7.5 years	186	12.6	9.0	0.1–50.0

[a]Based on Hollingshead Four Factor Index of Social Status (1975).
[b]Consumers only.

women reporting alcohol consumption at conception averaging at least 0.5 oz of absolute alcohol/day (AA/day or about one drink per day) were invited to participate. A random sample of approximately 5% of the remaining clinic women were recruited as controls. Because of a cocaine epidemic in Detroit at that time, we were concerned that many heavy alcohol users might also be using cocaine. To reduce the risk that alcohol would be confounded with cocaine exposure, 78 heavy cocaine (at least 2 days/week), light alcohol (< 0.5 oz AA/day) users were also included. This stratification subsequently enabled us to discriminate alcohol from cocaine effects. Mothers and their infants were seen in our laboratory at 6.5, 12, and 13 months postpartum and again when the children were 7.5 years of age. Examiners were blind to exposure.

In our research, we use multiple regression and analysis of covariance to control for potential confounding influences. The potential confounding variables include maternal education and IQ, smoking and illicit drug use during pregnancy, pregnancy and delivery complications, quality of intellectual stimulation provided by the parents, maternal depression and psychopathology, and current maternal drinking and drug use. Correlational analysis is used to determine the control variables that need to be included in multivariate analyses to control for potential confounding. A control variable cannot be the true cause of an observed deficit unless it is related to both exposure and outcome (Schlesselman, 1982). Control variables are selected in relation to outcome, which has the advantage of including covariates unrelated to exposure, thereby increasing precision (Kleinbaum, Kupper, & Muller, 1988). All control variables even weakly related to the outcome in question ($p < .10$) are entered first in the regression analyses, followed by alcohol exposure at the next step. An alcohol-related deficit is inferred only if the effect of exposure is significant (at $p < .05$), after adjustment for the effects of the control variables.

Processing Speed. The most consistent neurobehavioral effect of prenatal alcohol exposure in older children relates to attention. Poorer accuracy and slower reaction times were related to moderate prenatal alcohol exposure in a largely middle-class Seattle cohort at 4, 7, and 14 years (Streissguth et al., 1984, 1986; Streissguth, Bookstein, Sampson, & Barr, 1995), an effect also detected in children with FAS (Nanson & Hiscock, 1990). These findings led Streissguth to suggest an alcohol-related deficit in speed of central processing.

Several new paradigms for assessment of infant information processing have been advanced in recent years. Traditional infant tests, such as the Bayley Scales, focus on rate of progress through developmental milestones, an approach also taken by measures from the Uzgiris and Hunt (1975) Scales and complexity of play tasks (e.g., Belsky, Garduque, & Hrncir, 1984; Nicolich, 1977). Other tests based on habituation and paired-comparison paradigms focus more directly on information-processing capabilities (Bornstein & Sigman, 1986). Some investigators (Fagan & Singer, 1983; Rose, Feldman, & Wallace, 1988) have emphasized measurement of novelty preference in the paired-comparison paradigm, while others have recommended assessment of duration of attention and inattention (fixation duration) during familiarization (Colombo, Mitchell, & Horowitz, 1988). Novelty preference has been found to have markedly better predictive validity for later performance on standardized intelligence tests than the Bayley (Fagan & Singer, 1983; Rose & Wallace, 1985), and two studies have shown that shorter fixation duration during infancy also predicts higher childhood IQ (Rose, Slater, & Perry, 1986; Sigman, Cohen, Beckwith, & Parmelee, 1985). Shorter fixation duration, which has been related to superior performance on numerous infant tasks (e.g., Colombo et al., 1988; Mitchell & Colombo, 1989; Tamis-LeMonda & Bornstein, 1989), may indicate more efficient information processing (Colombo & Mitchell, 1990), which is often measured by reaction time (RT) paradigms in older children. Our research confirmed this hypothesized relation by being the first to show a direct link between fixation duration and RT in infants (S. Jacobson et al., 1992). Faster RTs on the Visual Expectancy Paradigm (VExP; Haith, Hazan, Goodman, 1988; described in detail subsequently) were related to shorter fixation duration on both the Fagan Test of Infant Intelligence (FTII) and cross-modal transfer test (rs ranged from .24 to .33, ps > .05).

Infants in our Detroit cohort were administered the FTII (Fagan & Singer, 1983) at 6.5 and 12 months and a cross-modal transfer test (Rose, Gottfried, & Bridger, 1978) at 12 months, both of which provide a measure of novelty preference (see S. Jacobson et al., 1992). In the FTII, the infant was seated on the mother's lap and shown two identical target photos, one of which is then presented together with a novel stimulus. Infant fixation to the stimuli was judged from corneal reflections of the stimulus targets observed through a peephole located halfway between the two target photos and recorded on a computer. The stimuli consisted of 10 pairs of faces. Preference for novelty was defined as the percent of total fixation to the novel target for each pair of photos. Mean preference for novelty was calculated by averaging percent of novelty preference for the 10 problems at each age and then, to increase reliability, across the two ages (see Colombo et al., 1988; DiLalla et al., 1990; Rose et al., 1988b; Thompson Fagan, & Fulker, 1991). In addition, Colombo and Mitchell (1990) suggested that mean duration of visual fixation on the FTII could provide a valid measure of speed of information processing or processing efficiency in infancy. Data from the FTII can readily be analyzed to yield a measure of length of visual fixation. Mean duration of visual fixation is computed by dividing total duration looking time divided by number of looks and averaging these across the problems at 6.5 months and 12 months and then across the two ages.

Cross-modal transfer was assessed using the procedure developed by Rose et al. (1978). The stimuli, modeled after those used by Rose, consisted of six pairs of acrylic objects, which differed primarily in shape (S. Jacobson et al., 1992). The infant was seated on the mother's lap in front of a stage. The examiner placed an object in the infant's hand, shielding it from view during the familiarization period. The object was then placed in full view with a novel object of the same color and size. Visual fixation to each of the stimuli was recorded on a computer by a second examiner. Preference for novelty was computed separately for each problem by dividing fixation time to the novel stimulus by total fixation time to the novel and familiar stimuli and then averaged across the six problems. Mean fixation duration was computed by dividing fixation duration by number of looks and averaging across the six problems.

We had expected that prenatal alcohol exposure, like PCBs (Jacobson, Fein, Jacobson, Schwartz, & Dowler, 1985), would be related to poorer recognition memory on the FTII. Much to our surprise, alcohol exposure was not related to novelty preference on either the FTII or the cross-modal transfer test but was associated instead with a pattern of significantly longer infant visual fixation (Table 3.2), suggesting that slower, less efficient information processing, previously only detected in older alcohol-exposed children, is already evident in infancy (S. Jacobson et al., 1993). Infants whose mothers drank on average 1.0 oz AA/day or 2 drinks/day exhibited longer fixations. This effect was dose-dependent and seen at two different ages, 6.5 and 12 months.

We also administered the VExP (Haith et al., 1988), which for the first time assesses RT and thus provides a direct assessment of speed of cognitive processing in infancy. This paradigm measures latency to shift visual fixation from one location to another in the context of a series of dynamic visual events, that is, when stimuli are displayed alternatively in two adjacent locations in the infant's visual field. This paradigm yields a measure of anticipation, based on the percentage of trials in which the infant shifts his or her gaze even before the stimulus appears in the adjacent visual field, which indicates that the infant is learning the alternating pattern. Two RT measures are computed: baseline or native RT, assessed prior to the alternating sequence, and postbaseline RT, which presumably reflects both native RT and the effect of expectations formed for the alternating sequence.

We adapted the VExP, originally designed for 3-month-olds, for use with our cohort at 6.5 months and administered it to 103 infants (S. Jacobson et al., 1992). Only a subsample was evaluated due to the extensive time needed to code each protocol and because the task was still considered experimental. After a brief baseline of random presentations, 60 stimuli appear in a predictable left–right alternating sequence with the entire series lasting 120.5 sec. The infant's eye movements are recorded on videotape, which is subsequently coded to determine speed of response, defined as latency between the onset of the stimulus and the time the infant's eye begins to move toward the stimulus. This measure is comparable to decision time defined as "the time from onset of the test phase of each trial to the initiation of a response" rather than as "the time from test onset to response completion" (Rose et al., 1997, p. 632). Anticipation was defined as a shift in gaze in the correct direction during the interstimulus interval before the event was displayed or within 200 milliseconds of stimulus onset. Percent anticipations were computed as follows: number of anticipations/number of events fixated. Percent fast (201–300 milliseconds) RTs were constructed by dividing the number of fast

TABLE 3.2
Relation of Maternal Drinking During and After Pregnancy to Infant Cognitive Outcome

| | | | | Maternal Drinking (oz AA/day) | | | |
| | | | | During Pregnancy | | Postpartum | |
	N	M	SD	r	β	r	β
Bayley Scales of Infant Development							
Mental Development Index[a]	375	109.6	13.3	-.17**	-.11*	-.09	-.05
Psychomotor Development Index[b]	368	105.7	13.6	-.13*	-.10+	-.08	-.04
Fagan Test of Infant Intelligence							
Novelty preference[c]	315	0.6	0.1	.08	.07	.01	-.01
Fixation duration(s)[d]	312	1.5	0.3	.15**	.12*	.12	.08
Cross-modal transfer							
Novelty preference[e]	361	0.5	0.1	.04	-.01	.12	.08
Fixation duration(s)[f]	362	1.2	0.3	.16**	.12*	.10	.03
Visual Expectancy Paradigm[g]							
Reaction time (ms)	103	322.9	46.6	.25***	.27**	.02	.02
Percent fast (. 300 ms)	103	49.1	18.8	-.31***	-.36****	-.07	-.09
Percent quick (% anticipations + fast)	103	55.2	16.8	-.30	-.32***	-.06	-.07
Play							
Spontaneous[h]	304	3.3	0.9	-.15**	-.09	-.04	.00
Elicited[i]	310	9.0	3.7	-.15**	-.15**	-.08	-.05
Mean SDA (sec)[j]	307	2.7	36.5	.13*	.11+	.06	.06
Object permanence[k]	354	8.7	1.7	-.02	-.05	-.03	-.04

[a]Adjusted for maternal age, number of prenatal visits, HOME, smoking and opiate use during pregnancy, age at visit, and examiner.
[b]Adjusted for parity, number of prenatal visits, HOME, age at visit, and examiner.
[c]Adjusted for parity and age at visit.
[d]Adjusted for maternal education, PPVT-R score, HOME, and maternal smoking.
[e]Adjusted for number of prenatal clinic visits, HOME, and examiner.
[f]Adjusted for age at visit, maternal smoking, opiates, and cocaine use during pregnancy, and examiner.
[g]Adjusted for sex of infant. Percent fast also adjusted for age at visit.
[h]Adjusted for mother's age, parity, welfare status, number of prenatal visits, smoking during pregnancy, age at visit, and examiner.
[i]Adjusted for welfare status, sex of infant, and examiner.
[j]Adjusted for number of prenatal visits, PPVT-R score, marijuana use during pregnancy, and examiner
[k]Adjusted for maternal age and PPVT-R score.
+p < .10. *p < .05. **p < .01. ***p < .001.

postbaseline RTs by the total number of postbaseline RTs. As expected, infants had shorter RTs and a higher percentage of anticipations at 6.5 months than reported by Haith et al. (1988) at 3 months.

Anticipations and shorter baseline RTs were both moderately related to FTII novelty preference (Table 3.3; S. Jacobson, et al., 1992). As indicated earlier, faster baseline and postbaseline RTs were related to shorter fixation duration on both the FTII and cross-modal transfer test, thereby confirming Colombo's premise (Colombo et al., 1988) that length of look reflects speed of processing. As in DiLalla et al. (1990), anticipation and RT were not related to Bayley Scale performance at 1 year. The relation of visual expectation to FTII recognition memory was examined further in a multiple regression analysis (Table 3.4). Percent anticipations and baseline RT each contributed independently to the prediction of novelty preference, suggesting that memory and processing speed constitute separate components of performance on the FTII. Prenatal alcohol exposure was also related to poorer performance on elicited play, which will be described later in this chapter.

As shown in Table 3.5, maternal drinking at conception and during pregnancy were associated with longer RTs on the VExP (Jacobson, Jacobson, & Sokol, 1994). More highly exposed infants had fewer fast RTs and a higher proportion of slow responses. Infant RT proved particularly sensitive, detecting effects at 0.5 oz AA/day (about 1 standard drink/day), the lowest level at which effects have been detected. These deficits are consistent with findings from neuroimaging studies of patients with FAS and FAE, which have demonstrated damage to the

TABLE 3.3
Correlations of Percent Anticipation and VExP RT With Infant Cognitive Measures

	Percent Anticipations	Baseline RT	Postbaseline RT
Fagan Test of Infant Intelligence			
Preference for novelty	.25*	-.32**	-.06
Mean fixation duration	-.02	.24*	.28**
Cross-modal transfer			
Preference for familiarity	-.09	-.00	.04
Mean fixation duration	-.20†	.33**	.33**
Play			
Mean SDA	.28*	-.05	-.11
Complexity of play			
Spontaneous	-.25*	.46***	.09
Elicited	.01	.14	-.06
Object permanence	-.05	.13	.14
Bayley Scales			
Mental Development Index	-.04	.09	.06
Psychomotor Development Index	-.08	-.11	.07

†$p < .10$. *$p < .05$. **$p < .01$. ***$p < .001$.

TABLE 3.4
Regression Analysis of FTII (Novelty Preference) on VExP Anticipation and RT ($N = 79$)

	r	β^a	p
Percent anticipation	.26	.27	.025
Baseline RT	-.32	-.34	.005
Postbaseline RT	-.06	.19	.138

[a]Standardized regression coefficient with the three visual expectation measures entered simultaneously.

TABLE 3.5
Effects of Maternal Drinking on Infant Anticipation and Reaction Time on the Visual Expectancy paradigm ($N = 103$)

			At Conception		During Pregnancy	
	M	SD	r	β	r	β
Percent anticipations	28.1	12.0	-.08	-.08	-.12	-.12
Baseline median RT (ms)[a]	344.9	70.3	.04	.07	.04	.07
Postbaseline median RT (ms)	322.9	46.6	.26**	.27**	.25**	.27**
Percent fast RTs (201-300 ms)	49.1	18.8	-.29**	-.30**	-.31***	-.34***
Percent quick responses[b]	55.2	16.8	-.26**	-.28**	-.29**	-.32***

Note. All outcomes adjusted for sex of infant. Percent fast responses also adjusted for age at visit.
[a]Baseline median RT missing for one infant.
[b]Percent quick responses combines percent anticipations and fast RTs.
$\dagger p < .10.$ $*p < .05.$ $**p < .01.$ $***p < .001.$

basal ganglia (Mattson et al., 1994), which may be involved in this type of visual reaction time.

Moderate prenatal alcohol exposure has been found to explain only about 1–2% of the variance in CNS function on most traditional cognitive outcome measures examined to date. Prenatal alcohol exposure explains a markedly greater percentage of the variance in these RT measures, with R^2s ranging between 8–12%.

Postpartum Maternal Drinking.   A correlation between pregnancy drinking and cognitive function is usually interpreted as teratogenic, that is, due to a direct effect of the drug on fetal CNS development. An alternative explanation, that the observed deficits are due to the socioenvironmental consequences of being raised by a drinking mother, can be evaluated by examining the relation of the deficit to postnatal maternal alcohol use (Jacobson, 1998). As can be seen in Table 3.2, none of the infant neurobehavioral deficits detected in our Detroit cohort were related to postpartum drinking by the mother or caregiver, indicating that these effects were related specifically to exposure during the prenatal period (J. Jacobson et al., 1993; S. Jacobson et al., 1993; S. Jacobson et al., 1994).

As indicated earlier, we expected that the more specific information-processing measures would be less affected by socioenvironmental factors than the more global developmental assessments. As shown in Table 3.6, they were related to fewer of the environment measures than were the Bayley Scales, suggesting that the abilities being assessed in the newer infant tests are less malleable and less influenced by interaction with the caregiver and other sources of environmental stimulation.

Thus, the effect of alcohol on processing speed was seen in three separate domains—recognition memory, cross-modal transfer, and visual expectancy—and at two different ages—6.5 and 12 months. These data suggest a specific effect of prenatal alcohol exposure on speed of information processing rather than general developmental delay or overall poorer performance on these tests and are consistent with Streissguth's suggestion of an alcohol-related deficit in "speed of central processing," previously seen only in older children (Streissguth et al., 1984, 1986, 1995). They are also consistent with recent findings showing a lack of recognition-memory deficits in children with FAS (M age = 10.0 years), but the time needed to recall the objects condition was significantly longer than for controls (Uecker & Nadel, 1996, 1998). Although recognition problems were not found, the children with FAS had poorer spatial memory.

Underlying Components Of Cognition. A detailed description of the battery administered to the infants in the Detroit cohort during the first 13 months is provided in S. Jacobson et al. (1993). In addition to the FTII at 6.5 and 12 months, the VExP at 6.5 months, and the cross-modal transfer test at 12 months, the Bayley Scales were administered at 13 months. Play was assessed at 12 months in terms of the highest level (most complex) spontaneous play by the infant and the highest level of elicited play, that is, play modeled by the examiner that the infant was able to imitate (Belsky et al., 1984). The play audiotapes were also coded on a tempo of play measure, sustained directed activity (SDA; Kagan, 1971), which is described as the amount of time spent in visually directed manipulation of a toy or toy group and which we defined as the mean of the two longest periods of directed attention. Object permanence (Uzgiris & Hunt, 1975) was also assessed at 12 months.

Mean FTII novelty preference was lower than the mean of 61–62% in Fagan and Singer's (1983) normative sample and middle-class, low-risk sample (Thompson et al., 1991) and similar to that reported for at-risk infants and lower SES fullterms (Fagan & Singer, 1983; Jacobson, Fein, Jacobson, Schwartz, & Dowler, 1985; Rose et al., 1988).

Whereas 84% of the infants exhibited novelty preference (i.e., looked more than 50% of the time at the novel stimulus) on the FTII, 74% preferred the familiar stimulus on the cross-modal transfer test. This reversed pattern of prefer-

TABLE 3.6
Relation of Control Variables With Infant Outcomes

	Maternal Age	Parity	Number of Prenatal Visits	HOME Inventory	PPVT-R	Beck Depression Inventory	Sex of Infant[a]
Bayley Scales (N = 382)							
Mental Development Index	-.21***	-.06	.14**	.19***	-.00	-.11*	.03
Psychomotor Development Index	-.12	-.14**	.11*	.14**	.02	-.13*	-.06
FTII (N = 315)							
Novelty preference	-.02	.09†	-.02	.04	.01	-.01	.08
Fixation duration	-.05	.05	-.04	-.12*	-.09†	.12*	.02
Cross-modal (N = 362)							
Novelty preference	-.04	.03	-.11*	.10†	.04	-.02	-.07
Fixation duration	.07	.07	-.04	.00	-.04	.04	.03
Processing speed[b] (N = 311)	.01	.07	-.04	-.07	-.08	.09	.04
VExP (N = 103)							
Reaction time	.00	.06	-.12	.12	-.05	.01	.21*
% anticipation	-.19	-.12	.08	-.08	.04	.00	.01
Spontaneous play[c] (N = 304)	-.14*	-.10†	.10†	-.01	-.03	.00	.01
Elicited play[c] (N = 310)	-.03	-.00	.04	.04	.05	-.05	.10†
Object permanence (N = 354)	.11*	.05	-.06	.08	.16**	-.05	-.03

[a]1 = male; 2 = female.
[b]Average fixation duration for the FTII and cross-modal transfer test.
[c]Belsky play level.
†p < .10. *p < .05. **p < .01. ***p < .001.

ence for the familiar stimulus is different from that seen in middle-class 12-month-olds, who prefer the novel stimulus, but consistent with that found in previous studies with lower-class, full-term infants at 12 months and younger (Rose et al., 1978, 1988; Rose, Feldman, McCarton, & Wolfson, 1988). The data suggest that the cross-modal problems were difficult for these infants.

Mean spontaneous play level on the Belsky, Garduque, and Hrncir (1984) play scale was between *functional relational* and *enactive naming*, indicating that much of the infant's play involved bringing together toys that belonged together, with only some very simple pretend behavior. The infants demonstrated more complex play in response to elicitation by the examiner; the mean response consisted of imitation of a series of single pretense acts, such as drinking from the cup and giving the doll a drink from the cup. The means and ranges for spontaneous play and SDA were very similar to those reported for comparable measures for a middle-class sample at 1 year (Tamis-LeMonda & Bornstein, 1990). On object permanence, the median highest step passed involved finding an object hidden under three superimposed screens, which is one step below the median level reported by Uzgiris and Hunt (1975) for their upper middle-class sample and comparable to performance by one at-risk preterm group (Rose & Wallace, 1985). Bayley scores were similar to those of 1-year-old infants from both lower and middle-class samples (Bradley et al., 1989; Lyons-Ruth, Connell, & Grunebaum, 1990).

A principal components analysis with varimax rotation of the FTII, the cross-modal transfer test, and the other developmental measures yielded four factors (Table 3.7). RT from the VExP and fixation duration on the FTII and cross-modal test loaded highly on the first factor, which we interpreted as indicating processing speed. The second factor on which the Bayley Scales, complexity of elicited play, and object permanence loaded most strongly, appears to reflect a symbolic developmental dimension. VExP anticipation and visual recognition memory (VRM) novelty preference loaded on a third memory–attention factor. The fourth factor was not readily interpretable.

Additional support for the independence of the processing speed and memory–attention components is provided by a second factor analysis based on a larger sample of 218 infants who had completed all the infant tests except the VExP test, which was only available for a subsample of the infants (Table 3.8). The McCall Index was constructed by averaging the 15 items loading on the first unrotated principal component from a factor analysis of the Bayley Scales (J. Jacobson et al., 1993). The McCall Index was constructed following McCall, Eichorn, and Hogarty (1977) by averaging the 15 items loading most strongly on the first (unrotated) principal component from a factor analysis of the Bayley Scales (see Jacobson, Jacobson, Sokol, et al., 1993). The McCall Index is designed to assess the most salient dimension of development, which at 13 months is the ability to imitate modeled behavior. It was, therefore, not surprising that the McCall Index loads together with elicited play, which is a measure of imitation. The finding that cross-modal novelty preference did not load with novelty preference on the FTII

TABLE 3.7
Varimax Rotated Factors ($N = 57$)

	Factor 1	Factor 2	Factor 3	Factor 4
	Processing Speed	Symbol Development	Memory/ Attention	
Postbaseline RT	.77	-.01	-.17	-.01
Baseline RT	.64	.02	-.17	.46
Cross-modal fixation duration	.64	.07	-.20	.10
VRM fixation duration	.63	.02	.43	-.13
Bayley MDI	.02	.79	-.10	-.10
Bayley PDI	-.16	.65	-.37	-.10
Elicited play	-.01	.65	.16	.55
Object permanence	.35	.63	.36	.06
Mean SDA	-.00	-.07	.74	-.11
VRM novelty preference	-.20	-.09	.60	.30
Percent anticipations	-.42	.16	.56	-.03
Cross-modal familiarity preference	-.03	-.26	.10	.76
Spontaneous play	.18	.17	-.32	.76
Eigenvalue	2.77	1.94	1.70	1.48
Variance explained (proportion)	.21	.15	.13	.11

suggests that the two are measuring different components of cognitive function; cross-modal transfer requires a mental transformation of the perceptual input not required by the FTII.

Note that method variance was not a problem in either of these factor analyses in that variables loaded on factors reflecting the underlying processes they were measuring rather than the test paradigm they came from. As indicated earlier (Table 3.6), the measures comprising the processing speed, memory–attention, and cross-modal transfer factors were markedly less influenced by socioenvironmental factors than those comprising the symbolic development factor.

Predictive Validity of the Infant Cognitive Component.   Preliminary data on the first 94 Detroit children seen at 7.5 years postpartum provide further evidence of the independent contribution of the three infant-cognitive components described previously in predicting later IQ on the WISC-III (Jacobson, Chiodo, & Jacobson, 1996). Mean FTII recognition memory at 6.5 and 12 months was a stronger predictor of WISC-III Verbal IQ than the Bayley Mental Developmental Index (MDI) at 13 months. This may be because the MDI during the first year primarily assesses sensorimotor function, which may explain why it was moderately predictive of WISC-III Performance IQ (Table 3.9). The highest level of play on the Belsky scale, a measure of early symbolic development, was also moderately predictive of 7.5-year

TABLE 3.8
Varimax Rotated Factors ($N = 218$)

	Factor 1	Factor 2	Factor 3	Factor 4
	Developmental Level	Processing Speed	Memory/ Attention	Cross-modal Transfer
Elicited play	.77	.01	-.02	-.10
Spontaneous play	.74	.12	-.00	-.13
McCall Index	.70	-.29	-.15	.15
Cross-modal fixation duration	.04	.76	.15	.02
VRM fixation duration	-.06	.72	-.04	-.10
Mean SDA	-.17	.20	.66	.11
VRM novelty preference	-.04	-.41	.65	-.29
Object permanence	.39	.19	.45	.24
Cross-modal novelty preference	-.10	.09	.04	.91
Eigenvalue	1.85	1.46	1.09	1.03
Variance explained (proportion)	.21	.16	.12	.12

TABLE 3.9
Correlations of Infant Outcomes With 7.5 Year IQ Scores

	WISC-III IQ		
	Verbal	Performance	Full
Bayley Scales			
Mental Development Index	0.18†	0.36***	0.30**
Psychomotor Development Index	0.15	0.16	0.17
Fagan Test of Infant Intelligence (FTII)			
Novelty preference[a]	0.24*	0.13	0.22†
Processing speed[b]	-0.15	-0.27**	-0.23*
Elicited play	0.34**	0.13	0.27*

Note. Values are Pearson product-moment correlation coefficients.
[a]Average of 6.5 and 12-month testing. [b]12-month test.
$†p < 0.10.$ $*p < 0.05.$ $**p < 0.01.$ $***p < 0.001.$

Verbal IQ. Although the 6.5-month fixation duration measure was unrelated to later outcome, longer fixations at 12 months were associated with poorer 7.5-year Performance IQ. Thus, as reported in earlier studies, FTII recognition memory predicted Verbal but not Performance IQ. By contrast, fixation duration was only related to Performance IQ.[1]

---

[1]To ensure that prenatal alcohol exposure did not unduly influence the results reported in this chapter, the correlation matrices on which these findings were based were recomputed as partial correlation matrices in which maternal alcohol consumption during pregnancy was held constant. None of the partial correlation coefficients were altered from their corresponding zero-order coefficients by values of more than .05, and all that had been significant remained so.

When examined simultaneously in a multiple regression analysis (Table 3.10), mean FTII novelty preference and highest level of play on the Belsky scale each contributed independently to Verbal IQ. By contrast, fixation duration, a measure of processing speed and the 13-month MDI, which is composed largely of fine motor manipulation and spatial ability items, are independently associated with Performance IQ at 7.5 years. These effects remain virtually unchanged when the Infant HOME (Caldwell & Bradley, 1979) and maternal Verbal IQ from the PPVT-R (Dunn & Dunn, 1981) are included in the regressions. Thus, these findings provide further evidence for the hypothesis that memory–attention, processing speed, and symbolic play during infancy represent relatively separate components of intellectual function in infants and children.

Longterm Effects of Prenatal Alcohol Exposure.   Preliminary data on the children of the first 244 moderately exposed women in our Detroit cohort assessed in our 7.5 years follow-up study showed no alcohol-related deficits on WISC-III Full

TABLE 3.10
Relation of Infant Measures to 7.5 Year IQ

		WISC-III	
	N	*r*	*β*
Verbal IQ			
FTII novelty preference[a]	66	.33**	.27*
Mental Development Index[b]	66	.15	.01
Highest level of play[c]	66	.35**	.30*
Performance IQ			
FTII mean fixation duration[d]	82	-.27**	-.23*
Mental Development Index[b]	82	.32**	.29**
Full IQ			
FTII mean fixation duration[d]	66	-.21†	-.24*
FTII novelty preference[a]	66	-.28*	.22†
Mental Development Index[b]	66	.27*	.14
Highest level of play[c]	66	.26*	.21†

[a]Averaged across 6.5- and 12-month assessment.
[b]Bayley Scales.
[c]Based on Belsky play measure.
[d]12-month assessment.
†$p < 0.10$. *$p < 0.05$. **$p < 0.01$.

Scale, Verbal, or Performance IQ (Table 3.11). Instead, specific deficits were seen in IQ subtests relating to attentional function, especially arithmetic and digit span, after control for confounds, including postnatal maternal alcohol use (Jacobson, Bihun, & Chiodo, 1999). These effects were strikingly similar to those found in the more middle-class Seattle moderate drinking cohort (Streissguth et al., 1993).

In addition to the WISC-III, we administered an expanded version of Mirsky's four-factor model of attention (sustain, encode, focus, and shift; Mirsky, Anthony, Duncan, Ahearn, & Kellam, 1991), which enabled us to examine the underlying components of attention that are impaired. Sustained attention refers to the ability to maintain focus and alertness over time. Focused attention is the ability to maintain attention in the presence of distractions. Executive function (called *shift* in the Mirsky model) involves the ability to coordinate, plan, and execute appropriate responses and modify behavior in response to feedback. Working memory (*encode*) is the sequential mental manipulation of information linking input from the environment with information retrieved from memory, including: (a) temporary storage of task-relevant information, as in the retention of strings of digits in the digit span test; and (b) *on-line* manipulation of that information to determine a response, as in arithmetic or mental rotation.

As shown in Table 3.12, we found that alcohol-exposed children perform normally on simpler tasks involving rote learning or simple reaction time but have particular difficulty on more complex speeded tasks involving the encode factor or working memory, such as, WISC-III arithmetic and digit span, magnitude estimation, mental rotation, and a short-term memory processing efficiency test, and on focused attention tasks, such as, digit cancellation (Jacobson et al., 1999). Although the effects differ from FAS in that global IQ is not implicated, the specific pattern of attention deficits is consistent with that seen in children with FAS (Nanson & Hiscock, 1990) and in other prospective studies of moderately exposed children (Coles et al., 1997; Streissguth et al., 1993).

TABLE 3.11
Relation of Maternal Drinking to WISC-III IQ Scores (N = 234)

	Maternal Drinking During Pregnancy		Caregiver Drinking at 7.5 Years	
	r	β	r	β
Full scale IQ	-.08	-.04	-.15*	-.07
Verbal IQ	-.06	-.04	-.19**	-.10†
Performance IQ	-.07	-.05	-.08	-.01
Freedom from distractibility/ Processing speed factor	-.18**	-.15*	-.15*	-.07

†p < .10. *p < .05. **p < .01.

TABLE 3.12
Relation of Prenatal Alcohol Exposure to Attention, Processing Speed, and Verbal Memory

	Drinking During Pregnancy	
	r	β
Mirsky Dimensions of Attention		
Sustain		
CPT—reaction time	.05	.08
CPT—number correct	-.04	-.07
CPT—errors of commission	.05	.04
Focus		
WISC-III coding	-.12†	-.12†
Digit cancellation	.07	.07
Digit cancellation w/interference	.17*	.16**
Working memory (encode)		
WISC-III arithmetic	-.15*	-.14*
WISC-III digit span	-.21**	-.18**
Seashore Rhythm	-.12†	-.12†
Executive function (shift)		
Wisconsin Card Sorting Test		
Categories	.01	.01
Perseverative errors	.01	.01
Tower of London	-.15*	-.15*
Verbal fluency	-.17*	-.15*
Processing speed		
Color naming	-.04	-.02
Sternberg short-term memory		
Yes	.17*	.14*
No	.06	.05
Mental rotation		
Forward	.23***	.18**
Backward	.23***	.22***
Magnitude estimation—numbers	.18**	.15*
Magnitude estimation—arrows	.20**	.18**
Verbal memory		
Verbal learning	-.02	-.03
Story memory	.03	.01

†$p < .10.$ *$p < .05.$ **$p < .01.$ ***$p < .001.$

Until recently, behavioral toxicology studies have focused mainly on effects on cognitive and attentional function. One important exception is the pioneering longitudinal studies conducted by Streissguth and her collaborators on adolescents and adults with FAS (Streissguth, 1997; Streissguth et al., 1991), who found deficits in the social domain, particularly poor interpersonal relations, lack of responsiveness to social cues, and poor social judgment. Relatively little information is available regarding socioemotional function in children exposed at lower levels. Using the Achenbach Child Behavior Checklist-Teacher's Report Form (TRF), Coles and her colleagues found poorer social competence and more aggressive and destructive behavior in children whose mothers drank throughout pregnancy than in those whose mothers had abstained or stopped in midpregnancy, after controlling for current maternal drinking (Brown et al., 1991). In the Seattle study at 14 years, prenatal alcohol exposure was associated with a more negative self-concept, increased aggression and delinquency, and greater use of alcohol, tobacco, and drugs (Carmichael Olson et al., 1997).

In our Detroit follow-up study at 7.5 years, prenatal alcohol exposure was associated with higher teacher ratings on three of the eight TRF problem syndromes—social, attention, and aggression—and greater inattention and impulsivity on the DuPaul-Barkley Attention Deficit Hyperactivity Disorder (ADHD) Scale, after controlling for potential confounders and current caregiver drinking (Table 3.13; Jacobson et al., 1999). Path analyses showed that the effect of alcohol on inattention was mediated by a composite attentional measure (average RTs for Sternberg short-term memory, mental rotation, and magnitude estimation) but that the effect on impulsivity was not. In addition, aggression and social problems were not merely by-products of the children's attentional deficits. These findings suggest that prenatal alcohol exposure impacts directly on diverse aspects of CNS function (Fig. 3.3). The severity of these problems is indicated by the high proportion of children whose scores fell in the borderline or clinical range (33% compared with 4–5% found in the population at large). These data are among the first to suggest that, in addition to its effects on cognition, moderate levels of prenatal alcohol may also disrupt CNS pathways that mediate affective response and emotional regulation and lead to attentional and disruptive behaviors similar to those found in the more heavily exposed FAS children and adolescents.

Brain Alterations Following Prenatal Alcohol Exposure. One of the main features of FAS is microcephaly, defined as head circumference 2–3 SDs or more below the mean. It had been believed that prenatal exposure to alcohol led to diffuse brain anomalies rather than a distinct pattern of brain damage. The advent of quantitative MRI and positron emission tomography (PET) scanning have permitted more detailed morphometric examinations of the brain than autopsies of children with FAS

TABLE 3.13
Relation of Prenatal Alcohol Exposure to Teacher Ratings in the Clinical Range

	r	β
TRF behavior problems		
Social	.19*	.23**
Attention	.27***	.27***
Aggression	.21**	.25**
Total	.21**	.17*
Internalizing	.03	.03
Externalizing	.21**	.18*
ADHD Scale	.28***	.29***

Note. 0 = normal; 1 = clinical or borderline.
*$p < .05$. **$p < .01$. ***$p < .001$.

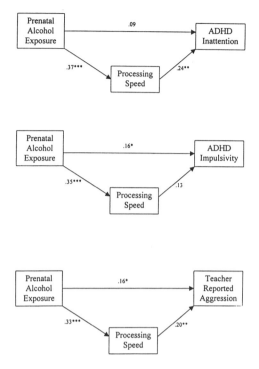

FIG. 3.3.   Path analyses examining mediation of the relation between prenatal alcohol exposure and child behavioral outcomes by processing speed.

and during the last 5 years, research on fetal alcohol effects has demonstrated specific neuropsychological effects and brain changes (Riley & Mattson, 1997).

Both autopsy and MRI studies indicate that the corpus callosum, which connects the neocortical hemispheres, is particularly sensitive to alcohol exposure. These studies have shown a high incidence of complete agenesis, partial agenesis, or cases with significantly thinned but present callosa (e.g., Mattson et al., 1996). Overall area and four of the five equiangular regions of the corpus callosum were reduced in size in children with FAS or a history of heavy alcohol exposure, and three of the four regions were significantly reduced after control for overall brain size. The affected areas included the genu, which links the prefrontal areas; the area anterior to the splenium, which links sensory areas; and the splenium, which links the visual areas. It is of interest that these areas have also been found to be affected in children with ADHD (Hynd et al., 1991), suggesting that they may be responsible for some of the similar neurobehavioral problems seen in FAS and ADHD (e.g., hyperactivity, attentional problems, and impulsivity) (Riley & Mattson, 1997). Abnormalities of the corpus callosum are also consistent with anomalies seen in animal studies of prenatal alcohol effects (Goodlett & West, 1992; Riley & Mattson, 1997).

Other areas affected by alcohol exposure include the hippocampus, basal ganglia, and cerebellum (Goodlett & West, 1992; Miller, 1992; Riley et al., 1997). MRI studies found that the basal ganglia may be especially affected since overall reduction in the volume of the basal ganglia and, in particular, the caudate were found, even after control for brain size (Mattson et al., 1992, 1994). Animal studies show that changes in the cerebellum occur in FAS cases in which binge drinking occurred during the third trimester (Goodlett & West, 1992). A recent MRI study also showed that the anterior (lobules I–V) regions of the cerebellar vermis were reduced (Sowell et al., 1995), which is also consistent with animal findings (Goodlett, Marcussen, & West, 1990). These reductions were found in children with full FAS and in children lacking the full facial features of FAS, suggesting that specific brain structures are more susceptible than others to alcohol exposure and that these brain changes can occur in the absence of the facial features upon which a diagnosis of FAS is made (Riley & Mattson, 1997). More research is needed on the relation between reduced structural volumes and functional outcomes in alcohol-exposed children.

The most consistent finding in animal research is gross reduction in brain weight. Changes at the microscopic level include generation, migration, and cell death; changes in glial cells; and changes in biochemical and electrophysiological properties of the CNS (for reviews see Goodlett & West, 1992; Riley, Thomas, Lafiette, Dominquez, 1997). Vulnerability of the cerebellar Purkinje cell changes depends on timing of exposure, but Purkinje cell loss can be permanent (Bonthius & West, 1991). Reductions in cerebellar granule cells, olfactory mitral cells, and pyramidal cells in the hippocampal CA1 region and neuronal connectivity also occur following alcohol exposure.

Functional Significance.   The 1996 Institute of Medicine (Stratton et al., 1996) report questioned the functional importance of the effects reported in the prospective, longitudinal studies of non-FAS, alcohol-exposed children on the grounds that the statistical associations reported in these studies were small. Because there are often marked individual differences in vulnerability to neurotoxic agents, however, a shift of a few test points in a group's average score may reflect a more substantial downward shift in the scores of more vulnerable individuals.

Although criteria for mental retardation (IQ < 70) and borderline retardation (70–79) are well established for IQ scores, there is little consensus regarding the functional importance of a 5- or 10-point decrement when scores fall within the normal range. For most assessment paradigms, particularly those focusing on specific domains of cognitive function, there is no information regarding the importance of test scores for the day-to-day function of the individual child. In the absence of established criteria, Streissguth et al. (1993) adopted the bottom 7.5 percentile to identify affected children and we have used the bottom 10th percentile or 1 standard deviation below the mean to indicate poor performance. These criteria are based on the premise that, although performance at these levels may fall within the normal range, it is so poor that it is likely to interfere with the child's day-to-day function.

Figure 3.4 illustrates the approach we have taken in evaluating the functional significance of the effects of prenatal alcohol exposure on five infant outcomes in the Detroit study. In our initial correlational (multiple regression) analyses, we found that the effects of prenatal alcohol exposure in our non-FAS, alcohol-exposed cohort were markedly stronger in infants born to women over 30 years of age (J. Jacobson et al., 1996). These findings are consistent with data from case studies of multiparous alcohol-abusing mothers with FAS children, which found that each successive born child is almost always more severely impaired than the previous one. This pattern has been shown in controlled animal experiments to be due to maternal aging rather than parity. The data in Fig. 3.4 were used to evaluate the functional significance of the infancy deficits found in the analyses in the Detroit study by examining whether pregnancy drinking above a threshold of 7 drinks/week was associated with an increased incidence of poor performance, defined as performance in the bottom 10th percentile of the distribution (see Jacobson et al., 1998, for a discussion of the basis of the 7 drink/week threshold).

For the first three outcomes shown in Fig. 3.4, there was no increased incidence of functionally significant deficit among the infants born to the younger mothers, whereas, for those born to older women, drinking above threshold was associated

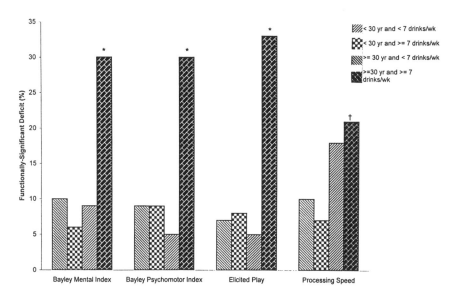

FIG. 3.4. Rate of functionally significant deficit among offspring of older and younger mothers prenatally exposed to alcohol above and below threshold (7 drinks per week during pregnancy). None of the differences among the younger mothers were significant. Significant differences between the offspring of the older mothers exposed above and below threshold are indicated as follows: †$p < .10$. *$p < .01$.

with 3- to 5-fold increases in functional impairment. The sole exception was processing speed; pregnancy drinking above threshold doubled the risk of functional deficit in processing speed in both age groups, an effect that was significant for the sample as a whole ($p = 0.05$). These data indicate that the relatively modest relations found in the multiple regression analyses (βs ranged from 0.17 to 0.31 for the infants born to older mothers) translated into a markedly greater risk of functionally significant impairment in all five domains tested. Thus, although correlational analyses are appropriate for an initial determination of whether there is an adverse effect from prenatal alcohol exposure, additional analyses directly examining the functional significance of such effects are necessary to fully understand their import.

Drinking Patterns During Pregnancy.   While reporting alcohol intake in terms of mean oz of AA/day or standard drinks/week permits cross-study comparisons, this measure may obscure the importance of pattern and concentration of alcohol exposure. Experimental animal studies indicate that this average is probably misleading since ingestion of a given dose of alcohol over a short time period generates a greater peak blood alcohol concentration and greater neuronal and behavioral impairment than when the same dose is ingested gradually over several days (Bonthius & West, 1990; Goodlett, Kelly, & West, 1987; Goodlett & Peterson, 1994; West & Goodlett, 1990).

Although the thresholds in our analyses are characterized in terms of oz of AA/day, only one of 480 mothers in the Detroit cohort actually drank every day and only three drank more than 4 days/week (Fig. 3.5). A mean of 0.5 oz AA/day exposure, therefore, typically represents higher doses of alcohol on those days on which drinking occurs. For the mothers who drank at least 0.5 oz AA/day, the lowest level at which deficits were consistently seen, the median drinking pattern was 3.0 oz AA/drinking day or 6 standard drinks on 2.3 days of the week, a sharp contrast in pattern to the women who drank an average of less than 0.5 oz AA/day (Table 3.14). These data are consistent with other studies (e.g., Streissguth et al., 1994), suggesting that much of the impairment is related to relatively high levels of drinking per occasion. On the other hand, adverse effects on neurobehavior were by no means limited to the children of alcoholics. The majority of the Detroit mothers (59.3%) who drank more than 0.5 oz AA/day were negative on the Michigan Alcoholism Screening Test (MAST), indicating that their drinking was not marked by the psychosocial or physiological sequelae of alcohol abuse.

We have reanalyzed the Detroit infant data to examine the relation of drinking pattern to developmental outcome (Jacobson et al., 1998). The principal variables included in these analyses were dose (average drinks/occasion ingested on those days during pregnancy when the mother drank) and frequency (average days/week of drinking during pregnancy). A functionally significant deficit was defined in these analyses as the bottom 10th percentile on one or more of the four infant developmental outcomes most strongly associated with prenatal alcohol exposure—Bayley MDI and PDI, elicited play, and processing speed.

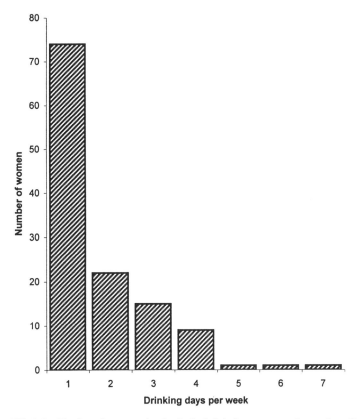

FIG. 3.5. Number of women who drank alcohol during pregnancy by number of days/week they drank alcohol.

Table 3.15 examines the relation of average drinks/occasion to functional deficit in the infants of mothers who drank at moderate-to-heavy levels (at least 7 drinks/week on the average). Sixteen of the 20 functionally impaired infants (80.0%) were born to women who averaged at least 5 drinks/occasion during pregnancy. These data are consistent with findings reported by Streissguth et al. (1993), who examined pattern of drinking correlationally and found that the measures of pregnancy drinking that have the greatest impact on developmental outcome are bingeing (defined as drinking at least 5 drinks on at least one occasion) and average number of drinks/occasion.

We also looked at the 11 infants in the sample whose mothers drank frequently (at least 4 days/week) during pregnancy. Functional impairment was seen in four of the five infants born to frequently drinking women who averaged at least 5 drinks/occasion but in none of the six who drank frequently at lower levels (range = 1.3–4.6 drinks/occasion). The one mother who drank every day was an

TABLE 3.14
Drinking Patterns During Pregnancy

	Oz AA/Day	
	0.5 or More	*< 0.5*
Standard drinks/occasion	6.00	1.90
Oz AA/drinking day	3.00	0.95
Frequency of drinking	2.3 days/week	once in 3 weeks
MAST positive	40.70%	0.00%

Note. Values are group medians.

TABLE 3.15
Incidence of Functionally Significant Deficit by Drinks/Occasion and Maternal MAST Score in
Infants Exposed at Moderate-to-Heavy Levels ($\geq$ 0.5 Oz AA/Day) (N = 47)

	Drinks/Occasion		MAST Score	
	< 5	*$\geq$ 5*	*$\leq$ 4*	*> 4*
Functional deficit				
Yes	4 (21%)	16 (57%)	11 (41%)	9 (45%)
No	15 (79%)	12 (43%)	16 (58%)	11 (55%)
χ^2		6.03*		0.09

*p = 0.014.

alcoholic, and her infant was born with FAS. By contrast, the infant of the frequently drinking mother who averaged only 1.3 drinks/occasion scored 12 points (1 standard deviation) above the sample mean on the Bayley Mental Index. The median drinking pattern of the mothers of the 20 children in Table 3.15 with functionally significant deficits was 7 drinks/occasion on 1–2 days/week. Although this level of drinking can be termed *moderate* in that 7–14 drinks are consumed per week, this pattern might be characterized more accurately as heavy recreational drinking on the weekend.

It should be emphasized that the 0.5 oz AA/day threshold represents a sample average and that more sensitive and reliable tests may detect even lower thresholds in the future. In light of individual differences in vulnerability to prenatal alcohol exposure and in the absence of information on synergistic effects with other substances, the 0.5 oz AA/day threshold should not be taken to imply that drinking below that level is safe. Analyses of our Detroit infant data (Jacobson et al., 1998) indicate that functionally significant deficits were seen primarily in infants born to mothers who averaged at least 5 drinks/occasion on an average of at least once/week during pregnancy. These findings underscore the significance of a recent Centers for Disease Control and Prevention survey that found that consumption of at least 7 drinks per week or 5 or more drinks per occasion increased four-fold among pregnant women between 1991 and 1995 (U.S. Public Health Service, 1997).

POLYCHLORINATED BIPHENYLS (PCBS)

Since 1980, we have been following a cohort of 313 children prenatally exposed to PCBs (Jacobson et al., 1985; Jacobson & Jacobson, 1997 for detailed description of the cohort and recruitment). They live near Lake Michigan, and their mothers were recruited into our study in the hospital, shortly after delivery on the basis of maternal consumption of PCB-contaminated Lake Michigan fish. PCBs are a family of polycyclic, synthetic hydrocarbons once used in a wide range of industrial products (e.g., transformers, capacitors, plastics, and carbonless copy paper). Although banned in the United States in the 1970s and subsequently elsewhere, they are among the most ubiquitous and persistent environmental contaminants. Residues are currently found in air, water, and soil samples and can be detected in biologic tissue in most residents of industrialized countries and in animals, including arctic mammals and the golden eagle. Levels in water are low but concentrations increase about one order of magnitude per link up the food chain, with man at the top. Because PCBs are lipophilic and difficult for humans to excrete, they tend to accumulate in the body. Lake Michigan sportsfish have been identified as a major dietary source of PCB exposure in humans with PCB body burden directly related to amount of contaminated fish consumed. Since PCBs cross the placenta, they are also a source of fetal exposure. Umbilical cord serum levels provide a biological record of intrauterine exposure.

The toxic effects of PCBs were first recognized in 1968 with the Yusho accident in Japan and in 1979 with the Yu-cheng accident in Taiwan. Infants of pregnant women who consumed rice oil contaminated with high levels of PCBs and polychlorinated dibenzofurans (PCDFs) showed elevated PCB and PCDF serum levels and a set of dermatological anomalies, which included chloracne, brown pigmentation of the skin, swollen eyelids, pigmentation of the gums and nails, and eruption of teeth at birth. They were called *cola-colored* babies because of the brown pigmentation of their skin (Fig. 3.6). Infants exposed in utero were smaller at birth, sluggish, hypotonic, and performed more poorly on IQ tests administered during childhood (Higuchi, 1976; Rogan et al., 1988; see review Jacobson & Jacobson, 1997).

While acute, high levels of PCB exposure result in clinically apparent disorders, our Michigan research provided the first opportunity to examine the effects of chronic, low to moderate level exposure on infants and children. Mothers were recruited from hospitals near Lake Michigan. Over 8000 women were screened the day after delivery in order to find 242 women who ate relatively large quan-

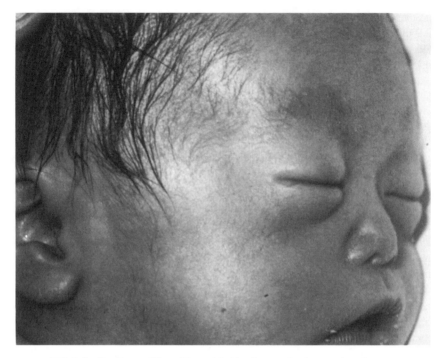

FIG. 3.6. Swollen eyelids and brownish skin pigmentation in a newborn born to a mother exposed to Yusho disease.

tities of Lake Michigan fish (at least 26 lbs over a 6-year period) and 71 women were recruited who did not eat Lake Michigan fish (Jacobson, Jacobson, Schwartz, & Fein, 1983). Although women were screened for fish consumption in order to locate higher exposed infants, the primary measure of prenatal exposure used in our analyses was PCB level in the umbilical cord serum.

Cord serum and breast milk samples were analyzed by the Michigan Department of Public Health by means of packed column gas chromatography, adapting the Webb-McCall method. As can be seen in Table 3.16, the levels of postnatal exposure in breast milk were dramatically higher than the prenatal levels. As in our alcohol research described previously, potential confounders are adjusted statistically in all evaluations of prenatal PCB effects, and effects are only presented after control for confounders.

Obvious and distinctive Yusho symptoms were not noted in the Michigan sample, and infants born to the Michigan women appeared clinically asymptomatic. They were somewhat smaller at birth, weighing about 200 g less, a reduction in size comparable to that of smoking but that, unlike smoking, persisted at 5 months and 4 years postpartum. Smaller head circumference was also related to PCB exposure at the three ages (Jacobson & Jacobson, 1997). The principal deficit in cognitive function seen in infancy was poorer visual recognition memory on the Fagan test

TABLE 3.16
PCB Levels in Cord and Maternal Sera and Breast Milk

	N	Mean	Range	
			Low	High
PCB levels (ppb)				
Cord serum	286	2.3	0.0	12.6
Maternal serum	208	5.3	0.2	23.1
Breast milk (fat basis)	138	732.7	185.7	2600.0

administered at 7 months postpartum (Jacobson et al., 1985). Preference for novelty was related to cord serum PCB level in a dose-dependent fashion, after controlling for potential confounds (Fig. 3.7). The most highly exposed infants spent only about half the time looking at the novel stimulus. The percent of unique variance explained by cord serum PCB level was 10.4%.

Examination of the tails of the distribution indicates that infants with elevated cord serum PCB levels (≥ 3 ppb) were three times more likely to score in the lower tail of the distribution ($< M - 1$ SD) than nonexposed or low-exposed infants. They were substantially less likely to score in the upper tail. While 29% of the

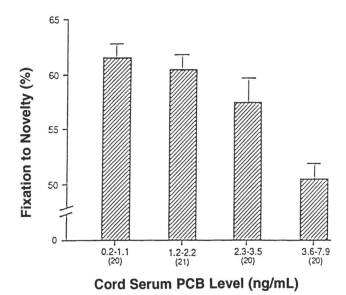

FIG. 3.7. Relation of cord serum PCB level to fixation to novelty on the Fagan Test of Infant Intelligence, adjusted for socioeconomic status, maternal age, and parity. Number of children in each group is given in parentheses.

nonexposed or low-exposed infants scored at least 1 SD above the mean, only one high-exposed infant (less than 4%) scored in this range.

It is important to note that by contrast to prenatal PCB exposure as indicated by cord serum levels, postnatal exposure from breastfeeding was unrelated to recognition memory performance, F (3,80) = 1.18, ns, even though absolute levels of postnatal exposure in the breast milk were much higher than in the cord serum (Table 3.16).

Yu-cheng

We will now present findings from the study on infants born to women exposed to Yu-cheng disease in Taiwan. The study was conducted in 1992 at the National Cheng Kung University Medical College, Tainan, in collaboration with Ko, Yao, Chang, and Hsu. We had demonstrated that PCBs are related to poorer novelty preference on the Fagan recognition memory test in our Michigan PCB-exposed cohort (Jacobson et al., 1985). No other study had, as yet, confirmed these findings, and we had not ruled out the possibility that PCB-exposed infants might also process information more slowly on the FTII. Due to the way the Michigan PCB data were collected, it was not possible to examine this hypothesis in our original cohort.

In the Yu-cheng accident in 1979, over 2000 Taiwanese ingested cooking oil accidentally contaminated with PCBs and PCDFs. Many of the exposed were young women, boarders at a school attached to the food processing plant where the accident occurred. Some of these Yu-cheng women were continuing to have babies in 1994. The Taiwanese Bureau of Disease Control maintains a registry of Yu-cheng cases and therefore was used to locate exposed women. Public health nurses located Yu-cheng women who were then pregnant and invited them to participate in this study.

This report is based on findings on 11 infants born to Yu-cheng women and 48 nonexposed controls, who were administered the FTII at 6.5 months (Ko et al., 1994). As shown in Table 3.17, the Yu-cheng exposed infants showed significantly poorer recognition memory, as indicated by less novelty preference, after controlling for the relevant potential confounders (parity, maternal education, and examiner), F (1,54) = 13.13, $p < .001$. The percent of unique variance explained by Yu-cheng exposure was high, 28.1%. By contrast to the Detroit alcohol-exposed infants, the Yu-cheng infants showed novelty preference deficits but no processing speed effects, F (1,54) = 0.57, ns. The results confirmed that PCB exposure is specifically related to a memory deficit rather than slower processing speed.

Longterm Effects of PCBs

In our follow-up study of the Michigan PCB cohort at age 4 years, we continued to find short-term memory deficits. At this age, effects were seen on the memory scale on the McCarthy Scales of Children's Abilities (Jacobson, Jacobson, &

TABLE 3.17
FTII Recognition Memory and Processing Speed by Exposure Group

	Yu-Cheng (N = 9)	Controls (N = 30)	F (1, 34)
Novelty preference (%)	56.9	64.9	4.96*
Mean fixation duration	1.9	1.9	0.06

Note. Values are means adjusted for maternal education, parity, and infant examiner.
*p < .05.

Humphrey, 1990) and on a simplified version of the Sternberg short-term memory test (Jacobson, Jacobson, Padgett, Brumitt, & Billings, 1992). By the 11-year follow-up (Jacobson & Jacobson, 1996), we found that prenatal exposure to PCBs was associated with lower Full Scale and Verbal IQ scores on the WISC-R, after control for potential confounders (Table 3.18), as well as poorer performance on an attentional factor derived from the WISC-R, known as freedom from distractibility. The most highly exposed children were three times as likely to have low average ($\leq M$—1 SD) IQ scores ($p < .001$) and twice as likely to be at least 2 years behind in reading comprehension on the Woodcock Reading Mastery Test ($p < .05$). Although larger quantities of PCBs are transferred by breast-feeding than in utero, there were deficits only in association with transplacental exposure, suggesting that the developing fetal brain is particularly sensitive to these compounds.

We were also able to compare these PCB findings to those found for children with low lead exposure in the cohort (Jacobson & Jacobson, 1996). We found that higher lead concentration obtained in blood assays at 4 years of age was associated with lower WISC-R Verbal IQ scores and poorer Woodcock Reading Comprehension scores at 11 years but not with poorer attention, as indicated by freedom of distractibility. The lead effects were evident primarily in children with blood lead concentrations of at least 10 μg per deciliter (.48 μmol per liter). They are consistent with findings of global IQ deficits rather than specific impairment in lead-exposed children (Bellinger et al., 1992). This pattern of effects is different from that found for alcohol, which affects attention and not Verbal IQ, and from PCBs, which affects both Verbal IQ and attention.

PCB Mechanisms of Action

The mechanisms of action responsible for the effects of prenatal PCB exposure on early CNS development are not well understood. A protein known as the aryl hydrocarbon (Ah) receptor has been identified in vitro as a mediator in the pro-

TABLE 3.18
Relation Between Prenatal Exposure to Polychlorinated Biphenyls (PCBs) and Performance on IQ
and Achievement Tests

	N	r	β^a	p
Wechsler Intelligence Scales for Children–Revised				
Full IQ	178	-.16	-.17	0.02
Verbal IQ[b]	178	-.15	-.16	0.02
Performance IQ[c]	178	-.14	-.13	0.08
Verbal comprehension[b]	178	-.15	-.16	0.02
Perceptual organization[d]	178	-.12	-.11	0.13
Freedom from distractibility[e]	178	-.17	-.17	0.02
Wide Range Achievement Test–Revised				
Spelling[f]	176	-.06	-.07	0.26
Arithmetic[g]	176	-.01	-.04	0.56
Woodcock Reading Mastery Tests–Revised				
Word comprehension[h]	177	-.18	-.17	0.01
Passage comprehension[i]	177	-.11	-.09	0.20
Reading comprehension[i]	177	-.14	-.13	0.06

[a]β is the standardized regression coefficient for prenatal exposure to polychlorinated biphenyls from a multiple regression analysis. All the regressions controlled for socioeconomic status, maternal education, vocabulary, and the HOME Inventory. In addition, we controlled for the covariates listed in the following footnotes.
[b]The additional covariates were maternal marital status and smoking during pregnancy.
[c]The additional covariates were number of children in the household, delivery complications, and prenatal exposure to polychlorinated biphenyls.
[d]The additional covariate was number of children in the household.
[e]The additional covarites were number of children in the household, child's sex, and exposure to mercury.
fThe additional covariates were child's sex and grade, drinking during pregnancy, smoking during pregnancy, and exposure to mercury.
[g]The additional covarites were maternal age, child's age and grade, drinking and smoking during pregnancy, and prenatal exposure to polychlorinated biphenyls.
[h]The additional covariates were parity, child's sex and grade, and drinking and smoking during pregnancy.
[i]The additional covarites were parity, stress within past year, child's sex and grade, drinking and smoking during pregnancy, and exposure to mercury.

duction of toxic compounds following exposure to TCDD and the structurally similar nonortho coplanar PCBs (Safe, 1990), but the role of the Ah receptor in PCB neurotoxicity has not been studied. Recently, considerable attention has been focused on the potential of PCBs to disrupt endocrine function. Several studies have provided evidence of endocrine disruption by PCBs and organochlorine pesticide contaminants in wildlife (Giesy et al., 1994; Guillette et al., 1994). Much of this research has focused on the estrogenic properties of these compounds although other hormones can be affected as well. With regard to the CNS deficits associated with prenatal PCB exposure, thyroid hormone seems the most likely candidate. Thyroid hormone is necessary to stimulate neuronal and glial proliferation and differentiation during the late gestation and early postnatal periods (Porterfield & Hendrich, 1993), and a thyroid hormone deficiency during this period causes spasticity and mental retardation (Frost, 1986). In utero, PCB exposure has been linked to reduced fetal brain concentrations of thyroid hormones in prenatally exposed Dutch infants (Koopman-Esseboom et al., 1994b), but these reductions are small relative to those found in cognitively impaired, thyroid-deficient infants. Given the vulnerability of the developing brain, there are numerous alternative mechanisms through which prenatal PCB exposure may also disrupt fetal CNS development. Migratory cells and cells undergoing mitosis are particularly sensitive to toxic insult (Annau & Eccles, 1986), the fetal blood-brain barrier is incomplete (Woodbury, 1974), and the fetus lacks important drug metabolizing detoxification capacities that are found postnatally (Dvorchik, 1981).

EFFECTS OF HEAVY PRENATAL COCAINE EXPOSURE

Numerous studies of cocaine exposure have reported the lack of effects on infant cognition, and a number of reviews have concluded that the link between in utero cocaine exposure and poor cognitive outcome is much less conclusive than expected (Hutchings, 1993; Mayes, Granger, Bornstein, & Zuckerman, 1992; Zuckerman & Frank, 1992). At least two factors need to be considered, however, before concluding that cocaine exposure does not affect infant cognitive function: the sensitivity of the outcome measures used and potential threshold effects. As indicated earlier, virtually all prospective studies on the effects of prenatal teratogenic exposure have used the Bayley Scales to assess neurobehavioral function in infancy. In the animal literature, attainment of developmental milestones, such as crawling or walking, which are roughly comparable to items measured on the Bayley, were also relatively unaffected by prenatal cocaine exposure (Dow-Edwards, 1993, 1997; Spear, Kirstein, & Bell, 1989). However, more cognitively challenging learning and memory behaviors were susceptible to alterations by prenatal cocaine exposure. Alternatively, some teratogenic effects may become apparent only when heavy exposure is involved, and inclusion of light and moderately exposed infants among the exposed may mask effects of heavy exposure.

As indicated earlier, our sample of inner-city, African American infants was originally recruited to study effects of prenatal alcohol exposure on cognitive development, but the co-occurrence of a cocaine epidemic necessitated the use of a stratified design and inclusion of a heavy cocaine, low alcohol-exposed group in the sample to permit statistical analysis of alcohol versus cocaine effects (Jacobson, Jacobson, Sokol, & Martier, 1996).

Table 3.19 summarizes data from regression analyses of cocaine on infant outcome. None of the infant cognitive outcomes were related to prenatal cocaine exposure, when the cocaine exposure was assessed using continuous measures. Cocaine exposure was next dichotomized by whether or not cocaine was used during pregnancy, as is typically done in studies of cocaine effects. In addition, a second

TABLE 3.19
Effects of Cocaine Use on Gestational Age and Cognitive Outcome Using Continuous Measures
of Exposure

	r	β
Gestational age[a]	-.20	-.12*
Neurobehavioral outcomes		
Bayley Scales[b]		
Mental Development Index	-.07	.04
Psychomotor Development Index	.00	.04
Fagan Test of Infant Intelligence[c]	-.05	-.04
Visual expectancy paradigm[d]		
Anticipations	-.11	-.11
Median RT	-.09	-.09
Percent fast	.17	.14
Percent quick	.13	.12

Note. r = simple correlation between cocaine exposure and the outcome measure; β = standardized regression coefficient from a multiple regression assessing the relation between cocaine exposure and the outcome measure after control for confounding.
[a]N = 464. Gestational age was adjusted for maternal age and education, parity, infant gender, number of prenatal clinic visits, and maternal alcohol use and smoking during pregnancy.
[b]N = 360 for MDI; N = 353 for PDI. MDI and PDI were adjusted for maternal age, prenatal visits, HOME, alcohol and smoking, and age at test. In addition, PDI was adjusted for parity and examiner.
[c]N = 302. Visual recognition memory was adjusted for parity and age at test.
*$p < .05$.

set of ANCOVAs was examined in which cocaine use was dichotomized into heavy (2 or more days/week) and light/none (< 2 days/week). No between-group differences for cocaine use were found in relation to any of the cognitive outcomes when cocaine exposure was dichotomized by use versus nonuse (Table 3.20). Similarly, no differences were found between heavy and low cocaine-exposed infants on the Bayley MDI or PDI, confirming earlier studies (e.g., Chasnoff, Griffith, Freier, & Murray, 1992). By contrast, heavy cocaine exposure was related to poorer novelty preference on the FTII, after control for confounding. A score of 53% preference for novelty is considered at risk on the FTII. Based on this criterion, two-thirds of the heavily cocaine-exposed infants (66.3%) were at risk, compared with 42.6% of those who were less exposed, χ^2 (1) = 15.84, $p < .0001$.

Heavy cocaine exposure was also related to faster responsiveness on the Haith VExP, after controlling for confounders (Table 3.20). These effects are consistent with prior findings, suggesting that cocaine-exposed infants may be hyperresponsive or prefer faster frequencies of stimulation but process information more poorly. The absence of an effect on anticipations indicates that the faster reactivity was not accompanied by improved learning of the alternating sequence.

None of the cognitive effects associated with in utero cocaine exposure were related to maternal postpartum use of cocaine assessed in terms of either the presence or absence of use or by heavy use, suggesting that the observed effects were related to prenatal exposure and not a consequence of environmental factors related to maternal substance abuse (S. Jacobson, Jacobson, Sokol, & Martier, 1996).

TABLE 3.20
Effects of Cocaine Use Dichotomized by Two Different Cut-Points

	Abstainer		User			Abstainer or Light User		Heavy User		
	N	Mean	N	Mean	F	N	Mean	N	Mean	F
Bayley Scales[a]										
Mental Development Index	257	109.6	91	109.7	0.01	293	109.2	55	111.8	1.82
Psychomotor Development Index	251	106.1	90	104.3	0.04	287	105.9	54	104.4	0.01
Fagan Test of Infant Intelligence[b] (Novelty preference %)	227	56.8	75	56.8	0.27	258	56.8	44	55.8	4.16*
Visual Expectancy Paradigm[c]										
Anticipations (%)	59	29.8	40	25.8	2.32	73	26.8	26	29.8	1.25
Median RT (msec)	59	323.5	40	322.9	0.00	73	328.2	26	309.6	3.20†
Fast responses (%)	59	48.0	40	50.0	0.42	73	47.0	26	55.0	4.32*
Quick responses (%)	59	54.2	40	56.2	0.31	73	53.2	26	61.2	5.08*

Note. Means are from ANCOVAS, adjusted for relevant potential confounders.
[a]MDI and PDI were adjusted for maternal age and depression, prenatal visits, HOME, alcohol and smoking, and age at test. In addition, PDI was adjusted for parity and examiner.
[b]Visual recognition memory was adjusted for parity and age at test.
[c]Anticipations, RT, and percent fast and quick responses were adjusted for sex of infant and maternal alcohol use. Percent fast responses were also adjusted for age at test.
†$p < .10$. *$p < .05$.

The cocaine-related CNS deficits, poorer novelty preference on the FTII, and faster reactivity on the VExP, were seen in relation to a measure of heavy exposure reported by the mothers at the initial prenatal clinic visit. Dose and timing of exposure may, in fact, be critical in understanding the impact of these cocaine effects. These findings are consistent with laboratory findings, suggesting that these deficits may be mediated by direct action of cocaine on the reuptake of neurotransmitters, norepinephrine and dopamine, resulting in increased synaptic availability of these neurotransmitters and a consequent exaggerated responsiveness or supersensitivity in animals (Dow-Edwards, 1993, 1997; Mayes et al., 1992; Spear et al., 1989).

SPECIFICITY OF INFANT EFFECTS

As shown in Table 3.21, these findings provide evidence that prenatal exposure to each of these substances is related to a specific pattern of effects: alcohol to slower infant processing speed but not poorer recognition memory; PCBs to poorer recognition memory but not poorer processing speed; and cocaine to faster but apparently poorer processing speed and poorer recognition memory. Because we did not have RT data on the PCB-exposed infants, we cannot rule out the possibility that the pattern for PCB- and cocaine-exposed infants may still look similar. However, there are several reasons why this possibility seems very unlikely. As indicated earlier, we have previously found a moderate correlation between the VExP RT measure and the processing speed measure (fixation duration) on the FTII and crossmodal test. We found no relation between PCBs and the processing speed measure on the FTII, and no indication of processing speed deficits in the Taiwanese Yucheng data. PCB-exposed infants and children have been described as hypotonic (Harada, 1976; Jacobson, Jacobson, Fein, Schwartz, & Dowler, 1984) rather than as aroused and hyperreactive, like cocaine-exposed children (Karmel & Gardner, 1996; Mayes, Bornstein, Chawarska, & Granger, 1995).

Furthermore, the specific pattern of infant findings in relation to each of these substances is consistent with the long-term outcomes we and others have found to be related to these substances and to findings from animal research.

TABLE 3.21
Effects of Three Neurotoxicants on Infant Information Processing Outcome

	PCBs	Alcohol	Cocaine
Novelty preference (%)	↓	←→	↓
Duration fixation (s)	←→	↑	←→
Reaction time (ms)	—[a]	↑	↓

[a]Not tested.

CORTISOL EFFECTS

The data summarized previously indicate that different neurocognitive patterns of effects emerge depending on type of prenatal exposure. A differential neurobehavioral pattern also appears when other systems, such as the neuroendocrine arousal system, is affected. Elevated corticosterone levels in response to stress have been found in adult rats exposed prenatally to alcohol, but little is known about the effects of prenatal alcohol or drug exposure on the cortisol response in humans. To date one study has found that crack–cocaine is related to depressed newborn cortisol levels following a heel-prick (Magnano, Gardner, & Karmel, 1992), and one study of 26 infants recently found that prenatal alcohol and cigarette exposure was related to higher prestressor cortisol levels at 2 and 6 months of age (Ramsey, Bendersky, & Lewis, 1996). In our Detroit study, saliva samples were obtained at arrival to our laboratory and 30 minutes after a blood draw for lead screening from 83 13-month-old infants (Jacobson et al., 1999). To examine effects of prenatal alcohol and drug exposure on infant cortisol levels, data were collected on a broad range of background characteristics including specific situational variables known to influence cortisol level. These included time of day when testing sample was obtained, time since last ingestion of milk, and whether the infant was cutting new teeth. No differences were found in relation to time of day or time since last drink of milk.

Post-blood drawn cortisol levels did not differ from basal levels in many of the infants, confirming recent studies indicating adaptation of the adrenocortical response to this type of stress at this age (Gunnar, Broderson, & Krueger, 1996; Lewis & Thomas, 1990; Ramsey & Lewis, 1994). As in other studies, cortisol levels were positively related to maternal depression (Field et al., 1988) and emergence of teeth (Gunnar, Mangelsdorf, Larson, & Hertsgaard, 1989).

It is of interest that a distinct pattern in basal cortisol levels emerged depending on type of prenatal exposure. Higher levels of maternal drinking at conception and during pregnancy were related to elevated basal levels, after control for potential confounders including cocaine (Table 3.22). By contrast, infants heavily exposed to cocaine had lower basal levels, after control for confounds including alcohol exposure.

As predicted from animal findings, heavy alcohol exposure was also related to elevated poststress cortisol levels. Prenatal alcohol exposure was not related to poststress levels using a continuous alcohol exposure measure. However, some teratogenic effects emerge only when heavy exposure is involved (S. Jacobson, Jacobson, Sokol, & Martier, 1996). Group differences in mean basal and poststress levels are shown in Fig. 3.8, in which alcohol, cocaine, and smoking were dichotomized into heavy users versus light users and abstainers. A repeated measures (basal and poststress) ANCOVA with one between-subjects factor (exposure group) was performed for each substance. The effect of heavy alcohol at conception (1 or more oz AA/day) on cortisol levels was significant. Post hoc F tests controlling for confounders showed that the heavy alcohol group exhibited high-

TABLE 3.22
Effects of Alcohol and Cocaine on Basal and Poststress Cortisol Levels

	Basal[a]		Poststress[b]	
	r	β	r	β
Alcohol				
At conception	.40***	.44***	.20†	.15
During pregnancy	.24*	.25*	.17	.12
MAST	.38***	.46***	.14	.11
Cocaine during pregnancy	-.28*	-.30**	-.04	-.04

[a] βs adjusted for pacifier use, cutting teeth, and caregiver welfare status and depression. The alcohol analyses included heavy cocaine use and the cocaine analyses included alcohol use during pregnancy as potential confounders. Data missing on cutting teeth for seven infants. $N = 64$.
[b] βs adjusted for cutting teeth, caregiver PPVT-R, infant age at visit, and basal levels. Data missing on cutting teeth for seven infants and PPVT-R for two caregivers. $N = 74$; for cocaine $N = 67$.
†$p < .10$. *$p < .05$. **$p < .01$. ***$p < .001$.

er cortisol levels at baseline, $F(1,57) = 11.95$, $p < .001$, and as predicted from the animal studies, poststress cortisol levels were also higher in this group, $F(1,62) = 3.15$, $p < .05$, one-tail. By contrast, only basal cortisol was significantly depressed among the heavy cocaine exposed compared with the light–nonexposed infants, $F(1, 57) = 6.42$, $p < .05$. There were no smoking effects on cortisol levels, even when heavy smoking was considered.

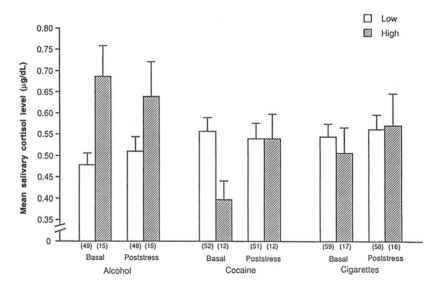

FIG. 3.8.   Mean basal and poststress cortisol levels dichotomized by heavy versus light/abstainer use of alcohol, cocaine, and smoking.

CONCLUSIONS

In the last 25 years, dramatic advances have been made in detecting and understanding the impact of environmental contaminants and of substances, such as alcohol and illicit drugs, on the development of the fetus. Moreover, the critical role of neurobehavioral defects as early indicators of danger to the infant and to humans more generally has been recognized. Even the public has become more aware of the potential consequences of prenatal exposure on behavioral deficits and human development. On Wednesday, May 11, 1994, the *New York Times* carried a front page headline that read, "Fetal Harm, Not Cancer, Cited as Primary Threat from Dioxin." Among the evidence supporting this statement, the article described our recent findings on the impact of PCBs—a substance related to dioxin—on infant neurobehavioral development at levels of exposure just above those found in the general population.

The findings presented here also support our hypothesis that the difficulty in detecting a behavioral profile may be an artifact of relying on more global measures like IQ. The advent of newer, more specific infant and child outcomes, such as the information processing measures used in our research, appear to facilitate the emergence of specific patterns of impairment that are related to specific behavioral teratogens. The picture that emerges is of distinct underlying dimensions of intellectual function, which are affected differentially by different teratogenic exposures. In addition, these data confirm the findings of Rose and her colleagues (Rose & Feldman, 1995; Rose et al., 1997) that memory and processing speed are pivotal constructs contributing to the relation between infant-information processing and later IQ. In an elegant longitudinal study, Rose et al. showed that 7-month visual recognition memory and 12-month cross-modal transfer predicted 11-year IQ and that this relation was largely attributable to speed and memory measures obtained at 11 years. Although there was a direct relation of infant recognition memory to 11-year recognition memory, this measure only partly explained the relation between the infancy measure and IQ (Rose & Feldman, 1995). The authors found that those aspects of 11-year recognition memory shared with other 11-year measures of memory accounted for the infancy-IQ relation (encoding and perceptual speed), not those unique to recognition or to retrieval speed (Rose et al., 1977). Our findings complement those of Rose and her colleagues. By breaking down the memory and speed measures inherent in the infant tests and by demonstrating the differential impact of these infant constructs in the factor analyses and prediction of later IQ.

The findings by Rose et al. (1997) also indicate that, while memory and attention are responsible for some of the infant-childhood continuities in cognition, other processes also play a role in the infant-IQ relations. In our study, we found that early symbolic development may constitute a third dimension that has predictive validity. The symbolic factor detected in our cohort bears much similarity to the representational competence construct suggested by Tamis-LeMonda and

Bornstein (1989). This factor, which reflects the ability to imitate modeled behavior, emerged from the Belsky play measure of symbolic development and as
the most salient dimension of development at 13 months on the Bayley Scales
using McCall et al. (1977) factor analytic procedure described earlier (S. Jacobson et al., 1992). The measures constituting this early symbolic dimension are related to a different and larger set of environmental confounds than those comprising the other two information-processing factors, processing speed and
memory. They may, therefore, be more influenced by environmental stimulation
and potentially amenable to therapeutic intervention.

Following Mirsky et al.'s (1991) four-factor model of attention (sustain, encode, focus, and shift), we have recently added an assessment of the infant's ability to shift attention, the A-not B test (Diamond, 1985, 1991) to the battery of infant tests we use to evaluate the impact of behavioral teratogens on specific
aspects of infant attention and memory. The infant's ability to shift attention is
presumably a precursor of executive function, which has been found to be disrupted by lesions of the dorsolateral prefrontal cortex in laboratory monkeys. We
have also added a more complicated version of Haith et al.'s (1988) VExP. Given
the socioemotional outcomes that are emerging from the TRF and CBCL
(Achenbach, 1991) data that we collected on the alcohol-exposed cohort at 7.5
years, we plan to conduct a more comprehensive clinical assessment of the children at 12.5 years to examine more closely the impact of prenatal exposure as a
predictor of behavioral and emotional disturbances and of early use of alcohol,
drugs, and smoking.

The findings presented in this chapter provide evidence that exposure to each
of the three teratogens that we have studied is related to a specific pattern of effects already seen in infancy. Findings in animal studies on prenatal PCB (Jacobson & Jacobson, 1997; Tilson, Jacobson, & Rogan, 1990) and cocaine (Dow-Edwards, 1997) exposure are consistent with the differential pattern of effects found
for these substances on the infant tests described here. The attentional and processing speed deficits detected on the infant tests in alcohol-exposed infants and
the short-term memory impairment detected in PCB-exposed infants are also
consistent with similar processing difficulties in older children (J. Jacobson et al.,
1990, 1992; Nanson & Hiscock, 1990; Streissguth et al., 1984, 1986, 1995). To
date, findings from our long-term follow-up of children prenatally exposed to
PCBs suggest a different pattern of impairment at 11 years than that seen in alcohol-exposed children, with PCB-related deficits detected primarily on Verbal
IQ and reading comprehension tests (Jacobson & Jacobson 1996). Study designs
comparing effects of alcohol exposure to those related to other teratogens to
which the fetus has been exposed may help clarify the manner in which neurotoxicants affect the developing CNS, both what they share in common and how
they differ. Timing of exposure is a known major determinant of which system
and outcomes will be affected. Bellinger (1995) suggested that, for some neurotoxicants, knowledge of the site and mechanism of action may permit the formu-

lation of specific predictions about the form in which toxicity will be expressed. As with lead, the primary neuropathological lesions underlying alcohol neurotoxicity have not yet been sufficiently characterized, probably because numerous mechanisms appear to be involved.

Our findings also show that exposure to different prenatal substances impact initially on specific cognitive abilities rather than on a singular, general factor, as measured by IQ or a single underlying infant-developmental index. The specificity of the teratogenic effects reported in this chapter for alcohol, cocaine, and PCBs suggests that these substances operate on different sites of action in the CNS or differentially alter neuronal cellular and synaptic development. This specificity also provides evidence for the independence of the underlying components of infant-information processing. This type of research has the potential to complement ongoing research in the neurosciences and psychology (e.g., Damasio, 1994; LeDoux, 1994, 1996; Nelson, 1995; Nelson & Bloom, 1997; Posner & Petersen, 1990), by attempting to identify the neurophysiological substrates of specific domains of cognitive and neurobehavioral function. To the degree that the developmental psychologist can provide relatively narrow band tests that identify specific domains of function, these tests can be useful in the effort to understand their underlying neurophysiological processes and to detect differential patterns of deficits previously only seen later in childhood.

ACKNOWLEDGMENTS

The alcohol research was supported by National Institute on Alcohol Abuse and Alcoholism grants (RO1-AA06966 and P50-AA0706), with supplemental support from a National Institutes of Health Minority Access to Research Careers grant (T34-GM08030) and a Minority Biomedical Research Support grant (SO6-RR08167). The PCB research was funded by grants from the United States Environmental Protection Agency, 1979–1982, and the National Institute of Environmental Health Sciences (RO1-ES03246 and RO1-ES05843); the Yu-cheng study by a grant from the National Science Council, Taiwan, 1992–1995. This work was also supported by a grant from the Joseph Young, Sr., Fund from the State of Michigan. Special thanks to Robert Sokol, Susan Martier, Joel Ager, Melissa Estrin-Kaplan, Greta Fein, Pamela Schwartz, H.-C. Ko, B.L. Yao, F.M. Chang, and C.C. Hsu, who collaborated on portions of this research; Joseph Fagan, Susan Rose, Jay Belsky, and Marshall Haith for their consultation regarding the infant tests; and Lisa Chiodo, Renee Berube, Sonia Narang, Jeannine Krupinski, Joan Bihun, and our staff for their contributions to the studies reported here. Portions of this paper were presented at the biennial meeting of the Society for Research in Child Development, Indianapolis, March, 1995, and the International Symposium on the Behavioral Effects in Children following Prenatal Alcohol Exposure, Missilac, France, 1996.

REFERENCES

Aase, J. M. (1994). Clinical recognition of FAS: Difficulties of detection and diagnosis. *Alcohol Health and Research World*, *18*, 5–9.

Achenbach, T. (1991). Manual for the Child Behavior Checklist. Burlington, VT: University of Vermont.

Alber, S. A., & Strupp, B. J. (1996). An in-depth analysis of lead effects in a delayed spatial alteration task: Assessment of mnemonic effects, side bias, and proactive interference. *Neurotoxicology and Teratology*, *18*, 3–15.

Annau, Z., & Eccles, C. U. (1986). Prenatal exposure. In Z. Annau (Ed.), *Neurobehavioral toxicology*. Baltimore: Johns Hopkins University Press.

Bayley, N. (1969). *Bayley Scales of Infant Development*. New York: Psychological Corporation.

Bellinger, D. (1995). Interpreting the literature on lead and child development: The neglected role of the "experimental system." *Neurotoxicology and Teratology*, *17*, 210–212.

Bellinger, D. C., Stiles, K. M., & Needleman, H. L. (1992). Low-level lead exposure, intelligence and academic achievement: A long-term follow-up study. *Pediatrics*, *90*, 855–861.

Belsky, J., Garduque, L., & Hrncir, E. (1984). Assessing performance, competence, and executive capacity in infant play: Relations to home environment and security of attachment. *Developmental Psychology*, *20*, 406–417.

Bonthius, D. J., & West, J. R. (1990). Alcohol-induced neuronal loss in developing rats: Increased brain damage with binge exposure. *Alcoholism: Clinical and Experimental Research*, *14*, 107–118.

Bonthius, D. J., & West, J. R. (1991). Acute and long-term neuronal deficits in the rat olfactory bulb following alcohol exposure during the brain growth spurt. *Neurotoxicology and Teratology*, *13*(6), 611–619.

Bornstein, M. H., & Sigman, M. D. (1986). Continuity in mental development from infancy. *Child Development*, *57*, 251–274.

Bradley, R. H., Caldwell, B. M., Rock, S. L., Ramey, C. T., Barnard, K. E., Gray, C., Hammond, M. A., Mitchell, S., Gottfried, A. W., Siegel, L., & Johnson, D. L. (1989). Home environment and cognitive development in the first 3 years of life: A collaborative study involving six sites and three ethnic groups in North America. *Developmental Psychology*, *25*, 217–235.

Brown, R. T., Coles, C. D., Smith, I. E., Platzman, K. A., Silverstein, J., Erickson, S., & Falek, A. (1991). Effects of prenatal alcohol exposure at school age. II. Attention and behavior. *Neurotoxicology and Teratology*, *13*, 369–376.

Butcher, R. E. (1976). Behavioral testing as a method for assessing risk. *Environmental Health Perspectives*, *18*, 75–78.

Butcher, R. E., Vorhees, C. V., & Kimmel, C. A. (1972). Learning impairment from maternal salicylate treatment in rats. *Nature in New Biology*, *236*, 211–212.

Caldwell, B. M., & Bradley, R. H. (1979). *Home Observation for Measurement of the Environment*. Little Rock: University of Arkansas Press.

Carmichael Olson, H., Streissguth, A. P., Sampson, P. D., Barr, H. M., Bookstein, F. L., & Tiede, K. (1997). Association of prenatal alcohol exposure with behavioral and learning problems in early adolescence. *Journal of the American Academy of Child and Adolescent Psychiatry*, *36*, 1187–1194.

Chasnoff, I. J., Griffith, D. R., Freier, C., & Murray, J. (1992). Cocaine/polydrug use in pregnancy: Two year follow-up. *Pediatrics*, *89*, 284–289.

Coles, C. D., Platzman, K. A., Raskind-Hood, C. L., Brown, R. T., Falek, A., & Smith, I. E. (1997). A comparison of children affected by prenatal alcohol exposure and attention deficit, hyperactivity disorder. *Alcoholism: Clinical and Experimental Research*, *20*, 150–161.

Colombo, J. (1993). *Infant cognition: Predicting later intellectual function*. Newberry Park, CA: Sage.

Colombo, J., & Mitchell, D. W. (1990). Individual differences in early visual attention: Fixation time and information processing. In J. Colombo & J. Fagen (Eds.), *Individual differences in infancy: Reliability, stability, prediction*, (pp. 193–227). Hillsdale, NJ: Lawrence Erlbaum Associates.

Colombo, J., Mitchell, D. W., & Horowitz, F. D. (1988). Infant visual attention in the paired-comparison paradigm: Test-retest and attention-performance relations. *Child Development*, *89*, 1198–1210.

Coyle, I., Wayner, M. J., & Singer, G. (1976). Behavioral teratogenesis: A critical evaluation. *Pharmacological Biochemical Behavior, 4*, 191–200.

Damasio, A. R. (1994). *Descartes' error: Emotion, reason, and the human brain.* New York: Grosset/Putnam.

Diamond, A. (1985). Development of the ability to use recall to guide action, as indicated by infants' performance on AB. *Child Development, 56*, 868–883.

Diamond, A. (1991). Frontal lobe involvement in cognitive changes during the first year of life. In K. R. Gibson & A. C. Peterson (Eds.), *Brain maturation and cognitive development.* New York: Aldine de Gruyter.

DiLalla, L. F., Thompson, L. A., Plomin, R., Phillips, K., Fagan, J. F., Haith, M. M., Cyphers, L. H., & Fulker, D. W. (1990). Infant predictors of preschool and adult IQ: A study of infant twins and their parents. *Developmental Psychology, 26*, 759–769.

Dow-Edwards, D. (1993). The puzzle of cocaine's effects following maternal use during pregnancy: Still unsolved. *Neurotoxicology & Teratology, 15*, 295–296.

Dow-Edwards, D. (1997). Comparability of human and animal studies of developmental cocaine exposure. *NIDA Research Monograph Series: Behaviors of drug-exposed offspring: Research update* (pp. 146–174). Washington, DC: Department of Health and Human Services, National Institutes of Health.

Dunn, L. M., & Dunn, L. M. (1981). *PPVT Manual for Forms L and M.* Circle Pines, NM: American Guidance Service.

Dvorchik, B. H. (1981). Nonhuman primates as animal models for the study of fetal hepatic drug metabolism. In L. F. Soyka & G. P. Redmond (Eds.), *Drug metabolism in the immature human.* New York: Raven.

Fagan, J. F. (1984). The relationship of novelty preferences during infancy to later intelligence and recognition memory. *Intelligence, 8*, 339–346.

Fagan, J. F., & McGrath, S. K. (1981). Infant recognition memory and later intelligence. *Intelligence, 5*, 121–130.

Fagan, J. F., & Singer, L. T. (1983). Infant recognition memory as a measure of intelligence. In L. P. Lipsitt (Ed.), *Advances in infancy research* (Vol. 2). Norwood, NJ: Ablex.

Field, T. M., Healy, B., Goldstein, S., Perry, S., Bendell, D., Schanberg, S., Zimmerman, E. A., & Kuhn, C. (1988). Infants of depressed mothers show "depressed" behavior even with non-depressed adults. *Child Development, 59*, 1569–1579.

Frost, G. J. (1986). Aspects of congenital hypothyroidism. *Child Care, Health and Development, 12*, 369–375.

Garavan, H., Morgan, R. E., Hermer-Vazquez, L., Levitsky, D. A., & Strupp, B. J. (in press). Enduring effects of early lead exposure: Evidence for a specific deficit in associative ability, *Neurotoxicology and Teraology.*

Giesy, J., Ludwig, J., & Tillitt, D. (1994). Deformities in birds of the Great Lakes region: Assigning causality. *Environmental Science and Technology, 28*, 128–135.

Goldschmidt, L., (1996). Prenatal alcohol exposure and academic achievement at age six: A nonlinear fit. *Alcoholism: Clinical and Experimental Research, 20*(4), 763–770.

Goodlett, C. R., Kelly, S. J., & West, J. R. (1987). Early postnatal alcohol exposure that produces high blood alcohol levels impairs development of spatial navigation learning. *Psychobiology, 15*, 64–74.

Goodlett, C. R., Marcussen, B. L., & West, J. R. (1990). A single day of alcohol exposure during the brain growth spurt includes microencephaly and cerebellar Purkinje cell loss. *Alcohol, 7*, 104–114.

Goodlett, C. R., & Peterson, S. D. (1994). The role of duration and timing of binge-like neonatal alcohol exposure in determining the extent of alcohol-induced deficits in spatial navigation and motor learning. *Alcoholism: Clinical & Experimental Research, 18*, 501.

Goodlett, C. R., & West, J. R. (1992). Fetal alcohol effects: Rat model of alcohol exposure during the brain growth spurt. In I. S. Zagon & T. A. Slotkin (Eds.), *Maternal substance abuse and the developing nervous system* (pp. 45–75). New York: Academic Press.

Guillette, L., Gross, T., Masson, G., Matter, J., Percival, H., & Woodward, A. (1994). Developmental abnormalities of the gonad and abnormal sex hormone concentrations in juvenile alligators from contaminated and control lakes in Florida. *Environmental Health Perspectives, 102*, 680–688.

Gunnar, M. R., Broderson, L., & Krueger, K. (1996). Dampening of adrenocortical responses during infancy: Normative changes and individual differences. *Child Development, 67*, 877–889.

Gunnar, M. R., Mangelsdorf, S., Larson, M., & Hertsgaard, L. (1989). Attachment, temperament, and adrenocortical activity in infancy: A study of psychoendocrine regulation. *Developmental Psychology, 25*, 355–363.

Haith, M. M., Hazan, C., & Goodman, G. S. (1988). Expectation and anticipation of dynamic visual events by 3.5-month-old babies. *Child Development, 59*, 467–479.

Harada, M. (1976). Intrauterine poisoning: Clinical and epidemiological studies and significance of the problem. *Bulletin of the Institute of Constitutional Medicine, Kumamoto University, 25* (Suppl), 1–69.

Higuchi, K. (Ed.). (1976). *PCB poisoning and pollution*. New York: Academic Press.

Hilson, J., & Strupp, B. J. (1997). Analyses of response patterns clarify lead effects in olfactory reversal and extra-dimensional shift tasks: Assessment of inhibitory control, associative ability, and memory. *Behavioral Neuroscience, 111*, 532–542.

Hutchings, D. E. (1978). Behavioral Teratology: Embryopathic and behavioral effects of drugs during pregnancy. In G. Gottlieb (Ed.), *Studies on the development of behavior and the nervous system* (Vol. 4). New York: Academic Press.

Hutchings, D. E. (1993). The puzzle of cocaine's effects following maternal use during pregnancy: Are there reconcilable differences? *Neurotoxicology & Teratology, 15*, 281–286.

Hynd, G. W., Semrud-Clikeman, M., Lorys, A., Novey, E., et al. (1991). Corpus callosum morphology in attention deficit-hyperactivity disorder: Morphometric analysis of MRI. *Journal of Learning Disabilities, 24*, 141–146.

Jacobson, J. L., & Jacobson, S. W. (1994). Prenatal alcohol exposure and neurobehavioral development: Where is the threshold? *Alcohol Health and Research World, 18*, 30–36.

Jacobson, J. L., & Jacobson, S. W. (1996). Intellectual impairment in children exposed to polychlorinated biphenyls in utero. *New England Journal of Medicine, 335*, 783–789.

Jacobson, J. L., & Jacobson, S. W. (1997). Teratogen update: Polychlorinated biphenyls. *Teratology, 55*, 338–347.

Jacobson, J. L., Jacobson, S. W., Fein, G. G., Schwartz, P. M., & Dowler, J. K. (1984). Prenatal exposure to an environmental toxin: A test of the multiple effects model. *Developmental Psychology, 20*, 523–532.

Jacobson, J. L., Jacobson, S. W., & Humphrey, H. E. B. (1990). Effects of *in utero* exposure to polychlorinated biphenyls and related contaminants on cognitive functioning in young children. *Journal of Pediatrics, 116*, 38–45.

Jacobson, J. L., Jacobson, S. W., Padgett, R. J., Brumitt, G. A., & Billings, R. L. (1992). Effects of prenatal exposure to polychlorinated biphenyls on cognitive processing efficiency and sustained attention. *Developmental Psychology, 28*, 297–306.

Jacobson, J. L., Jacobson, S. W., & Sokol, R. J. (1996). Increased vulnerability to alcohol-related birth defects in the offspring of mothers over 30. *Alcoholism: Clinical and Experimental Research, 20*, 359–363.

Jacobson, J. L., Jacobson, S. W., Sokol, R. J., & Ager, J. W. (1998). Relation of maternal age and pattern of pregnancy drinking to functionally significant cognitive deficit in infancy. *Alcohol Health & Research World, 22*, 354–351.

Jacobson, J. L., Jacobson, S. W., Sokol, R. J., Martier, S. S., Ager, J. W., & Kaplan-Estrin, M. G. (1993). Teratogenic effects of alcohol on infant development. *Alcoholism: Clinical and Experimental Research, 17*, 174–183.

Jacobson, S. W. (1998). Assessing the impact of maternal drinking during and after pregnancy on child neurobehavioral outcome. *Alcohol Health and Research World, 21*, 199–203.

Jacobson, S. W., Bihun, J. T., & Chiodo, L. M. (1999). Effects of prenatal alcohol and cocaine exposure on infant cortisol levels. *Development & Psychopathology, 11,* 195–208.

Jacobson, S. W., Chiodo, L. M., & Jacobson, J. L. (1996). Predictive validity of infant recognition memory and processing speed to 7-year IQ in an inner-city sample. *Infant Behavior and Development, 19,* 524.

Jacobson, S. W., Fein, G. G., Jacobson, J. L., Schwartz, P. M., & Dowler, J. K. (1985). The effect of intrauterine PCB exposure on visual recognition memory. *Child Development, 56,* 853–860.

Jacobson, S. W., Jacobson, J. L., O'Neill, J. M., Padgett, R. J., Frankowski, J. J., & Bihun, J. T. (1992). Visual expectation and dimensions of infant information processing. *Child Development, 63,* 711–724.

Jacobson, S. W., Jacobson, J. L., Schwartz, P. M., & Fein, G. G. (1983). Intrauterine exposure of human newborns to PCBs: Measures of exposure. In F. M. d'Itri & M. Kamrin (Eds.), *PCBs: Human and environmental hazards.* Boston: Butterworth.

Jacobson, S. W., Jacobson, J. L., & Sokol, R. J. (1994). Effects of fetal alcohol exposure on infant reaction time. *Alcoholism: Clinical and Experimental Research, 18,* 1125–1132.

Jacobson, S. W., Jacobson, J. L., Sokol, R. J., & Martier, S. S. (1996). New evidence of neurobehavioral effects of in utero cocaine exposure. *The Journal of Pediatrics, 129,* 581–590.

Jacobson, S. W., Jacobson, J. L., Sokol, R. J., Martier, S., & Ager, J. W. (1993). Prenatal alcohol exposure and infant information processing ability. *Child Development, 64,* 1706–1721.

Jensh, R. P. (1983). Behavioral testing procedures: A review. In E. M. Johnson & D. M. Kochlar (Eds.), *Teratogenesis and reproductive toxicology.* New York: Springer-Verlag.

Jones, K. L., & Smith, D. W. (1973). Recognition of the fetal alcohol syndrome in early infancy. *Lancet, 2,* 999–1001.

Kagan, J. (1971). *Change and continuity in infancy.* New York: Wiley.

Karmel, B. Z., & Gardner, J. M. (1996). Prenatal cocaine effects on arousal modulated attention during neonatal period. *Developmental Psychobiology, 29,* 463–480.

Kleinbaum, D. G., Kupper, L. L., & Muller, K. E. (1988). *Applied regression analysis and other multivariable methods* (2nd ed.). Boston: PWS-Kent.

Ko, H., Yao, B., Chang, F. -M., Hsu, C. -C., Jacobson, S. W., & Jacobson, J. L. (1994). Preliminary evidence of recognition memory deficits in infants born to Yu-cheng exposed women. In H. Fiedler, O. Hutzinger, L. Birnbaum, G. Lambert, L. Needham, & S. Safe (Eds.), *Dioxin '94.* Kyoto, Japan: Kyoto University.

Koopman-Esseboom, C., Huisman, M., Weisglas-Kuperus, N., Van der Paauw, C. G., Tuinstra, L. G. M. T., Boersma, E. R., & Sauer, P. J. J. (1994). PCB and dioxin levels in plasma and human milk of 418 Dutch women and their infants: Predictive value of PCB congener levels in maternal plasma for fetal and infant's exposure to PCBs and dioxins. *Chemosphere, 9,* 1721–1732.

Koopman-Esseboom, C., Morse, D. C., Weisglas-Kuperus, N., LutkeSchipholt, J., Van der Paauw, C. G., Tuinstra, L. G. M. Th., Brouwer, A., & Sauer, P. J. J. (1994). Effects of dioxins and polychlorinated biphenyls on thyroid hormone status of pregnant women and their infants. *Pediatric Research, 36,* 468–473.

LeDoux, J. E. (1994). Emotion, memory, and the brain. *Scientific American,* 50–57.

LeDoux, J. E. (1996). *The emotional brain.* New York: Simon & Schuster.

Lemoine, P., & Lemoine, P. H. (1992). Avenir des enfants de meres alcooliques (Etude de 105 cas retrouves a l'age adulte) et quelques constatations d'interet prophylatique. *Annuals of Pediatrics, 39,* 226–235.

Lewis, M., & Thomas, D. (1990). Cortisol release in infants in response to inoculation. *Child Development, 9,* 106.

Lyons-Ruth, K., Connell, D. B., & Grunebaum, H. W. (1990). Infants at social risk: Maternal depression and family support services as mediators of infant development and security of attachment. *Child Development, 61,* 85–98.

Magnano, C. L., Gardner, J. M., & Karmel, B. Z. (1992). Differences in cortisol levels in cocaine-exposed and noncocaine-exposed NICU infants. *Developmental Psychobiology, 25,* 93–103.

Mattson, S. N., Riley, E. P., & Jernigan, T. L. (1994). MRI and prenatal alcohol exposure: Images provide insight into FAS. *Alcohol Health & Research World, 18*, 49–54.

Mattson, S. N., Riley, E. P., Jernigan, T. L., Ehlers, C. L., Delis, D. C., Jones, K. L., Stern, C., Johnson, K. A., Hesselink, J. R., & Bellugi, U. (1992). Fetal alcohol syndrome: A case report of neuropsychological, MRI, and EEG assessment of two children. *Alcoholism: Clinical and Experimental Research, 16*, 1001–1003.

Mattson, S. N., Riley, E. P., Sowell, E. R., Jernigan, T. L., Sobel, D. F., & Jones, K. L. (1996). A decrease in the size of the basal ganglia in children with fetal alcohol syndrome. *Alcoholism: Clinical and Experimental Research, 20*, 1088–1093.

Mayes, L. C., Bronstein, M. H., Chawarska, K., & Granger, R. H. (1995). Information processing and developmental assessments in 3-month-old infants exposed prenatally to cocaine. *Pediatrics, 95*, 539–545.

Mayes, L. C., Granger, R. H., Bornstein, M. H., & Zuckerman, B. (1992). The problem of prenatal cocaine exposure: A rush to judgment. *JAMA, 267*, 406–408.

McCall, R. B., & Carriger, M. S. (1993). A meta-analysis of infant habituation and recognition memory performance as predictors of later IQ. *Child Development, 64*, 57–79.

McCall, R. B., Eichorn, D. H., & Hogarty, P. S. (1977). Transitions in early mental development. *Monographs of the Society for Research in Child Development, 42*(3).

Miller, M. W. (1992). Development of the CNS: Effects of alcohol and opiates. New York: Wiley-Liss.

Mirsky, A. F., Anthony, B. J., Duncan, C. C., Ahearn, M. B., & Kellam, S. G. (1991). Analysis of the elements of attention: A neuropsychological approach. *Neuropsychology Review, 2*, 109–145.

Mitchell, D. W., & Colombo, J. (1989). Fixation time as a predictor of 3- and 4-month-olds' learning, retention and transfer. *Abstracts of the Society of Research in Child Development, 6*, 321.

Nanson, J. L., & Hiscock, M. (1990). Attention deficits in children exposed to alcohol prenatally. *Alcoholism: Clinical and Experimental Research, 14*, 656–661.

Nelson, C. A. (1995). The ontogeny of human memory: A cognitive neuroscience perspective. *Developmental Psychology, 31*, 723–738.

Nelson, C. A., & Bloom, F. E. (1997). Child development and neuroscience. *Child Development, 68*, 970–987.

Nicolich, L. M. (1977). Beyond sensorimotor intelligence: Assessment of symbolic maturity through analysis of pretend play. *Merrill-Palmer Quarterly, 23*, 89–99.

Porterfield, S. P., & Hendrich, C. E. (1993). The role of thyroid hormones in prenatal and neonatal neurological development—Current perspectives. *Endocrine Reviews, 14*, 94–106.

Posner, M. I., & Petersen, S. E. (1990). The attention system of the human brain. *Annual Review of Neuroscience, 13*, 25–42.

Ramsey, D. S., Bendersky, M. I., & Lewis, M. (1996). Effects of prenatal alcohol and cigarette exposure on two- and six-month-old infants' adrenocortical reactivity to stress. *Journal of Pediatric Psychology, 21*, 833–840.

Ramsey, D. S., & Lewis, M. (1994). Developmental changes in infant cortisol and behavioral response to inoculation. *Child Development, 65*, 1491–1502.

Riley, E. P., & Mattson, S. N. (1997). Behavioral deficits and brain following prenatal alcohol exposure. *Extramural Scientific Advisory Board Meeting on FAS.*

Riley, E. P., Thomas, J. D., Lafiette, M., & Dominquez, H. D. (1997). Nonbehavioral and animal behavioral presentations of FAS/ARBD. *Extramural Scientific Advisory Board Meeting on FAS.*

Riley, E. P., & Vorhees, C. V. (1986). *Handbook of Behavioral Teratology*. New York: Plenum.

Rogan, W. J., Gladen, B. C., Hung, K., Koong, S., Shih, L., Taylor, J. S., Wu, Y., Yang, D., Rogan, N. B., & Hsu, C. (1988). Congenital poisoning by polychlorinated biphenyls and their contaminants in Taiwan. *Science, 241*, 334–336.

Rose, S. A., & Feldman, J. F. (1995). Prediction to IQ and specific cognitive abilities at 11 years from infancy measures. *Developmental Psychology, 31*, 685–696.

Rose, S. A., & Feldman, J. F. (1997). Memory and speed: Their role in the relation of infant information processing to later IQ. *Child Development, 68*, 630–641.

Rose, S. A., Feldman, J. F., Futterweit, L. R., & Jankowski, J. J. (1997). Continuity in visual recognition memory: Infancy to 11 years. *Intelligence, 24*, 381–392.

Rose, S. A., Feldman, J. F., McCarton, C. M., & Wolfson, J. (1988). Information processing in seven-month-old infants as function of risk status. *Child Development, 59*, 589–603.

Rose, S. A., Feldman, J. F., & Wallace, I. F. (1988). Individual differences in infants' information processing: Reliability, stability, and prediction. *Child Development, 59*, 1177–1197.

Rose, S. A., Gottfried, A. W., & Bridger, W. H. (1978). Cross-modal transfer in infants: Relationship to prematurity and socioeconomic background. *Developmental Psychology, 14*, 643–652.

Rose, S. A., Slater, A., & Perry, H. (1986). Prediction of childhood intelligence from habituation in early infancy. *Intelligence, 10*, 251–263.

Rose, S. A., & Wallace, I. F. (1985). Visual recognition memory: A predictor of later cognitive functioning in preterms. *Child Development, 56*, 843–852.

Safe, S. (1990). Polychlorinated biphenyls (PCBs), dibenzo-*p*-dioxins (PCDDs), dibenzofurans (PCDFs) and related compounds: Environmental and mechanistic considerations which support the development of toxic equivalency factors (TEFs). *CRC Critical Reviews in Toxicology, 21*, 51–88.

Schlesselman, J. (1982). *Case-control studies: Design, conduct, analysis*. New York: Oxford University Press.

Sigman, M. D., Cohen, S. E., Beckwith, L., & Parmelee, A. H. (1985, July). *Infant attention in relation to intellectual abilities in childhood*. Paper presented at the International Society for the Study of Behavioural Development, Tours, France.

Sokol, R. J., & Clarren, S. K. (1989). Guidelines for use of terminology describing the impact of prenatal alcohol on the offspring. *Alcoholism: Clinical and Experimental Research, 13*, 597–598.

Sowell, E. R. (1995). Abnormal development of the cerebellar vermis in children prenatally exposed to alcohol: Size reduction in lobules I through V. *Alcoholism: Clinical and Experimental Research, 19*(6).

Spear, L. P., Kirstein, C. L., & Bell, J. (1989). Effects of prenatal cocaine exposure on behavior during the early postnatal period. *Neurotoxicology & Teratology, 11*, 57–63.

Spohr, H., Willms, J., & Steinhausen, H. (1993). Prenatal alcohol exposure and long-term developmental consequences. *The Lancet, 341*, 907–910.

Spyker, J. M. (1975). Assessing the impact of low level chemicals on development: Behavioral and latent effects. *Federation Proceedings, 34*, 1835–1844.

Stratton, K., Howe, C., & Battaglia, F. (1996). *Fetal alcohol syndrome: Diagnosis, epidemiology, prevention, and treatment*. Washington, DC: National Academy Press.

Streissguth, A. P. (1997). *Fetal alcohol syndrome*. Baltimore: Paul H. Brookes.

Streissguth, A. P., Aase, J. M., Clarren, S. K., Randels, S. P., LaDue, R. A., & Smith, D. F. (1991). Fetal Alcohol Syndrome in adolescents and adults. *Journal of the American Medical Association, 265*, 1961–1967.

Streissguth, A. P., Barr, H. M., Sampson, P. D., Parrish-Johnson, J. C., Kirchner, G. L., & Martin, D. C. (1986). Attention, distraction and reaction time at age 7 years and prenatal alcohol exposure. *Neurobehavioral Toxicology and Teratology, 8*, 717–725.

Streissguth, A. P., Bookstein, F. L., Sampson, P. D., & Barr, H. M. (1993). The enduring effects of prenatal alcohol exposure on child development, birth through 7 years: A partial least squares solution. Ann Arbor: University of Michigan Press.

Streissguth, A. P., Bookstein, F. L., Sampson, P. D., & Barr, H. M. (1995). Attention: Prenatal alcohol and continuities of vigilance and attentional problems from 4 through 14 years. *Developmental Psychopathology, 7*, 419–446.

Streissguth, A. P., Martin, D. C., Barr, H. M., Sandman, B. M., Kirchner, G. L., & Darby, B. L. (1984). Intrauterine alcohol and nicotine exposure: Attention and reaction time in 4-year-old children. *Developmental Psychology, 20*, 533–541.

Streissguth, A. P., Sampson, P. D., Carmichael Olson, H., Bookstein, F. L., Barr, H. M., Scott, M., Feldman, J., & Mirsky, A. F. (1994). Maternal drinking during pregnancy: Attention and short-term memory in 14-year-old offspring—A longitudinal prospective study. *Alcoholism: Clinical and Experimental Research, 18,* 202–218.

Strupp, B. J., Driscoll, L., Beaudin, S., Hermer-Vazquez, L., Morgan, R. E., & Garavan, H. (In press). Early lead (Pb) epxousre: The emerging cognitive profile. *Neurotoxicology and Teratology.*

Tamis-LeMonda, C. S., & Bornstein, M. H. (1989). Habituation and maternal encouragement of attention in infancy as predictors of toddler language, play, and representational competence. *Child Development, 60,* 738–751.

Tamis-LeMonda, C. S., & Bornstein, M. H. (1990). Language, play, and attention at one year. *Infant Behavior and Development, 13,* 85–98.

Thompson, L. A., Fagan, J. F., & Fulker, D. W. (1991). Longitudinal prediction of specific cognitive abilities from infant novelty preference. *Child Development, 67,* 530–538.

Tilson, H. A., Jacobson, J. L., & Rogan W. J. (1990). Polychlorinated biphenyls and the developing nervous system: Cross-species comparisons. *Neurotoxicology and Teratology, 12,* 239–248.

Tuchmann-Duplessis, H. (1975). *Drug effects on the fetus.* Monographs on drugs, 2. Littleton, MA: Publishing Sciences Group.

Uecker, A., & Nadel, L. (1996). Spatial locations gone awry: Object and spatial memory deficits in children with fetal alcohol syndrome. *Neuropsychologia, 34,* 209–223.

Uecker, A., & Nadel, L. (1998). Spatial but not object memory impairments in children with fetal alcohol syndrome. *American Journal on Mental Retardation, 103,* 12–18.

U.S. Public Health Service. (1997). Alcohol consumption among pregnant and childbearing-aged women—United States, 1991 and 1995. *Mortality and Morbidity Weekly, 46,* 346–350.

Uzgiris, I. C., & Hunt, J. McV. (1975). *Assessment in infancy: Ordinal scales of psychological development.* Urbana: University of Illinois Press.

Vorhees, C. V. (1986). Principles of behavioral teratology. In E. P. Riley & C. V. Vorhees (Eds.), *Handbook of behavioral teratology* (pp. 23–48). New York: Plenum.

Vorhees, C. V., Brunner, R. L., & Butcher, R. E. (1979). Psychotropic drugs as behavioral teratogens. *Science, 205,* 1220–1225.

Weiss, B., & Spyker, J. M. (1974). Behavioral implication of prenatal and early postnatal exposure to chemical pollutants. *Pediatrics, 53,* 851–856.

Werboff, J., & Gottlieb, J. S. (1963). Drugs in pregnancy: Behavioral teratology. *Obstetrical and Gynecological Survey, 18,* 420–423.

West, J. R., & Goodlett, C. R. (1990). Teratogenic effects of alcohol on brain development. *Annuals of Medicine, 22*(5), 319–25.

Wilson, J. G. (1977). Current status of teratology. In J. G. Wilson & F. C. Fraser (Eds.), *Handbook of teratology* (Vol. 1). New York: Plenum.

Woodbury, B. M. (1974). Maturation of the blood-brain and blood-CSF barriers. In A. Vernadakis & N. Weiner (Eds.), *Advances in behavioral biology* (Vol. 8). New York: Plenum.

Zuckerman, B., & Frank, D. (1992). "Crack kids": Not broken. *Pediatrics, 89,* 337–339.

4

▼▼▼▼▼▼▼▼

Medical and Developmental Sequelae of Early Childhood Institutionalization in Eastern European Adoptees

Dana E. Johnson
University of Minnesota

As the world celebrated Christmas 1989, Nicolae and Elena Ceausescu faced a firing squad and paid for 24 years of tyranny with their lives (Kifner, 1989). As despotic as their regime appeared (Blumenthal, 1989), few were prepared for the horrors revealed following their deaths. One of the Ceausescus' most heinous legacies was a system of 600–800 (Battiata, 1991) institutions for abandoned children. Although Romanian government officials acknowledged only 14,000 orphans in their care in 1990 (Hilton, 1990), a more realistic figure was 100,000–130,000 (Battiata, 1991; Hunt, 1991), with estimates ranging as high as 200,000–300,000 (Jamieson, 1991; Williams, 1990).

Following liberalization of the Romanian adoption laws in August of 1990, thousands of Western Europeans and North Americans traveled to Romania with hopes of adopting one or more of these children (Hunt, 1991). In fiscal year (FY) 1989, the final year of Ceausescu's rule, the United States Immigration and Naturalization Service issued two orphan visas for Romanian children (Immigration and Naturalization Service, 1998). In FY 1991, 2,594 immigrated to the United States. These Romanian children were the vanguard of close to 40,000 children adopted by American parents from orphanages and related institutions since 1991 (Immigration and Naturalization Service, 1998).

According to United States Immigration and Naturalization statistics, 15,774 children were adopted from abroad by Americans in FY 1978, up 16% from FY 1997, and up 120% from FY 1990 (Immigration and Naturalization Service, 1998).

Reasons for this dramatic increase in international adoptions include a shortage of adoptable children in the United States with the most desired age and racial characteristics, and family or emotional ties to a specific country. Parents are also very concerned about real or perceived uncertainties inherent in domestic adoption; e.g., a birth parent failing to relinquish rights or returning to claim a child already placed in an adoptive home. In the words of one adoptive mother, "There are no Baby Richards in China" (King & Hamilton, 1997, p. 62). With keen interest in adopting internationally and traditional placement countries such as Korea reducing the number of children available, the countries of Eastern Europe (33%) and China (27%) have become the source of the majority of children placed in American families (Immigration and Naturalization Service, 1998).

More important than changes in countries of origin has been a dramatic deterioration in the level of care received by international adoptees early in life, prior to arrival in the United States. In 1989, two-thirds of adoptees came from Korea, a country with a high standard of living where children were reared in foster homes and had access to excellent health care. In FY 1998, 88% of children adopted from abroad came from institutional-care settings in countries where per capita income was low and appropriate levels of health care and nutrition were difficult to provide (Immigration and Naturalization Service, 1998).

The sheer number of children arriving from Eastern European countries since 1989 coupled with media attention publicizing the inhumane conditions under which they lived focused national attention on a concept that for most professional had been relegated to dusty library stacks—institutional care for infants. Studies conducted decades earlier when orphanages were still extant in the United States foretold what physicians, psychologists, and educators observed as they confronted the pervasive medical and developmental problems afflicting these children. No group illustrates better the concept of the importance of the first few years of life for facilitating healthy brain and behavioral development.

Well into the modern era, placement of an infant in an orphanage was tantamount to a death sentence. Mortality rates within foundling homes exceeded 90% during the first year of life into the early 20th century in major European and American cities (Chapin, 1908, 1911, 1915, 1917; English, 1984; Frank, Klass, Earls, & Eisenberg, 1996; Gardner, 1972; Langer, 1972). Significant improvement was not seen until the 1940s when mortality rates dropped to 10%, primarily through improved nutrition using cow's-milk-based infant formulas, suppression of diarrheal and respiratory disease through rigid isolation techniques, and the development of the first generations of antibacterial agents (Frank et al., 1996). Recent experience reinforces how dangerous orphanage care for infants continues to be even in countries with extensive resources. From 1987–89, 2,000 infants and toddlers were placed in congregate-care settings in New York City. Poorly trained workers, spoiled food, and disease spread by unhygienic conditions led to repeated outbreaks of diarrhea and other infectious diseases as well as the death of two infants (Ford & Kroll, 1995).

Although the negative effects of environmental and social deprivation on infant well-being had been recognized for some time, deviations from normal development in institutionalized children could not be carefully studied until survival through infancy was assured. Consequently, it was not until the late 1930s and early 1940s that investigators reported on developmental delays and suppressed growth and immune functioning within congregate care settings for infants (Bowlby, 1951; Freud & Burlingham, 1944; Gesell & Amatruda, 1947; Goldfarb, 1943b; Spitz, 1945). Through the next three decades, investigators documented an increasingly wider array of problems in children institutionalized during infancy, including:

- Delays in emotional, motor, social, speech, and physical development, diminished ability to make smooth transitions from one developmental state to another, and impairment in play and exploratory behavior (Bowlby, 1951; Brodbeck & Irwin, 1946; Collard, 1971; Freud & Burlingham, 1944; Gesell & Amatruda, 1947; Goldfarb, 1943a, 1943b, 1945; Provence & Lipton, 1962; Wolkind, 1974).
- Interruption of normal adult–child bonding cycles and risk of attachment disorders (Bowlby, 1951; Dennis, 1973; Kaler & Freeman, 1994; Provence & Lipton, 1962; Spitz, 1945; Tizard & Rees, 1974).
- Severe behavior and emotional problems with aggressive or antisocial behavior (Goldfarb, 1943a, 1943b, 1945; Lowrey, 1940).
- Learning problems including reading difficulties, problems in critical thinking, especially establishing cause and effect, and impulsivity (Goldfarb, 1943a, 1945; Mapstone, 1969; Pringel & Bossio, 1960; Wolkind, 1974).

In response, in part to these studies, this era of investigation witnessed the end of institutional infant care in the United States in favor of foster placement. The problems observed in current international adoptees, most of which developed within institutional-care settings, refocuses attention on the effects of severe deprivation on early childhood development.

CHARACTERISTICS OF CHILDREN IN EASTERN EUROPEAN ORPHANAGES

The term *orphanage* is truly a misnomer since most children housed within institutions are not parentless. In 252 sequential referrals from Eastern Europe orphanages evaluated for prospective adoptive families by our clinic, the reasons for children being available for adoption could be determined in 75% of cases (Johnson et al., 1996a). These included: (a) the child was a foundling (5%); (b) courts terminated parental rights because of neglect, abuse, or both (15%); and (c) parent(s) relinquished or abandoned their rights to the child for social or economic reasons (76%). Only 4% of children were placed in institutional care because of the death of both parents and were truly orphans, a figure almost identical to the one quoted by UNICEF for the Russian Federation (UNICEF, 1997).

Therefore, almost all children within institutional care in Central and Eastern Europe have one or more living parent(s) at the time they entered the orphanage. These *half orphans* or *social orphans* are similar to children found in institutional care in the United States between the Civil War and the Great Depression, a time when more children received care within orphanages and related institutions than any other means (Hacsi, 1997; Olasky, 1999). During this period of immigration and industrialization, the United States sustained a dramatic increase in population and urban poverty. The only social service safety net that existed for most families in dire economic straits was to place one or more of their children in orphanages operated by churches or benevolent organizations with the hope of reclaiming the child when economic conditions improved (Hacsi, 1997).

This pattern of overpopulation, poverty, dissolution of extended family units, and paucity of social service options was replicated 100 years later in Eastern Europe. In 1966, one year after coming to power, Ceausescu promulgated Romanian State Decree #770 (Nachtwey & Hunt, 1990). This edict and others that followed, known as the pronatalist laws, were enacted to build a larger workforce through controlling the reproductive behavior of an entire country. In essence, women 45 years or younger were compelled to have children. Taxes of childless couples were increased and all means of birth control were banned, as were abortions— the major mode of birth control where birth control pills, IUDs, and condoms were either expensive or unattainable. Sex education was forbidden (Hilton, 1990) and a woman could not renew her driver's license without a pregnancy test (Olszewski, 1990). Gynecologists conducted periodic examinations within the workplace and were required to report those who were pregnant and those who sought emergency care for the complications of illegal abortion (Williams, 1990). In 1965, in order to qualify for a legal abortion, a woman had to have four children, 18 or under, living at home. In 1989, in an attempt to reverse a falling birthrate, this number was increased to five. Despite these attempts, Ceausescu failed to reach his goal of increasing the population from 23 to 30 million by the year 2000 (Hilton, 1990; Shinkle, 1991). At the time of his death, the population of Romania was unchanged and the average number of children per family was three (Williams, 1990).

If the Romanian orphanage system was fathered by the pronatalist laws, it was nurtured to maturity by economic conditions within Romania, which, under Ceausescu, had the lowest standard of living in Europe (Blumenthal, 1989; Rothman & Rothman, 1990). With little maternity leave, few tax breaks for large families and totally inadequate childcare services (Rothman & Rothman, 1990), many families and most single women were unable to provide for their normal children. Aggravating these problems was destruction of ties to extended family in small villages through a process of rural collectivization and relocation of workers to urban industrial areas. Handicapped children fared even worse since corrective surgery and treatment for chronic disease was generally unavailable. Immediately after the revolution, a survey of infants and young children in Romanian Baby Homes revealed 19% had a disability or malformation (The Children's Health Care Collaborative Study Group, 1994).

Similar economic conditions existed within the Soviet Union during the final years and continue to persist within the Russian Federation. The fall of communism brought high unemployment levels and a breakdown of social and medical services (Feshbach, 1995). Handicapped children also make up a disproportionate percentage of institutionalized children in Russia as health care professionals actively encourage placement of handicapped children in orphanages (Human Rights Watch, 1998). Even if a family wished to care for a disabled child at home, they faced social ostracism, an inability to find a caretaker for their child during the work day, and probable poverty since the government pays only a $30 per month stipend for home care for a handicapped child (Human Rights Watch, 1998).

While governments and political philosophies have changed since 1989, economic conditions for most citizens of Romania and Russia have remained static or have deteriorated. Since most placements by families are economically driven, the institutionalized populations in both countries remain robust. One out of every 60 children in Romania is institutionalized—one of the largest per capita populations of institutionalized children in the world (Tabacaru, 1998). The situation is similar in the Russian Federation. UNICEF estimated that in 1997, 611,034 children were without parental care. Of these, 337,527 were cared for within institutional settings (UNICEF, 1997).

The economic conditions that force children into institutional-care settings also predict much of the morbidity observed in this population. Most women who place children within orphanages receive no prenatal care, have a nutritionally inadequate diet, and are often unimmunized against preventable teratogenic agents such as rubella. In 1992, it was estimated that 75% of women suffered a medical disorder during pregnancy (Feshbach, 1995). Mean birth weight of the 252 children in the aforementioned study was low at 2,509 grams (Johnson et al., 1996a). Forty-eight percent were low birth weight infants (BW < 2500 g), and of these, 15% ($n = 17$) were very low birth weight (< 1500 g). The low birth weight could partially be accounted for by prematurity that was noted in 82 referrals (27%). However, low birth weight was nutritional as well, since the mean birth weight-by-length for infants ≥ 49 cm in length at birth was one standard deviation below normal. Children referred for adoption represented the first pregnancy for only 25% of birth mothers where pregnancy history was documented. The child was $\geq$ 4th pregnancy for 44% of birth mothers. Analysis of gravidity and measurements of the child at birth by ANOVA showed a significant relationship between increasing maternal parity and lower birth-weight-by-length z scores.

Alcohol is a major factor in morbidity and mortality for Eastern European women and their children. Combining estimates of the numbers of chronic alcoholics and heavy drinkers, 30% of the population may chronically abuse alcohol in the Russian Federation (Davis, 1994). Since the end of Gorbachev's sobriety campaign, per capita alcohol consumption has increased 600%, to 38 liters of 100-proof vodka per year per adult. Deaths from alcohol poisoning have increased by 300% and deaths from cirrhosis by 250% (Feshbach & Prokhorov, 1995). Perhaps the most ominous statistic is the 48.1% increase in the incidence of alcoholism among women since 1989. Though economic conditions are grim, alcoholic beverages are readily available and affordable. In girls 15–17 years old, 80–94% drank sometimes and 17% drank often (Feshbach & Prokhorov, 1995). A popular method of distribution of vodka and other high-proof beverages is in pop-top cans. Since these containers cannot be resealed, opening a can encourages consumption of the entire 12 ounces at one sitting.

Maternal alcoholism was mentioned in 17% of referral documents, particularly in those cases where parental rights were terminated by the courts for neglect, abuse, or both (Johnson et al., 1996a). A recent review of 105 Russian adoptees revealed that 43/47 maternal histories noted alcohol consumption (McGuinness, 1998). The incidence of fetal alcohol syndrome (FAS) in a group of Eastern European adoptees examined in this country was 1.6% (Albers, Johnson, Hostetter, Iverson, & Miller, 1997). However, this figure almost certainly underestimates the incidence of FAS in the institutionalized population since children with a history of alcohol exposure may not be referred for adoption, and those with growth failure and the characteristic phenotype may be turned down by potential adoptive families. Within the group of 252 referred children (Johnson et al., 1996a), the diagnosis of FAS had been made in the country of origin in 16% ($n = 8$) of known alcohol-exposed pregnancies (2.6% of all referrals). In a separate review of 265 sequential referrals from Eastern Europe where medical information was accompanied by a video of the child, 9% had histories, physical features, and growth patterns that strongly suggested alcohol exposure in utero. Whatever figures one accepts, an incidence of possible alcohol exposure between 17% and 91% is chilling. An incidence of FAS–fetal alcohol effect (FAE) between 1.6% and 9% is 9 to 47 times higher than the incidence in the United States and most countries in Western Europe (Abel & Sokol, 1987).

Since families are encouraged to place handicapped children within institutions, medically and developmentally disabled children are overrepresented within Eastern European orphanages. In this same study, an additional 14% of children had clear medical problems such as hepatitis B and C, developmental delays far more severe than could be explained by orphanage confinement, cerebral palsy, autistic-like behavior, severe microcephaly, etc. This was undoubtedly an underestimate of the true incidence of significant preexisting problems, since 59% of the children reviewed had insufficient information to accurately assess their medical and developmental status. Normal growth and development could be confirmed in only 9% of children.

By any definition, institutionalized children constitute a special-needs population whose requirements for medical, developmental, and educational services parallel those of our domestic population of children with the same spectrum of prenatal and postnatal problems (Johnson, 1997b; Johnson & Dole, 1999). Ironically, fear of adopting a special-needs child is one reason many parents choose to adopt internationally. This high incidence of biologic risk factors must be taken into account when assessing the outcome of this population of institutionalized children.

ORPHANAGE CARE

With similar political philosophies and an expanding population of social orphans, the evolution of custodial child-care systems within Romania and the Russian Federation followed similar courses. Belief in central control and the ability of the State to replace the family inevitably led to focusing care within large state-sponsored institutions utilizing a model that relied on regimentation and discipline, and segregated children by age and projected outcome (UNICEF, 1997). For the first years of life, all children are housed within *Baby Homes* operated by the Ministry of Health that provide a basic level of food, clothing, medical care, and shelter (Hunt, 1991; Nachtwey & Hunt, 1990; Rothman & Rothman, 1990; UNICEF, 1997). However, since orphanage space is at a premium in both Romania and the Russian Federation, infants abandoned in hospitals, where care is even less attentive than orphanages, often remain there for months waiting for a space to open up in Baby Homes. The Baby Homes (Dom Rebyoka) in the Russian Federation house 18–20,000 children (Ministry of Labor and Social Development of the Russian Federation, 1997) and those in Romania (Leagane), approximately 9–10,000 (Fig. 4.1) (Tabacaru, 1998). Children within Baby Homes are more likely to have involved parents since these facilities represent a major part of the social service safety net in these countries. Single mothers or victims of domestic abuse place children in the Baby Homes for several months while looking for housing, jobs, or alternative living conditions. Mothers who are students or working commonly place their children within these institutions during the week and take them home on the weekends.

Organization of most orphanages for infants and toddlers conforms to a model in which groups of children, segregated by age, occupy a suite of two to four large rooms. Orphanages, depending on size, may have many of these child-care units, each with their own staff of caregivers, teachers, and even a physician. Except for outdoor play, all activities take place within a room where children sleep or nap and a common play area–dining room where all other activities take place. All food other than snacks is prepared in a central kitchen and delivered to each unit. How each facility functions is highly dependent on three factors: (a) the resources allocated by the governmental unit responsible for institutional maintenance; (b) the training and motivation of each orphanage director; and (c) the mental and physical well-being of the staff directly responsible for infant and child care.

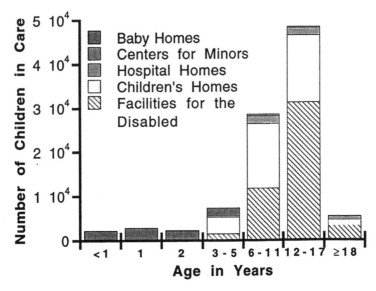

FIG. 4.1. Distribution and number of Romanian children in institutional care in
1997. From unpublished data (C. Tabacaru, personal communication, October, 1998).

Resources have a direct impact on the ratio of caregivers to children, and are
rarely sufficient within Baby Homes to staff at a level (1:3) where developmental
scores remain within the normal range though still significantly lower than
matched groups in home care (Hansen, 1971). Faced with the responsibility for
10–20 infants, workers must place the efficient completion of life-sustaining
tasks above the developmental needs of those entrusted to their care. Consequently, infants are most often relegated to cribs (Jamieson, 1991) (Fig. 4.2) with
limited access to their peers and, for caregiver convenience, remain there much
longer than is age appropriate (Fig. 4.3). With little time to directly interact with
the children in their care, there is little laughter or music and few sounds of play
in these facilities—only silence (Eicher, 1990; Shinkle, 1991).
    Resources also have a direct effect on diet. UNICEF estimated that rickets in-
creased 13%, malnutrition disorders 20% and anemia 75% in Russian Baby
Homes between 1989 and 1994 (UNICEF, 1997). Infants are generally fed com-
mercially available cow's-milk-based formulas in which the ratio of powdered
formula-to-water at any one time is directly dependent on the fiscal state of the
orphanage. Later in the first year, fermented dairy products such as yogurt may
replace some milk, and cereal may be added either to the bottle or fed by spoon.
Due to low caregiver-to-child ratios, bottles are often propped and solids spooned
into a child's mouth as quickly as possible (Fig. 4.4). Infants are transitioned to
solids and cup feedings after 12 months and children are expected to feed themselves with minimal adult supervision as soon as they can bring a spoon to their
mouths (Fig. 4.5). Since food must be both inexpensive and readily consumed by

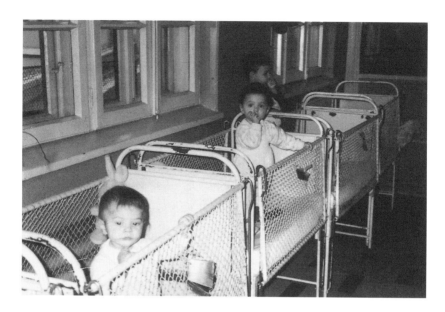

FIG. 4.2.   Romanian Baby Home (1993).

FIG. 4.3.   Romanian Neuropsychiatric Institute (1998).

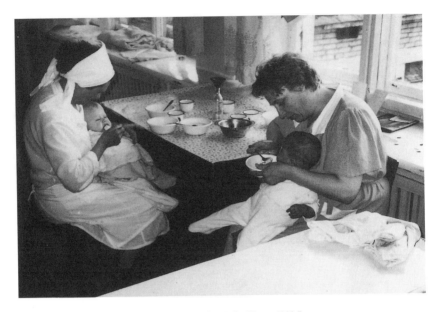

FIG. 4.4. Russian Baby Home (1996).

FIG. 4.5. Romanian Baby Home (1993).

young children, a toddler's diet commonly consists of soup, bread, and a main dish of potatoes or rice into which is incorporated available meat and vegetables in minced, ground, or pureed form (Fig. 4.5).

All daily activities including toileting are strictly regimented with little possibility for accommodating individual needs (Jamieson, 1991) (Fig. 4.6). Play outside the crib is often limited to unsupervised time with few accessible toys (Fig. 4.7, 4.8). Additional avenues for productive interpersonal connection, such as contact with older children and competent peers, are also restricted because of age segregation and overrepresentation of children with profound handicaps in institutional-care settings.

Since the Ministry of Health in both Romania and the Russian Federation administers Baby Homes, most directors are trained as health care providers and, understandably, focus on this aspect of infant care. Few are trained in child development. Therefore, the environment of most Baby Homes, especially for children less than 1 year of age, resembles the sterile environment of a hospital rather than the nurturing environment of a home. This approach is poignantly illustrated in a mural on the outside of Leagane, which shows a nurse holding eight children, approximately the ratio of children to caregivers in the orphanage (Fig. 4.9). Caregiver mental and physical well-being is probably the most important factor in determining the quality of interaction between child and adult within the orphanage. Stressed by the magnitude of their responsibilities in the workplace, underpaid, often clinically depressed, and living in countries where life is difficult,

FIG. 4.6. Romanian Baby Home (1993).

FIG. 4.7.   Russian Baby Home (1996).

FIG. 4.8.   Romanian Baby Home (1993).

FIG. 4.9.   Wall mural outside a Romanian Baby Home (1998).

many caregivers are so overwhelmed with the drudgery and difficulty of life that they have little energy left to nurture their charges.

Traditionally, at the age of 3 (Romania) (Battiata, 1990a; Rothman & Rothman, 1990) and 4 (Russian Federation) (Human Rights Watch, 1998), children are examined by a team of psychologists and pediatricians and separated into two major groups. Children judged to be physically and developmentally normal or mildly delayed are placed in institutions run by the Ministry of Education where they are provided limited educational and medical services. Children felt to be significantly developmentally or physically impaired are relegated to pediatric Neuropsychiatric Hospitals in Romania and Internat in the Russian Federation where care is abysmal and educational opportunities unavailable (Battiata, 1990a; Human Rights Watch, 1998; Olszewski, 1990; Rothman & Rothman, 1990).

Determining the current population of these two arms of the Romanian and Russian institutional-care system for older children is difficult. Figures quoted by Human Rights Watch place 30,000 children within Internat in Russia, leaving approximately 287,000 children within institutions for normal and mildly impaired children (Human Rights Watch, 1998). In Romania in 1997, 35,165 children (36%) were within Children's Homes (Casa Copi) and 47,107 (48%) were within homes for the disabled, although this figure probably includes children with both severe and mild disabilities (Fig. 4.1) (Tabacaru, 1998). Considering the known effects of prolonged neglect on development during the first 3 to 4 years of life, it is not surprising that many of the children placed within these latter facilities had the misfortune of early childhood institutionalization compounded by being misdiagnosed as mentally deficient (Battiata, 1990b; Human Rights Watch, 1998; Johnson, Aronson, Cozzens, Federici, et al, 1999; Shirks, 1991).

Life is much harder in facilities that care for individuals considered handicapped (Human Rights Watch, 1998). In the utilitarian view of former governments of Romania and the Russian Federation, nonproductive individuals were irrelevant and child-care resources were allocated as such. In Romania, children were fed on as little as 14¢ a day (Nachtwey & Hunt, 1990). Bread and fatty sausage (Williams, 1990), tripe gruel with wormy apples (Olszewski, 1990), or bread heels stewed with tomatoes (Battiata, 1990a) constituted typical meals. Facilities were unheated; medical care, educational services, and rehabilitation programs were nonexistent; and institutional sanitation and personal hygiene were ignored (Battiata, 1990a; Olszewski, 1990; Williams, 1990). Not only were the physical needs of these children disregarded, but also a ratio of 40–60 children to one caregiver, a typical situation in these facilities, ensured that none of the children received any emotional sustenance (Shirks, 1991; Williams, 1990).

In Romanian facilities prior to 1990, the prevalence of human immunodeficiency virus-1 (HIV-1) and hepatitis B virus (HBV) infection reached shocking levels. Zaknun et al. (1991) reported an incidence of western blot-confirmed HIV-1 seropositivity of 52% and a 60% incidence of hepatitis B surface antigen (HbsAg) positivity in one such institution. Eighty percent of this population showed evidence of maternal deprivation syndrome (Zaknun et al., 1991). Eventually, many children surrendered their will to live or succumbed to starvation or disease. In these asylums, the mortality rate reached 25–50% a year (Battiata, 1990a, 1991; Williams, 1990), the same as in the English parish workhouses of the mid-18th century (Langer, 1972).

Unfortunately, despite the attention and humanitarian aid focused on such institutions in the early 1990s, conditions have improved only marginally. Visits to three Neuropsychiatric Institutes in Romania in June and December 1998 revealed persistence of the same tragic living conditions described previously. In one institution, over 500 children were segregated into large rooms that housed beds, a large table, and a television set. All activities took place within this room except for brief trips to the playground (Fig. 4.10). Children who were profoundly disabled were placed on the ground in a walled courtyard where they remained until moved indoors by their caregivers (Fig. 4.11). Irrespective of where the children were, we observed essentially no caretaker-child interaction. Heads were shaved, children were dressed in ragged clothing, and it was difficult to determine each child's gender.

In two similar though somewhat smaller institutions visited during the winter, children spent all day within their rooms sitting against the wall on mattresses, or in their beds, huddled under blankets or bundled in clothing to remain warm (Fig. 4.12, 4.13). The only diversion available to children in one institution, and only to those who could walk, was 30 minutes per day in the *Disco* room where a sound system blasted 1970s dance classics and a flashing, rotating, ceiling-mounted *disco*

FIG. 4.10.   Romanian Neuropsychiatric Institute (1998).

FIG. 4.11.   Romanian Neuropsychiatric Institute (1998).

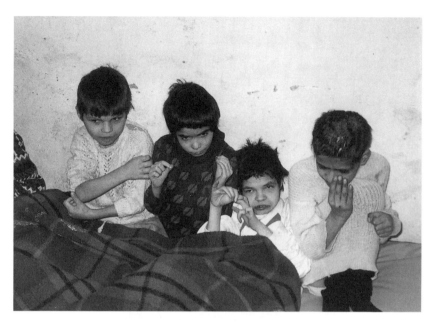

FIG. 4.12.   Romanian Neuropsychiatric Institute (1998).

FIG. 4.13.   Romanian Neuropsychiatric Institute (1998).

128

ball challenged the seizure threshold of everyone present. We observed rooms of stroller-bound children, many of whom showed signs of severe depression and withdrawal (Fig. 4.14). Crib-bound children were found isolated in barren rooms (Fig. 4.15), lying on plastic sheets, and plagued by flies (Fig. 4.16). Food was of extremely poor quality; in one case, milk *soup* with crackers sufficed for the morning meal (Fig. 4.17, 4.18). For those children who could feed themselves, food was piled on plates and eaten without utensils (Fig. 4.19) or consumed wherever the child happened to be at that moment (Fig. 4.17). These children appeared in the best condition since they could ask for more from the caregivers or steal it from their neighbor's plate. Children dependent on others to feed them fared the worst and appeared in dire nutritional condition (Fig. 4.18). Evidence of injuries both accidental and perpetrated by others was observed frequently (Fig. 4.20). Virtually identical conditions were recently documented by Human Rights Watch within Russian Internat (Human Rights Watch, 1998).

There are, of course, exceptions to the situations described previously. Every country has orphanages where children are provided the best care possible. In these situations, directors place as much emphasis on development as health, validate the importance of the work of their staff, and inspire workers to develop innovative programs. Schedules that include movement and music (Fig. 4.21), supervised outdoor exercise (Fig. 4.22), swimming (Fig. 4.23), and massage vastly expand the sensory diet and the amount of adult-child interaction for institutionalized children. In orphanages with sufficient resources, adequate staffing allows

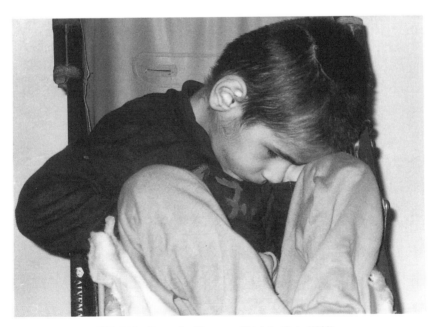

FIG. 4.14.   Romanian Neuropsychiatric Institute (1998).

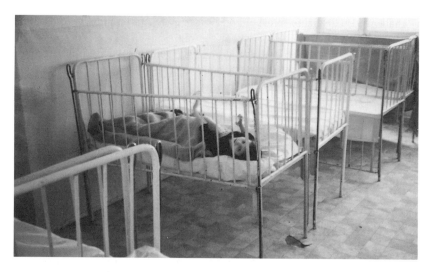

FIG. 4.15.   Romanian Neuropsychiatric Institute (1998).

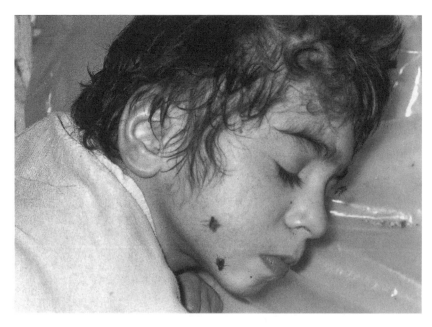

FIG. 4.16.   Romanian Neuropsychiatric Institute (1998).

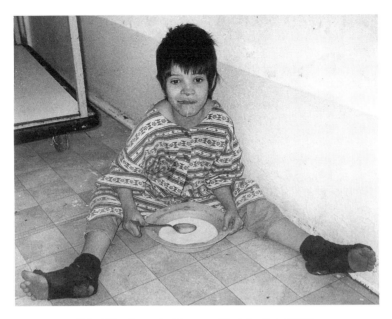

FIG. 4.17.   Romanian Neuropsychiatric Institute (1998).

FIG. 4.18.   Romanian Neuropsychiatric Institute (1998).

131

FIG. 4.19.   Romanian Neuropsychiatric Institute (1998).

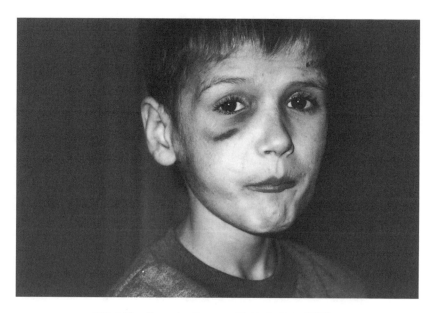

FIG. 4.20.   Romanian Neuropsychiatric Institute (1998).

FIG. 4.21. Music lesson in a Russian Baby Home (1996). The various surfaces used in this exercise expand the sensory diet of these children.

FIG. 4.22. Romanian Baby Home (1998).

FIG. 4.23.   Russian Baby Home (1996).

caregivers to attend to the individual needs of children (Fig. 4.24). In some orphanages, the staff will bring children to their homes during the weekend. Even
better are orphanages based on the *cottage system* where consistent adults provide
care for a group of children of varying ages in a home-like suite of rooms. In
these situations, not only is there cohesive care giving, but children have expanded opportunities to learn new skills from older children in the group.

HEALTH AND DEVELOPMENT STATUS
OF INSTITUTIONALIZED CHILDREN UPON ARRIVAL

Infectious Diseases

The prevalence of readily transmissible infectious agents within congregate-care
settings for infants and young children is a major factor in institutional medical
morbidity (Frank et al., 1996). While perhaps not as prevalent as other problems
observed in institutionalized children (Johnson & Traister, 1999), infectious diseases place the child and adoptive family at risk for long-term complications,
many of which are treatable or preventable (Hershow, Hadler, & Kane, 1987;
Hostetter, Iverson, Dole, & Johnson, 1989; Hostetter & Johnson, 1989, 1996;
Hostetter et al., 1991; Jenista, 1993; Jenista & Chapman, 1987; Johnson, 1997a;
Johnson & Hostetter, 1997; Miller, Kiernan, Mathers, & Klein-Gitelman, 1995;
Mitchell & Jenista, 1997a, 1997b).

FIG. 4.24   Russian Baby Home (1996).

Hepatitis B

As hepatitis B infection is common in most countries of origin, an incidence of HBsAg positivity (chronic infection) that is tenfold higher (5%) than United States-born children of similar age has been recognized in international adoptees for some time (Hershow et al., 1987; Hostetter et al., 1989, 1991; Jenista & Chapman, 1987). The incidence in Romanian adoptees from 1990–91 was much higher. In a cohort of 57 infants and children adopted from Romania (Johnson et al., 1992), 53% showed serologic evidence of infection with the HBV. The overall prevalence of HBsAg positivity was 20% in all children tested ($n = 64$). Children who had serologic evidence of infection with HBV were older than noninfected children (seronegative for ≤ 6 months of age and seropositive for anti-HBs, anti-HBc alone, or both) [32.7 ± 21.0 months vs. 9.4 ± 9.7 months ($p < 0.001$)] and had spent significantly more time within the orphanage system [27.9 ± 20.0 months vs. 5.6 ± 8.5 months ($p < 0.001$)]. These findings strongly suggested horizontal transmission via contaminated needles or biological preparations within these institutions as opposed to vertical transmission at the time of birth. Only one infant ≤ 6 months of age showed clear evidence of infection, while 83% of children > 18 months of age had been or were infected with the virus. Similar high incidences of surface antigen positivity in the initial wave of Romanian adoptees were reported by other investigators: 27% (Benoit, Jocelyn, Moddemann, & Embree, 1996), 28% (Ames, 1997), and 40% (Jenista, 1992). This problem with chronic hepatitis B infection in Romanian institutions persists. A recent survey of

51 children revealed that 35% had chronic hepatitis B (Johnson, Aronson, Cozzens, Daunauer, Faber et al., 1999). For unknown reasons, the problem with hepatitis B is not as severe in Russian institutions. Among 56 adoptees screened from 1991–95, 89% of which came from the Republics of the former Soviet Union, 16% had contracted hepatitis B and only 2% had chronic infection.

Intestinal Parasites

Intestinal parasites were found in 33% of Romanian children who were screened ($n = 61$). Infected children were significantly older (38.9 ± 19.6 months) than noninfected children (16.0 ± 18.1) ($p < 0.001$). Fifty-eight percent of children > 18 months of age were infected, in contrast to 0/17 infants ≤ 6 months of age. Among infected children, *Giardia lamblia* (55%), *Hymenolepsis nana* (30%), and *Ascaris lumbricoides* (25%) were identified most commonly, followed by *Strongyloides stercoralis* (15%), *Entamoeba histolytica* (15%), *Blastocystis hominis* (10%), and *Trichuris trichiura* (10%). Forty-five percent of infected children had two or more pathogens identified. Similar rates of infection were observed by other investigators: 31% (Ames, 1997), 23% (Benoit et al., 1996), and 70% (Jenista, 1992). Children from the Republics of the former Soviet Union had a slightly higher incidence of infestation (45–51%) (Albers et al., 1997; Johnson et al., 1996b), primarily with the water-borne parasite *Giardia*, which was identified in 95% of infected children (Johnson et al., 1996b).

Other Infectious Diseases

Despite the epidemic of syphilis in Eastern Europe, particularly the Russian Federation, few children were positive on arrival. Only one of 59 children from Romania was found to have congenital syphilis with inflammatory change in the long bones and retina, hepatosplenomegaly, and microcephaly (Johnson et al., 1992). No Russian child in our published series was positive (Albers et al., 1997). Tuberculosis is a disease that is endemic in most countries that place children for adoption in the United States. In a historical sample of 293 children adopted prior to 1990, the incidence of tuberculin reactivity (3%, positive skin tests alone) and active disease (1%) was 150-fold greater than a comparable United States population (Hostetter et al., 1991). The incidence (5%) among adoptees from Eastern Europe is even higher (Albers et al., 1997; Benoit et al., 1996; Hostetter et al., 1991).

An unexpected finding, in view of the reported overall incidence of HIV-1 positivity in Romanian hospitals and orphanages of 10% (Vita, 1990), with higher incidences in specific institutions (Patrascu, Constantinescu, & Dublanchet, 1990; Rudin et al., 1990; Zaknun et al., 1991), was that none of our subjects from Romania or countries of the former Soviet Union were positive for the acquired immunodeficiency syndrome (AIDS) virus (Albers et al., 1997; Johnson et al., 1992). Since children are usually screened for HIV-1 prior to placement for adoption, seropositive children may have been excluded from the selection process. Three of 11 Romanian adoptees tested positive for HIV-1 in Britain (Kurtz, 1991), 1/22 in Canada (Benoit et al., 1996), and 1/10 in the United States (Jenista, 1992). A recent survey of 105 children in a Romanian Neuropsychiatric Institute showed an 8% infection rate with HIV.

Immunizations

Review of all written immunization certificates from postinstitutionalized children from Eastern Europe and China over a 17-month period disclosed several irregularities including vaccinations antedating the birthdate, vaccinations given repetitively on the same day of successive months, or vaccinations exceeding the recommended number for age. Testing for protective titers against diphtheria and tetanus in all children who had been institutionalized and who presented written evidence of three or more DPT (diphtheria/pertussis/tetanus) vaccinations in their country of origin ($n = 17$) revealed that only 12% had protective titers to both agents. Therefore, records are being falsified, vaccines are impotent, or there is blunting of the immune response due to prolonged institutionalization (Hostetter & Johnson, 1998).

Growth

Poor growth within institutional care settings has been recognized for centuries (Chapin, 1908, 1915; English, 1984; Gardner, 1972; Spitz, 1945). Careful studies in hospitals and orphanages in New York by pioneers in this field such as Bakwin, Ribble, Spitz and Wolf in the 1940s documented poor weight gain in institutionalized children despite receiving adequate calories (Gardner, 1972). Perhaps the most dramatic demonstration of how an adverse environment affects growth occurred after World War II in Germany when British nutritionist Elsie Widdowson studied 50 children between the ages of 4 and 14 years in two small municipal orphanages within the British zone of occupation (Widdowson, 1951). A young, cheerful woman who was fond of children cared for one group of children and an older, stern woman who was a strict disciplinarian to all children except for a small group of favorites cared for the second group.

During the first 6 months of observation, the children cared for by the younger woman gained weight and height far better than those in the orphanage governed by the strict matron, with the exception of her favorites who did quite well. During the second 6 months, arrangements were made to provide additional rations to one of the orphanages and, concurrent with the improvement in daily calories, the caretakers shifted as well, creating an unintended crossover study. During the second 6 months, despite receiving additional calories, the children in the orphanage managed by the stern matron grew poorly. Her favorites, who accompanied her to the other institution, again were the exception and gained weight and height better than either of the other two groups in the study. The children previously cared for by the strict matron and now cared for by the cheerful woman during the second 6 months rapidly gained weight and height despite no increase in calories.

Height and Weight

Growth failure is a universal finding in institutionalized children from Eastern Europe. Romanian adoptees exhibited a high incidence of growth failure, the severity of which correlated with the length of time within the orphanage system. Two patterns of growth failure we observed closely resemble the two subtypes of psychosocial short stature defined by Blizzard and Bulatovic, 1996. Both occur in association with prolonged psychological harassment or emotional deprivation by the child's caregiver(s). Type I, or the infantile form, is characterized by a generalized failure to thrive. In this condition, infants are often depressed with a poor appetite (Bakwin, 1949; Rutter, 1981), usually do not exhibit bizarre behavior, and have normal growth hormone secretion (Blizzard & Bulatovic, 1996). In these children, lack of tactile stimulation may make the use of nutrients less efficient (Field, 1995). Among our patients, the infants clearly had generalized failure to thrive. Length/height, weight, and weight-for-height all appeared adversely affected by institutionalization. Length/height ($r = -0.34$. $p < 0.05$), weight ($r = -0.59$, $p < 0.001$), and weight-for-height ($r = -0.40$, $p < 0.025$) z scores all decreased as the length of institutionalization increased (Fig. 4.25). Of the four parameters, weight-for-length remained within the normal range and appeared least affected.

Type II, the childhood variety, affects primarily stature. This pattern of growth failure is characteristic of psychosocial short stature, a condition known by a number of terms including abuse dwarfism (Widdowson, 1951). As defined by Blizzard and others (Powell, Brasel, & Blizzard, 1967; Powell, Brasel, Raiti, & Blizzard, 1967; Widdowson, 1951), psychosocial short stature is a syndrome of short stature that occurs in childhood and adolescence, in association with psychological harassment or emotional deprivation by the child's caregiver(s), and for which there is no other explanation. In this syndrome, failure to thrive is often not present and some children may be overweight. Children are often depressed and exhibit bizarre behaviors such as polyphagia and polydypsia, retarded speech, solitary play, temper tantrums, shyness, and enuresis. Growth hormone secretion is decreased or absent. In Romanian adoptees 15 months and older, weight, head circumference, and weight-for-height z scores remained stable with increasing length of institutionalization. Weight-for-height was well within the normal range. However, the negative association between length of institutionalization and length/height z scores ($r = -0.40$, $p < 0.05$) persisted (Fig. 4.26). Linear growth failure in institutionalized infants and children is best illustrated by plotting linear growth lag (height age–actual age) versus length of time within the orphanage ($r = -0.79$, $p < 0.001$) (Fig. 4.27).

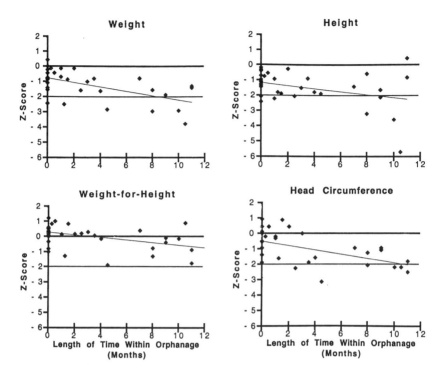

FIG. 4.25. Linear regression analysis of weight ($r = -.59$, $p < .001$, $y = -0.77-0.14x$ [x equals the length of orphanage confinement in months]); length ($r = -34$, $p < .05$, $y = -1.17-0.09x$); head circumference ($r = -.54$, $p < .001$, $y = -0.50-0.14x$); and weight-for-height ($r = -.40$, $p < .02$, $y = -0.28-0.08x$) z scores for Romanian adoptees younger than 15 months versus length of institutionalization within the Romanian orphanage system. From "The health of children adopted from Romania" by D. E. Johnson, L. C. Miller, S. Iverson, W. Thomas, B. Franchino, K. Dole, M. T. Kiernan, M. K. Georgieff, and M. K. Hostetter, 1992, *Journal of the American Medical Association, 268*, 3446–3451. © 1992 by the American Medical Association, reprinted by permission.

Other investigators have documented this high incidence of growth failure in institutionalized children in Eastern Europe as well. In a study where 475 adopted families responded to a questionnaire, 72% of children were below normal in weight and 80% below normal in height at the time of arrival in their adoptive families (mean age 1.7 years) (Groze & Ileana, 1996). A study of 22 children arriving at a mean age of 15.5 months from Romania to Manitoba revealed that 36% were less than the 5th percentile in weight, 32% in height, and 45% in head circumference (Benoit et al., 1996). In a cohort of 111 children arriving to the United Kingdom from Romania at a mean age of 6.6 months, 51% were less than the 3rd percentile in length, 34% in weight, and 38% in head circumference (Rutter, 1998). In a study of the health of 56 institutionalized children from Eastern

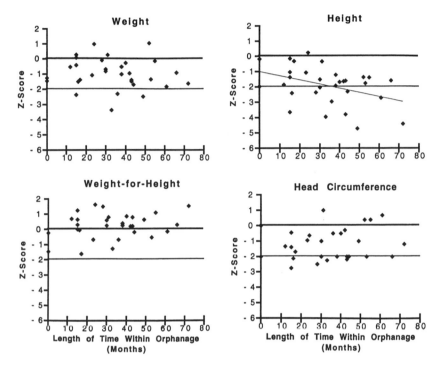

FIG. 4.26.   Linear regression analysis of weight ($r = -.59, p < .001, y = -0.77 - 0.14x$
[x equals the length of orphanage confinement in months]); length (not significant): head circumference (not significant) and weight-for-height (not significant);
z scores for Romanian adoptees aged 15 months or older versus length of institutionalization within the Romanian orphanage system. From "The health of children
adopted from Romania" by D. E. Johnson, L. C. Miller, S. Iverson, W. Thomas, B.
Franchino, K. Dole, M. T. Kiernan, M. K. Georgieff, and M. K. Hostetter, 1992,
Journal of the American Medical Association, 268, 3446–3451. © 1992 by the
American Medical Association, reprinted by permission.

Europe, 44% of children were below one standard deviation in weight, 68% in
height, and 43% in head circumference at the time of arrival (26 months). The adverse effects of the orphanage environment on linear growth are remarkably consistent worldwide. Whether a child is institutionalized in Romania (Ames, 1997;
Johnson et al., 1992), the Former Soviet Union (Albers et al., 1997), or China
(Johnson et al., 1996c; Johnson & Traister, 1999), analysis of growth data from a
variety of orphanage systems indicates that children lose 1 month of linear
growth for approximately every 3 months spent in institutional care (Fig. 4.27).

As is predicted by the simple regression line, children who spend their entire
childhood within institutional care are at greatest risk for growth stunting. At the
request of the Romanian government, 59 children in two Neuropsychiatric Institutes located in central and north-central Romania were examined. All had been

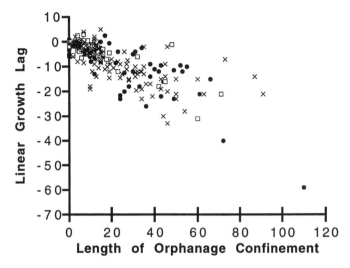

FIG. 4.27. Effect of orphanage confinement on linear growth (linear growth lag = height age – chronological age)

• = Romanian orphans ($n = 77$) [($r = -0.82$, $p < .001$, $y = -0.45-0.38x$) [x equals the length of orphanage confinement in months]). One month of linear growth loss for every 2.63 months of institutional care.

□ = Chinese orphans ($n = 78$) [($r = -0.82$, $p < .001$, $y = -0.43-0.33x$) [x equals the length of orphanage confinement in months]). One month of linear growth loss for every 3.03 months of institutional care.

X = Russian orphans ($n = 130$) [($r = -0.72$, $p < .001$, $y = -1.79-0.30x$) [x equals the length of orphanage confinement in months]). One month of linear growth loss for every 3.36 months of institutional care.

institutionalized since the 1st year of life. Growth was profoundly affected: height [mean -3.56 ± 2.0 *SD* (range -11.2 to -1.1], weight [mean -2.47 ± 1.29 *SD* (range -6.04 to -0.1)]. Height was affected more than length.

Head Growth

The effect of orphanage confinement on head growth deserves special attention in view of the poor cognitive outcome described in institutionalized children. Measuring head circumference cannot provide the detailed picture of brain structure and function that MRI and functional neuroimaging (e.g., fMRI) can. However, a measuring tape is inarguably cheaper and more portable than either of these techniques, and head circumference has been shown to correlate well with postnatal brain growth in normal and malnourished infants (Winick & Rosso, 1969). Brain growth, as determined by measuring head circumference z scores, decreased in direct relationship to the length of orphanage confinement during early infancy ($r = -0.54$, $p < 0.005$) (Fig. 4.25) (Johnson et al., 1992). This early effect on head growth persisted into early childhood. Only 7% of infants < 10 months of age ($n = 27$) had head circumference z score -2 versus 41% of those 10 months of age ($n = 37$) ($p < 0.005$ by χ^2) (Fig. 4.26).

In a cross-sectional analysis of head circumference in a cohort of 252 referrals evaluated by our clinic (Johnson et al., 1996a), head circumference reached its nadir between 8 and 12 months of age at a z score of -1.83 (95% confidence interval) (Fig. 4.28) and, though recovering some, remained significantly below normal during early childhood. Not surprisingly, children within Neuropsychiatric Institutes fared the worst in terms of head growth. At a mean age of 11.75 years, mean head circumference z score was -2.04 ± 1.6 (Johnson et al., 1996b). Head circumference was significantly greater in children judged developmentally competent (head circumference z score -1.5 ± 1.4) vs. those judged developmentally incompetent [head circumference z score -2.5 ± 1.5 ($p < 0.02$ t test)] (Johnson et al., 1999b).

Growth Failure: Neglect or Diet?

Within institutional-care settings, children are neglected and abused but are also nutritionally deprived. Which is a more important factor in their growth failure? The fact that weight is consistently higher than height in these children is most compatible with a larger role for stress than nutritional deprivation (Johnson et al., 1992, 1996b). Analysis of growth parameters in referred children revealed a significant increase in weight-for-length z scores [-0.95 ± 0.86 vs. -0.46 ± 0.4 ($p < 0.02$, paired t test)] between the time of birth and the time the child was offered for placement

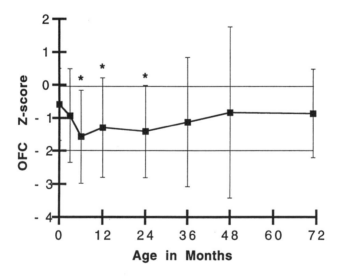

FIG. 4.28.   Cross-sectional analysis of Russian adoptees referred for adoption ($n = 236$) ($* = p < .01$, t test vs. birth head circumference z score).

(Johnson et al., 1996a). Anthropomorphic measurements lend additional support. Up to 6 years of age, only 7% of Romanian adoptees (initial screening) had arm fat area less than the 5th percentile. However, 24% had abnormally low arm muscle area (Fig. 4.28) compared to European and American norms (Fig. 4.29) (Frisancho, 1981; Sann, Durand, Picard, Lasne, & Bethenod, 1988). Among those 13/42 children whose height was more than two standard deviations below the mean at the time of arrival, only one had an arm fat area but five had arm muscle areas less than the 5th percentile at arrival (Fig. 4.29). Within the Neuropsychiatric Institutes, the same pattern persisted even in the face of more profound nutritional deprivation (Johnson, Aronson, Federici, et al., in press). Again, height was affected significantly more than weight. Triceps skinfold thickness was less than the 5th percentile in 55% and mid-arm circumference below normal in 85% of children. Institutionalization results in a more profound effect on linear growth and muscle accretion than on total weight and fat accretion. This abnormal growth pattern suggests a mixed etiology of protein-energy malnutrition and abnormal growth hormone secretion–responsiveness due to psychosocial deprivation. In light of the profound stunting and lack of lean body mass, the latter etiology appears predominant.

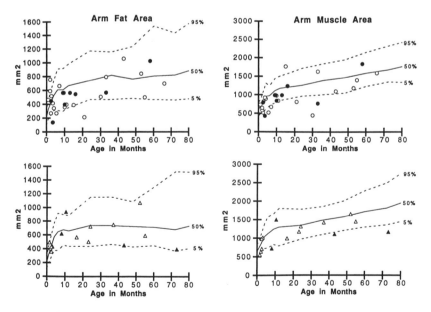

FIG. 4.29   Arm fat and muscle areas in Romanian adoptees at the time of arrival (1990–91).
O Female with height z scores −2
△ Males with height z scores −2
● Females with height z scores < −2
▲ Males with height z scores < −2

Sensory Integration Difficulties

In addition to numerous biologic risk factors that imperil important sensory functions, institutional care places children at risk for acquiring hearing and vision problems. The incidence of upper respiratory infections and subsequent middle ear pathology in congregate-care settings is high (Frank et al., 1996; Osterholm, Reves, Murph, & Pickering, 1992). Children with chronic middle ear disease early in life are at clear risk for speech and language delays (Roberts, Burchinal, Davis, Collier, & Henderson, 1991; Wallace, Gravel, McCarlton, & Ruben, 1988). Parents of 3.8% of Romanian adoptees reported deafness or hearing impairment (Groze & Ileana, 1996).

Parents of 5.1% of Romanian adoptees reported blindness or visual impairment (Groze & Ileana, 1996). Biologic risk factors such as prematurity and unmonitored exposure to supplemental oxygen increase the risk that refractive errors, retinal abnormalities, or both will be found. Strabismus is quite common in institutionally reared children (Spitz, 1965), being mentioned in 10% of 252 sequential referrals reviewed by our clinic (Johnson et al., 1996a). Personal observations in one Romanian orphanage revealed that 25% of the children had obvious strabismus (Fig. 4.30).

In addition to sustaining damage to important organs of sensation, institutionalized infants spend the majority of their time in silent, colorless rooms, receive

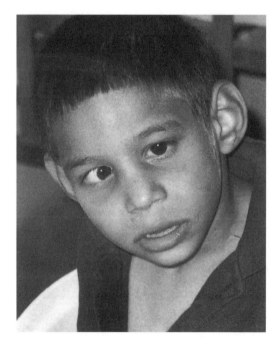

FIG. 4.30.   Child with strabismus in Romanian Neuropsychiatric Institute (1998).

a bland diet of liquid or ground food, are rarely spoken to, and may only be touched during bathing and clothing changes. It is therefore understandable that abnormalities in sensory processing and integration in Romanian and Russian adoptees are common. Provence and Lipton (1962) noted that the environment in which their infants lived was sensory deprived. In noting that their subjects had a low rate of initiating contact with their own bodies, other persons, or toys, and had poor modulation when attempting a movement, they suggested that sensory stimulation is important in building a repertoire of experience from which a person can organize and interpret external stimulation to produce a voluntary motor act. This concept, further refined by Ayers (1979) into a theory termed *sensory integration*, involves a child's synthesizing environmental information (e.g., body position, body movement, and touch) to produce an adaptive response or output. These adaptive responses serve as building blocks for further sensory integration, which in turn leads to more adaptive responses (Cermak & Daunhauer, 1997).

Children with sensory integration difficulties may present with tactile, auditory, visual, olfactory, and vestibular defensiveness. Their overresponsiveness when faced with the offending stimulus may lead to either shutdown and withdrawal or aggressiveness because of fear or anxiety when the sensory information is misinterpreted as a threat (Cermak & Daunhauer, 1997). Infants with sensory integration abnormalities may have problems attaining developmentally appropriate skills (Cermak & Daunhauer, 1997) and commonly present with behaviors consistent with regulatory disorders, difficult temperament, or poor state modulation (Lewerenz & Schaaf, 1996).

Within the contemporary group of institutionalized children, abnormalities in sensory processing and adaptive behavior as compared to normal American children were first described in 1994 in a cohort of 22 institutionalized Romanian infants aged 4–9 months (Haradon, Bascom, Dragomir, & Scripcaru, 1994). Cermak and Daunhaurer (1997) studied 73 Romanian adoptees and a matched-control group of 72 American children developing normally. Significantly greater problems existed in the Romanian adoptees in five of six sensory-processing domains: touch, movement-avoids, movement-seeks, vision, and audition; and four of five behavioral domains: activity level, feeding, organization, and social-emotional.

Speech Delays

Profound delays in normal speech acquisition in neglected children have been recognized since the 13th century when Frederick II, Emperor of the Holy Roman Empire, and therefore not subject to review by a Human Subjects Committee, isolated infants from human speech in an attempt to determine that language was innate (Gardner, 1972). Reportedly, none of the infants developed any language and all died, a significant finding even without the aid of statistical analysis. Since the 1940s, studies in which this issue was addressed have consistently found language delays in institutionalized children (Allen & Oliver, 1982; Brodbeck & Irwin, 1946; Culp, Lawrence, Letts, Kelly, & Rice, 1991; Fox, Calkins, & Bell, 1994; Haggerty, 1959; Tizard, Cooperman, Joseph, & Tizard, 1972; Whitehurst, 1997). In 1962, Province and Lipton concluded that during the 1st year of life, "The speech of institutionalized infants showed signs of maldevelopment early, became progressively worse and was the most severely retarded of all functions that could be measured on the tests." (pp. 91–92)—perhaps the most succinct and accurate description of language delays in institutionalized children yet written. When their children were placed in family situations, development of language abilities took longer than other areas of development. Disturbances in articulation were not a common problem, but the period of mimicking the words of adults and use of phrases related to the child's needs and routine matters of life was prolonged. Spontaneous verbalization and the use of language for asking questions, expressing ideas and fantasies, and verbalizing feelings were delayed.

Since language mediates most psychological competencies such as perception, memory, cognition, goal-oriented behavior, etc., language deficits have a profound effect on a child's competence (Gindis, 1999). The first 2 years of life is a particularly sensitive period for language development. Therefore, it is not surprising that residential care for infants and toddlers leads to deficits in verbal skills that persist into school age and adolescence. As with most problems noted in this population, deficits are worst in those children institutionalized early and longest (Allen & Oliver, 1982; Pringle & Bossio, 1958; Saltz, 1973).

Contemporary studies of institutionalized children from Eastern Europe reveal essentially the same findings. A study performed within a Russian Baby Home revealed that 60% of 2-year-olds had no language at all. When retested at 3 years of age, only 4% used two-word sentences (Dubrovina, 1991). A survey of 154 families who adopted internationally found that 57% had significant concerns about their child's speech and language development (Hough, 1999). Another study surveying parents of 475 Romanian adoptees found that 30% reported delayed language skills (Groze & Ileana, 1996). In 56 children adopted from the former Soviet Union and Eastern Europe, 57% had language delays at the time of arrival in the United States (Albers et al., 1997).

Developmental Delay

After 2 years within institutional care, young children in Eastern Europe tested in-country are universally and severely delayed in all cognitive and social domains (Kaler & Freeman, 1994) and in motor skills (Sweeney & Bascom, 1995). Therefore, it is not surprising that all but the youngest children coming from institutional settings are developmentally abnormal at the time of arrival in their adoptive homes. Delays are progressive in that severity of developmental delays in institutionalized children at arrival correlates directly with the length of orphanage confinement. The majority of infants less than 6 months of age adopted in 1990–91 from Romania were developmentally normal. However, if children spent more than 12 months within institutional-care settings, 90% were abnormal in one or more developmental areas (Johnson et al., 1992). Developmental delays are also pervasive. Examination of 57 institutionalized children adopted from Eastern Europe from 1991 to 1995 revealed that a majority of children had developmental delays affecting gross (70%) and fine motor (82%) abilities, and social skills (53%) (Albers et al., 1997).

Physical and Sexual Abuse

Unfortunately, institutional-care settings are magnets for adults who prey upon children and are a common site for child physical and sexual maltreatment (Frank et al., 1996). The recent report on conditions in Russian orphanages (Human Rights Watch, 1998) confirms the pervasive nature of abuse within institutional-care settings in this country. Mistreatment of orphans by adults listed in this report include slapping or striking, shoving heads into the toilet, squeezing hands or testicles during interrogation, stripping off clothing in front of peers, locking children in a freezing, unheated room for days, rape, and sending children to a Psychiatric Institute to punish them for misdeeds such as attempting to run away (Human Rights Watch, 1998). In addition, children are subjected to abuse perpetrated by older or stronger orphans, often with the approval of staff members. Such actions include: beating children on the neck, forehead and cheeks; throwing them out of the window in a wooden chest; wiring a metal bed to electricity and shocking a child forced to lie on it; and forcing a child to beg or steal for them (Human Rights Watch, 1998).

Such treatment is not confined to school-aged inmates of orphanages in one corner of the world. In 1982, institutionalized children under the oversight of the Oklahoma Department of Human Services were subject to severe physical and sexual abuse including being bound and manacled for extended periods, solitary confinement, being coerced into performing homosexual acts with staff members, and being recruited into a prostitution ring (Ford & Kroll, 1995). Little literature exists regarding sexual and physical abuse for infants and toddlers within orphanages (Frank et al., 1996). However, anecdotal evidence from parents regarding behaviors in 2- to 3-year-old children strongly suggests premature sexualization. Physical evidence of healing fractures and even a severe rectal tear in a young infant examined in our clinic suggests that all children within institutional-care settings are at risk.

OUTCOME IN INSTITUTIONALIZED CHILDREN

Growth Postarrival

Most children with psychosocial short stature have an immediate and dramatic surge in growth when removed from their hostile environment, probably due to both improved nutrition and improved growth hormone secretion (Powell, Brasel,

& Blizzard, 1967; Powell, Brasel, Raiti, & Blizzard, 1967; Widdowson, 1951). This pathonomonic finding of rapid growth following removal from the harsh environment of the orphanage was observed in all Romanian children ($n = 15$), with arrival height–length more than two standard deviations below the mean (Johnson et al., 1993) (Fig. 4.31). Height–length velocity z scores were markedly elevated in all subjects (mean + 5.5). In children ≤ 18 months at arrival, 78% had reached a height–length in the normal range within 9 months of arrival. Growth velocity in children greater than 18 months at arrival was virtually identical to younger children; however, because more absolute growth was required to exceed the 3rd percentile, none of these children had reached height–length within the normal range during the period of observation.

Longer follow-up confirms that catch-up growth is excellent in most postinstitutionalized children. However, the length of time within institutional care does have a moderating effect. Benoit et al. observed that 12 months after arrival, all children adopted at 6 months of age were greater than 5th percentile. Growth was also excellent in children adopted at greater than 6 months of age, but 13% were less than 5th percentile in height and 6% in weight (Benoit et al., 1996). Rutter et al. found that despite a high incidence of growth failure on arrival (see earlier), at 4 years of age only 2% were less than 3rd percentile in weight and 1% in height.

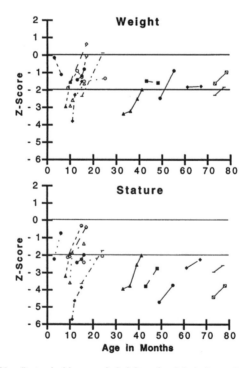

FIG. 4.31.   Postarrival increase in height and weight in Romanian adoptees.

Despite being in the normal range, they found that children adopted at ≥ 6 months of age were slightly shorter and lighter than their control group of adoptees within the United Kingdom (Rutter, 1998). Ames et al. also noted that children who had spent 8 months or more in institutional care were 2 inches shorter than their Canadian-born control group and 1 inch shorter than children institutionalized ≤ 4 months (Ames, 1997). While these results are encouraging, the odds for achieving innate growth potential may be diminished in children within long-term institutional care because of a combination of prenatal growth deficiency, psychosocial growth retardation, and an increased incidence of precocious puberty (Tuvemo & Proos, 1993).

Brain Growth

Catch-up head growth was also noted in 85% of Eastern European orphans (n = 34) after arrival (Fig. 4.32). Mean head circumference z scores increased an average of 0.67 ± 0.82 from arrival (−1.07 ± 0.9, mean age 13.2 ± 5.2 months, range 5.5–32 months) to follow-up (−0.40 ± 1, mean age 26 ± 7 months, range 5.5–32 months) ($p < 0.01$ paired t test) (Aronson & Johnson, in press). The length of time of institutionalization appears to have a very strong effect on eventual head size. Benoit et al. (1996) found that 13% of children institutionalized more than 6 months had a head circumference less than 5th percentile an average of 12 months after arrival while all children adopted at 6 months or less were within the normal range. Rutter et al. (1998) found significant differences in mean head circumference z scores at 4 years of age in children adopted at 6 months of age or

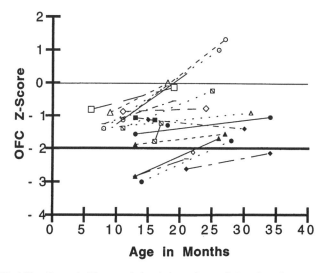

FIG. 4.32.   Postarrival increase in head circumference in Russian adoptees.

more (−1.5 ± 1.0), children adopted prior to 6 months (−1.1 ± 1.0), and their control group of children adopted to the United Kingdom (−0.5 ± 0.8).

Development

Placement of institutionalized orphans within adoptive families in North America and Western Europe provides a unique opportunity to observe what happens when children, neglected and abused in their early years, are parented by educated, highly motivated, economically well-to-do parents who have been carefully screened to assure their capabilities. In the transition from the worst to arguably the best environment for developmental gains, deficits that persist are more likely linked to early life in the orphanage rather than inadequate experience in the adoptive home. In this regard, review of the observations of Province and Lipton (1962) on 14 infants institutionalized within the first month of life and placed with adoptive–foster families between 12 and 24 months of age foretell the recovery and persistent deficits expected in postinstitutionalized children from Eastern Europe.

Motor Skills.   Gross and fine motor skills recovered quickly but lacked the smoothly flowing, well-modulated movements seen in children raised in birth families. Periods of excitement or stress elicited hand tremors or mild breakdown of coordination.

Language.   Language remained the greatest area of retardation, as noted earlier. Perhaps the most significant finding was that using language in an abstract rather than a concrete context was very delayed and by school age was still not as well developed as in a family-reared child.

Reactions To People.   Children were less likely to use adults for problem solving or comfort seeking even after many months with the same caregiver. During periods of stress, children often reverted to stereotyped behaviors observed in the orphanage. Children were also likely to be indiscriminately friendly. Relationships were superficial and one adult could easily substitute for another in the care of the child as long as the child's immediate needs were met.

Impulse Control And Delay Of Gratification.   Passivity, depression, and lack of energy and interest characterized the first months of placement. Gradually there was a shift and children began to express their feelings, and make their needs and wishes known. However, along with increased expression of pleasure, love, excitement, and anger, problems with impulse control and ability to delay gratification were recognized.

Difficulty In Making Transitions.   Postinstitutionalized children had diminished capacity to shift from one situation, activity, or thought to another. The authors had the impression of rigidity in thought process and personality structure, and speculated that it might reflect a reduction in the number of adaptive and defensive strategies available to the child.

Impairment In Thinking. Postinstitutionalized children learned best by imitation and rote memory but had great difficulty with thinking through a situation and anticipation. This led to problems in any predicament that required logical and sequential thought. Children also had problems in generalizing, in overcoming obstacles, and with excessive concreteness of thought.

Since the influx of Romanian adoptees in 1990–91 predated increased placements from the remainder of Eastern Europe, almost all contemporary studies have focused on these children. Ames et al. (1997) have followed two groups of Romanian children adopted to British Columbia during 1990–91 and a Canadian-born control group of children living with their birth parents (Ames, 1997). One study group consisted of 29 Romanian children who were adopted prior to 4 four months of age and had never been institutionalized. The second group included 46 children who had been institutionalized for 8 months or more (median 17.5 months, range 8–53 months), generally spending almost their entire lives within the orphanage. Children were studied twice: the first time when the institutionalized group had spent a median time of 11 months (4–25 months) in their adoptive homes, and again 3 years later when most children were 4.5 years or older. In general, the outcome of the group of Romanian children adopted prior to 4 months of age did not differ significantly from the Canadian-born control group at the second time period. Both of these groups differed significantly from the group of Romanian adoptees who had spent considerable time within institutional care. Their observations are strikingly similar to those of Province and Lipton (1962).

Cognitive Outcome

When adopted, every institutionalized child was developmentally delayed and 78% were delayed in all areas tested (fine and gross motor, personal-social, and language). Fewer areas of delay were noted in children who had experience with toys in the orphanage, had been kept clean, had been favorites of their caretakers, or had been in the orphanage a shorter time. Most children made rapid progress during the first years after arrival, with average increases of 2 developmental quotient points per month.

After 3 years of age, the length of time in the orphanage and delays at 11 months correlate negatively with IQ scores. In children who spent at least 8 months within institutional care, mean overall IQ was 90, with a range from 65 to 127 ($n = 31$). In children who spent 2 years or more within institutional care, mean overall IQ was 69, with a range from 52 to 98 ($n = 12$). Older institutionalized children who had been adopted after 2 years of age had lower IQ scores than those children adopted prior to 2 years of age. Compared to children adopted prior to 2 years of age, these older children were also more likely to have school readiness scores (56% vs. 17%) that indicated they were not ready for the school grade appropriate to their age.

Attachment

Low attachment scores were seen at the time of the first evaluation in the group institutionalized for 8 months. At the time of the second evaluation, fewer in this group had formed secure attachment relationships and one-third displayed atypical, insecure attachment patterns, particularly those children with lower IQs, more behavior problems, and families with lower socioeconomic status. Indiscriminately friendly behavior with new adults was seen more often in this group and did not decrease between the first and second evaluation.

Behavior and Social Problems

At the time of the first evaluation, institutionalized children exhibited internalizing behaviors; e.g., failure to make their needs known, stereotyped behavior, refusing solid food, and avoiding or withdrawing from siblings and peers. Three years after arrival, at the time of the second evaluation, externalizing behavior problems predominated. Children were more aggressive, antisocial, undercontrolled, rageful, and oppositional. According to both parents and teachers, institutionalized children had more social behavior problems, with 36% scoring above the clinical cutoff on the Child Behavior Check List (CBCL). They also continued to have more stereotyped behavior.

The theme of marked improvement but persistent deficits in postinstitutionalized children is repeated in all longitudinal studies of Romanian orphans. Benoit et al. (1996) followed 22 children adopted at 15.5 ± 13 SD months of age. When reexamined at an age of 35 ± 13 months of age, these children had significant increases in gross and fine motor, cognitive, and language abilities. Abnormal behavioral findings such as self-stimulating behavior, failure to initiate eye contact, preference for objects, and abnormal play behavior decreased, but not significantly. Fifty-five percent of these children had abnormal behavioral findings initially, and these persisted in 36% of subjects at the time of follow-up.

Marcovitch et al. (1997) studied 56 Romanian adoptees in Ontario and compared the 37 who spent less than 6 months in institutions prior to adoption to 19 who had been institutionalized longer than 6 months. Scores on the CBCL, while within the normal range, were higher for those children institutionalized longer. Mean developmental quotients were also within the normal range for both groups, but those children institutionalized less than 6 months were in the high-normal range (mean = 110.6) while those institutionalized 6 months or longer scored in the low-normal range (mean = 89.5). Scores on the Vineland for communication, daily living, and social and motor skills were also consistently higher in those institutionalized less than 6 months. Rutter (1998) compared 111 Romanian children adopted to the United Kingdom prior to 2 years of age to 55 United Kingdom-adopted children placed before 6 months of age. At the time of arrival, 59% of Romanian adoptees had a Denver Developmental Quotient less than 50 (retarded range) and another 15% were 50–69 (mildly impaired). When tested at age 4 years, cognitive function in children adopted from Romania at less than 6 months of age had improved to a level that was not significantly different from the United Kingdom adoptees. For those children older than 6 months at placement, catch-up was impressive but not complete. While average scores in this group were in the normal range, Denver Quotient and McCarthy General Cognitive Index (GCI) averaged 19 and 14 points less, respectively. The strongest predictor of cognitive functioning at 4 years of age is the child's age at entry to the United Kingdom; i.e., duration of institutionalization. Variations in degree of malnutrition on arrival were not felt to be a major determinant of cognitive outcome.

The effects of institutionalization in Russia are essentially the same. Sloutsky (1997) studied developmental outcomes in 52 6- and 7-year-old Russian children living in orphanages and compared them to 45 kindergarten students living with their working-class families. Overall, verbal and performance Wechsler IQ scores averaged 17–21 points higher in the kindergarten children, who also exhibited a lower level of conformity and higher level of empathy. Outcomes were correlated with the age at placement in the orphanage and the duration of institutionalization.

In the first study of adoptees from the former Soviet Union, 105 children were studied at an average of 7.7 years of age with the CBCL and the Vineland Adaptive Behavior Scales (McGuinness, 1998). Mean Vineland scores were 87.8 ± 15.4 (range 51–131). While 65% scored ≥ 85, the adequate range, twice as many children than expected scored lower. On the CBCL, the increase in the percentage scoring in the clinical range on conduct competence scores (Externalizing Score: 10%) was no more than would be expected in a normal control population. However, the mean total-problem score that gives an overall idea of difficulties facing the child and family was 33, higher than would be expected in a control population (20) and similar to that found in Romanian adoptees institutionalized for 8 months or more (39) (Ames, 1997). Most children (85%) attended regular classrooms, but 57% attended at least one special class, usually speech–language therapy.

Autistic patterns of behavior (institutional autism) have also been noted in those children coming from the worst circumstances in Eastern Europe. As described by Federici (1998), this syndrome is characterized by poor growth, regressive or absent language, problems with attention and concentration, self-stimulating behaviors, and deficient memory. Rutter et al. (1999) found that 6% of 111 Romanian children adopted by families in the United Kingdom and assessed at the ages of 4 and 6 years had autistic-like patterns of behavior. An additional 6% had isolated autistic features. These behavior patterns were associated with a longer duration of severe deprivation and a greater degree of cognitive impairment. Marked improvement was seen in these children between 4 and 6 years of age.

POSTINSTITUTIONALIZED EASTERN EUROPEAN
ADOPTEES WITHIN FAMILIES AND AS ADULTS

Many families adopted from Romania in 1990–1991, believing that lots of love and good food would change the skinny, floppy waif they found in the orphanage into the child of their dreams. While naïve, the innate resilience of children coupled with parental love and attentiveness has helped this become true in many situations. The popular press has concentrated on the negative aspects of adopting institutionalized children including severe attachment disorders, adoption disruption, and profound behavioral and cognitive problems (Bogert, 1994; Deane, 1997; Horn, 1997; King & Hamilton, 1997; Talbot, 1998). However, a survey of adoptive parents of children from Romania showed that 91% felt the overall impact of the adoption on the family was very or mostly positive and 93% never thought about disrupting the placement. Only 3% felt mostly or very negative about their adoption or thought about disrupting the placement frequently or most of the time (Groze & Ileana, 1996).

All children present challenges to their parents, and postinstitutionalized children are no exception. Therefore, equating parental satisfaction with absence of problems is incorrect. Overall outcome 3 years after arrival in Ames' (1997) study showed that institutionalized children fell into one of three groups. The first group (35%) had made wonderful progress. The second group (35%) were making progress but had one or two of the following serious problems: IQ 85, atypical insecure attachment, severe behavior problems, and ongoing stereotyped behavior. The third group (30%) had three to four of these serious problems and were challenging children to parent. A similar breakdown emerged from Groze's (1996) parental questionnaire study. Twenty percent of children, termed *resilient rascals*, displayed no obvious ill effects of institutionalization. *Wounded wonders*, the largest group (60%), were behind their peers in social and developmental growth but had managed to make substantial gains in their adoptive homes. Approximately 20% were *challenged children* who had been severely affected and had significant emotional problems and developmental delays up to 4 years after placement (Talbot, 1998, p. 30).

In Ames' (1997) study, predictors of major problems 3 years after arrival included: length of time in the orphanage, the number of children adopted, younger adoptive mother, lower socioeconomic status of the mother, and the father alone selected the child. Children institutionalized during infancy are needy children who conspicuously consume family financial resources, as well parental time and energy. Presumably, adopting more than one child at a time, having an inexperienced primary caretaker, few financial resources, and lack of a strong bond to the primary caretaker overtaxes an already fragile system, contributing to poorer outcomes. Parents whose children had a larger number of serious problems were more likely to feel incompetent, to be depressed, to be less invested in parenting, and to be more likely to use harsh means to deal with their child's problems (Ames, 1997).

Following children into adolescence who had spent at least the first 2 years of their lives within congregate care, Hodges and Tizard (1989) found that postinstitutionalized children at age 16 were more likely to have more social and emotional problems than other children and more disruptions in their lives. There was no effect, however, of early institutionalization on IQ. A study of 81 adult women who were institutionalized before the age of five, of which 90% had spent 4 years of more in care, generally showed poor outcomes (Quinton, Rutter, & Liddle, 1984). Twenty-five percent exhibited a personality disorder, and many had serious failure in parenting and experienced poor social circumstances. The authors concluded that "Only a minority of women with a stable harmonious pattern of upbringing exhibited poor parenting when subjected to chronic stress and disadvantage in adult life, but the majority of those who lacked good rearing in childhood did so" (p. 122). Institutionalization appeared to leave women ". . . less well prepared to deal with adult adversities" (Quinton et al., 1984, p. 122).

It may be difficult to infer from these studies how Eastern European adoptees will function as teenagers and adults. One finding by Hodges and Tizard (1989) that should be comforting to adoptive families demonstrated that children who had been adopted were doing better in their adolescent years than those reunited with their biologic family. The authors speculated that adopted children did better because of the adoptive parents' strong desire for the child, superior financial resources, and a strong desire to build a relationship with the adopted child. However, the large number of biologic risk factors present in this population and a degree of deprivation in Eastern European orphanages far exceeding that sustained by children in previous studies suggest outcomes may be worse than described earlier.

Ongoing Need for Institutional Care

Unfortunately, a system of child care must remain in place in Eastern Europe as the majority of children within institutional-care settings are more than 4 years of age (Fig. 4.1) and unlikely to be placed within adoptive homes in their country of origin or abroad (Hostetter & Johnson, 1989). During the past 5 years (since 1994), Secretary of State Christian Tabacaru, the head of the Romanian Adoption Committee, and his staff have begun to aggressively address the problems of institutionalized children within their country (Tabacaru, 1998).

By far the most important goal is to limit the number of children entering orphanage care. Not only is there tremendous human cost, but institutional care is expensive. Caring for a child in an orphanage in Romania averages two to three times the cost of foster care. During the 12 months between June 1997 and June 1998, over 40,000 requests were made to institutionalize children in Romania. Previously, all would have entered orphanages, but by providing maternal financial assistance, kindergarten daycare, and other social services, 70% of abandonments were prevented. An additional 16% were placed in family care, leaving only 14% to enter orphanages. An example of the innovative programs that reduce the need for child placement is the Leagane in Suceava, Romania, which reno-vated space, previously occupied by children, into small apartments for homeless women or victims of domestic abuse. Mother and child live together until alter-native living situations can be found, thereby eliminating the need to abandon the child to the orphanage.

A second priority is reducing the number of children within orphanages. Through family reunification, domestic and international adoption, and place-ment of competent older children within group homes, sheltered work environ-ments or trade schools, the overall orphanage population decreased 8% during the same time period, from 100,000 to 92,0000 children. Part of this process involves teams of psychologists and physicians identifying competent children misclassi-fied as handicapped or severely developmentally delayed within Neuropsychiatric Institutes. For the first time in the history of the Romanian orphanage system, a small number of inmates from the worst institutions have left to join adoptive families or enter group homes.

The third priority is improving the competency of orphanages to facilitate normal development. Partnerships with a variety of nongovernmental organizations has helped increase the number of caregivers and improve training of orphanage work-ers and living standards within some orphanages. Finally, some of the most inhu-mane institutions are being closed and children transferred to better living situations.

In conclusion, the problems observed in postinstitutionalized adoptees from Eastern Europe do not differ qualitatively from those predicted by studies of in-stitutionalized children performed from 1959 to 1979, though quantitative differ-ences exist due to a greater degree of early deprivation. However, current studies do add an exclamation point to the concept that nothing replaces a family (or at least a consistent, devoted caregiver) in promoting normal development in early childhood. Though institutionalization of hundreds of thousands of children is clearly a tragedy, it is happening at a time when neuroscientists are devoting con-siderable attention to how early life experiences affect brain development. A new generation of investigators now has the opportunity to examine the effects of se-vere deprivation on critical periods in human development using psychometric, electrophysiologic and functional brain imaging techniques unavailable in 1962. The knowledge forthcoming may improve the outcome of these children who sus-tained neglect more severe and of longer duration than groups previously studied, and assist in the effort to permanently end institutional care for infants and young children worldwide.

REFERENCES

Abel, E. L., & Sokol, R. J. (1987). Incidence of fetal alcohol syndrome and economic impact of FAS-related anomalies. *Drug and Alcohol Dependence, 19*, 51–70.

Albers, L. H., Johnson, D. E., Hostetter, M. K., Iverson, S., & Miller, L. C. (1997). Health of children adopted from the former Soviet Union and Eastern Europe. *Journal of the American Medical As-sociation, 278*, 922–924.

Allen, R., & Oliver, J. (1982). The effects of child maltreatment on language development. *Child Abuse and Neglect, 6*, 299–305.

Ames, E. W. (1997). *The development of Romanian orphanage children adopted to Canada.* Burnaby, BC: Simon Fraser University.

Aronson, J. E., & Johnson, D. E. (in press). Catch-up brain growth in children adopted from Eastern Europe and Russia. Manuscript.

Ayres, A. J. (1979). *Sensory integration and the child.* Los Angeles: Western Psychological Services.

Bakwin, H. (1949). Emotional deprivation in infants. *Journal of Pediatrics, 35*, 512–521.

Battiata, M. (1990a, June 7). A Ceausescu legacy: Warehouses for children. *The Washington Post,* pp. A1(Col. 2)–A34.

Battiata, M. (1990b, October 5). '20/20': Inside Romanian orphanages. *The Washington Post,* p. D3(Col. 2).

Battiata, M. (1991, January 7). Despite aid, Romanian children face bleak lives. *The Washington Post,* pp. A1(Col. 3)–A20.

Benoit, T. C., Jocelyn, L. J., Moddemann, D. M., & Embree, J. E. (1996). Romanian adoption: The Manitoba experience. *Archives of Pediatrics and Adolescent Medicine, 150*, 1278–1282.

Blizzard, R. M., & Bulatovic, A. (1996). Syndromes of psychosocial short stature. In F. Lifshitz (Ed.), *Pediatric Endocrinology* (pp. 83–93). New York: Marcel Dekker.

Blumenthal, R. (1989, December 26). The Ceausescus: 24 years of fierce repression, isolation and independence. *The New York Times,* p. A18(Col.1).

Bogert, C. (1994, November 21). Bringing back baby. *Newsweek, 124*, 78–79.

Bowlby, J. (1951). *Maternal care and mental health* (World Health Organization Monograph No. 2). Geneva, Switzerland: World Health Organization.

Brodbeck, A., & Irwin, O. (1946). The speech behaviors of infants without families. *Child Development, 17*, 146–156.

Cermak, S. A., & Daunhauer, L. A. (1997). Sensory processing in the post-institutionalized child. *The American Journal of Occupational Therapy, 51*, 500–507.

Chapin, H. D. (1908). A plan of dealing with atrophic infants and children. *Archives of Pediatrics, 25*, 491–496.

Chapin, H. D. (1911). The proper management of foundlings and neglected infants. *Medical Record, 79*, 283–288.

Chapin, H. D. (1915). Are institutions for infants necessary? *Journal of the American Medical Association, 64*, 1–3.

Chapin, H. D. (1917). Systematized boarding out vs. institutional care for infants and young children. *New York Medical Journal, 105*, 1009–1011.

Collard, K. K. (1971). Exploratory and play behavior of infants reared in an institution and in lower- and middle-class homes. *Child Development, 42*, 1003–1015.

Culp, R., Lawrence, H., Letts, D., Kelly, D., & Rice, M. (1991). Maltreated children's language and speech development: Abused, neglected, and abused and neglected. *First Language, 11*, 377–389.

Davis, R. B. (1994). Drug and alcohol use in the former Soviet Union: Selected factors and future considerations. *International Journal of the Addictions, 29*, 303–323.

Deane, B. (1997, April 22). International adoptions: Can love beat the odds. *Woman's Day, 60*(8), 95–98.

Dennis, W. (1973). *Children of the Creche.* New York: Appleton-Century-Crofts.

Dubrovina, I. (1991). *Psychological development of children in orphanages (Psichologicheskoe Razvitie Vospitanikov v Detskom Dome).* Moscow: Prosveschenie Press.

Eicher, D. (1990, June 22). Throwaway children fall behind. *Denver Post,* pp. E1(Col. 1)–E2.

English, P. C. (1984). Pediatrics and the unwanted child in history: Foundling homes, disease and the origins of foster care in New York City, 1860–1920. *Pediatrics, 75*, 699–711.

Federici, R. (1998). *Help for the hopeless child: A guide for families.* Alexandria, VA: Dr. Ronald S. Federici and Associates.

Feshbach, M. (1995). *Ecological disaster: Cleaning up the hidden legacy of the Soviet Regime.* New York: Twentieth Century Fund Press.

Feshbach, M., & Prokhorov, B. (1995). *Environmental and health atlas of Russia*. Moscow, Russia: PAIMS.

Field, T. (1995). Massage therapy for infants. *Journal of Developmental and Behavioral Pediatrics, 16*, 105–111.

Ford, M., & Kroll, J. (1995). *There is a better way: Family-based alternatives to institutional care*. St. Paul, MN: North American Council on Adoptable Children.

Fox, N., Calkins, S., & Bell, M. (1994). Neural plasticity and development in the first two years of life: Evidence from cognitive and socioemotional domains of research. *Development and Psychopathology, 6*, 677–698.

Frank, D. A., Klass, P. E., Earls, F., & Eisenberg, L. (1996). Infants and young children in orphanages: One view from pediatrics and child psychiatry. *Pediatrics, 97*, 569–578.

Freud, A., & Burlingham, D. T. (1944). *Infants without families*. New York: International Universities Press.

Frisancho, A. R. (1981). New norms of upper limb fat and muscle areas for assessment of nutritional status. *American Journal of Clinical Nutrition, 34*, 2540–2545.

Gardner, L. I. (1972). Deprivation dwarfism. *Scientific American, 227*(1), 76–82.

Gesell, A., & Amatruda, C. S. (1947). *Developmental diagnosis*. New York: Hoebar.

Gindis, B. (1999). Language-related issues for international adoptees and adoptive families. In T. Tepper, L. Hannon, & D. Sandstrom (Eds.), *International adoption: Challenges and opportunities* (pp. 98–107). Meadow Lands, PA: Parent Network for the Post-Institutionalized Child.

Goldfarb, W. (1943a). Effects of early institutional care on adolescent personality. *Journal of Experimental Education, 12*, 106–129.

Goldfarb, W. (1943b). Infant rearing and problem behavior. *American Journal of Orthopsychiatry, 13*, 249–265.

Goldfarb, W. (1945). Psychological privation in infancy and subsequent adjustment. *American Journal of Orthopsychiatry, 14*, 247–255.

Groze, V., & Ileana, D. (1996). A follow-up study of adopted children from Romania. *Child and Adolescent Social Work Journal, 13*, 541–565.

Hacsi, T. A. (1997). *Second home: Orphan asylums and poor families in America*. Cambridge, MA: Harvard University Press.

Haggerty, A. (1959). The effects of long-term hospitalization or institutionalization upon the language development of children. *The Journal of Genetic Psychology, 94*, 205–209.

Hansen, A. B. (1971). Short term differences of infant development in nursery homes and in private families. *Acta Pediatrica, 60*, 571–77.

Haradon, G., Bascom, B., Dragomir, C., & Scripcaru, V. (1994). Sensory functions of institutionalized Romanian infants: A pilot study. *Occupational Therapy International, 1*, 250–260.

Hershow, R. C., Hadler, S. C., & Kane, M. A. (1987). Adoption of children from countries with endemic hepatitis B: Transmission risks and medical issues. *Pediatric Infectious Disease Journal, 6*, 431–437.

Hilton, B. (1990, February 11). Romania: Politics can kill. *San Francisco Examiner*, p. D19(Col.6).

Hodges, J., & Tizard, B. (1989). IQ and behavioural adjustment of ex-institutionalized adolescents. *Journal of Child Psychology and Psychiatry, 30*, 53–75.

Horn, M. (1997, August 14). A dead child, a troubling defense. *U.S. News & World Report, 123*, 24–28.

Hostetter, M. K., Iverson, S., Dole, K., & Johnson, D. E. (1989). Unsuspected infectious diseases and other medical diagnoses in the evaluation of internationally adopted children. *Pediatrics, 83*, 559–564.

Hostetter, M. K., Iverson, S., Thomas, W., McKenzie, D., Dole, K., & Johnson, D. E. (1991). Medical evaluation of internationally adopted children. *New England Journal of Medicine, 325*, 479–485.

Hostetter, M. K., & Johnson, D. E. (1989). International adoption: An introduction for physicians. *American Journal of Diseases of Children, 143*, 325–332.

Hostetter, M. K., & Johnson, D. E. (1996). Medical examination of the internationally adopted child. *Postgraduate Medicine, 99*, 70–82.

Hostetter, M. K., & Johnson, D. E. (1998). Immunization status of adoptees from China, Russia and Eastern Europe [Abstract]. *Pediatric Research, 43*, 147A.

Hough, S. D. (1999). Risk factors for speech and language development in children adopted from Eastern Europe and the former USSR. In T. Tepper, L. Hannon, & D. Sandstrom (Eds.), *International adoption: Challenges and opportunities* (pp. 108–128). Meadow Lands, PA: Parent Network for the Post-Institutionalized Child.

Human Rights Watch. (1998). *Abandoned to the State: Cruelty and neglect in Russian orphanages.* New York: Author.

Hunt, K. (1991, March 24). The Romanian baby bazaar. *The New York Times Magazine, 140*, pp. 24–53.

Immigration and Naturalization Service. (1998). *Immigrant orphans admitted to the United States by country of origin or region of birth 1989–1998.* Washington, DC: U.S. Department of Justice.

Jamieson, F. (1991, August 28). The forgotten children. *Nursing Times, 87*, 39–42.

Jenista, J. A. (1992). Disease in adopted children from Romania. *Journal of the American Medical Association, 268*, 601–602.

Jenista, J. A. (1993). Infectious disease and the internationally adopted child. *Current Opinion on Infectious Diseases, 6*, 576–584.

Jenista, J. A., & Chapman, D. (1987). Medical problems of foreign-born adopted children. *American Journal of Diseases of Children, 141*, 298–302.

Johnson, D. E. (1997a). Medical issues in international adoption: Factors that affect your child's pre-adoption health. *Adoptive Families, 30*, 18–20.

Johnson, D. E. (1997b). Adopting the institutionalized child: What are the risks? *Adoptive Families, 30*, 26–29.

Johnson, D. E., Albers, L. H., Iverson, S., Mathers, M., Dole, K., Georgieff, M. K., Hostetter, M. K., & Miller, L. C. (1996a). Health status of Eastern European orphans referred for adoption [Abstract]. *Pediatric Research, 39*, 134A.

Johnson, D. E., Albers, L. H., Iverson, S., Mathers, M., Dole, K., Georgieff, M. K., Hostetter, M. K., & Miller, L. C. (1996b). Health status of US-adopted Eastern European orphans [Abstract]. *Pediatric Research, 39*, 134A.

Johnson, D. E., Aronson, J. E., Cozzens, D., Daunauer, L., Faber, S., Federici, J., Federici, R., Pearl, P., Sbordone, R., Storer, D., Windsor, M., Zeanah, P., & Zeanah, C. (1999). *Incidence of HBsAg- and HIV-positivity in children within the Neuropsychiatric Institute in Videle, Romania.* Unpublished manuscript.

Johnson, D. E., Aronson, J. E., Cozzens, D., Federici, J., Federici, R., Pearl, P., Sbordone, R., Storer, D., Zeanah, P., & Zeanah, C. (1999). Growth parameters help predict neurologic competence in profoundly deprived institutionalized children in Romania. *Pediatric Research, 45*, 126A.

Johnson, D. E., Aronson, J. E., Federici, R., Faber, S., Tartaglia, M., Daunauer, L., Windsor, M., & Georgieff, M. K. (1999). Profound, global growth failure afflicts residents of pediatric neuropsychiatric institutes in Romania. *Pediatric Research, 45*, 126A.

Johnson, D. E., & Dole, K. (1999). International adoption: Implication for early intervention. *Infants and Young Children, 11*, 34–45.

Johnson, D. E., & Hostetter, M. K. (1997). Post-arrival evaluations. *Adoptive Families, 30*, 14–17.

Johnson, D. E., Miller, L. C., Iverson, S., Thomas, W., Franchino, B., Dole, K., Kiernan, M. T., Georgieff, M. K., & Hostetter, M. K. (1992). The health of children adopted from Romania. *Journal of the American Medical Association, 268*, 3446–3451.

Johnson, D. E., Miller, L. C., Iverson, S., Thomas, W., Franchino, B., Dole, K., Kiernan, M. T., Georgieff, M. K., & Hostetter, M. K. (1993). Post-placement catch-up growth in Romanian orphans with psychosocial short stature [Abstract]. *Pediatric Research, 33*, 89A.

Johnson, D. E., & Traister, M. (1999). Micronutrient deficiencies, growth failure and developmental delays are more prevalent than infectious diseases in US-adopted Chinese orphans. *Pediatric Research, 45*, 126A.

Johnson, D. E., Traister, M., Iverson, S., Dole, K., Hostetter, M. K., & Miller, L. C. (1996). Health status of US adopted Chinese orphans [Abstract]. *Pediatric Research, 39*, 135A.

Kaler, S. R., & Freeman, B. J. (1994). An analysis of environmental deprivation: Cognitive and social development in Romanian orphans. *Journal of Child Psychology and Psychiatry, 35*, 769–81.

Kifner, J. (1989, December 26). Army executes Ceausescu and wife for 'genocide' role, Bucharest says. *The New York Times*, A1(Col. 6)–A16.

King, P., & Hamilton, K. (1997). Bringing kids all the way home. *Newsweek, 129*, 60–65.

Kurtz, J. (1991). HIV infection and hepatitis B in adopted Romanian children. *British Medical Journal, 302*, 1399.

Langer, W. L. (1972). Checks on population growth: 1750–1850. *Scientific American, 226*(2), 93–99.

Lewerenz, T. L., & Schaaf, R. C. (1996). Sensory processing in at-risk infants. *Sensory Integration, 19*, 1–4.

Lowrey, L. G. (1940). Personality distortion and early institutional care. *American Journal of Orthopsychiatry, 10*, 576–585.

Mapstone, E. (1969). Children in care. *Concern, 3*, 23–28.

Marcovitch, S., Goldberg, S., Gold, A., Washington, J., Wasson, C., Krekewich, K., & Handley-Derry, M. (1997). Determinants of behavioural problems in Romanian children adopted in Ontario. *International Journal of Behavioral Development, 20*, 17–31.

McGuinness, T. M. (1998). Risk and protective factors in children adopted from the former Soviet Union. *The Parent Network for Post-Institutionalized Children, 18*, 1–5.

Miller, L. C., Kiernan, M. T., Mathers, M. I., & Klein-Gitelman, M. (1995). Developmental and nutritional status of internationally adopted children. *Archives of Pediatrics and Adolescent Medicine, 149*, 40–44.

Ministry of Labor and Social Development of the Russian Federation. (1997). *On the situation of children in the Russian federation: Annual report for 1996*. Moscow: Author.

Mitchell, M. A., & Jenista, J. A. (1997a). Health care of the internationally adopted. Part 1. Before and at arrival into the adoptive home. *Journal of Pediatric Health Care, 11*, 51–60.

Mitchell, M. A., & Jenista, J. A. (1997b). Health care of the internationally adopted child. Part 2: Chronic care long term medical issues. *Journal of Pediatric Health Care, 11*, 117–126.

Nachtwey, J., & Hunt, K. (1990, June 24). Romania's lost children. *The New York Times Magazine, 139*, 28–33.

Olasky, M. (1999). The rise and fall of American orphanages. In R. B. McKenzie (Ed.), *Rethinking orphanages for the 21st Century* (pp. 65–78). Thousand Oaks, CA: Sage.

Olszewski, L. (1990, December 10). Bay group helping Romanian orphans. *San Francisco Chronicle*, p. A5(Col. 1).

Osterholm, M. T., Reves, R. R., Murph, J. R., & Pickering, L. K. (1992). Infectious diseases in child day care. *Pediatric Infectious Disease Journal, 11*, S31–S41.

Patrascu, I. V., Constantinescu, StN., & Dublanchet, A. (1990). HIV-1 infection in Romanian children. *Lancet, 335*, 672.

Powell, G. F., Brasel, J. A., & Blizzard, R. M. (1967). Emotional deprivation and growth retardation simulating idiopathic hypopituitarism. I. Clinical evaluation of the syndrome. *New England Journal of Medicine, 26*, 1271–1278.

Powell, G. F., Brasel, J. A., Raiti, S., & Blizzard, R. M. (1967). Emotional deprivation and growth retardation simulating idiopathic hypopituitarism. II. Endocrinologic evaluation of the syndrome. *New England Journal of Medicine, 276*, 1279–1283.

Pringel, M. L., & Bossio, V. (1960). Early, prolonged separation and emotional adjustment. *Journal of Child Psychology and Psychiatry, 1*, 37–48.

Pringle, M. L. K., & Bossio, V. (1958). Intellectual, emotional and social development of deprived children. *Vita Human, 1*, 66–92.

Provence, S., & Lipton, R. C. (1962). *Infants in institutions: A comparison of their development with family reared infants during the first year of life*. New York: International Universities Press.

Quinton, D., Rutter, M., & Liddle, C. (1984). Institutional rearing, parenting difficulties and marital support. *Psychological Medicine, 14*, 107–124.

Roberts, J. E., Burchinal, M. R., Davis, B. P., Collier, A. M., & Henderson, F. W. (1991). Otitis media in early childhood and later language. *Journal of Speech and Language Research, 34*, 1158–1168.

Rothman, D. J., & Rothman, S. M. (1990, November 8). How AIDS came to Romania. *The New York Review of Books*, 5–7.

Rudin, C., Berger, R., Tobler, R., Nars, P. W., Just, M., & Pavic, N. (1990). HIV-1, hepatitis (A, B, and C), and measles in Romanian children. *Lancet, 336,* 1592–1593.

Rutter, M. (1981). *Maternal deprivation reassessed.* New York: Penguin.

Rutter, M. (1998). Developmental catch-up, and deficit, following adoption after severe global early privation. English and Romanian Adoptees (ERA) Study Team. *Journal of Child Psychology & Psychiatry, 39,* 465–476.

Rutter, M., Andersen-Wood, L., Beckett, C., Bredenkamp, D., Castle, J., Groothues, C., Kreppner, J., Keaveney, L., O'Connor, T. G., & the English and Romanian Adoptees (E.R.A.) Study Team. (1999). Quasi-autistic patterns following severe early global privation. *Journal of Child Psychology and Psychiatry,* 537–549.

Saltz, R. (1973). Effect of part-time "mothering" on IQ and SQ of young institutionalized children. *Child Development, 44,* 166–170.

Sann, L., Durand, M., Picard, J., Lasne, Y., & Bethenod, M. (1988). Arm fat and muscle areas in infancy. *Archives of Disease in Childhood, 63,* 256–260.

Shinkle, F. (1991, May 22). Pilgrimage to Romanian orphanage. *St. Louis Post-Dispatch,* p. E3(Col. 1).

Shirks, M. (1991, May 20). Sifting through the 'unrecoverables' in search of the children underneath. *St. Louis Post-Dispatch,* p. B1(Col. 1).

Sloutsky, V. M. (1997). Institutional care and developmental outcomes of 6- and 7-year old children: a contextualist perspective. *International Journal of Behavioral Development, 20,* 131–151.

Spitz, R. (1945). Hospitalism. An inquiry into the genesis of psychiatric conditions in early childhood. In A. Freud, H. Hartmann, & E. Kris (Eds.), *The psychoanalytic study of the child* (pp. 53–74). New York: International Universities Press.

Spitz, R. (1965). *The first year of life: A psychoanalytic study of normal and deviant development of object relations.* New York: International Universities Press.

Sweeney, J. K., & Bascom, B. (1995). Motor development and self-stimulatory movement in institutionalized Romanian children. *Pediatric Physical Therapy, 7,* 124–132.

Tabacaru, C. (1998). *Institutionalization care and problems in Romania: A special case.* Address delivered at Post-Institutionalization: The Internationally Adopted Child, Children's National Medical Center, Washington, DC.

Talbot, M. (1998, May 24). Attachment theory: The ultimate experiment. *New York Times Magazine,* 24–54.

The Children's Health Care Collaborative Study Group. (1994). The causes of children's institutionalization in Romania. *Child: Care, Health and Development, 20,* 77–88.

Tizard, B., Cooperman, O., Joseph, A., & Tizard, J. (1972). Environmental effects on language development: A study of children in long-stay residential nurseries. *Child Development, 43,* 337–358.

Tizard, B., & Rees, J. (1974). A comparison of the effects of adoption, restoration to the natural mother, and continued institutionalization on the cognitive development of four-year-old children. *Child Development, 45,* 92–99.

Tuvemo, T., & Proos, L. A. (1993). Girls adopted from developing countries: A group at risk of early pubertal development and short final height. Implications for health surveillance and treatment. *Annals of Medicine, 25,* 217–219.

UNICEF. (1997). *Children at risk in Central and Eastern Europe: Perils and promises, regional monitoring report No. 4.* Florence, Italy: International Child Development Center.

Vita, M. C. (1990, July 1). AIDS taking deadly toll among abandoned Romanian babies. *The Atlanta Journal and Constitution,* p. C2(Col. 1).

Wallace, I., Gravel, J., McCarlton, C., & Ruben, R. (1988). Otitis media and language development at 1 year of age. *Journal of Speech and Hearing Disorders, 53,* 245–252.

Whitehurst, G. (1997). Language processes in context: Children reared in poverty. In L. Adamson & M. Romski (Eds.), *Communication and language acquisition* (pp. 233–265). Baltimore: Paul Brookes Publishing.

Widdowson, E. M. (1951). Mental contentment and physical growth. *Lancet, 1,* 1316–1318.

Williams, C. (1990, December 10). The unwanted children: casualties left by a tyrant. *Los Angeles Times,* pp. A1(Col. 5)–A17.

Winick, M., & Rosso, P. (1969). Head circumference and cellular growth of the brain in normal and marasmic children. *Journal of Pediatrics, 74*, 774–778.

Wolkind, S. N. (1974). The components of "affectionless psychopathy" in institutionalized children. *Journal of Child Psychology and Psychiatry, 15*, 215–220.

Zaknun, D., Oswald, H.-P., Zaknun, J., Mayersbach, P., Sperl, W., Schmitzberger, R., Fuchs, D., & Sailer, M. (1991). Auswirkungen von hygienischer and mudizinischer unterversorgung auf den klinischen zustand und das soziale verhalten bei säuglingen and kleinkindern in einem rumänischen kinderheim. *Pädiatrie und Pädologie, 26*, 65–67.

5

▼▼▼▼▼▼▼▼

Early Adversity and the Development of Stress Reactivity and Regulation

Megan R. Gunnar
Institute of Child Development
University of Minnesota

In this chapter, I will first describe a general model in which the reactivity and regulation of stress physiology serves as a common pathway through which many aspects of early adversity may converge. In this model, caregiving characteristics function to mediate and moderate the impact of early adverse conditions on the activity of stress systems. After a brief discussion of the physiology of stress, I review the animal data that support this model and consider whether and how the animal models may need to be altered when researchers attempt to apply them to human development in adverse contexts. I then review the limited data available on human infants and children and argue that it is largely consistent with the proposed model.

Adversity is conceptualized broadly as conditions that threaten physical or emotional well-being. The argument made in this chapter is that many adverse conditions may influence neurobehavioral development, in part, through affecting the reactivity and regulation of stress-sensitive physiological systems. This is shown in Fig. 5.1 and is consistent with many views of early experience and stress responsivity (Coplan et al., 1996; Davidson, 1994; Rosenblum et al., 1994; Smotherman & Bell, 1980). Contact with and proximity to caregivers serves to regulate and reduce stress-system reactivity to potentially noxious stimulation (Coe, Rosenberg, Fischer, & Levine, 1987; Levine & Wiener, 1988; Mendoza, Coe, Smotherman, Kaplan, & Levine, 1980). In addition, *hidden regulators* within relationships, to use Hofer's terminology, stimulate the development of neural systems that regulate stress physiology (Caldji et al., 1998; Hofer, 1987). As a result, disturbances within the caregiving system should have pervasive effects on the neurobiology of

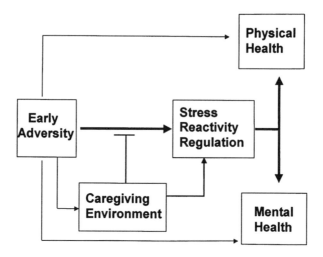

FIG. 5.1.   Model of the role of stress-sensitive physiological systems in mediating impact of early adverse life condition on physical and emotional health. The caregiving environment is described as potentially both mediating and moderating the impact of adverse conditions on stress-system reactivity and regulation.

stress. An important aspect of this conceptual model is the expectation that stress affects physical and mental health (Borysenko, 1984; Nemeroff, 1996). Before discussing early experiences, it is necessary to briefly define stress, its physiology, and general models of its associations with health.

THE PSYCHOBIOLOGY OF STRESS

Stress is notoriously difficult to define (Engle, 1985). It results when there are actual (reactive) or potential (proactive) threats to homeostasis or physical well-being, in the context of a lack of certainty about one's capacity to cope with or effectively manage the threat (Chrousos & Gold, 1992; Johnson, Kamilaris, Chrousos, & Gold, 1992). Challenges to well-being come in many forms. Successful adaptation often requires integrated action of most of the regulatory systems of the body, including emotional and cognitive systems, the autonomic nervous system, the neuroendocrine system, and the immune system (Strand, 1999b). In addition, in young organisms whose regulatory systems are organized to function within a caregiving context, successful adaptation to stressors requires appropriate actions and responses by caregivers (Kraemer, 1992). Stress has been studied both behaviorally and physiologically. In this chapter, I will emphasize the central role of physiological stress systems in the orchestration of stress responses. However, given the emphasis on behavioral definitions in human developmental research, a brief discussion of the challenges of defining and studying stress behaviorally will be included.

The Physiology of Stress

While most regulatory systems are involved in managing threats to well-being, the corticotropin-releasing hormone hypothalamic-pituitary-adrenocortical (CRH-HPA) system (see Fig. 5.2) appears to play a central, coordinating role (Chrousos & Gold, 1992; Kalin, 1990; Strand, 1999b). CRH produced in the paraventricular nuclei (PVN) of the hypothalamus, together with the synergistic actions of vasopressin (VP), stimulates the secretion of adrenocorticotropic hormone (ACTH) and endorphins by the anterior pituitary (see Fig. 5.2). Cells on the

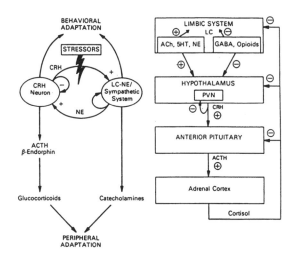

FIG. 5.2.   The stress system and neurotransmitter as well as neurohormonal control mechanisms modulating CRH secretion. (Left) CRH neurons stimulate both pituitary ACTH secretion and the central autonomic arousal system (LC-NE system), leading, respectively, to glucocorticoid and NE secretion. The positive reverberating loop between the CRH neuron and the autonomic arousal centers is under ultra-short-loop feedback control, respectively, by CRH and NE presynaptic inhibition. Plus signs represent stimulation; minus signs indicate inhibition. (Right) Hypothalamic CRH neurons receive positive NE input from the central limbic system, cholinergic and serotonergic stimulation, and opiate and γ-aminobutyric acid (GABA)ergic inhibition. Circled plus signs represent stimulatory pathways; circled minus signs, inhibitory pathways. ACh = acetylcholine; 5HT = 5-hydroxytryptamine (serotonin); GABA = γ-aminobutyric acid; PVN = paraventricular nucleus. From "The stress-response and the regulation of inflammatory disease," by E. M. Sternberg, G. P. Chrousos, R. L. Wilder, and P. W. Gold, 1992, *Annals of Internal Medicine, 117*, pp. 854–866. Copyright 1992, by American College of Physicians—American Society of Internal Medicine. Reprinted with permission.

cortex of the adrenal gland respond to ACTH resulting in the release of gluco-corticoids. Cortisol is the primary glucocorticoid in primates, including humans, while corticosterone is the primary glucocorticoid in rodents. Glucocorticoids are regulated through complex feedback loops operating at the level of the pituitary, hypothalamus, hippocampus, and frontal cortex (de Kloet, 1991; de Kloet & Reul, 1987; Diorio, Viau, & Meaney, 1993; Sarrieau et al., 1988).

Glucocorticoids affect almost every organ and tissue of the body (Munck, Guyre, & Holbrook, 1984). At low, basal levels, their actions tend to permit or re-store processes that prime homeostatic defense mechanisms (Munck & Naray-Fejes-Toth, 1994). Increases in glucocorticoids in this basal range generally pro-mote mental and physical health and development (de Kloet, Rots, van den Berg, & Oitzl, 1994). At higher levels, glucocorticoids have suppressive and potential-ly destructive effects (Munck & Naray-Fejes-Toth, 1994; Sapolsky, 1994; Sapol-sky, 1997). They tend to suppress the body's defense mechanisms (e.g., immune system) and produce actions on the central nervous system that threaten its in-tegrity. It is assumed that these opposing classes of effects (protective vs. sup-pressive) operate, in part, through different receptor systems (Munck & Naray-Fejes-Toth, 1994; Sapolsky, 1997). However, to some extent they are the result of differing, sometimes opposing, effects of glucocorticoids, ACTH, and CRH (de Kloet & De Wied, 1980).

There are two receptors that bind glucocorticoids: MR and GR (de Kloet, 1991). MR are largely occupied when glucocorticoids are low or in basal ranges. These receptors mediate many of the protective functions of the hormone (also sometimes called *permissive* functions). GR are bound when glucocorticoids are at high concentrations and at the peak of the daily cycle in basal hormone pro-duction. GR mediate many of the suppressive–destructive actions of glucocorti-coids. Permissive and suppressive functions of glucocorticoids have different time-courses of onset and decay, with suppressive, potentially destructive effects becoming more pronounced when GR are occupied for longer periods of time (Munck & Naray-Fejes-Toth, 1994; Sapolsky, 1997). As a result, an inverted U-function has been found for many effects of glucocorticoids. Small increases in the hormone, or brief elevations even to high levels, often enhance behavioral per-formance and support health-promoting or sustaining physiological processes. Larger increases, particularly if they result in prolonged occupation of GR, lead to impairments and threats to health.

It follows that both overactivity (hyperresponsiveness) and underactivity (hy-poresponsiveness) of the CRH-HPA system may have deleterious effects on health and development (McEwen et al., 1992; Munck & Naray-Fejes-Toth, 1994). A hyperresponsive CRH-HPA system influences the development of hy-pertension and cardiovascular disease, immunosuppression and vulnerability to inflammatory disease, suppression of the reproductive system at all levels leading to amenorrhea and loss of libido, and the accumulation of visceral fat leading to hyperinsulinism and insulin resistance (Stratakis & Chrousos, 1995). Many of these stress-related disorders are observed more in aging, as counter-regulatory processes that promote restoration and resistance wane in their efficacy (Lupienet al., 1994; McEwen, 1988; Seeman, Berkman, Blazer, & Rowe, 1994). In addition, glucocorticoids often participate in the age-related impairments in restorative functioning (e.g., glucocorticoids stimulate age-related involution of the thymus resulting in decreased immunocompetence, Strand, 1999a). Hyperresponsivity of this system also suppresses growth (Grigoriadis, Insel, Heroux, & De Souza, 1993; Koob, 1992). For the developing organism, this can have drastic effects as observed in the growth retardation and developmental delay of children reared under extreme conditions of deprivation (see Johnson, chap. 4, this volume) or in the offspring of stressed pregnancies (see Schneider and Moore, chap. 6, this volume). Hyperactivity of this system is also believed to foster activity in the central nervous system that forms the diathesis for anxiety disorders and depression (Nemeroff, 1996; Rosen & Schulkin, 1998). While a hyperresponsive system is a threat to healthy functioning, so is a hyporesponsive CRH-HPA system. Hyporesponsivity of the CRH-HPA system is associated with chronic fatigue, somnolence, and increased susceptibility to autoimmune and inflammatory diseases such as rheumatoid arthritis and asthma (Stratakis & Chrousos, 1995).

The CRH-HPA system interacts at many levels with the other major regulatory systems of the body, including the immune and autonomic nervous system (Borysenko, 1984). Its interactions with the autonomic nervous system (ANS) support many of the behavioral adjustments necessary to manage threats to well-being (Schulkin, McEwen, & Gold, 1994). In the central nervous system, interactions with the ANS take place both within and outside of the hypothalamus. Some of these interactions are modulatory, as observed in the hippocampus where elevated glucocorticoids reduce neural sensitivity to norepinephrine (NE) (Diamond & Rose, 1994; McEwen & Gould, 1990). Some of them are stimulatory. For example, CRH from the PVN stimulates brainstem nuclei regulating the sympathetic adrenomedullary (SAM) system or sympathetic arm of the ANS (Rosen & Schulkin, 1998; Strand, 1999b). This results in an increase in catecholamine action in the periphery. Centrally, CRH also stimulates the locus ceruleus (LC)-NE system (Valentio, 1990). Activation of the SAM/LC-NE system supports the shift from anabolic, growth-promoting processes to catabolic, energy-depleting processes that is the hallmark of the stress response (Mason, 1968). It also supports changes in the central nervous system that narrow attention, increase alertness, and lower thresholds for threat perception (Chrousos & Gold, 1992).

CRH is not only produced in the hypothalamus, but in most neural cells (Strand, 1999b). The central nucleus of the amygdala has some of the highest concentrations of CRH-producing cells (Makino, Gold, & Schulkin, 1994). Similarly, receptors for glucocorticoids are not only found in the hypothalamus and pituitary, but also are widespread in the brain, with high concentrations in the hippocampus and medial (cingulate) frontal cortex (Bohus, de Kloet, & Veldhuis, 1982; Brooke, de Haas-Johnson, Kaplan, & Sapolsky, 1994; de Kloet, 1991). This extrahypothalamic CRH and glucocorticoid receptor system appears to be particularly involved in coordinating anticipatory, proactive stress responses that support reactivity to novelty and avoidance of and proactive management of situations that could pose threats to homeostasis or the organism's well-being (Diorio, Viau, & Meaney, 1993; Feldman, Conforti, & Weidenfeld, 1995). These proactive responses have been described as allostatic adjustments that protect the organism from immediate threat, but carry hidden costs mediated through the potential deleterious effects of frequent or prolonged activation of both the CRH-HPA system and the SAM/LC-NE system (McEwen, 1998). As with other neuroactive peptides, the actions of this extrahypothalamic CRH system are immensely complex, interact with other neurotransmitters and neuropeptides, change with development in ways only beginning to be understood, and modulate the organism's responses to stimulation more so than causing particular cognitive, emotional, or physiological patterns (Strand, 1999b). It is this extrahypothalamic CRH-HPA system that appears to be particularly sensitive to experiences early in life in rodents, and possibly also in primates (Caldji et al., 1998; Meaney et al., 1996; Plotsky & Meaney, 1993).

Behavioral Measures of Stress Reactivity

In behavioral research, stress responses are typically measured in reaction to emotionally threatening situations. Except in situations where reactions to pain are being examined (e.g., studies of circumcision, childhood immunizations, and so on), the situations used are typically ones that some individuals perceive as threatening and others do not. In research on infants and young children, these situations often include brief separations from attachment figures, the approach of strangers, or exposure to strange, novel objects (see Nachmias, Gunnar, Mangelsdorf, Parritz, & Buss, 1996; Spangler & Schieche, 1998). The behaviors used to assess reactivity to the threat are those that reflect whether the individual is responding to the situation as threatening or not. These behaviors vary with the context, but typically include measures of negative emotion (fuss, cry), withdrawal, or attempts to escape the potentially threatening event–object, and in young children, attempts to increase proximity to parents or other caregivers.

These behaviors can be used effectively to examine thresholds for interpreting events as threatening. However, because stress results when events are actually or potentially threatening *and* they are experienced as overwhelming one's capacity to manage threat (Lazarus & Folkman, 1984), taken alone they are not adequate indices of stress. To be adequate they need to be evaluated in light of their effectiveness in regulating threat. Furthermore, numerous studies have demonstrated that it is the individual's perceptions of the behavior's effectiveness, and not the behavior's actual effectiveness that is associated with stress (Lazarus & Folkman, 1984). This makes it challenging, particularly in nonverbal or preverbal organisms, to move from assessing behaviors indicating that events are perceived as threatening to interpretation of these behaviors as indices of stress reactivity.

One way this has been accomplished in animals is to provide experiences that train the animal that nothing it does will affect aversive outcomes. Paradigms using these procedures (e.g., *learned helplessness* paradigms) are associated with intense activation of the stress system, often accompanied by behavioral passivity (Maier, Ryan, Barksdale, & Kalin, 1986). Another technique used with both animals and humans is to alter environmental cues in ways that enhance or diminish expectations that attempts to manage threat will be effective. In animals, providing a signal that indicates that a response has effectively prevented a shock from occurring has been shown to determine whether the response is associated with increased catecholamines and glucocorticoids (no signal) or not (signal) (Weiss, 1971).

Because, with rare exception, infant primates cannot effectively manage threat on their own, these manipulations in young primates typically involve varying access to attachment figures or varying the responsiveness of adult caregivers. For example, different conditions of separation in rhesus infants have been used that should alter expectancies that behavioral responses will lead to reestablishment of contact with the mother. In one study, infants were separated under conditions in which they could see, hear, and smell their mothers (high expectancy of reestablishing contact) or under conditions in which all contact was prevented (low expectancy of reestablishing contact) (Bayart, Hayashi, Faull, Barchas, & Levine, 1990). The more proximal conditions resulted in intense coo vocalizations (a retrieval call), behavioral agitation, and attempts to break through the barrier that separated mother and infant. These behaviors were less frequent under the condition where all contact with the mother was prevented. In that condition, passivity and a different vocalization (isolation call) were observed. Animals in both conditions exhibited elevations in cortisol, but these responses were much larger in the isolated condition. In human infants, the sensitivity and responsiveness of substitute caregivers has been experimentally manipulated as a means of altering whether the infant's behavior can function to reduce threat (Gunnar, Larson, Hertsgaard, Harris, & Brodersen, 1992). In the presence of a responsive caregiver, separation from the mother failed to produce increases in cortisol, on average. Fussing, crying, and other behaviors reflecting distress at the mother's departure were not correlated with posttest cortisol levels in this condition. In the presence of an unresponsive caregiver, significant average increases in cortisol were noted and distress behaviors were positively correlated with the magnitude of the increase.

As will be discussed, control and cues predicting safety are critical factors that determine the extent to which a potentially threatening event is experienced as stressful. Distress vocalizations and proximity seeking are the primary way that infants and young children increase safety under conditions of threat. Therefore, it should come as no surprise that when these behaviors are assessed as measures of stress responsivity in the absence of attempts to examine their potential effectiveness, they are often poor reflections of the degree of stress the child is actually experiencing.

ADVERSE CONDITIONS INFLUENCE
THE DEVELOPMENT OF THE CRH-HPA SYSTEM

Adverse conditions early in life may influence the development of the CRH-HPA system (Ogilvie & Rivier, 1997; Smythe, McCormick, Rochford, & Meaney, 1994; Weiner & Levine, 1978). As noted, receptors for glucocorticoids are widely distributed in the brain, with the highest concentrations in the hippocampus (pyramidal and granulae cells), cortex, hypothalamus, septum, amygdala, raphe nucleus, and LC (de Kloet, 1991; McEwen, de Kloet, & Rostene, 1986; Meaney et al., 1993). The GR receptor system is highly responsive to increasing levels of glucocorticoids. Approximately 20 minutes after a large rise in glucocorticoids over half of GR receptors are bound. These receptors stay bound for 2 to 4 hours. Binding of GR receptors is associated with termination of CRH production by the PVN of the hypothalamus, reduction of ACTH from the pituitary, and consequently the termination of glucocorticoid production (Liu et al., 1997). Levels of glucocorticoids in circulation, however, wane only gradually as their clearance involves uptake and degradation (breakdown) by the liver and excretion through the kidneys (Tepperman & Tepperman, 1987).

Containing and controlling the CRH-HPA axis response largely depends on a healthy and robust GR system (de Kloet, 1991; de Kloet & Reul, 1987). As with many receptor systems, high levels of its hormone tend to reduce receptor numbers (Strand, 1999a; Strand, 1999b). Some of these effects are transitory. Early in the life of the organism, the development of this receptor system appears to be affected by growth-promoting factors such as the level of thyroid hormone and neurotransmitters, including serotonin (Meaney et al., 1994). Events during development can have long-term impact on gene expression and the robustness of the glucocorticoid receptor system. GR also mediate activity in neurons that threaten their integrity (McEwen, 1988; McEwen et al., 1986). When GR are stimulated, this reduces NE uptake by neural cells, alters the capacity of the neuron to use glucose, increases the activity of excitatory amino acids (e.g. glutamate), and facilitates the actions of N-methyl-D-aspartate (NMDA) receptors that result in actions that are highly energy-demanding. The result is to increase the vulnerability of the neuron to overstimulation that can result in cell death. These actions of glucocorticoids are seen most prevalently in the hippocampus. Although elevated glucocorticoids may initially help foster hippocampal activity involved in memory storage, high or prolonged elevations in glucocorticoids have been associated with cell death, altered dendritic growth, and impairment in the cognitive functions served by the hippocampus and its related structures.

Early experiences that elevate glucocorticoids, reduce thyroid hormone and serotonin, or both, appear to have profound effects on the hippocampal GR system. Elevated glucocorticoids and early experiences (e.g. early handling, maternal separation, malnutrition, and endotoxins) also influence the extrahypothalamic CRH system. There is some evidence that elevated glucocorticoids increase activity of CRH-producing neurons in the central nucleus of the amygdala (Makino et al., 1994). Likewise, early experiences that are associated with the development of a more hyperresponsive CRH-HPA axis are also associated with increased vigilance, inhibition of behavioral responses in novel settings, and increased CRH activity in the amygdala (Caldji et al., 1998).

The GR system and the central CRH system may be affected by many components of adverse early life conditions. Elevations in glucocorticoids are only one route through which these effects may operate, although this route may be significant during both prenatal and postnatal development. Prenatal stress to the mother affects GR numbers and the development of the hippocampus (Barbazanges, Piazza, Moal, & Maccari, 1996; Clarke, Wittwer, Abbott, & Schneider, 1994; Schneider et al., 1998; Schneider, Coe, & Lubach, 1992). This has been demonstrated in rodents, and is consistent with the effects observed in nonhuman primates (see Schneider and Moore, chap. 6, this volume). In rodents, preventing elevations in maternal glucocorticoids through removal of the mother's adrenal gland and replacement with controlled levels of corticosterone largely eliminates the glucocorticoid receptor development effects of stressing the mother during pregnancy (Barbazanges et al., 1996). Prenatal alcohol exposure in the rat and monkey is also known to increase reactivity and reduce regulation of the HPA axis (Ogilvie & Rivier, 1997). As noted earlier, manipulations of thyroid hormone and serotonin levels in early development have also been shown to influence the development of the GR system in rodents (Meaney et al., 1994). Although acute periods of malnutrition in the preweanling rat do not appear to produce long-term effects on the HPA axis (Weiner & Levine, 1978), malnutrition does tend to lower thyroid levels and increase glucocorticoid levels and thus might be expected to increase the vulnerability of the developing stress neuraxis (van Haasteren et al., 1996). Finally, cytokines, the chemical messengers of the immune system, are potent stimulators of the HPA axis (Besedovsky, Del Rey, Sorkin, & Dinarello, 1986; Cacioppo, 1994; Maes, Bosmans, Meltzer, Scharpe, & Suy, 1993; Maier, Watkins, & Fleshner, 1994; Strand, 1999a). Exposure to an endotoxin in early development has been shown, in rats, to reduce GR numbers and increase behavioral and neuroendocrine responses to stressors (Shanks, Laroque, & Meaney, 1995). Thus the development of an efficient CRH-HPA system (one that expresses moderate basal levels, responds with elevations to stressors when needed, and terminates its response quickly) may be threatened by many factors that are components of adverse early life conditions (e.g., prenatal stress and alcohol exposure, malnutrition, illness). Importantly, however, the impact of these conditions on the development of the CRH-HPA axis appears to be strongly affected by early experiences within the caregiver–infant relationship (Ogilvie & Rivier, 1997; Smythe et al., 1994; Weiner & Levine, 1978).

CAREGIVER MEDIATION OF EARLY ADVERSE LIFE CONDITIONS

The evidence that early experiences, whether adverse or protective, have long-term effects on the HPA axis comes almost entirely from animal research, most from rodents. The timing of HPA axis development relative to the timing of birth differs markedly between rodents and primates (Reynolds, 1981; Vazquez, 1998). Indeed, the period of postnatal development during which most of the early experience research has been conducted with rat pups (e.g., 4 to 14 days postnatal) corresponds roughly to the 23rd week of gestation in humans (Fitzgerald & Anand, 1993). Thus it is not at all clear how or whether this research bears on our understanding of human infants developing under adverse early life conditions. Nonetheless, there is a literature on nonhuman primates whose CRH-HPA axis development approximates our own at birth. This work also shows that experiences in the infancy period, particularly those related to caregiving, affect long-term responsivity of the axis. The rodent research may have more applicability to our understanding of human development than it might at first appear. In the following section, the rodent research will be briefly reviewed with particular emphasis on the evidence that maternal behavior may mediate many of the early experience effects that have been reported. The smaller, but perhaps more directly applicable work on nonhuman primates, will then be described. Finally, the emerging literature in humans will be discussed. This literature, too, indicates that adverse early life conditions can produce long-term changes in glucocorticoid levels, and that the nature of the social environment plays a significant role in regulation of glucocorticoid levels in early development. While the animal data on early social experience is often couched in terms of maternal stimulation, it is noteworthy that the same animal data points to the efficacy of stimulation that mimics stimulation typically provided by the mother. Thus, it appears that caregiving stimulation plays the critical role, and that may or may not be provided by the mother.

Rodent Studies

There are a plethora of paradigms that have been used to study the acute and chronic impact of stress on development in rodents. Most have involved some form of maternal separation. Sometimes these paradigms are called *maternal separation* (Plotsky, Thrivkraman, & Meaney, 1993). Sometimes they are not (Levine, 1957). These various separation paradigms produce acute and long-term effects that differ with the age of the pup (Levine, 1994). Attempts to explain the impact of these manipulations by focusing primarily on characteristics of the experimental manipulations have largely failed. Over 20 years ago, Levine (1975) raised the possibility that these paradigms might be producing their effects, in part, through altering mother–infant interactions. Levine (1975) made this argument in speculating on the mechanisms that produce early handling effects in rodents.

The early handling paradigm was one of the first widely studied rodent separation paradigms (Denenberg, Brumaghim, Haltmeyer, & Zarrow, 1967; Levine, 1957). In this paradigm, the infant or pup is removed from the nest daily for 3–15 minutes throughout the preweaning period. A variant of this procedure involves removal of the mother or dam (Meaney, Aitken, van Berkel, Bhatnagar, & Sapolsky, 1988). The effects of early handling are remarkable and robust. Compared to offspring from nests that were never disturbed, those from the handled nests show significantly less fearful behavior in open-field testing as adults, exhibit smaller and less prolonged glucocorticoid responses to restraint stress, grow physically larger, and reach maturity slightly earlier (Liu et al., 1997; Levine, 1975; Meaney et al., 1996; Plotsky & Meaney, 1993). The handled rats also exhibit decreased CRH activity in the hypothalamus and central nucleus of the amygdala and increased GR expression in the hippocampus and frontal cortex. Alterations have also been reported in neurotransmitter systems (serotonin, dopamine, and norepinephrine). These effects are more marked if handling begins earlier in the preweaning period (e.g. week 1) rather than later (week 2), suggesting that there is a sensitive period for the effects of these early experiences on stress-system organization (Meaney, 1996; Meaney et al., 1994). Importantly, these early experiences appear to affect response to stressors such as restraint and novel environments, more so than physical stressors such as ether and pain (Ladd et al., in press). That is, they appear to influence the central circuits involved in proactive stress response more than those involved in reactive response to homeostatic challenge.

While the handling paradigm appears to help organize a less stress-reactive-proactive central stress system, other early separation paradigms produce the opposite effects. When the daily separation period is lengthened to 3 hours, it produces hyperstress reactivity (Plotsky, Thrivkraman, & Meaney, 1993). Rats subjected to this paradigm, actually termed *maternal separation*, as adults show larger and longer glucocorticoid responses to restraint stress and novel environments, reduced GR numbers, increased CRH activity, and larger central norepinephrine reactions to threat (Liu et al., 1997). Less frequent, but more prolonged (12 to 24 hours) periods of separation have also been studied. The effects of these more drastic manipulations vary with the age of the pups (Levine, 1994; Suchecki, Mazzafarian, Gross, Rosenfeld, & Levine, 1993; Suchecki, Nelson, Van Oers, & Levine, 1995; van Oers, de Kloet, & Levine, 1997). In addition to impacts on the HPA axis and its central regulation, Robbins and his colleagues noted that 10, 6-hour removals from the nest performed randomly between postnatal days 5 and 20 produced alterations in the adult ventral striatal dopamine reward system (Hall et al., 1998). This paradigm also reduces behavioral reactions to food rewards, and thus creates a neurobiology reminiscent of human depression (Matthews, Wilkinson, & Robbins, 1996).

Although Levine (Levine, 1975; Levine & Thoman, 1970) suggested the maternal mediation hypothesis decades ago, recently it has received renewed interest (Liu et al., 1997). Studies in the 1960s and 1970s demonstrated that increasing maternal stimulation during the early development of the rodent pup reduced adult responsiveness of the adrenocortical system (see review by Smotherman & Bel, 1980). Furthermore, it was shown that handling, while it did not affect how much time the mother spends with her pups, altered how much she licked and groomed them and how well she assumed the nursing posture (Liu et al., 1997).

The vigorous tactile stimulation provided by maternal licking influences central nervous system development in rat pups and modulates the production of enzymes essential for physical growth (Kuhn, Butler, & Schanberg, 1978; Schanberg, Evoniuk, & Kuhn, 1984). Maternal licking in rodents also helps to maintain the HPA axis in relative quiescence through influencing ACTH activity in the pituitary (Rosenfield, Suchecki, & Levine, 1992). Feeding (milk into the gut) maintains the adrenal in a relatively quiescent state (Levine, 1994). Thus, components of maternal behavior that are critically important to keeping the pup alive (feeding and stimulating elimination of waste products through licking of the anogenital region) profoundly regulates the CRH-HPA axis in the developing rodent. Furthermore, procedures that disturb these aspects of maternal behavior result in significant alterations in the development of the pup's CRH-HPA system and its behavioral responses to conditions associated with potential threat in adulthood (Plotsky et al., 1993).

Several studies have now shown that natural variations in maternal care correlate with the development of neural systems mediating stress reactivity in rats (Caldji et al., 1998; Liu et al., 1997). Pups reared by mothers who engage in less licking and grooming, in adulthood show larger HPA axis responses to restraint stress, reduced glucocorticoid receptor-mediated negative feedback containment of the glucocorticoid stress response, heightened fear (freezing) in open-field testing, reduced sensitivity to anxiety-reducing drugs, and heightened amygdala-LC activity. Several strains of rodents have been bred to be hyperstress reactive. Mothers in these strains engage in less licking and grooming of their offspring than do mothers from less reactive strains (Anisman, Zaharia, Meaney, & Merali, 1998; Zaharia, Kulczycki, Shanks, Meaney, & Anisman, 1996). If pups from high fearful strains are cross-fostered to mothers from less fearful strains who are, in addition, high *lickers and groomers*, fearful behavior and neuroendocrine activity in adulthood is reduced. Similar findings were reported earlier when mice were cross-fostered to rat mothers (Denenberg et al., 1968). Thus, in rodents, it appears that the neural systems mediating the stress response, although genetically biased, are also highly plastic in early development and can be strongly influenced by variations in stimulation provided under natural conditions by the mother.

Studies in Nonhuman Primates

Monkeys have also been used to study the effects of early experiences on stress reactivity and regulation (Champoux, Byrne, DeLizio, & Suomi, 1992; Coe, Lubach, & Ershler, 1989; Coplan et al., 1996; Kalin & Carnes, 1984; Levine & Wiener, 1988; Suomi, 1995). However, because it takes much longer for monkeys than rodents to grow to adulthood, and most primate facilities cannot afford to maintain animals for years merely to examine early history effects, there are very few studies of the impact of early experiences on adult stress physiology. Those that exist, however, are consistent with the rodent work. Suomi and his colleagues studied rhesus infants reared only with peers and compared them to mother-reared infants (Higley, Suomi, & Linnoila, 1992).[1] Compared to mother-reared infants, peer-only reared monkeys as adults show larger cortisol responses to psychosocial stressors. Behavioral differences produced by peer-only rearing also persist into adulthood; with peer-only reared animals consuming more alcohol than mother-reared infants (Fulke et al., 1998). These differences in alcohol consumption presumably reflect the impact of rearing history on the neural substrate mediating fear and stress reactions. Indeed, independent of rearing history, monkeys who showed larger cortisol responses to social stress as infants and juveniles drank more alcohol when given the opportunity.

While peers undoubtedly make poor caregivers, peer-only reared infants also make poor playmates (Suomi, 1991a). Long-term effects of peer-only rearing on stress physiology and fearful behavior may be due to alterations in caregiving stimulation, peer experiences, or both. The variable foraging paradigm is an early experience paradigm in which long-term effects are more likely to be caregiver mediated (Coplan, Rosenblum, & Gorman, 1995). In this paradigm, adult female monkeys and their young live in social groups. The adult females must forage for their food. Infants can slip through a small hole into a feeding station, and thus are never food deprived. The caregiver's foraging demands are manipulated experimentally by varying the number of feeding slots that are baited with monkey chow. In the high and low demand conditions, respectively, either a small or large percentage of slots contain chow. High demand requires that the mothers spend more time searching for food than does low demand. But despite this, infants in the two conditions do not differ in emotional behavior or physiological responses. The social relations of the adult females also do not differ in these two conditions. In both the high and low demand conditions, the females establish stable dominance relationships, sit near one another, and engage in social grooming.

There is a third, variable demand condition. In this condition, the group is switched between high and low demand, alternating every 2 weeks. Variable schedules produce marked disruptions in the social group. Females cease to groom one another, hierarchies become unstable, and maternal behaviors appear to suffer as a consequence (Rosenblum & Andrews, 1994). If given the opportunity, mothers in the variable foraging condition avoid their infants, are unresponsive to their signals, and rarely hold them. The paradigm is highly stressful for

---

[1]In peer-only rearing infants are housed together, 4 to a group, and do not have access to their own cloth surrogate. All clinging and contact seeking, thus, requires the response or acquiescence of another infant monkey. This type of rearing appears to produce more dramatic effects than surrogate-peer rearing. In surrogate-peer rearing, infants are housed singly with their cloth surrogate; however, beginning at 1 month of age they are placed for 2 hours per day in a group care with 3 other infants to play. Provision of the playmates appears to improve the infants' abilities to interact with other monkeys and to mate and rear young in adulthood. In both types of rearing, it is assumed that it is not the lack of the biological mother that produces alterations in development, but the lack of a consistent, animate and responsive caregiver.

both mothers and infants, producing prolonged increases in ACTH and cortisol for all members of the social group (Champoux, Zanker, & Levine, 1993.) A mere 10 weeks of such disturbance in the first year of life appears to produce long-term effects on behavior and stress physiology (Andrews & Rosenblum, 1994; Coplan et al., 1996; Rosenblum et al., 1994). Similar to rats reared by mothers who provided inadequate licking and stimulation, in adulthood, monkeys reared by mothers subjected to variable foraging demands have higher cerebrospinal fluid levels of CRH. When placed in social groups as adults, the monkeys from variable foraging conditions typically end up occupying the lowest positions of dominance.

While many caregiver-mediated effects on stress-system organization appear to be produced through maternal licking and grooming in rodents, it is not clear that tactile stimulation is the primary or sole route of transmission in primates. Certainly monkey mothers provide their infants with such stimulation. Tactile stimulation in the form of deep massage has also been shown in human newborns to stimulate growth and in children and adults to lower cortisol levels (Field, 1995; Kuhn et al., 1991). Tactile stimulation probably does play an important role in organizing the stress system in primates, at least early in development. However, it is difficult in the two monkey paradigms just described to imagine how the effects on stress physiology could have been mediated solely through tactile stimulation. Peer-only reared infants cling to one another, sleep together, and provide each other with often quite vigorous tactile stimulation (Suomi, 1991a, 1991b). In the variable foraging paradigm, to insure that the infants get enough to eat, the paradigm is not introduced until monkey infants are old enough to get their sustenance from solid foods (Rosenblum & Andrews, 1994). By this age, infants typically spend much of their day off the mother (Mason, 1970). Introduction of the paradigm, thus, does not result in much reduction of tactile stimulation. What is reduced in both peer-only rearing and variable foraging is the contingency of stimulation.

Stimulation must be contingent on infant actions in order for it to be controllable. Control and predictability are key psychological variables affecting perception of threat in human adults (Breier et al., 1987). In numerous studies, controllable noxious stimulation has been shown in rats, monkeys, and humans to produce smaller neuroendocrine and catecholamine responses than has uncontrollable noxious stimulation (Averill, 1973; Hanson, Larson, & Snowdon, 1976; Pervin, 1968; Weiss, 1971). Control does not need to be exercised in order for it to reduce perceived threat, physiological responses to stressors, or both (Glass & Singer, 1972). Simply the expectation that the noxious event can be controlled is stress reducing. Contingent, responsive stimulation may be an important aspect of the early experience in primates that influences the development of stress-system reactivity and regulation. While such stimulation is probably most likely to be experienced through interactions with caregivers, it is not clear that it must be experienced within the caregiving context in order to influence stress-system responsivity and regulation. Note that similar conclusions have been made for the role of tactile stimulation in the developing rodent (Denenberg, 1999).

For example, in a study conducted with peer-only reared monkeys, Mineka, Gunnar, and Champoux (1986) provided some groups of infants with daily access to levers and pulleys that they could use to obtain treats. Yoked groups received the same treats, independent of their control. These experiences with response-contingent stimulation had significant effects on the monkeys' behavioral responses to novelty. When introduced into a novel playroom, monkeys who grew up experiencing more controllable, contingent stimulation were less fearful, explored more, and played more. Reduced inhibition or freezing in novel contexts is the behavioral hallmark of the early experience effects in rodents (Denenberg, 1999). As adults, the monkeys studied by Mineka et al. (1996) showed smaller neuroendocrine reactions to an anxiety-producing drug (Insel, Scanlan, Champoux, & Suomi, 1988).

Naturally occurring variations in mother–infant relationships in primates have also been shown to relate to stress-system responses. Rhesus infants who have experienced more responsive mothering show larger initial responses to experimental separation, but recover more rapidly and show a marked lowering of cortisol levels upon reunion (Gunnar, Gonzales, & Levine, 1981). In contrast, infants who have experienced less responsive, more rejecting mothering, while exhibiting less immediate behavioral distress upon separation, show marked increases in cortisol levels 24 hours after reunion. Similar results have also been reported for Goeldi's monkeys (Dettling, Pryce, Martin, & Döbeli, 1998). Thus, in primate infants, the responsiveness of the caregiving environment appears to be at least as important as the tactile stimulation received during caregiving in organizing the reactivity and regulation of the infant's stress system.

STUDIES WITH HUMAN INFANTS AND CHILDREN

The animal data clearly show that early experiences can produce long-term alterations in CRH-HPA axis functioning, but do they have implications for human development? If they do, they suggest the following model. As discussed earlier, many components of early adverse life conditions (e.g., prenatal stress, malnutrition, toxin exposure, and illness) may affect the organization of the infant's CRH-HPA system. This may be reflected in the development of hyperresponsivity or hyporesponsivity, either of which may have deleterious, albeit different, consequences for emotional and physical health and development. Events embedded in day-to-day, mundane interactions between caregivers and infants should also affect the development of CRH-HPA system, and the impact of the adverse events listed previously should be more marked in the absence of a supportive, caregiving environment. Although the nature of human caregiver–infant interactions that foster the development of a less reactive and better regulated stress system are not known, based on the animal studies, both tactile stimulation and experience with response-contingent or controllable stimulation are likely to be important. Caregiving contexts that provide healthy doses of both may be expected to counteract or reduce the effects of early adversity on the CRH-HPA axis, while caregiving contexts that are deficient should promote the development of a less well-organized stress system, even in the absence of other adverse conditions.

As yet, there are relatively few data available to test this model. Several retrospective studies have found that adults who as children suffered loss of a parent or attachment figure have altered catecholamine and glucocorticoid activity as adults if, in addition, the rearing environment was hostile and rejecting (Breier, 1989; Luecken, 1998). Also, as noted in Dawson and Ashman (chap. 7, this volume), there is evidence that maternal depression during the 1st year of life is associated with reduced interactions between infant and mother and higher basal glucocorticoid levels several years later in childhood. There is also evidence that will be reviewed later suggesting that global deprivation in infancy and early childhood is associated with elevated levels of cortisol in children many years after removal from the depriving environment (Gunnar, Morison, Chisholm, & Schuder, 2000). Finally, there is a reasonably large amount of literature showing that activity of the CRH-HPA axis in infants and young children varies with characteristics of the caregiving environment and the security of the child's relationship with the caregiver (Gunnar, Brodersen, Nachmias, Buss, & Rigatuso, 1996b; Gunnar, Mangelsdorf, Larson, & Hertsgaard, 1989; Nachmias et al., 1996; Spangler & Schieche, 1994; Spangler & Schieche, 1998).

Postinstitutionalized, Romanian Children

In order to ascribe differences in CRH-HPA system functioning to early adverse experiences two conditions need to pertain. First, we need to have a clearly demarcated period of adversity. If the adverse conditions noted early in development persist, it is difficult to disentangle the effects of early experiences from the continued threats to well-being experienced by the child. Second, we need a control group similar to our experimental group in all but exposure to the adverse conditions. Internationally adopted, postinstitutionalized children offer an unfortunate, yet unique, opportunity to meet these two conditions. As Johnson discussed in chap. 4, this volume, in the last decade we have seen a marked increase in the number of young children adopted from institutions or orphanages into middle- to upper-middle class homes in the United States, Canada, and Western Europe. The conditions in the institutions range from horrific to adequate, but most fail to provide the level or quality of stimulation and interaction with caregivers that a child would experience growing up in a family. In the absence of a reliable, sensitive, and responsive caregiving system, other threats to well-being, including malnutrition, abuse, illness, and painful stimulation should all have their most marked effects on the development of stress reactivity and regulation.

My students and I have had the opportunity to examine cortisol levels in a group of internationally adopted children in a recent collaboration with Ames in

British Columbia. Ames and her students collected a sample of all of the children adopted from orphanages in Romania into homes in British Columbia (Ames, 1997). These children were adopted in the first 2 years after the fall of the Romanian communist regime. Forty-six of the children had been adopted after 8 months or more of institutional care (RO: Romanian Orphanage group). Thirty were destined for orphanage rearing, but because of when they were born relative to the political events in their country, were able to be adopted early, within 4 months of birth (EA: Early Adopted group). These children were presumably similar to the RO children with regard to prenatal and perinatal factors, but lacked the long-term exposure to institutional care. Finally, 46 children reared in their families of origin in British Columbia (CB: Canadian Born group) were matched to the RO children in age, sex, and adoptive family's socioeconomic level. As reported by Ames (1997), adoptive families of the EA children tended to be financially more secure and somewhat better educated than adoptive families of the RO children. However, as is typical in international adoption, families of both the RO and EA children were at least middle-class and most had some college education. Variation in education and socioeconomic class, however, were controlled when comparisons were made between RO and CB or Canadian-born control children.

Ames and her students (1997) collected behavioral data on these children after they had been with their adoptive families for approximately a year, and again several years later when the majority were 4- to 5-years-old. These data revealed few differences between the CB and EA children. In contrast, the RO showed significant cognitive deficits and emotional problems. Many of the RO children had low IQs (below 85), atypical attachment behavior, and clinical levels of behavior problems, particularly externalizing problems. The likelihood of problems increased with the length of institutionalization. Ames' data are highly consistent with findings by Rutter and his colleagues in their epidemiological study of Romanian children adopted in the United Kingdom (Rutter, 1996, 1998; Rutter et al., 1999). Similar to Ames' group, Rutter and his colleagues found that children adopted out of institutions before 6 months of age showed little evidence of persistent effects of institutional rearing, while those adopted beyond 6 months showed deficits, although they also showed remarkable recuperative abilities.

To some extent, the problems displayed by both the long-term institutionalized children in the UK study and the British Columbia study could be due to age at adoption and health at adoption, rather than length of institutional experience. These factors are difficult to disentangle. Children older at adoption had somewhat less time to acculturate prior to testing and may have been more challenged by tasks that required use of their new, English language. However, Ames (1997) noted that the RO children were equally delayed in cognitive tasks that were nonverbal as they were on verbal tasks. Rutter and his group (1988a) also examined whether growth retardation at the time of adoption, a proxy measure of health, predicted cognitive and behavioral functioning several years postadoption and found no significant association. Finally, prenatal and perinatal factors might account for the effects observed. However, the fact that the EA children in Ames' sample were drawn from the same group, who, were it not for the timing of their birth surrounding the fall of the communist regime, would have been institutionalized, tends to reduce the viability of attributing the children's problems to prenatal and perinatal factors. In all, the most parsimonious explanation of the behavioral findings is that length of institutionalization and the conditions the children were exposed to during their time in the institution affected their capacity to return to a normative developmental trajectory in the first years following adoption.

Six years after adoption, with the help of Ames and her students, we invited the parents to participate in a study of home salivary cortisol levels (Gunnar et al., 1999). Approximately two-thirds of the parents agreed to be contacted by our research group. From these families, we obtained complete cortisol data on 21 RO, 16 EA, and 29 CB children. Table 5.1 shows the age at adoption and age at cortisol sampling for this subsample. By design, the RO and EA groups differed on age at adoption. For the long-term institutionalized children, age at adoption ranged from 9 to 68 months, and averaged 22 months or 1.8 years. For the EA group, adoption age ranged from shortly after birth to 4 months and averaged 2.3 months. Baseline cortisol levels are not known to vary during the school-age years (Davis, Donzella, Krueger, & Gunnar, 1999; Dettling, Gunnar, & Donzella, 1999), thus in deciding on when to sample the children we were more concerned with equating time postadoption than in equating age of cortisol sampling. As can be seen, we were successful. Cortisol levels in the Romanian children were sampled when they had been in a family setting for approximately 6 to 7.5 years with a mean of 6.7 years for the RO group and 6.5 years for the EA group. Using this design, age at sampling necessarily varied for the RO and EA children. The CB children, however, were roughly comparable in age to the RO children.

The Ames group had completed their second session of behavioral testing on these children between 2 and 3 years before we obtained the cortisol data. We ex-

TABLE 5.1
Sample Demographics of Postinstitutionalized Romanian Children Adopted Into Canada

	RO	EA	CB
	9–68 mos	0–4 mos	NA
n	21/46	16/29	29/46
Age	8.5 (1 year)	6.7 (.3 year)	7.8 (.7 year)
Years postadoption	6.7 (.4 year)	6.5 (.3 year)	NA
Stanford Binet IV	84.2 (16.3)	104.3 (10.2)	106.6 (7.7)

Note. n refers to the number of children participating in the cortisol collection, relative to the total number in Ames' sample. RO = Romanian Orphans, adopted after 9-68 months of institutionalization; EA = Early Adopted, adopted after 4 or less months of institutionalization; CB = Canadian Born controls. Stanford Binet IV reflects full-scale score from testing an average of 3 years prior to saliva sampling. Means and (standard deviations).

amined these behavioral data to determine whether our subsample was comparable to the total sample. These data also help characterize the children we were able
to test. Similar to the total sample, the RO children in our subsample had lower
IQs (although, of course, IQ may have changed in the years between the Ames'
testing and our sampling) with 10 of our 22 children exhibiting IQs below 85. The
range of IQ was quite marked, however, with the highest being 110. Ames found
that about one-third of the total sample of RO children exhibited three or more serious problems. With 21 RO children in our subsample, we should have had about
7 children drawn from this subgroup. We had 9. Thus, although the families self-
selected to take part in this cortisol study, we seem to have obtained a group that
was roughly comparable to the total sample. As the Ames sample consisted of all
of the children in British Columbia adopted from Romanian orphanages in the
early years of this decade, despite our relatively small sample size, the results
should be reasonably representative.

Parents collected saliva samples for cortisol determination on 3 days when the
children were not in school. They were instructed to collect the samples 20–30
minutes after the children awoke in the morning before they had breakfast, at
noon before lunch, and in the evening within 30 minutes of bedtime. Sampling
times varied among the children, but did not differ across the groups. Following
standard procedures in studies of cortisol, we log transformed the cortisol data to
normalize the distributions, and averaged the samples across the 3 days. Using
Cronbach's alpha, we then examined the reliability of these measures. The reliability of these assessments tended to be low for Wakeup (.44) and Noon (.43) estimates, but were moderately high and acceptable for Evening (.72) estimates. We
then examined differences among the groups using repeated measures ANOVA.
The results are shown in Fig. 5.3. All three groups showed the expected circadian rhythm in cortisol production. High levels were obtained in the morning
around the time of awakening and decreasing levels were noted over the day. Similar to the behavioral data, the EA and CB children did not differ in cortisol levels,
despite their presumed differences in prenatal and perinatal conditions. In addition,
while the RO children had a higher mean cortisol level, many were still well within the range of values shown by EA and CB children. This is also consistent with
the behavioral data reported by Ames and her colleagues (1997). We were struck,
however, that while there were many RO children within the EA and CB range,
none of the RO children had levels in the lowest (e.g. bottom one-third) of the control children's distributions. Thus, both the average and the entire distribution of the
RO children's cortisol values appeared to have been shifted upwards.

To examine further the association between cortisol levels and institutional
rearing, we correlated length of time in an institution with morning, noon, and
evening cortisol levels for the RO children. Evening levels, in particular, were
higher the longer the children spent in institutional care (see Fig. 5.4). Remarkably, RO children with the longest institutional experience had evening levels that
were close to the average of the wakeup or peak levels shown by EA and CB children. The many children in the RO group with low IQs might have produced this

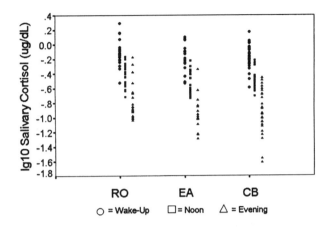

FIG. 5.3. Salivary cortisol levels in children adopted after 8 months or more in a Romanian orphanage (RO), less than 4 months of orphanage experience (EA), or Canadian-born (CB) family-reared children. Samples were obtained 6 years after adoption for RO and EA children. Individual values are reflected at wakeup, noon, and evening. RO children had levels that were significantly higher than EA and CB children. This was particularly true for evening cortisol levels. From "Cortisol levels in orphanage-reared Romanian children 6 years after adoption," by M. R. Gunnar, S. J. Morison, K. Chisholm, and M. Schuder, 2000. Manuscript in preparation.

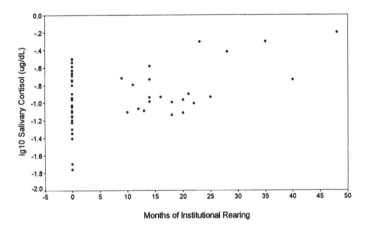

FIG. 5.4. Evening levels of salivary cortisol for CB children all with 0 institutional experience, and RO children all with 8 months or more of experience in an institution prior to adoption. Length of institutionalization was significantly associated with evening cortisol levels (partial $r = .48$, $p < .05$, controlling statistically for total IQ). From "Cortisol levels in orphanage-reared Romanian children 6 years after adoption," by M. R. Gunnar, S. J. Morison, K. Chisholm, and M. Schuder, 2000. Manuscript in preparation.

182

effect. To rule this out, we recomputed the evening cortisol correlation controlling statistically for IQ as measured by Ames' group. The partial correlation was still significant (partial $r = 0.48$, $p = .05$). Thus, the longer the children were institutionalized, the higher their cortisol levels, particularly in the evening when cortisol should be approaching the nadir or lowest point in the daily cycle. Higher evening levels of cortisol may be a noteworthy finding, as the failure to bring cortisol levels to near zero concentrations near the nadir of the daily cycle is seen as highly indicative of dysregulation of the CRH-HPA system.

We do not know, of course, that the effects we observed were due to an inadequately stimulating and responsive caregiving environment early in development. Malnutrition, frequent illness, and prolonged periods of discomfort, likely also contributed to these findings. In addition, the challenge of making the transition from the institution in Romania to a family in British Columbia, with all the novelty and strangeness this must have entailed, may have produced elevations in cortisol that could have affected the long-term functioning of the CRH-HPA system. Finally, in none of the animal studies reviewed earlier were baseline levels particularly affected, although theoretically, with sufficient adverse stimulation baseline should be elevated. It is important to note that none of the animal paradigms have combined inadequate caregiving, malnutrition, low stimulation, and physical abuse, as may have been experienced by some of these children. Thus, it is likely that these postinstitutionalized children experienced more extreme adversity in early rearing than has been, or could ethically be, imposed in the animal paradigms. In fact, there are a few more extreme animal paradigms in which elevated baseline levels have been noted (e.g., Gilles, Shultz, & Baram, 1996). We still do not know, however, whether changes in postadoption cortisol levels were due, in any way, to alterations in CRH-HPA axis functioning while the children were still in the institutions. In order to ascribe the effects to events occurring within the institutions, it is essential that HPA axis activity be examined in children still living in those institutions.

Cortisol Levels for Children in Institutional Care

There is relatively little information on activity of the HPA axis among children living in institutional environments. The most complete information comes from a study conducted by Carlson and colleagues on 2- to 3-year-old children living in a Leagane or infant home in Romania (Carlson, et al., 1995; Carlson & Earls, 1997). Carlson obtained salivary cortisol samples on these children over 2 days when the children woke up (between 7 and 8 a.m.), at noon before lunch, and in the late afternoon–early evening (5 to 7 p.m.). Their levels were compared to Romanian children who attended a center-based, full-day childcare program run by the same government organization. The childcare children were sampled at comparable times on 2 childcare days and 2 weekend days when they were with their families all day. One of the most striking results reported by Carlson was the lack of a strong circadian rhythm in the Leagane or orphanage children. Many of the Leagane children had relatively low wakeup cortisol values and showed their peak or highest cortisol level at noon. While not particularly elevated, cortisol levels in orphanage were associated with developmental delay as assessed using the Bayley (1993) Scales. All of the Leagane or orphanage children were delayed to some degree, with many being nearly a year delayed in both physical and mental development. Higher cortisol levels were associated with greater developmental delays. Indeed, the children showing the least delay had cortisol levels that were quite low across the day. If these associations reflect a causal relationship between CRH-HPA axis functioning and developmental delay, the direction of effect can still not be determined. However, if no relationship had been found it would call into question the proposed model.

The children in Carlson's sample had been part of an experimental intervention study when they were between approximately 9 and 22 months of age. As part of that study they were randomly assigned to Intervention or Control conditions. The Control children experienced the usual care, which consisted of constantly changing caregivers, a roughly 1:20 ratio of caregivers to children, and low stimulation. Children in the Intervention condition were assigned to one constant caregiver. This person provided their care from 9 a.m. to 5 p.m. on weekdays. Each caregiver had 4 infants in her care and the caregivers were trained to stimulate the babies with toys. Over the 13 months of the intervention, despite being fed the same meals and spending nights and weekends under care conditions similar to the Control group, the Intervention group grew better and showed significant catch-up in behavioral development as assessed using the Denver Developmental Scales. Approximately 6 months before Carlson and colleagues obtained the cortisol measures, funding for the intervention ran out, and all the children reverted to the standard care provided by the institution. Although few of the benefits of the intervention persisted, M. Carlson (personal communication, October, 1998) noted that Control children tended to have higher cortisol levels, particularly at noon.

The results from the Romanian Leagane are quite similar to pilot data we have obtained on 11 children, 3 to 51 months of age, living in what might be considered a model orphanage or Baby Home in the Russian Federation (Kroupina, Gunnar, & Johnson, 1997). Thus Carlson's data were probably not specific to Romanian institutions. In the Russian Baby Home, the children were housed in smaller groups than in the Romanian institution studied by Carlson. Beginning at 3 months of age when they entered this particular, and unusual, Russian Baby Home, the children were provided with a daily routine that included massages, music classes, swimming classes, herbal therapy, and dance (see Johnson, chap. 4, this volume). Each child was assigned to one adult who was that child's special person. This adult provided additional care and attention, often taking the child home with her on weekends or including the child in family vacations. On a recent trip to this Baby Home, a Russian graduate student in the Institute of Child Development, Maria Kroupina, obtained salivary cortisol samples from a number of these children. As in the Carlson study, the samples were taken at 8 a.m., noon before lunch, and late in the afternoon, around 4 p.m. The children Kroupina sampled were chosen simply because they were available. We have little background information on the 11 children, aged 3 months to 4.5 years, although all had been in this Baby Home or another institution for most of their lives. Despite the difference in the structure of this Russian Baby Home and Carlson's Romanian Leagane, these Russian Baby Home children showed a blunted circadian rhythm (see Fig. 5.5). Samples Kroupina obtained on one Russian preschool-aged child who was living with his parents, however, conformed to the expected circadian pattern (0.30 μg/dL at 9 a.m, 0.21 μg/dL at noon, and 0.15 μg/dL at 4 p.m.).

Remarkably, the blunting of the daily rhythm in cortisol production may not be peculiar to human infants and young children living in institutional settings. In a study of surrogate-peer-reared rhesus infants, we noted a very similar finding (Boyce, Champoux, Suomi, & Gunnar, 1995). These rhesus infants live in a nursery for the first month after birth. In the nursery, they are hand-fed several times a day by human caretakers. They then are housed with a cloth surrogate in individual cages, although they are put into playgroups of similar-aged peers for several hours each day. Boyce et al. (1995) collected multiple days of saliva samples from 5 such infants when they were around 5 to 7 months of age (comparable to 20 to 28 months of development for humans). The daily production of cortisol was low early in the morning shortly after lights-on, tended to rise over the morning hours, and fall in the afternoon. Subsequent work has shown that the rise over the morning hours is likely due to cortisol responses to disturbances that are common in any

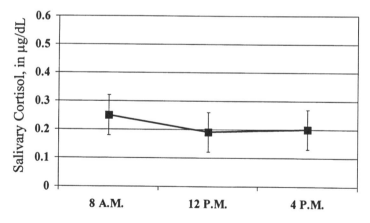

FIG. 5.5   Salivary cortisol levels for 11 children, ages 3 months to 4.5 years, living in an institution in Russia. Repeated measures analysis failed to yield evidence of a significant change in levels over the daytime hours ($p > .10$). Bars reflect standard deviations. Unpublished raw data, M. Kroupina, M. Gunnar, and D. Johnson, Institute of Child Development, University of Minnesota.

animal facility during the morning hours (e.g. cage cleaning, the setting up of experiments, and humans talking in the adjacent treatment room). The more typical decrease in cortisol over the morning hours and somewhat higher early morning cortisol levels were obtained when, through design, activity in the animal facility was reduced to a minimum (Champoux, Shannon, Gunnar, & Suomi, 1996). Thus, unlike mother-reared infant rhesus who are known to show no increase in cortisol to even fairly threatening, chaotic events (e.g. capture) if they can maintain contact with their mothers (Coe, Weiner, & Levine, 1993), these surrogate-reared infants appear to respond to even minor disturbances with elevations in cortisol.

Returning to Carlson's Romanian data, the comparisons she made of the Leagane or orphanage children with the childcare children revealed that Romanian children, when they were with their families, showed the expected circadian variation in cortisol. Nonetheless, these children, like the Leagane children, showed a blunted daily rhythm in cortisol when they are sampled at childcare. Clearly, children do not have to grow up in an institution in order to show the blunting of the daily cortisol rhythm when they are in group-care.

Sensitivity of the HPA Axis to Caregiving Contexts in Early Childhood

The Romanian childcare center was not assessed using measures of childcare quality. However, the caregivers in the center, like the caregivers in the Leagane, had no training in child development. Eating, napping, and toileting were highly regimented. There were few toys available, and playtime consisted of having the children sit at tables after which they were each handed a toy. While the quality of childcare may influence activity of the HPA axis (see Legendre & Kortinus, 1996), we have evidence from center-based childcare contexts in the United States suggesting that the altering of cortisol production over the day is seen even when quality indices are quite high. Figure 5.6 shows salivary cortisol levels in children from two center-based childcare programs in Minneapolis, Minnesota (Tout, de Haan, Kipp-Campbell, & Gunnar, 1998). Standard indices of quality were assessed for these centers (Arnett, 1989; Harms & Clifford, 1980) and both scored above average, with one scoring at ceiling on nearly all scales. The cortisol values shown are for 10–11 a.m. and 3–4 p.m. Rather than decreasing between these times as would be expected, cortisol levels rise from morning to afternoon. The rise differed by center, with a larger increase being observed at the center with poorer quality indices.

The children in our childcare study were between 3 and 5 years of age. Unlike in the Carlson et al. (1995) study, we did not have home data from days when the children were not at daycare. These data were obtained in a second study in which we sampled children on two days at childcare at 10 a.m. and 4 p.m. using the center that scored near ceiling on the quality indices (Dettling et al., 1999). We then had the parents sample these children at comparable times on weekend days. We also included data from older children who were attending full-day, center-based

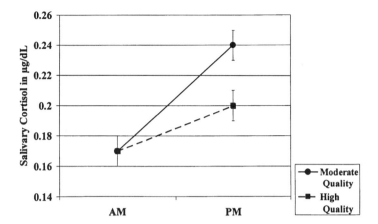

FIG. 5.6.   Salivary cortisol levels in children in two full-day childcare centers. The centers differed slightly in standard quality assessments from moderate quality to high quality. Values depicted are the average of median cortisol concentrations obtained midmorning and midafternoon. Each child's median score was based on between 10 and 20 days of sampling (*M* = 16 days). Bars reflect standard errors of the mean. From "Social behavior correlates of adrenocortical activity in daycare: Gender differences and time-of-day effects," by K. Tout, M. de Haan, E. Kipp-Campbell, and M. R. Gunnar, 1998, *Child Development, 69*(5), p. 1253. Copyright 1998 by the Society for Research in Child Development, Inc. Adapted with permission.

care during summer months when school was not in session. These data are shown in Fig. 5.7. The results of this study showed us that it was primarily the 3- and 4-year-old children who showed the rising pattern of cortisol over the day at childcare. By 5 years of age, the children in the preschool center exhibited levels that were comparable to the 6-year-old children in the school-age center. By 7 to 8 years of age, most of the children showed a clear decrease in cortisol from morning to afternoon when at childcare. Furthermore, home levels showed the expected circadian decrease for most of the children, regardless of age.

We do not know what it is about being in group or institutional care that influences the pattern of daily cortisol production and elevations in cortisol over home levels later in the day. The ubiquity of the effect, being observed in institutionally reared children, home-reared children, and rhesus infants, and its emergence in contexts differing markedly in many aspects of quality, suggests that the infant primate's CRH-HPA axis is highly sensitive to characteristics differing between these contexts and the home environment. Furthermore, sensitivity to these context effects seems marked in early childhood, declining by the school-age years. At this point, there is no evidence that this blunting or altering of the daily pattern of cortisol production and the elevation over home levels observed in the afternoon in group-care settings have any effect on children's development. Cer-

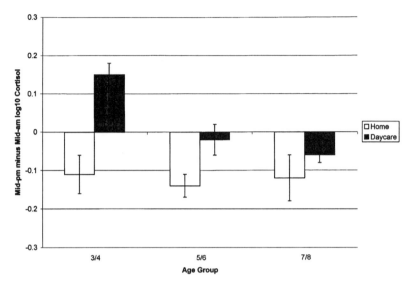

FIG. 5.7. Changes in salivary cortisol concentrations from midmorning to midafternoon at home and in full-day childcare. A positive value reflects a rise in level from morning to afternoon, while a negative value reflects the expected circadian decrease from morning to afternoon. Bars reflect *SEM*. Adapted from *Psychoneuroendocrinology, 24*(5) by A. Dettling, M. R. Gunnar, and B. Donzella, "Cortisol levels of young children in full-day childcare centers: Relations with age and temperament," p. 529. Copyright (1999), with permission from Elsevier Science.

tainly, for children who live at home but attend childcare, these effects appear transitory. The expected pattern of cortisol production over the day is readily observed when the children are with their families all day.

We also do not know what aspects of these childcare settings produce the rising pattern of hormone production. Group-care settings confront the young child with the need to manage interactions with multiple same-aged peers. They also involve the lack (in institutional rearing) or absence (in childcare) of the children's primary attachment figure(s). These factors, or others yet to be identified, may be involved. There are no studies examining how the number of peers or the duration of peer contact each day may influence activity of the HPA axis. There are studies, however, of how the quality or security of children's attachment relationships is associated with responsivity of cortisol to stressful events.

Attachment Security and Cortisol Response

A number of studies have now shown that secure attachment relationships are associated with inhibition of elevations in cortisol to potentially distressing events. Many, but not all, of these studies have used the *strange situation* itself as the stressor. As recently reviewed by Spangler and Schieche (1998), regardless of whether the child is distressed during the strange situation procedures or not, elevations in cortisol are not seen among those children classified as securely attached. Indeed, the pattern typically observed is one of decreasing cortisol levels from the beginning to 30 minutes after the end of the procedure. In contrast, children classified as insecurely attached, especially if they are highly distressed during the procedures, show a rising pattern of hormone production. In addition, two of the three studies examining disorganized patterns of attachment behavior, patterns often observed in maltreated infants, have found that these children produce larger increases in cortisol than do other children classified as insecurely attached.

Using the strange situation to assess both attachment security and the relations between security and hormone production somewhat confounds these two measures. Of greater interest are studies in which attachment security has been used to predict hormone responses to other threatening, potentially stressful events. Elevations in cortisol to stressors have been shown to decrease markedly over the first year of life. Using well-child physical exams followed by inoculations for childhood immunizations, several research groups have shown that it is difficult to observe increases in cortisol by the second year (see Fig. 5.8). This is true, despite the fact that children show intense behavioral distress when given their inoculations (Gunnar, Broderson,

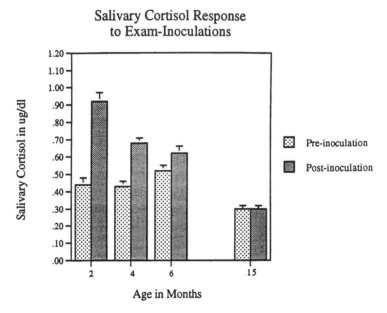

FIG. 5.8.   Salivary cortisol levels before and after a physical examination and inoculation examined longitudinally for infants at 2, 4, 6, and 15 months. Bars reflect *SEMs*. From "Dampening of adrenocortical responses during infancy: Normative changes and individual differences," by M. R. Gunnar, L. Brodersen, K. Krueger, and J. Rigatuso, 1996, *Child Development, 67,* p. 882. Copyright 1996 by the Society for Research in Child Development, Inc. Adapted with permission.

Krueger, & Rigatuso, 1996b; Jacobson & Bihun, 1994; Lewis & Ramsay, 1995; Ramsay & Lewis, 1994). It is perhaps noteworthy that the inhibition of the cortisol response emerges most strongly between 6 and 12 months, the period when children are organizing security-seeking behavior around one or more attachment figures. Some children, however, fail to show the inhibition or buffering of the cortisol response. In a longitudinal study of children followed during their 2-, 4-, 6-, and 15-month exam-inoculations and assessed at 18-months in the strange situation we found the following (Gunnar et al., 1996a). Nearly all of the children failed to show elevations in cortisol at 15 months to the exam-inoculation procedure, in marked contrast to what was observed in the 2- to 6-month testing. As in most middle-class samples, nearly 75% of the children were classified as securely attached. The few children who failed to exhibit this buffering of the CRH-HPA system were significantly more likely to have an insecure attachment relationship with the parent who accompanied them at 15 months during the doctor's visit, than were children who exhibited a buffering or lack of cortisol response.

Likewise, in Nachmias et al. (1996), we found that 18-month-olds who responded fearfully to a series of strange, novel events were likely to show elevations in cortisol only if they were insecurely attached to the parent who accompanied them and helped them to manage their emotional responses to those events (see Fig. 5.9). No differences in fearful or wary behavior was noted as a function of attachment security. These data tend to be more consistent with the view that secure relationships buffer the CRH-HPA axis in early children, rather than the view that temperamental differences in fearfulness or inhibition produce the differences in attachment classification, elevations in cortisol, or both, to strange and potentially threatening events.

In both the exam-inoculation (Gunnar et al., 1996a) and Nachmias et al. (1996), there was evidence that parental behavior was associated with the organization of a secure relationship and with the buffering or inhibiting of cortisol response for distressed or fearful children. In the exam-inoculation study (Gunnar et al., 1996a), children who were classified as securely attached at 18 months had parents who had been more sensitive and responsive to them during the doctor exams and inoculations at 2, 4, 6, and 15 months. In Nachmias et al. (1996), parents of children classified as securely attached were less likely to try to make their fearful toddler approach and act bold in the presence of the strange events. Parents of securely attached toddlers followed their children's lead more and were more supportive of the child's own attempts to manage their emotional reactions to the fear-eliciting situation.

Thus, similar to the nonhuman primate data, it appears that a sensitive and responsive caregiving system provides a powerful HPA-axis buffer for the human infant and toddler. With this system in place, the young child appears to be able to experience conditions that elicit behavioral distress and that produce inhibition of approach or fearfulness, without at the same time producing increases in glucocorticoids. We cannot tell from these data, of course, whether the variations in

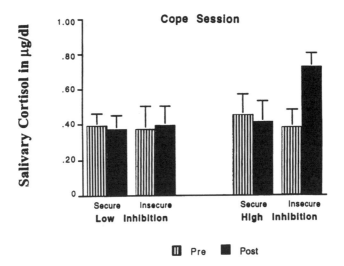

FIG. 5.9. Salivary cortisol concentrations in 18-month-olds before and after a session in which they had to cope with 3 strange, potentially fear-eliciting events. Elevations in cortisol were noted only for children who were fearful or inhibited during the session and who were also in insecure attachment relationships with the parent who accompanied them. Bars reflect *SEM*s. From "Behavioral inhibition and stress reactivity: The moderating role of attachment security," by M. Nachmias, M. R. Gunnar, S. Mangelsdorf, R. H. Parritz, & K. Buss, 1996, *Child Development, 67*, p. 516. Copyright 1996 by the Society for Research in Child Development, Inc. Reprinted with permission.

sensitivity and responsiveness associated with the normative variations in attachment security will have any long-term effects on the reactivity and regulation of the child's stress system. However, as shown by Dawson and Ashman (chap. 7, this volume), significant alterations in responsiveness, as noted in some clinically depressed mothers, may have lasting effects.

SUMMARY AND CONCLUSIONS

In this chapter, I have argued that many adverse conditions in early life may affect neurobehavioral development, at least in part, through effects on the development of the stress neuraxis. Research, primarily in animals, has shown that prenatal, postnatal, or both, exposure to a variety of conditions that threaten homeostasis or organism well-being (e.g., prenatal stress, toxin exposure, malnutrition, and painful or noxious stimulation) affect activity of stress-sensitive systems. These effects, which include elevations in catecholamines and glucocorticoids, are often essential for survival, but may have long-term impacts on development. In animal models, effects have been observed in heightened fearfulness and physiological vulnerability to stressful events encountered in adulthood.

Importantly, again in research using rodents and nonhuman primates, the caregiving context appears to both mediate and moderate many of the effects of early adversity. Adequate caregiving typically can often reverse or reduce the impact of early adverse conditions on stress physiology. Similarly, improving the quality of stimulation provided in the caregiving context tends to shape a less reactive behavioral and physiological stress system, while disrupting the quality of caregiving produces a more hyperresponsive stress system. Thus, in rodents and monkeys, stimulation provided by the caregiver early in life seems to shape responsivity of the stress system and to exacerbate, if inadequate, and modify, if adequate, the impact of adverse conditions.

As yet, there are relatively few human studies with which to evaluate the applicability of the model to human development. Most of the available data deal with the role of the caregiving context in modifying activity of the CRH-HPA system as reflected in peripheral measures of cortisol. These data are largely consistent with the model based on the animal work. Adverse conditions (malnutrition, illness, and possibly abuse) experienced by children in institutions where they lack adequate caregiving are associated with elevated cortisol levels years after removal from these institutions. Group-care settings are associated with altered daily cortisol patterns in younger (2- to 4-year-olds), but not older (5- to 9-year-olds), that rise to levels higher than those seen at home over the day. Secure attachment relationships tend to buffer or prevent elevations in cortisol among toddlers, even when the toddler is behaviorally distressed.

If the proposed model proves to apply to human development, it suggests that a variety of early adverse conditions may affect development, in part, through common stress-system mediated pathways. It also suggests that early adverse life events may foster vulnerability to stress-related conditions later in life. As with all research on human infants and children, the research on stress physiology is largely based on correlations. Isolating causal relationships remains a daunting task. However, the consistency of the findings with the experimentally rigorous animal research is encouraging and argues that this approach may indeed provide insights into the pathways through which early adverse conditions affect human biobehavioral development.

ACKNOWLEDGMENTS

The author wishes to thank Bonny Donzella for her help in manuscript preparation. This review was supported by an Independent Scientist Research Award from the National Institute of Mental Health (MH00946).

REFERENCES

Ames, E. (1997). *The Development of Romanian Orphanage Children Adopted to Canada* (Final Report to the National Welfare Grants Program: Human Resources Development Canada). Burnaby, British Columbia, Canada: Simon Fraser University.

Andrews, M. W., & Rosenblum, L. A. (1994). The development of affiliative and agonistic social patterns in differentially reared monkeys. *Child Development, 65*(5), 1398–1404.

Anisman, H., Zaharia, M. D., Meaney, M. J., & Merali, Z. (1998). Do early-life events permanently alter behavioral and hormonal responses to stressors? *International Journal of Developmental Neuroscience.* Vol. 16(3–4), 149–164.

Arnett, J. (1989). Caregivers in day-care centers: Does training matter? *Journal of Applied Developmental Psychology, 10*, 541–552.

Averill, J. R. (1973). Personal control over aversive stimuli and its relationship to stress. *Psychological Bulletin, 80*(4), 286–303.

Barbazanges, A., Piazza, P. V., Moal, M. L., & Maccari, S. (1996). Maternal glucocorticoid secretion mediates long-term effects of prenatal stress. *The Journal of Neuroscience, 16*(12), 3943–3949.

Bayart, F., Hayashi, K. T., Faull, K. F., Barchas, J. D., & Levine, S. (1990). Influence of maternal proximity on behavioral and psychological responses to separation in infant rhesus monkeys (Macaca mulatta). *Behavioral Neuroscience, 104*(1), 98–107.

Bayley, N. (1993). *Bayley Scales of Infant Development* (2nd ed.). San Antonio, TX: The Psychological Corporation.

Besedovsky, H., Del Rey, A., Sorkin, E., & Dinarello, C. A. (1986). Immunoregulatory feedback between interluekin-1 and glucocorticoid hormones. *Science, 233*, 652–654.

Bohus, B., de Kloet, E. R., & Veldhuis, H. D. (1982). Adrenal steroids and behavioral adaptation: Relationship to brain corticoid receptors. In D. Granten & D. W. Pfaff (Eds.), *Current topics in neuroendocrinology* (pp. 107–148). Berlin, Germany: Springer-Verlag.

Borysenko, J. (1984). Stress and coping, and the immune system. In J. D. Matarazzo, S. M. Weiss, J. A. Herd, N. E. Miller, & S. M. Weiss (Eds.), *Behavioral health* (pp. 248–260). New York: Wiley.

Boyce, W. T., Champoux, M., Suomi, S. J., & Gunnar, M. R. (1995). Salivary cortisol in nursery-reared Rhesus monkeys: Reactivity to peer interactions and altered circadian activity. *Developmental Psychobiology, 28*(5), 257–267.

Breier, A. (1989). Experimental approaches to human stress research: Assessment of neurobiological mechanisms of stress in volunteers and psychiatric patients. *Biological Psychiatry, 26*, 438–462.

Breier, A., Albus, M., Pickar, D., Zahn, T. P., Wolkowitz, O. M., & Paul, S. M. (1987). Controllable and uncontrollable stress in humans: Alterations in mood and neuroendocrine and psychophysiological function. *American Journal of Psychiatry, 144*(11), 1419–1425.

Brooke, S. M., de Haas-Johnson, A. M., Kaplan, J. R., & Sapolsky, R. M. (1994). Characterization of mineralocorticoid and glucocorticoid receptors in primate brain. *Brain Research, 637*, 303–307.

Cacioppo, J. T. (1994). Social neuroscience: Autonomic, neuroendocrine, and immune responses to stress. *Psychophysiology, 31*, 113–128.

Caldji, C., Tannenbaum, B., Sharma, S., Francis, D., Plotsky, P. M., & Meaney, M. J. (1998). Maternal care during infancy regulates the development of neural systems mediating the expression of fearfulness in the rat. *Proceedings of the National Academy of Sciences of the United States of America, 95*(9), 5445–5340.

Carlson, M., Dragomir, C., Earls, F., Farrell, M., Macovei, O., Nystrom, P., & Sparling, J. (1995). Effects of social deprivation on cortisol regulation in institutionalized Romanian infants. *Society of Neuroscience Abstracts, 21*, 524.

Carlson, M., & Earls, F. (1997). Psychological and neuroendocrinological sequelae of early social deprivation in institutionalized children in Romania. *Annals of the New York Academy of Sciences, 807*, 419–426.

Champoux, M., Byrne, E., DeLizio, R., & Suomi, S. (1992). Motherless mothers revisited: Rhesus maternal behavior and rearing history. *Primates, 33*(2), 251–255.

Champoux, M., Shannon, C., Gunnar, M., & Suomi, S. J. (1996, August). *Minor disturbances mask the circadian decrease in salivary cortisol in nursery-reared rhesus infants.* Paper presented at the Poster at the American Society of Primatologists, Madison, WI.

Champoux, M., Zanker, D., & Levine, S. (1993). Food search demand effort effects on behavior and cortisol in adult female squirrel monkeys. *Physiology and Behavior, 54*(6), 1091–1097.

Chrousos, G. P., & Gold, P. W. (1992). The concepts of stress and stress system disorders: Overview of physical and behavioral homeostasis. *Journal of the American Medical Association, 267*(9), 1244–1252.

Clarke, A. S., Wittwer, D. J., Abbott, D. H., & Schneider, M. L. (1994). Long-term effects of prenatal stress on HPA axis activity in juvenile rhesus monkeys. *Developmental Psychobiology, 27*(5), 257–269.

Coe, C. L., Lubach, G., & Ershler, W. B. (1989). Immunological consequences of maternal separation in infant primates. In M. Lewis & J. Worobey (Eds.), *Infant stress and coping* (pp. 65–91). San Francisco: Jossey-Bass.

Coe, C. L., Rosenberg, L. T., Fischer, M., & Levine, S. (1987). Psychological factors capable of preventing the inhibition of antibody responses in separated infant monkeys. *Child Development, 58,* 1420–1430.

Coe, C. L., Weiner, S. G., & Levine, S. (1993). Psychoendocrine responses of mother and infant monkeys to disturbance and separation. In L. A. Rosenblum & H. Moltz (Eds.), *Symbiosis in parent-offspring interactions* (pp. 189–214). New York: Plenum.

Coplan, J. D., Andrews, M. W., Rosenblum L. A., Owens, M. J., Friedman, S., Gorman, J. M., & Nemeroff, C. B. (1996). Persistent elevations of cerebrospinal fluid concentrations of corticotropin-releasing factor in adult nonhuman primates exposed to early-life stressors: Implications for the pathophysiology of mood and anxiety disorders. *Proceedings of the National Academy of Sciences of the United States of America, 93,* 1619–1623.

Coplan, J. D., Rosenblum, L. A., & Gorman, J. M. (1995). Primate models of anxiety: Longitudinal perspectives. *Pediatric Clinics of North America, 18,* 727–743.

Davidson, R. J. (1994). Asymmetric brain function, affective style, and psychopathology: The role of early experience and plasticity. *Development and Psychopathology, 6,* 741–758.

Davis, E. P., Donzella, B., Krueger, W. K., & Gunnar, M. R. (1999). The start of a new school year: Individual differences in salivary cortisol response in relation to child temperament. *Developmental Psychobiology, 35*(3), 188–196.

de Kloet, E. R. (1991). Brain corticosteroid receptor balance and homeostatic control. *Frontiers in Neuroendocrinology, 12*(2), 95–164.

de Kloet, R., & De Wied, D. (1980). The brain as target tissue for hormones of pituitary origin: Behavioral and biochemical studies. In L. Martini & W. F. Ganong (Eds.), *Frontiers in neuroendocrinology* (Vol. 6, pp. 157–201). New York: Raven.

de Kloet, E. R., & Reul, J. M. (1987). Feedback action and tonic influence of corticosteroids on brain function: A concept arising from the heterogeneity of brain receptor systems. *Psychoneuroendocrinology, 12*(2), 83–105.

de Kloet, E. R., Rots, N. Y., van den Berg, D. T., & Oitzl, M. S. (1994). Brain mineralocorticoid receptor function. *Annals of the New York Academy of Sciences, 746,* 8–20.

Denenberg, V. H. (1999). Commentary: Is maternal stimulation the mediator of the handling effects in infancy? *Developmental Psychobiology, 34*(1), 1–3.

Denenberg, V. H., Brumaghim, J. T., Haltmeyer, G. C., & Zarrow, M. X. (1967). Increased adrenocortical activity in the neonatal rat following handling. *Endocrinology, 81,* 1047–1052.

Denenberg, V. H., Rosenberg, K. M., Paschke, R., Hess, J. L., Zarrow, M. X., & Levine, S. (1968). Plasma corticosterone levels as a function of cross-species fostering and species differences. *Endocrinology, 83,* 900–902.

Dettling, A., Gunnar, M. R., & Donzella, B. (1999). Cortisol levels of young children in full-day child-care centers: Relations with age and temperament. *Psychoneuroendocrinology, 24*(5), 519–536.

Dettling, A., Pryce, C. R., Martin, R. D., & Döbeli, M. (1998). Physiological responses to parental separation and a strange situation are related to parental care received in juvenile Goeldi's monkeys (Callimico goeldii). *Developmental Psychobiology, 33,* 21–31.

Diamond, D. M., & Rose, G. M. (1994). Stress impairs LTP and hippocampal-dependent memory. *Annals of the New York Academy of Sciences, 746,* 411–414.

Diorio, D., Viau, V., & Meaney, M. J. (1993). The role of the medial-prefrontal cortex (cingulate gyrus) in the regulation of hypothalamic-pituitary-adrenal responses to stress. *The Journal of Neuroscience, 13*, 3839–3847.

Engle, B. T. (1985). Stress is a noun! No, a verb! No, an adjective. In T. Field, P. McCabe, & N. Sneiderman (Eds.), *Stress and coping* (Vol. 1, pp. 3–12). Hillsdale, NJ: Lawrence Erlbaum Associates.

Feldman, S., Conforti, N., & Weidenfeld, J. (1995). Limbic pathways and hypothalamic neurotransmitters mediating adrenocortical responses to neural stimuli. *Neuroscience and Biobehavioral Reviews, 19*(2), 235–240.

Field, T. (1995). Massage therapy for infants and children. *Journal of Developmental and Behavioral Pediatrics, 16*(2), 105–111.

Fitzgerald, M., & Anand, K. J. S. (1993). The developmental neuroanatomy and neurophysiology of pain. In N. Schechter, C. Berde, and M. Yaster (Eds.), *Pain management in infants, children and adolescents* (pp. 11–32). Baltimore: Williams & Williams.

Fulke, C., Lorenz, J. G., Long, J., Champoux, M., Suomi, S. J., & Higley, J. D. (1998). *Rearing experiences and plasma cortisol as early risk factors for alcohol consumption in non-human primates.* Manuscript submitted for publication.

Gilles, E. E., Shultz, L., & Baram, T. Z. (1996). Abnormal corticosterone regulation in an immature rate model of chronic stress. *Pediatric Neurology, 15*, 114–119.

Glass, D. C., & Singer, J. W. (1972). *Urban stress: Experiments on noise and social stressors.* New York: Academic Press.

Grigoriadis, D. E., Insel, T. R., Heroux, J. A., & De Souza, E. B. (1993). Corticotropin-releasing hormone receptors and the developing nervous system. In I. S. Zagon & P. J. McLaughlin (Eds.), *Growth factors and hormones* (Vol. 1, pp. 147–161). New York: Chapman & Hall.

Gunnar, M. R., Broderson, L., Krueger, K., & Rigatuso, J. (1996a). Dampening of adrenocortical responses during infancy: Normative changes and individual differences. *Child Development, 67*, 877–889.

Gunnar, M. R., Brodersen, L., Nachmias, M., Buss, K., & Rigatuso, J. (1996b). Stress reactivity and attachment security. *Developmental Psychobiology, 29*(3), 191–204.

Gunnar, M. R., Gonzales, C., & Levine, S. (1981). Behavioral and pituitary-adrenal responses during a prolonged separation period in infant Rhesus maques. *Psychoneuroendocrinology, 6*(1), 65–75.

Gunnar, M. R., Larson, M., Hertsgaard, L., Harris, M., & Brodersen, L. (1992). The stressfulness of separation among 9-month-old infants: Effects of social context variables and infant temperament. *Child Development, 63*, 290–303.

Gunnar, M. R., Mangelsdorf, S., Larson, M., & Hertsgaard, L. (1989). Attachment, temperament and adrenocortical activity in infancy: A study of psychoendocrine regulation. *Developmental Psychology, 25*, 355–363.

Gunnar, M. R., Morison, S. J., Chisholm, K., & Schuder, M. (1999). *Cortisol levels in orphanage-reared Romanian children 6 years after adoption.* Manuscript in preparation.

Hall, F. S., Wilkinson, L. S., Humby, T., Inglis, W., Kendall, D. A., Marsden, C. A., & Robbins, T. W. (1998). Isolation rearing in rats: Pre- and postsynaptic changes in striatal dopaminergic systems. *Pharmacology, Biochemistry and Behavior, 59*(4), 859–872.

Hanson, D., Larson, E., & Snowdon, T. (1976). The effects of control over high intensity noise on plasma cortisol levels in rhesus monkeys. *Behavioral Biology, 16*, 333–340.

Harms, T., & Clifford, R. M. (1980). *Early Childhood Environment Rating Scale.* New York: Teachers College Press.

Higley, J. D., Suomi, S. J., & Linnoila, M. (1992). A longitudinal study of CSF monoamine metabolite and plasma cortisol concentrations in young rhesus monkeys: Effects of early experience, age, sex, and stress on continuity of individual differences. *Biological Psychiatry, 32*, 127–145.

Hofer, M. A. (1987). Early social relationships: A psychobiologist's view. *Child Development, 58*, 633–647.

Insel, T. R., Scanlan, J., & Champoux, M., & Suomi, S. J. (1988). Rearing paradigm in a nonhuman primate affects response to beta-CCE challenge. *Psychopharmacology, 96*, 81–86.

Jacobson, S., & Bihun, J. L. (1994). Elevated poststress cortisol in infants exposed prenatally to alcohol [Abstract]. *Infant Behavior and Development, 17*, 722.

Johnson, D. E. (in press). Psychosocial and pediatric sequelae of institutionalized adoption. In C. A. Nelson (Ed.), *The Effects of Adversity on Neurobehavioral Development. Minnesota Symposia on Child Psychology, Volume 31*. Mahwah, NJ: Lawrence Erlbaum Associates.

Johnson, E. O., Kamilaris, T. C., Chrousos, G. P., & Gold, P. W. (1992). Mechanisms of stress: A dynamic overview of hormonal and behavioral homeostasis. *Neuroscience and Biobehavioral Reviews, 16*, 115–130.

Kalin, N. H. (1990). Behavioral and endocrine studies of corticotropin-releasing hormone in primates. In E. B. de Souza & C. B. Nemeroff (Eds.), *Corticotropin-releasing factor: Basic and clinical studies of a neuropeptide* (pp. 276–289). Boca Raton, FL: CRC Press Inc.

Kalin, N. H., & Carnes, M. (1984). Biological correlates of attachment bond disruption in humans and nonhuman primates. *Progress in Neuro-Psychopharmacology & Biological Psychiatry* (Vol. 8, pp. 459–469). Oxford: Pergamon.

Kaufman, I. C., & Rosenblum, L. A. (1967). The reaction to separation in infant monkeys: Anaclitic depression and conservation-withdrawal. *Psychosomatic Medicine, 29*(6), 648–675.

Koob, G. R. (1992). The behavioral neuroendocrinology of corticotropin-releasing factor, growth hormone-releasing factor, somatostatin and gonadotropin-releasing hormone. In C. B. Nemeroff (Ed.), *Neuroendocrinology* (pp. 353–364). Boca Raton, FL: CRC Press.

Kraemer, G. W. (1992). A psychobiological theory of attachment. *Behavioral and Brain Sciences, 15*, 493–541.

Kroupina, M., Gunnar, M., & Johnson, D. (1997). [Report on salivary cortisol levels in a Russian baby home.] Unpublished raw data.

Kuhn, C. M., Butler, S. R., & Schanberg, S. M. (1978). Selective depression of serum growth hormone during maternal deprivation in rat pups. *Science, 201*, 1034–1036.

Kuhn, C. M., Schanberg, S. M., Field, T., Symanski, R., Zimmerman, E., Scafidi, F., & Roberts, J. (1991). Tactile-kinesthetic stimulation effects on sympathetic and adrenocortical function in preterm infants. *Journal of Developmental and Behavioral Pediatrics, 119*(3), 434–440.

Ladd, C. O., Huot, R. L., Thrivikraman, K. V., Nemeroff, C. B., Meaney, M. J., & Plotsky, P. M. (in press). Long-term behavioral and neuroendocrine adaptations to adverse early experience. In E. Mayer & C. Saper (Eds.), *Progress in Brain Research: The Biological Basis for Mind Body Interactions*. Amsterdam, Netherlands: Elsevier.

Lazarus, R. S., & Folkman, S. (1984). *Stress, appraisal, and coping*. New York: Springer.

Legendre, A., & Kortinus, M. (1996, August). *Differences in stress susceptibility among toddlers in day-care centers: Relationships with frequency of diseases*. Paper presented at the International Society for the Study of Behavioural Development, Quebec City, Quebec, Canada.

Levine, S. (1957). Infantile experience and resistance to physiological stress. *Science, 126*, 405–406.

Levine, S. (1975). Psychosocial factors in growth and development. In L. Levi (Ed.), *Society, stress and disease* (pp. 43–50). London: Oxford University Press.

Levine, S. (1994). The ontogeny of the hypothalamic-pituitary-adrenal axis: The influence of maternal factors. *Annals of the New York Academy of Sciences, 746*, 275–288.

Levine, S., & Thoman, E. B. (1970). Maternal factors influencing subsequent adrenocortical activity in the offspring. In S. Kazda & V. H. Denenberg (Eds.), *Postnatal development of phenotype* (pp. 111–122). Prague, Czechoslovakia: Academia.

Levine, S., & Wiener, S. G. (1988). Psychoendocrine aspects of mother-infant relationships in nonhuman primates. *Psychoneuroendocrinology, 13*(1&2), 143–154.

Lewis, M., & Ramsay, D. S. (1995). Developmental change in infants' responses to stress. *Child Development, 66*, 657–670.

Liu, D., Dorio, J., Tannenbaum, B., Caldji, C., Francis, D., Freedman, A., Sharma, S., Pearson, D., Plotsky, P. M., & Meaney, M. J. (1997). Maternal care, hippocampal glucocorticoid receptors, and hypothalamic-pituitary-adrenal responses to stress. *Science, 277,* 1659–1662.

Luecken, L. J. (1998). Childhood attachment and loss experiences affect adult cardiovascular and cortisol function. *Psychosomatic Medicine, 60,* 765–772.

Lupien, S., Lecours, A. R., Lussier, I., Schwartz, G., Nair, N. P. V., & Meaney, M. J. (1994). Basal cortisol levels and cognitive deficits in human aging. *The Journal of Neuroscience, 14*(5), 2893–2903.

Maes, M., Bosmans, E., Meltzer, H. Y., Scharpe, S., & Suy, E. (1993). Interleukin 1B: A putative mediator of HPA axis hyperactivity in major depression? *American Journal of Psychiatry, 150*(8), 1189–1193.

Maier, S. F., Ryan, S. M., Barksdale, C. M., & Kalin, N. H. (1986). Stressor controllability and the pituitary-adrenal system. *Behavioral Neuroscience, 100*(5), 669–674.

Maier, S. F., Watkins, L. R., & Fleshner, M. (1994). The interface between behavior, brain, and immunity. *American Psychologist, 49*(12), 1004–1017.

Makino, S., Gold, P. W., & Schulkin, J. (1994). Corticosterone effects on corticotropin-releasing hormone mRNA in the central nucleus of the amygdala and the parvocellular region of the paraventricular nucleus of the hypothalamus. *Brain Research, 640,* 105–112.

Mason, J. W. (1968). A review of psychoendocrine research on the sympathetic-adrenal medullary system. *Psychosomatic Medicine, 30,* 631–653.

Mason, W. A. (1970). Motivational factors in psychosocial development. In W. J. Arnold & M. M. Page (Eds.), *Nebraska Symposium on Motivation* (pp. 35–67). Lincoln: University of Nebraska Press.

Matthews, K., Wilkinson, L. S., & Robbins, T. W. (1996). Repeated maternal separation of preweanling rats attenuates behavioral responses to primary and conditioned incentives in adulthood. *Physiology and Behavior, 59*(1), 99–107.

McEwen, B. S. (1988). Destructive hormonal influences on brain aging: A result of interacting modulators? In G. Pepeu, B. Tomlinson, & C. M. Wischik (Eds.), *New trends in aging research* (Vol. 15, pp. 75–84). New York: Springer-Verlag.

McEwen, B. S. (1998). Stress, adaptation, and disease: Allostasis and allostatic load. *Annals of the New York Academy of Science, 840,* 33–44.

McEwen, B. S., Angulo, J., Cameron, H., Chao, H. M., Daniels, D., Gannon, M. N., Gould, E., Mendelson, S., Sakai, R., Spencer, R., & Woolley, C. (1992). Paradoxical effects of adrenal steroids on the brain: Protection versus degeneration. *Biological Psychiatry, 31,* 177–199.

McEwen, B. S., de Kloet, E. R., & Rostene, W. (1986). Adrenal steroid receptors and actions in the nervous system. *Physiological Review, 66*(4), 1121–1188.

McEwen, B. S., & Gould, E. (1990). Adrenal steriod influences on the survival of hippocampal neurons. *Biochemical Pharmacology, 40*(11), 2393–2402.

Meaney, M. J., Aitken, D. H., van Berkel, C., Bhatnagar, S., & Sapolsky, R. M. (1988). Effect of neonatal handling on age-related impairments associated with the hippocampus. *Science, 239,* 766–768.

Meaney, M. J., Diorio, J., Francis, D., LaRocque, S., O'Donnell, D., Smythe, J. W., Sharma, S., & Tannenbaum, B. (1994). Environmental regulation of the development of glucocorticoid receptor systems in the rat forebrain: The role of serotonin. *Annals of the New York Academy of Sciences, 746,* 260–274.

Meaney, M. J., Diorio, J., Francis, D., Widdowson, J., La Plante, P., Caldui, C., Sharma, S., Seckl, J., & Plotsky, P. (1996). Early environmental regulation of forebrain glucocorticoid receptor gene expression: Implications for adrenocortical responses to stress. *Developmental Neuroscience, 18,* 49–72.

Meaney, M. J., O'Donnell, D., Viau, V., Bhatnagar, S., Sarrieau, A., Smythe, J., Shanks, N., & Walker, C. D. (1993). Corticosteroid receptors in the rat brain and pituitary during development and hypothalamic-pituitary-adrenal function. In I. S. Zagon & P. J. McLaughlin (Eds.), *Receptors in the developing nervous system: Growth factors and hormones* (Vol. 1, pp. 163–201). New York: Chapman & Hall.

Mendoza, S. P., Coe, C. L., Smotherman, W. P., Kaplan, J., & Levine, S. (1980). Functional consequences of attachment: A comparison of two species. In R. W. Bell & W. P. Smotherman (Eds.), *Maternal influences and early behavior* (pp. 235–252). New York: Spectrum.

Mineka, S., Gunnar, M. R., & Champoux, M. (1986). Control and early socio-emotional development: Infant Rhesus monkeys reared in controllable vs. uncontrollable environments. *Child Development, 57,* 1241–1256.

Munck, A., Guyre, P. M., & Holbrook, N. J. (1984). Physiological functions of glucocorticoids in stress and their relation to pharmacological actions. *Endocrine Review, 5*(1), 25–44.

Munck, A., & Naray-Fejes-Toth, A. (1994). Glucocorticoids and stress: Permissive and suppressive actions. *Annals of the New York Academy of Sciences, 746,* 115–130.

Nachmias, M., Gunnar, M., Mangelsdorf, S., Parritz, R., & Buss, K. (1996). Behavioral inhibition and stress reactivity: Moderating role of attachment security. *Child Development, 67,* 508–522.

Nemeroff, C. B. (1996). The corticotropin-releasing factor (CRF) hypothesis of depression: New findings and new directions. *Molecular Psychiatry, 1*(4), 336–342.

Ogilvie, K. M., & Rivier, C. (1997). Prenatal alcohol exposure results in hyperactivity of the hypothalamic-pituitary-adrenal axis of the offspring: Modulation by fostering at birth and postnatal handling. *Alcoholism, Clinical & Experimental Research, 21,* 424–429.

Pervin, L. A. (1968). The need to predict and control under conditions of threat. *Journal of Personality, 31,* 570–585.

Plotsky, P. M., & Meaney, M. J. (1993). Early, postnatal experience alters hypothalmic corticotropin-releasing factor (CRF) mRNA, median eminence CRF content and stress-induced release in adult rats. *Molecular Brain Research, 18,* 195–200.

Plotsky, P. M., Thrivkraman, K. V., & Meaney, M. J. (1993). Central and feedback regulation of hypothalamic corticotropin-releasing factor secretion. *Ciba Foundation Symposium, 172,* 59–84.

Ramsay, D. S., & Lewis, M. (1994). Developmental changes in infant cortisol and behavioral stress response to inoculation. *Child Development, 65,* 1491–1502.

Reynolds, J. W. (1981). Development and function of the human fetal adrenal cortex. In M. J. Novy & J. A. Resko (Eds.), *Fetal endocrinology* (pp. 35–52). New York: Academic Press.

Rosen, J. B., & Schulkin, J. (1998). From normal fear to pathological anxiety. *Psychological Review, 105*(2), 325–350.

Rosenblum, L. A., & Andrews, M. W. (1994). Influences of environmental demand on maternal behavior and infant development. *Acta Paediatrica, 397,* 57–63.

Rosenblum, L. A., Coplan, J. D., Friedman, S., Bassoff, T., Gorman, J. M., & Andrews, M. W. (1994). Adverse early experiences affect noradrenergic and serotonergic functioning in adult primates. *Biological Psychiatry, 35*(4), 221–227.

Rosenfield, P., Suchecki, D., & Levine, S. (1992). Multifactorial regulation of the hypothalamic-pituitary-adrenal axis during development. *Neuroscience and Biobehavioral Reviews, 16,* 553–568.

Rutter, M. (1996, June). *Profound early deprivation and later social relationships in early adoptees from Romanian orphanages followed at age 4.* Paper presented at the International Conference on Infant Studies, Providence, RI.

Rutter, M. (1998). Developmental catch-up, and deficit, following adoption after severe global early privation. English and Romanian Adoptees (ERA) Study Team. *Journal of Child Psychology and Psychiatry, 39*(4), 465–476.

Rutter, M., Anderson-Wood, L., Beckett, C., Bredenkamp, D., Castle, J., Groothues, C., Kreppner, J., Keaveney, L., & O'Connor, T. G. (1999). Quasi-autistic patterns following severe early global privation. English and Romanian Adoptees (ERA) Study Team. *Journal of Child Psychology and Psychiatry, 40*(4), 537–549.

Sapolsky, R. M. (1994). The physiological relevance of glucocorticoid endangerment of the hippocampus. *Annals of the New York Academy of Sciences, 746,* 294–307.

Sapolsky, R. M. (1997). McEwen-induced modulation of endocrine history: A partial review. *Stress, 2*(1), 1–12.

Sarrieau, A., Dussaillant, M., Sapolsky, R. M., Aitken, D. H., Olivier, A., Lal, S., Rostene, W. H., Quirion, R., & Meaney, M. J. (1988). Glucocorticoid binding sites in human temporal cortex. *Brain Research, 442*, 159–163.

Schanberg, S. M., Evoniuk, G., & Kuhn, C. M. (1984). Tactile and nutritional aspects of maternal care: Specific regulators of neuroendocrine function and cellular development. *Proceedings of the Society of Experimental Biology and Medicine, 175*, 135–146.

Schneider, M. L., Clarke, A. S., Kraemer, G. W., Roughton, E. C., Lubach, G. R., Rimm-Kaufman, S., Schmidt, D., & Ebert, M. (1998). Prenatal stress alters brain biogenic amine levels in primates. *Development and Psychopathology, 10*(3), 427–440.

Schneider, M. L., Coe, C. L., & Lubach, G. R. (1992). Endocrine activation mimics the adverse effects of prenatal stress on the neuromotor development of the infant primate. *Developmental Psychobiology, 25*(6), 427–439.

Schulkin, J., McEwen, B. S., & Gold, P. S. (1994). Allostasis, amygdala, and anticipatory angst. *Neuroscience and Behavioral Reviews, 18*(3), 385–396.

Seeman, T. E., Berkman, L. F., Blazer, D., & Rowe, J. W. (1994). Social ties and support and neuroendocrine function: The MacArthur studies of successful aging. *Annals of Behavioral Medicine, 16*(2), 95–106.

Shanks, N., Larocque, S., & Meaney, M. J. (1995). Neonatal endotoxin exposure alters the development of the hypothalamic-pituitary-adrenal axis: Early illness and altered responsivity to stress. *Journal of Neuroscience, 15*, 376–384.

Smotherman, W. P., & Bell, R. W. (1980). Maternal mediation of early experience. In R. W. Bell & W. P. Smotherman (Eds.), *Maternal influences and early behavior* (pp. 201–210). New York: Spectrum.

Smythe, J. W., McCormick, C. M., Rochford, J., & Meaney, M. J. (1994). The interaction between prenatal stress and neonatal handling on nociceptive response latencies in male and female rats. *Physiology and Behavior, 55*, 971–974.

Spangler, G., & Schieche, M. (1994, July). *The role of maternal sensitivity and the quality of infant-mother attachment for infant biobehavioral organization.* Paper presented at the 9th International Conference on Infant Studies, Paris, France.

Spangler, G., & Schieche, M. (1998). Emotional and adrenocortical responses of infants to the Strange Situation: The differential functions of emotion expression. *International Journal of Behavioral Development, 22*(4), 681–706.

Strand, F. L. (1999a). Neuropeptides, stress, and the immune system. *Neuropeptides: Regulators of physiological processes* (pp. 141–164). Cambridge, MA: MIT Press.

Strand, F. L. (1999b). Hypophysiotropic neuropeptides: TRH, CRH, GnRH, GHRH, SS, PACAP, DSIP. *Neuropeptides: Regulators of physiological processes* (pp. 179–228). Cambridge, MA: The MIT Press.

Stratakis, C. A., & Chrousos, G. P. (1995). Neuroendocrinology and pathophysiology of the stress system. *Annals of the New York Academy of Sciences, 771*, 1–18.

Suchecki, D., Mazzafarian, D., Gross, G., Rosenfeld, P., & Levine, S. (1993). Effects of maternal deprivation on the ACTH stress response in the infant rat. *Neuroendocrinology, 57*(2), 204–212.

Suchecki, D., Nelson, D. Y., Van Oers, H., & Levine, S. (1995). Activation and inhibition of the hypothalamic-pituitary-adrenal axis of the neonatal rat: Effects of maternal deprivation. *Psychoneuroendocrinology, 20*(2), 169–182.

Suomi, S. J. (1991a). Adolescent depression and depressive symptoms: Insights from longitudinal studies with rhesus monkeys. *Journal of Youth and Adolescence, 20*(2), 273–287.

Suomi, S. J. (1991b). Early stress and adult emotional reactivity in rhesus monkeys. In D. Barker (Ed.), *The childhood environment and adult disease* (Ciba Foundation Symposium #156, pp. 171–188). Chichester, England: Wiley.

Suomi, S. J. (1995). Influence of attachment theory on ethological studies of biobehavioral development in nonhuman primates. In S. Goldberg, R. Muir, & J. Kerr (Eds.), *Attachment theory: Social, developmental, and clinical perspectives* (pp. 185–201). Hillsdale, NJ: The Analytic Press.

Tepperman, J., & Tepperman, H. M. (1987). *Metabolic and endocrine physiology: An introductory text* (5th ed.). Chicago: Year Book Medical Publishers.

Tout, K., de Haan, M., Kipp-Campbell, E., & Gunnar, M. R. (1998). Social behavior correlates of adrenocortical activity in daycare: Gender differences and time-of-day effects. *Child Development, 69*(5), 1247–1262.

Valentio, R. J. (1990). Effects of CRF on spontaneous and sensory-evoked activity of locus ceruleus neurons. In E. B. de Souza & C. B. Nemeroff (Eds.), *Corticotropin-releasing factor: Basic and clinical studies of a neuropeptide* (pp. 218–231). Boca Raton, FL: CRC Press.

van Haasteren, G. A., Linkels, E., Klootwijk, W., Kaptein, E., deJong, F. H., Reymond, M. J., Visser, T. J., & deGreef, W. J. (1996). Efffects of long-term food restriction on the hypothalamus-pituitary-thyroid axis in male and female rats. *Journal of Endocrinology, 150*(20), 169–178.

van Oers, H. J. J., de Kloet, E. R., & Levine, S. (1997). Persistent, but paradoxical, effects on HPA regulation of infants maternally deprived at different ages. *Stress: The International Journal on the Biology of Stress, 1*(4), 249–263.

Vazquez, D. M. (1998). Stress and the developing limbic-hypothalamic-pituitary-adrenal axis. *Psychoneuroendocrinology, 7,* 663–700.

Weiner, S. G., & Levine, S. (1978). Perinatal malnutrition and early handling: Interactive effects on the development of the pituitary-adrenal system. *Developmental Psychobiology, 11*(4), 335–352.

Weiss, J. M. (1971). Effects of coping behavior with and without a feedback signal on stress pathology in rats. *Journal of Comparative and Physiological Psychology, 77*(1), 22–30.

Zaharia, M. D., Kulczycki, J., Shanks, N., Meaney, M. J., & Anisman, H. (1996). The effects of early postnatal stimulation on Morris water-maze acquisition in adult mice: Genetic and maternal factors. *Psychopharmacology, 128*(3), 227–239.

6

▼▼▼▼▼▼▼

Effect of Prenatal Stress on Development: A Nonhuman Primate Model

Mary L. Schneider
Departments of Kinesiology and Psychology
University of Wisconsin-Madison

Colleen F. Moore
Department of Psychology
University of Wisconsin-Madison

The idea that early experiences can have a profound influence on functioning during a later developmental period has been a fundamental theme in developmental theories. More recent theories have expanded on this idea, suggesting that early experiences may actually be incorporated into the individual's biology by altering neural processes. These altered neural substrates then influence the way the individual meets new experiences (Boyce et al., 1998; Cicchetti & Tucker, 1994). No one doubts that exposure to substances in utero via maternal intake can alter behavioral development (for example, cigarette smoking, alcohol, and many other drugs are acknowledged to have deleterious effects on offspring). Researchers have long been interested in the idea that even experiences during the fetal period can influence later development (Carmichael, 1970; Kuo, 1976). In spite of this long-standing interest, the issue of whether environmental events experienced by the mother during gestation can alter behavior and the neural substrates of behavior in the offspring has received only limited research attention.

In this chapter, we explore the question of whether repeated psychologically stressful events during pregnancy can alter offspring behavioral development. Before embarking on this endeavor, it is important to consider some approaches to conceptualizing and measuring psychosocial stress in both humans and animals. The ideas outlined here are drawn from several sources (Chrousos & Gold, 1992; Lobel, 1994). One difficulty is that in research some of the measures of stress that are used differ between humans and animals. Nevertheless, a common theme underlying most concepts of stress is that stress is a state of disharmony or threatened homeostasis (Chrousos & Gold, 1992). Stressors set in motion a complex of behavioral and physiological responses to reestablish homeostasis. Thus, stress involves three elements: (a) a stressor or event that induces changes in the homeostatic regulation of the organism; (b) the state of stress or the disharmony itself; and (c) the organism's response to the stress.

In research with humans, stressors are often measured by life-event questionnaires in which respondents indicate what events occurred (e.g., changing or losing one's job, getting married, or death of a loved one), without any evaluation of the events. In animal research, the stressors are specific manipulations administered to the animals (e.g., saline injections and loud noises). Because of the dynamics of any homeostatic system, the disharmony induced by a stressor and the stress responses to the imbalance are intertwined. In humans and animals, some of the physiological measures are similar (e.g., heart rate, blood pressure, and levels of glucocorticoids and catecholamines); while in animal studies, manipulations can be employed that would not be permitted in human studies (e.g., maternal adrenalectomy to investigate biological substrates or assessment of type I and type II corticosteroid receptors in the hippocampus of offspring) (Barbazanges, Piazza, Le Moal, & Maccari, 1996). In addition, with animal studies, the timing and the intensity of the stressor can be systematically manipulated. However, in human research, self-reports of the psychological effects of stressors are also available (e.g., anxiety questionnaires and perceived stressfulness of events) as well as self-reports of coping (Gruen, Folkman, & Lazarus, 1988). In animals, where self-reports are unavailable, there is reliance on variables of behavioral patterns (e.g., *freezing* in rats and clinging to conspecifics in primates).

The issue of prenatal stress is of practical importance in modern societies where daily life often involves much psychological stress. If maternal stress does have long-term behavioral effects on offspring, then perhaps stress should be added to the list of behavioral teratogens such as alcohol, cigarettes, lead, and mercury. At a public policy level, this issue has important implications in a society where many commodities, including uncontrollable psychological stressors, are not equitably distributed. That is, the economically underprivileged sector of our society is likely to be subjected to excesses of psychological stress. If psychological stress during pregnancy does have deleterious long-term effects on offspring, then it has far-reaching implications ranging from the nature of treatment programs for pregnant drug and alcohol users (and other aspects of prenatal care) to educational programs for children who are likely or known offspring of stressed pregnancies.

In a series of prospective longitudinal studies with nonhuman primates as subjects, we will provide evidence suggesting that if a mother experiences repeated stressful events during pregnancy, those experiences can have long-term effects on her offspring that persist into adulthood. More specifically, our studies suggest that how an individual copes within the context of a changing environment can be influenced by a trajectory laid down in fetal life. The broad developmental issue underlying this research concerns the plasticity of the fetal nervous system and the way the fetal nervous system incorporates information from the environment, in part, through changes in its organization. Such changes can cascade postnatally as the individual interprets and acts on new experiences; these new experiences can then lead to an increasing divergence in developmental outcomes, which then significantly impact later development and function (Boyce et al., 1998). Thus, we do not view prenatal events as determining later outcome in a lock-step mechanistic fashion. Instead, we view such events as one influence on the dynamic processes that influence behavior. This conceptual framework forms the background theme in our interpretations of our work on the behavioral and physiological development of prenatally stressed monkeys across infancy and into adulthood.

What kind of evidence would be needed to show that prenatal stress has important developmental effects? Notice that we argue here that any single source of evidence by itself is incomplete. In a way that is similar to arguments put forth by other researchers (e.g., Paarlberg, Vingerhoets, Dekker, Van Geijn, 1995), we think that the following types of evidence in combination will allow a conclusion that prenatal stress does alter behavioral development in the long term. First, correlational evidence in humans should suggest an association of prenatal stress with behavioral and psychological effects later in life. Such correlational research with humans is never definitive because a variety of confounding variables could be involved.

A second question is whether experimental animal research shows that prenatal stress has effects on the behavioral development of offspring. But with animal research we are constantly vexed by the question of its direct relevance to humans. What kinds of stress and severity of psychological stresses create what kinds of behavioral effects, and do those stresses and behavioral effects have analogues in humans? Because of these issues of relevance to humans, we believe that behavioral research with nonhuman primates has a greater potential to provide evidence that will be relevant to human behavior than does research with other species less closely related to humans. Although all mammals share certain biological processes related to psychological stress, different mammalian classes share fewer behavioral traits. By examining the behavioral (and some of the biological effects) of prenatal stress in rhesus monkeys, and using some behavioral measures that are directly analogous to measures of human behavioral development, the findings we describe should have relevance to humans. The argument can be simply stated this way: if behavioral effects of prenatal stress were found in rodent offspring, but not in monkey offspring, most of us would doubt the relevance of the rodent findings to humans. However, a pattern of results that extends across mammalian species and includes our primate cousins would be persuasive evidence for most of us.

A third requirement for concluding that prenatal stress has effects on behavioral development is that there are plausible biological mechanisms through which maternal stress during pregnancy could influence later behavior in the offspring. Here animal research on the biological effects of prenatal stress on off-spring is indispensable because, in the current mores of society, certain types of invasive measurements cannot be done with humans but can be with animals.

In this chapter, we cannot review all three types of evidence thoroughly. The plan of this chapter is as follows: first, we briefly consider the problem of prenatal stress in humans, that is, whether stress during pregnancy affects behavioral development. Do the data from human correlational studies support this relationship? Second, we briefly review the evidence from experiments with nonprimate animals (primarily rodents) regarding the effects of psychosocial stressors on behavioral development. The nonprimate animal research also provides very important evidence regarding the likely biological processes involved. We focus on empirical data suggesting that dysregulation of the hypothalamic-pituitary-adrenal (HPA) axis and corticotrophin-releasing hormone (CRH) overactivity may subserve some of the behavioral abnormalities associated with prenatal stress. Finally, we consider our own primate findings on prenatal stress. Because this work is longitudinal, covering birth to early adulthood, we can ask whether early behavioral markers of prenatal stress can be useful not only for early identification of prenatally stressed individuals, but we ask whether these early signs can shape the direction in which subsequent development is likely to unfold. This issue holds promise for increasing our understanding of the effects of prenatal stress, and may ultimately contribute information useful for intervention with infants and children influenced by maternal stress during gestation.

HUMAN STUDIES

There are a variety of findings in the literature that suggest (but do not definitively show) that psychosocial stress during pregnancy may cause alterations in the later psychological functioning of the offspring. There are two lines of relevant evidence from human studies. One source of evidence comes from retrospective studies that have compared the reported prenatal conditions of individuals with various psychiatric diagnoses to other individuals without those diagnoses, or that have compared groups of individuals with different prenatal backgrounds (e.g., war victims or refugees vs. those not subjected prenatally to those conditions). A second source of evidence comes from making a logical leap between two separate research findings: (a) psychosocial stress during pregnancy is associated with adverse gestational and birth outcomes such as preterm delivery and low birth weight, and (b) adverse gestational and birth outcomes are associated with increased rates of developmental problems. Only a couple of prospective studies have followed the children longitudinally to examine the later effects of prenatal stress. Each of these areas is briefly reviewed here.

The first line of evidence is the most intriguing, but is also methodologically the weakest. Wadhwa (1998) pointed out that in a few retrospective studies some very striking differences due to prenatal stress conditions have been obtained. In one study in Finland, paternal death during pregnancy was found to be associated with an increased risk of schizophrenia and criminality compared to a group whose fathers died during their first year after birth (Huttenen & Niskanen, 1978). Another more recent retrospective study compared children diagnosed with attention deficit hyperactivity disorder (ADHD) and undifferentiated attention deficit disorder (UADD) with normal children (McIntosh, Mulkins, & Dean, 1995). The results showed that self-reported stress during pregnancy was one of four significant predictors of diagnosis (other significant variables were an index of medical risk variables, smoking during pregnancy, and months to term). Stress was one of the many variables included in a questionnaire retrospectively assessing both medical conditions before and during pregnancy and lifestyle variables. Ward (1990, 1991) conducted two retrospective studies of a sample of children hospitalized with psychiatric disorders. The research team audited the medical charts of the children's mothers for their prenatal conditions. The 1990 study by Ward found an association between family discord and risk of autism. The Ward (1991) study included a comparison group of normal children sampled from the same hospital. The study found evidence of an association between risk of severe emotional disturbance and stresses such as family discord and unplanned pregnancy in an unmarried mother. Lastly, Meijer (1985) compared a cohort of boys born in Israel in the year of the Six-Day War of 1967 to a cohort born 2 years later. The war cohort showed later speech development, were later in achieving toilet training, were rated by their teachers as showing more social withdrawal and less consideration of peers, and were reported by their mothers to lie more often than the comparison cohort. However, the war cohort included children from mothers subjected to war stress during the prenatal period and the postnatal period as well.

These studies were all retrospective and carry the usual methodological problems of retrospective studies (Dawes, 1994). One particular problem is that because memory is reconstructive, retrospective self-report data can be unintentionally reconstructed by participants to fit preconceptions. Thus, a parent whose child shows developmental problems might be more likely to report prenatal stress or other negative events than a parent whose child does not show developmental problems. Moreover, scores on questionnaires tend to show a skewed distribution, in that a small number of women score extremely high (Paarlberg, 1995). Additionally, in human research there are many potential confounding variables (e.g., behavioral changes in response to stress such as use of alcohol, tobacco, etc., differential reporting of pregnancy events by those who have had a problem birth or child, and different parenting by mothers who experienced prenatal stress). Thus, these studies do not allow a firm conclusion that prenatal stress is a cause of psychological problems in offspring. Nevertheless, these findings raise the importance of research on prenatal stress and offspring psychological functioning.

Birth Outcomes

Most research on prenatal stress with humans has focused on what are called *birth outcomes*. Studies of birth outcomes deal with variables such as preterm labor, length of labor, delivery complications (forceps, caesarian, etc.), gestation length (or preterm delivery), birth weight, and neonatal Apgar scores. This literature has been reviewed in detail by a number of authors (Lobel, 1994; Paarlberg et al., 1995; Wadhwa, 1998). Our interest is not in birth outcomes per se, but in the possible developmental sequelae of adverse birth outcomes. Therefore, we only briefly summarize the main conclusions that have been drawn by other reviewers.

Both Wadhwa (in press) and Lobel (1994) concluded that in spite of a variety of methodological issues in the research on birth outcomes and prenatal stress (including when and how prenatal stress is measured, whether important confounding variables such as maternal parity, gender of the child, socioeconomic status (SES), and smoking and alcohol consumption are statistically controlled), the general conclusion is that there is some relationship between high prenatal stress and both low birth weight and shorter gestation duration (or preterm birth). In many of the studies reviewed by Wadhwa and Lobel, prenatal stress was measured with some form of life events survey. Paarlberg et al. (1995) also concluded that, "The results of research on the relation between maternal exposure to stressful events and preterm labour are rather consistent and unambiguous. Preterm deliveries have often been preceded by stressful situations" (p. 579). For low birth weight, Paarlberg et al. (1995) concluded that, "The findings of most studies, however, suggest that the contribution of maternal stressor exposure to low birth weight, either directly or mediated through health-risk behaviours, such as cigarette smoking, should be considered seriously" (p. 574). These authors also suggested that future research on prenatal stress should attend to the endocrine and immunological responses to stress that are the likely mechanisms for low birth weight.

One important gap is in the study of the timing of prenatal stress. Most of the human studies that have been prospective have examined perceived prenatal stresses at one point in time, usually after the 20th week of gestation, and sometimes as late as after the 30th week of gestation. Pregnancies that ended in miscarriage are excluded from analyses, presumably because the cause could be a severe fetal malformation unrelated to stress. But we know from the study of many teratogenic substances that the timing of a teratogen is a key factor in what the impact is on the developing fetus and later functioning of the child. For prenatal stress, the same principles would be expected to apply. The neuroendocrine system is thought to be the most vulnerable system to prenatal stress because it is the system that is influenced most directly by stress hormones and neurotransmitters released during stress. Therefore, studies that relate the timing of the prenatal stress to the developing state of the neuroendocrine system might increase our understanding of the effects of stress on later psychological functioning. But such studies are lacking in the human research.

The relationships between prenatal stress and low birth weight and preterm delivery that have been found do not, by themselves, necessarily imply an association between prenatal stress and later psychological functioning. Hence, we describe this line of evidence as requiring a logical leap. Low birth weight and preterm delivery are associated with an increase in medical risks during infancy (Wadhwa, 1998). Low birth weight infants are also at risk for various physical developmental problems as well as problems in psychological functioning (such as seizures, central nervous system defects, and low scores on standardized cognitive and developmental tests) (Brown, 1993; see also Rose and Feldman, chap. 2, this volume). Of course, high psychosocial stress is only one of many factors that has an association with low birth weight and preterm delivery. Others include cigarette smoking, alcohol and drug use, poor weight gain, lack of social support, low maternal education, young maternal age, and nonwhite race (Brooke, Anderson, Bland, Peacock, & Stewart, 1989; McCormick et al., 1990). Unfortunately, very few studies have actually followed individuals from gestation to a point beyond the neonatal period in order to assess later psychological functioning.

Those few prospective studies of the effects of prenatal psychosocial stress on later functioning do have interesting results. For example, Oyemade et al. (1994) conducted a prospective study of African-American women that included measures of prenatal stress (trait anxiety, stressful life events, and daily hassles) and measures of neonatal neurobehavioral development (Brazelton Neonatal Behavioral Assessment Scale, the BNBAS, 1984). Oyemade and colleagues concluded that maternal prenatal stress was negatively associated with the attention and habituation measures of the BNBAS.

Although Oyemade's results are intriguing, it is apparent that there is a paucity of prospective studies with humans on the effects of prenatal stress on later psychological functioning. This is understandable given the difficulties of doing a lengthy longitudinal prospective study. The topic of prenatal stress has attracted research with human populations mainly because of the medical consequences of a variety of labor and delivery complications. Thus, the conclusions that can be drawn from the human research remain largely at the level of "A is associated with B. B is associated with C. Therefore, A must also be associated with C." But in behavioral science with correlational data, such an inference is speculative. For this reason, we turn to the experimental animal research.

ANIMAL STUDIES

Thus far, we have concentrated on studies of humans. An important finding of these studies has been that women who experience stress and anxiety during pregnancy have higher rates of adverse birth outcomes, such as low birth weight and preterm deliveries. However, the complex interrelationship between SES, ethnicity, stress, smoking, substance abuse, and personal resources prevent firm causal conclusions. The essential role of animal models is that they afford investigators the opportunity to isolate prenatal stress from other lifestyle factors that accompany stress in human studies. Animal models also permit the administration of a standard stress treatment during a specific period of pregnancy. This enables study of the important developmental variable of the timing of the stressful experience. In addition, longitudinal studies can be conducted more easily than with humans, allowing a full assessment of the long-term effects of prenatal stress on offspring outcome. Also, the behavioral and hormonal measurements conducted on the offspring can be standardized and performed under baseline and challenging conditions repeatedly across the lifespan in order to assess whether long-term effects of prenatal stress can be detected.

Another difference between research on human prenatal stress and animal models of prenatal stress is the nature of the stressors. In humans, psychosocial stress is measured using interviews or questionnaires about life events or anxiety. In animal prenatal stress research, investigators use unpleasant, unexpected, and uncontrollable events (ranging from saline injections to noise blasts) with pregnant animals. It is not possible to directly compare the kinds of stressors used in animal research to the life-event stress that may be experienced by people. In any animal model, however, direct comparison to humans is not the goal. Rather, the goal of the animal model is to elucidate the mechanisms involved in the phenomenon of interest.

Rodent Behavioral Studies

Most of the studies of the behavioral effects of prenatal stress have been conducted in rodents. We will summarize primarily those findings pertinent to our primate research on prenatal stress. In rodent studies, pregnant dams have been exposed to a variety of stressors (Koehl, Barbazanges, Moal, & Maccari, 1997; Peters, 1990). Stressors have been administered across a wide array of times during pregnancy (Koehl et al., 1997; McCormick, Smythe, Sharma, & Meaney, 1995; Peters, 1982; Takahashi & Kalin, 1991; Williams, Hennessy, & Davis, 1995). One of the most robust findings is that prenatally stressed males exhibit marked reductions in male-typical sexual behavior (see Ward & Ward, 1985, for a review). Subsequent studies showed that not only are prenatally stressed males demasculinized, but females, at least in certain behaviors, are partially masculinzed (Kinsley & Bridges, 1988) and show fertility disturbances (Herrenkohl, 1979).

In addition to the effects of stress on gender-related behavior, prenatal stress has been found to be associated with increased emotional behavior of the pups (Thompson, 1957). Specifically, pups born to mothers exposed to stress during pregnancy showed a decrease in ambulatory behavior, and an increase in latency to move in an open-field test. More recent studies suggest that the sensitive period for this effect in the rodent is prenatal stress during the first trimester (first week) of pregnancy. Weinstock and others also reported heightened behavioral responsivity to stress in prenatally stressed rodents in the form of decreased ambulation in the open field, increased defensive freezing, and altered vocalizations (see Weinstock, 1997, for a review). Others have found that while certain behaviors do not differ between prenatally stressed and control rats under normal conditions (e.g., maternal behavior and food seeking after deprivation), the same behaviors are markedly disrupted in the prenatally stressed rats under stressful conditions (Fride, Dan, Feldon, Halevy, & Weinstock, 1986; Fride, Dan, Gavish, & Weinstock, 1985). Thus, it seems that prenatally stressed animals are more sensitive to stress and are most likely to show behavioral reactions that differ from control animals when tested under conditions of stress. That is, the prenatally stressed animals are more behaviorally reactive to stress than the control animals.

Biological Mechanisms

Animal experiments have yielded important findings regarding the likely biological processes behind the altered behavioral reactivity of prenatally stressed animals. Before reviewing some of these results, we first present a brief synopsis of the biology of stress.

There is no single universally accepted definition of stress. However, there are commonalities in the way different investigators define or describe stress. Since Selye (1936), most investigators have included in their viewpoints that stress is a state of disharmony or threatened homeostasis (see Chrousos & Gold, 1992). According to this view, a network of regulatory processes exists to maintain the organism's homeostasis in the face of continually changing environmental conditions and demand. Once the individual's homeostasis is threatened, adaptational responses attempt to counter the perturbation and return the organism to a state of stability or homeostasis. It is important to remember, however, that, according to Selye (1936), stressful states are not all negative. In fact, mild, brief, and controllable stressful events can be experienced as positive in that they are thought to stimulate cognitive and emotional processes. On the other hand, severe, prolonged and uncontrollable stress is believed to result in maladaptation (Selye, 1936).

As mentioned previously, the adaptation response is triggered under stress conditions. It involves numerous central and peripheral responses that are activated to reinstate homeostasis. The central responses include enhancement of the neural pathways that subserve arousal, alertness, cognition, focused attention, and appropriate aggression. At the same time, stress inhibits neural pathways that subserve feeding and reproduction (see Chrousos & Gold, 1992, for more details). From the perspective of the peripheral response, oxygen and nutrients are routed to the central nervous system and the region of the body experiencing stress. The peripheral responses include increases in cardiovascular tone, elevations in blood pressure and heart rate, increases in respiratory rate, gluconeogenesis, and lipolysis, all biological processes that increase the availability of vital energy.

The two main divisions of the adaptation response are the corticotropin-releasing hormone (CRH) system (including the hypothalamus, pituitary, and adrenal cortex, or HPA axis) and the locus ceruleus-norepinephrine (LC-NE)/autonomic (sympathetic) nervous systems. Response to stress is associated with an increase in release of CRH, which activates the pituitary-adrenal axis. This then causes the anterior lobe of the pituitary to release adrenocorticotrophic hormone (ACTH) (see Johnson, Kamilaris, Chrousos, & Gold, 1992, for a more detailed review). In humans, CRH shows a distinct circadian rhythm such that ACTH is normally highest at about 8 a.m. and lowest at around midnight. When ACTH is released, glucocorticoids (cortisol and 11-deoxycortisol in primates and humans and corticosterone in rodents) are secreted by the adrenal cortex. Thus, when a stressful event occurs, CRH is produced, which leads to release of ACTH and, in turn, cortisol. There is a negative feedback loop such that circulating glucocorticoids inhibit the release of ACTH by the pituitary and also the further release of CRH by the hypothalamus (Keller-Wood & Dallman, 1984). The hippocampus, which has a high density of glucocorticoid receptor cells, also plays an important role in dampening HPA activation (Sapolsky, 1992; Sapolsky, Krey, & McEwen, 1985).

CRH also stimulates the arousal and sympathetic centers through projections to the brain stem and the LC-NE system (Valentino, Cha, & Foote, 1986). Activation of the LC-NE system results in widespread release of NE throughout the brain. This release results in increased arousal and vigilance, and increased anxiety. The CRH and LC/NE systems function so that activation of one system facilitates the activity of the other. In other words, the release of NE can stimulate the release of CRH and vice versa (Calogero, Gallucci, Chrousos, & Gold, 1988).

Rodent studies have led to the conclusion that CRH can be conceptualized as coordinating not only the metabolic and circulatory stress responses as discussed earlier, but also behavioral responses to stress (Sutton, Koob, Le Moal, Rivier, & Vale, 1982). CRH receptor neurons are widely distributed in the brain (De Souza et al., 1985), perhaps underlying the wide-ranging effects of CRH on behavior. CRH produces behavioral arousal, manifested as increased locomotor activity in familiar settings and freezing in novel settings (Sutton et al., 1982). High levels of CRH can also cause bizarre repetitive behavior (Koob & Bloom, 1985). Interestingly, ACTH reduces exploration in a novel environment without affecting overall locomotion and can also cause excessive grooming behavior (File, 1978; Gipsen, van der Poel, & van Wimersma Greidanus, 1973). These results were established by administering CRH or ACTH directly to animals.

With all this as background, we are ready to take a brief look at what data from a number of rodent studies have shown regarding the likely biological processes that might be altered by exposure to prenatal stress. The most important finding seems to be an abnormal regulation of the HPA axis in the adult offspring of gestationally stressed females. The terms *dysregulation* and *abnormal regulation* are usually used to denote either hypofunctioning or hyperfunctioning of aspects of the HPA system that results in either physical health impacts or behavioral alterations (Chrousos &

Gold, 1992). Abnormal regulation or dysregulation of the HPA axis has been shown under baseline conditions in some studies (Fride et al., 1986; Peters, 1982) but not in others (Takahashi, Turner, & Kalin, 1992). Dysregulation of the HPA axis has been found to be more pronounced after exposure to stress, in that prenatally stressed offspring show enhanced or more prolonged elevation of corticosterone after stressful events (novel environment, restraint, or saline injections) compared to controls (Fride et al., 1986; McCormick et al., 1995; Takahashi et al., 1992).

The first question to ask about the reported heightened sensitivity to stressors in prenatally stressed offspring concerns its developmental origin. The mechanisms that subserve the enhanced stress reactivity and dysregulation of the HPA axis are not fully understood at present. The basic idea is that stress during pregnancy alters some aspects of the brain during development that are either part of the HPA axis or its feedback processes. Among the mechanisms suggested by research are: (a) altered oxygenation of the fetus during episodes of stress, and (b) glucocorticoids or other substances produced in the mother as a stress response that then cross the placenta during stress episodes and influence the fetus.

Effects of stress on fetal oxygenation have been shown in studies with rhesus monkeys. Myers (1975) used indwelling catheters placed in the femoral arteries of pregnant monkey mothers and their fetuses and showed that short periods of maternal stress caused fetal heart rate slowing, depression of fetal blood pressure, and impairment in fetal oxygenation. Similarly, Morishima, Pederson, and Finster (1978) found that maternal agitation was associated with a decrease in fetal heart rate and arterial oxygenation. Additionally, infusing catecholamines (epinephrine or norepinephrine) into the maternal circulation reduced fetal oxygenation (Adamsons, Mueller-Heubach, & Myers, 1971).

A number of animal experiments have supported the hypothesis that hormones transported from the maternal blood to the placenta are involved as mediators of prenatal stress effects. For example, when stress-induced glucocorticoid secretion was blocked in rodent dams, the effects of prenatal stress on the offspring were similarly suppressed (Barbazanges et al., 1996). Another study showed that when pregnant dams were injected with CRH from day 14–21 of gestation, the pups showed effects similar to those observed from prenatally stressed females (Williams et al., 1995). Moreover, injecting the dams with ACTH during the last third of pregnancy altered the developing HPA axis and decreased dopaminergic activity in the pups while increasing serotonergic activity (Fameli, Kitraki, & Stylianopoulou, 1994).

Elevated levels of glucocorticoids in the rodent dam have been shown to cross the placental barrier. In humans, it is known that during pregnancy the concentration of maternal plasma ACTH rises progressively (Weir et al., 1971); this rise leads to an increase in maternal plasma concentrations of cortisol. Although normally a rise in cortisol will lead to a decrease in ACTH (a negative feedback), during pregnancy it appears that the normal feedback linkage is lost, at least in maternal plasma levels of these hormones (see Jacobs, 1991, for a good summary of

HPA-axis function during pregnancy). Through most of pregnancy, the fetal tissues convert cortisol to the inactive metabolite, cortisone (to protect the fetus from inappropriate early fetal maturation), but late in pregnancy there is a shift in fetal metabolism such that there is a surge in fetal cortisol levels. This surge in cortisol is thought to have a role in maturation of the fetal lungs, and may also be important in initiating labor. Because in humans the placenta converts most maternal cortisol to cortisone, the mechanisms through which prenatal stress influences the fetus are not completely understood. Perhaps there is a threshold for cortisol conversion above which it passes the placental barrier without being converted into cortisone. Because glucocorticoids have been shown to cross the placental barrier in animals, they are likely to be part of the process by which prenatal stress influences development in humans as well.

What areas of the developing brain might be influenced by glucocorticoids? Some research has shown that in rodents when glucocorticoids cross the placenta they affect areas of the brain that contain glucocorticoid receptors, especially the hippocampus (Henry, Kabbaj, Simon, Le Moal, & Maccari, 1994; Maccari et al., 1995). The hippocampus is important because it is known that hippocampal glucocorticoid receptors regulate, at least partially, the negative feedback on the HPA axis in adult animals (De Kloet & Reul, 1987; McEwen, De Kloet, & Rostene, 1986). Moreover, research has demonstrated that chronic stress exposure in adult animals can reduce hippocampal neuronal density (Sapolsky, 1992), disrupting the HPA axis feedback mechanisms such that subsequent stressors may result in greater behavioral and physiological responses (Plotsky & Meaney, 1993).

One of the important mechanisms for the behavioral and neuroendocrine stress-response abnormalities in prenatally stressed offspring is an alteration in the cholinergic neurons found in the offspring's limbic system (specifically the septum and the hippocampus) (Day, Koehl, Deroche, Le Moal, & Maccari, 1998). This conclusion is based on recent evidence indicating that prenatally stressed rodents showed increased hippocampal acetylcholine release when tested under the stress of saline injections (Day et al., 1998). Other evidence suggests that cholingergic neurons regulate the hippocampal glucocorticoid receptors that are involved in the feedback inhibition of glucocorticoid secretion (McEwen et al., 1986). Therefore, Day et al. (1998) suggested that hypersensitivity of the cholinergic neurons of the septum and hippocampus could be at least partially responsible for the abnormalities in HPA axis activity found in prenatally stressed rats.

In addition to potential affects on cholinergic neurons, prenatal stress has been shown to impact other neurotransmitters in the brain. For example, compared to control animals, prenatally stressed rodents exhibit increased dopaminergic (DA) activity in the right prefrontal cortex and decreased DA activity in the right nucleus accumbens, indicating that prenatal stress may alter the cerebral lateralization of DA activity. It has also been shown that prenatal stress causes long-term alterations in DA receptors in the striatum as well as increased sensitivity to the behavioral effects of DA agonists (DA agonists include substances such as amphetamines) (Henry et al., 1995). Another study suggests that DA innervation of the nucleus accumbens (which is considered to be part of the reward system of the brain) could subserve the relationship between behavioral despair and altered motor lateralization reported in female offspring of stressed mothers. Specifically, prenatally stressed females showed an increase of DA and a decrease of 3,4 dihydroxyphenylacetic acid (DOPAC) and homovanillic acid (HVA) levels (metabolites of DA) in the nucleus accumbens of the right side of the brain (Alonso, Navarro, Santana, & Rodriguez, 1997). Others have reported that prenatal stress produces increased concentrations of NE and its metabolite, 3-methoxy-4-hydroxyphenylglycol (MHPG), in the rat cerebral cortex and LC and reduced DA and increased DOPAC in the LC (Takahashi, Turner, & Kalin, 1992). These might be interpreted as indicators of a chronic activation of the sympathetic nervous system. Finally, Peters (1986, 1988) reported altered development of 5-HT (or serotonin) neurons in several brain regions in prenatally stressed rats, possibly due to increased levels of plasma tryptophan expressed by the stressed mother (Peters, 1990).

Alterations in neurotransmitter systems contribute to various forms of psychopathology in humans. Thus, one way of summarizing these findings is to say that prenatal stress in animals not only induces depressive-like behaviors, but also modifies brain chemistry in ways that are similar to those that have been reported in depressed human patients. Indeed, a number of researchers have suggested that prenatal stress may serve as a predisposing factor to mental illness (Alonso, Navarro, & Rodriguez, 1994). It is well known that in humans, stress can trigger depression in predisposed individuals. Elevated glucocorticoids are commonly found in depressed individuals (Murphy, 1991) and brain dopaminergic neurotransmission is decreased in depression as well (Van Praag, 1982). Thus the observed effects of prenatal stress hormones on offspring motor behavior (locomotor and exploratory behaviors) could be mediated by directly affecting the maturation of the developing dopaminergic system.

PRIMATE STUDIES

Having discussed how rodent studies have contributed to the prenatal stress literature, we turn our attention to the nonhuman primate studies, which have received remarkably little attention to date. Nonhuman primate models, however, provide rich opportunities for prenatal stress studies because of their slow-paced fetal growth rates, long gestations, enriched placental nourishment, and single births—all features that make them more similar to humans (Newell-Morris & Fahrenbruch, 1985). Also, the slower postnatal growth rates in nonhuman primates allow more extensive examination of the neurobehavioral integrity of the infant than is possible in rapidly developing rodents (Goldman-Rakic & Brown, 1982). Furthermore, nonhuman primate offspring are similar enough to humans during the neonatal period to allow the use of instruments originally developed for humans (Schneider & Suomi, 1992). The richness of their behavioral and social organization and their ability to perform complex cognitive tasks makes them a superior model of behavioral development compared to the rodent.

Since at least 1979, researchers have been evaluating the influence of psychosocial stress on physiological and behavioral systems in nonhuman primates (Coe et al., 1978). Recently, Coe[1] and his colleagues have focused on the effects of prenatal stress on immune responses in rhesus monkey offspring (see Coe, Lubach, & Karaszewski, 1999). Sackett (1981) has studied birth outcomes in pigtailed macaques, reporting that exposure to prenatal stress increased fetal loss in female pigtailed macaques that, based on their prior breeding history, were considered to be at low risk for fetal loss. Interestingly, there was no effect on the abortion rate of those females at high risk for a poor pregnancy outcome. Also, compared to unstressed offspring, prenatally stressed pigtailed macaques showed morphological alterations that are associated with a higher incidence of infant mortality (Newell-Morris, Fahrenbruch, & Sackett, 1989). These primate studies laid the groundwork for a series of prenatal stress studies that we have been conducting at the University of Wisconsin Harlow Primate Laboratory. The following section will review these studies in some detail.

PRENATAL STRESS IN RHESUS MONKEYS

In our studies, we administered a mild daily stressor to the pregnant female monkeys, and conducted repeated observations of the infants' development, especially during developmental transitions, such as separation from the mother. With the exception of one study, the nonhuman primate species we chose to study is the rhesus macaque, an Old World monkey. We chose this primate species for several reasons. First, the normative pattern of rhesus monkey behavioral development is well-known and thoroughly documented in the literature (see Suomi, 1997, for a review). Also, rhesus monkeys breed well in captivity, they are responsive to mild stress, yet they produce viable offspring that are available for prospective longitudinal observations. In addition, our past research provided measures of neonatal development that are closely analogous to those used with humans.

We review the results of both published and recently completed but unpublished research, concentrating on the data from two studies of prenatal stress in rhesus monkeys (Schneider, 1992a, 1992b, 1992c; Schneider, Roughton, Koehler, & Lubach, 1999). In addition, where appropriate, we also discuss the results of two other studies conducted in collaboration with Coe at the Harlow Primate Laboratory (Schneider & Coe, 1993; Schneider, Coe, & Lubach, 1992). One of those studies involved a sample of squirrel monkeys (Schneider & Coe, 1993), and the other involved rhesus monkeys that were not exposed to prenatal stress, but instead were

---

[1]We are grateful to Dr. Christopher Coe for kindling our interest in the topic of prenatal stress.

administered ACTH during pregnancy to simulate some of the physiological effects of stress (Schneider et al., 1992). In our two studies with rhesus monkeys, we varied the rearing conditions (hand-reared in the Harlow Primate Lab nursery in Experiment 1, and mother-reared in Experiment 2), and the timing of the prenatal stressor (midgestation in Experiment 1, and either early or midgestation in Experiment 2). In all of the studies we discuss, we have conducted assessments of neonatal and infant neurobehavioral functioning modeled after Brazelton's (1984) neonatal test battery. In addition, across the studies we conducted a variety of other behavioral and physiological measures of functioning including object permanence, behavior in a novel environment, behavior during separation from an attachment figure (either mother or peers), maternal–infant interaction behaviors (when infants were reared with their mothers), peer interaction behaviors, plasma cortisol and ACTH, and concentrations of neurotransmitters in cerebrospinal fluid. In addition, we weighed the infant monkeys when they were tested during infancy, and maternal weight gain during pregnancy was measured.

Females for our study were selected from a large breeding colony at the Harlow Primate Lab. The stressor employed in our two studies of prenatal stress in rhesus monkeys consisted of removing the pregnant female from her home cage, transporting her to a darkened room, and administering three noise bursts (115 dB sound at 1 m, 1300 Hz) randomly over a 10-minute period. The stress treatment was chosen as a model of recurrent daily episodic stress. Noise has also been used as a prenatal stressor in rodent animal studies (Fride & Weinstock, 1988). Also, studies with humans show that uncontrollable noise (such as aircraft, highway traffic, and construction noise) is a source of psychological stress (Evans, Hygge, & Bullinger, 1995; Ising, Rebentisch, Poustka, & Curio, 1990; Kryter, 1990). Our data show that the stressor does activate the HPA axis in the mother, significantly raising plasma cortisol levels (in Experiment 1, baseline = 25.2 ± 2.2 µg/dl; post stress = 34.8 ± 2.4 µg/dl [mean $\pm$ *SEM*]). All females receiving the stressor were removed from their home cages at the same time of day and were placed in individual transport cages. The stressor was administered five times per week at 1600 hours for females in the stress condition. Controls were undisturbed during pregnancy, except for normal animal husbandry.

For our first study, the stressor was administered to pregnant females on days 90 to 145 of a 165-day gestation period. We refer to this timing of the stressor as midgestation stress. In both studies, we specifically avoided the very early gestation period (conception to day 45) in order to minimize the risk of inducing early fetal loss. Similarly, we avoided administering the stressor during late gestation to reduce the induction of early parturition, which could complicate the interpretation of our data (see Schneider, 1992a, 1992b, 1992c, for details).

Twenty-four infant monkeys (12 prenatally stressed and 12 controls) were born to these mothers in our first study. After the infants were born, they were separated from their mothers and hand-reared in the laboratory primate nursery. All infants were reared according to standard nutritional protocol (free access to Similac formula) (see Schneider, 1992a). In order to minimize any potential negative effects associated with hand-rearing, each infant cage was enriched with toys and climbing devices (see Schneider & Suomi, 1992, for details). The infants were also socialized in play groups with another infant from the same experimental condition for 15 minutes four times each week until they were approximately 30 days of age. At 30 days of age, the infants were then housed in mixed-sex groups of 3 monkeys from the same prenatal condition. Hand-rearing in the nursery, while labor intensive, was done to prevent confounding the prenatal stress condition with differential maternal treatment that could potentially result from maternal exposure to stress during pregnancy. This rearing procedure also enabled continuous access to the infant for testing.

In our second study (Schneider et al., 1999), we examined the timing of prenatal stress in order to determine whether a sensitive period for these effects would emerge. There were two groups of prenatally stressed infants: an early stress group of 10 monkeys, another group of 8 monkeys that experienced prenatal stress during midgestation as in the first study, and a control group of 13 monkeys. Prenatal stress was administered to the early stress group between days 45 to 90 postconception according to the same procedure as described for our first study. In the second study, the monkeys were mother-reared.

We describe the results of these studies later, proceeding longitudinally through the assessments. A key issue is that of the processes of developmental continuity—do the differences in infant functioning that we have found influence later functioning? These longitudinal issues are explored using primarily the data of our two studies of prenatal stress in rhesus monkeys. Where appropriate, we also describe the results of two other studies: one study was with rhesus monkeys who were not prenatally stressed, but were given ACTH to simulate stress, and the other was with squirrel monkeys who were prenatally stressed with a different procedure (maternal stress due to social relocation).

Measures of Gestation Variables and Birth Weight

Because the human literature suggests that prenatal stress is associated with preterm birth (short gestation duration) and low birth weight, we tested for condition differences in these variables. Gestation duration did not differ significantly across conditions in any of our studies. This was a result that we hoped would occur. We wanted to create an animal model for prenatal stress effects that did not involve deleterious effects on the pregnancy itself. The birth weights of all infants in both of our studies were within one standard deviation of what is considered normal for rhesus monkeys ($M \pm SD = 501 \pm 64$ for males and 478 ± 61 for females based on 1,270 rhesus monkeys at the Harlow Primate Laboratory from 1973 through 1997). Thus, none of our monkeys would fall in a category analogous to clinically low birth weight in humans. Birth weight did differ significantly across conditions in both studies. In our first study (hand-reared monkeys), the mean weight of the prenatal stress monkeys was less than that of the control monkeys. In Study 2, our results suggest that the timing of prenatal stress could influence its effect on birth weight. The early stress condition infants had slightly smaller birth weights ($M = 474$ g) than either the midgestation-stressed infants ($M = 560$ g) or the control infants ($M = 516$ g) in Study 2.

Infant Sensorimotor Development

At birth, rhesus macaque infants demonstrate neuromotor capabilities and temperamental characteristics that are remarkably similar to human neonates (Schneider & Suomi, 1992). This facilitates the use of tests that can be adapted directly from human tests, such as the BNBAS (Brazelton, 1984). In fact, prior factor analytic studies with a large sample of typically developing rhesus infants have identified four areas of functioning that are remarkably similar to those factors identified in human studies (Schneider, Moore, Suomi, & Champoux, 1991). These four domains are: Orientation, Motor Maturity, Motor Activity, and State Control.

All infants were tested several times across the first month of life on this test battery, and were weighed at each testing. Results of our first study (hand-reared monkeys) indicated the prenatally stressed infants scored significantly lower on Motor Maturity and Motor Activity, and marginally lower on Orientation compared to controls. These differences occurred even though there were no group differences in gestation duration. When individual items that comprise the clusters were examined, it was found that the prenatally stressed infants performed worse than controls on tests of muscle tonus, coordination, balance, and had slower response speeds. They were also more distractible and passive. These results are shown in Fig. 6.1.

It should be noted that in the study described earlier, the monkey infant was removed from its mother at birth and hand-reared in a primate nursery. While we have shown that rhesus monkeys reared in this environment develop well physically (i.e., gain weight rapidly and score well on tests of motor maturity), they have been found to display behavioral abnormalities (Harlow and Harlow, 1966). Nonetheless, this rearing procedure was implemented in order to eliminate potential effects from differential maternal treatment that might confound prenatal stress treatment and render our results difficult to interpret. Thus, the next logical step was to determine whether a similar profile would emerge in prenatally stressed infants reared with their mothers (Schneider & Coe, 1993; Schneider et al., 1992; Schneider et al., in press).

In Study 2 (mother-reared rhesus infants), a very similar pattern of scores occurred on the infant tests (Schneider et al., 1999). These results are shown in Fig. 6.2. Again there were effects of prenatal stress on motor maturity, motor activity, and orientation. The effects were also significant when birth weight was entered as a covariate. The infants who experienced prenatal stress early during gestation appear to be more strongly affected than the midgestation-stress infants. These results replicate the main findings of our first experiment, and show that they gen-

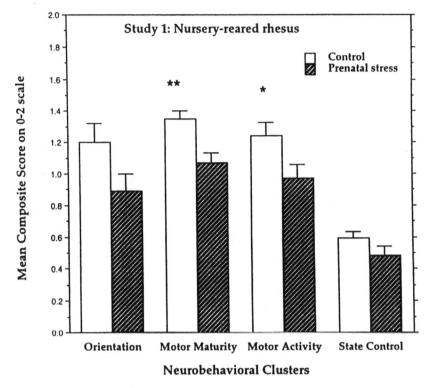

FIG. 6.1.   Infant Behavioral Assessment Scale (IBAS) composite scores for infants from two pregnancy conditions (control N = 12, mid-late stress N = 12). Bars represent standard errors. *$p < .05$, **$p < .01$.

eralize to a mother-reared sample. In addition, the results suggest that the timing of prenatal stress may be very important. While infants from both early and mid-late gestation stress conditions scored lower than controls on measures of attention and neuromotor maturity, infants from early gestation stress had more pervasive and pronounced neuromotor impairments. Moreover, a condition X day of testing interaction indicated that the pattern of development for controls differed across groups. While controls showed rapid developmental changes across testing days, the early and mid-late gestation stressed monkeys showed a flat or variable developmental trajectory (see Schneider et al., 1999, for details).

    We also have data on the infant neurobehavioral functioning of rhesus monkeys from a study conducted in collaboration with Coe. In this study, pregnant female rhesus monkeys were exposed to a 2-week period of ACTH (Schneider et al., 1992). As noted previously, rodent studies have indicated that ACTH treatments to the pregnant dam resulted in effects on the offspring that were similar to prenatal stress effects. When the rhesus infants in this study were tested with the identical neonatal test battery used in the previously described studies, we de-

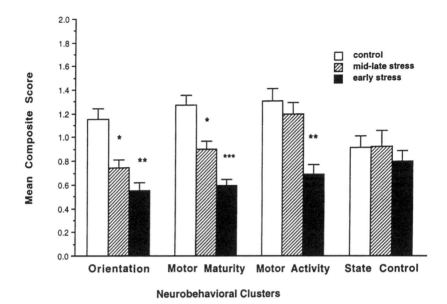

FIG. 6.2. IBAS composite scores for infants from three different pregnancy conditions (control $N = 10$, mid-late stress $N = 8$, early stress $N = 10$). Bars represent standard errors. *$p < .05$, **$p < .001$. From "Growth and development following prenatal stress exposure in primates: An examination of ontogenetic vulnerability," by M. L. Schneider et al., 1999, *Child Development, 70*(2), pp. 263–274. Copyright 1999. Reprinted with permission.

tected a strikingly similar behavioral profile across the three prenatal conditions that included a shorter attention span and motor impairments. In addition, the prenatal ACTH treated monkeys showed increased irritability and decreased consolability in the infants (see Fig. 6.3).

Since the first study from our lab had detected a shortened attention span in prenatally stressed monkeys, we also videotaped the infants in the ACTH study immediately after maternal separation for neurobehavioral testing. This allowed more detailed quantification of state regulation. This research was part of the Master's Thesis of the late Elizabeth Roughton. Using a computer-assisted continuous scoring coding system, the amount of time spent in drowsy, alert, and irritable states was coded. The infants from ACTH-treated mothers spent more time in a drowsy state than controls, especially during the postseparation period when acute stress was the highest. In contrast, controls spent more time in an active alert state, presumably searching for their mothers, a species-typical adaptive response to maternal separation (Roughton, Schneider, Bromley, & Coe, 1998). The results are displayed in Fig. 6.4.

As will be shown later, we have also found an increase in sleep in the nursery-reared prenatally stressed infants when they were tested in the playroom (an open

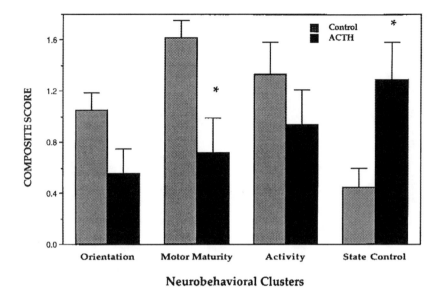

Neurobehavioral Clusters

FIG. 6.3.   IBAS scores obtained at 2 weeks of age; $n = 6$ for each condition. Bars represent standard errors. $*p < .05$. From "Endocrine activation mimics the adverse effects of prenatal stress on the neuromotor development of the infant primate" by M. L. Schneider et al., 1992, *Developmental Psychobiology*, *25*(6), pp. 427-439. Copyright 1992. Reprinted with permission.

field) at 6 months of age. This increase in drowsiness and sleep may be similar to a phenomenon documented by Emde and colleagues (1971) who reported that human infants showed an increase in non-rapid eye movement (NREM) sleep following circumcision. Their interpretation was that NREM sleep or quiet sleep served as a coping mechanism after a stressful event, to assist recovery from the perturbation. Similarly, Gunner and her colleagues (1985) found that newborn human infants showed increases in quiet or NREM sleep after circumcision. Moreover, they demonstrated an association between quiet sleep and the reestablishment of baseline adrenocortical hormone levels. One interpretation of our results is that the adaptation response of the ACTH-exposed monkeys is exhausted more quickly than in the controls.

Finally, in an experiment with squirrel monkeys not only were the infants reared with their mothers for the first 6 months of life, but disruption of the social relationships of the pregnant female was the stressful manipulation (Schneider & Coe, 1993). This manipulation was based on previous studies indicating that changes in the composition of monkey social groups result in marked changes in behavior, autonomic, and endocrine activity that persisted for several weeks (Kaplan, Manuck, & Gatsonis, 1990; Mendoza, Coe, & Levine, 1979). Moreover, naturalistic studies on monkeys have shown that dominance relations during pregnancy can influence reproductive success and infant development as

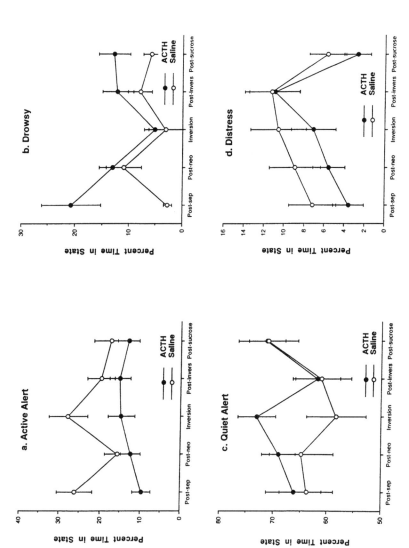

FIG. 6.4. Mean proportional time in neonatal state for infants from two pregnancy conditions (saline, *n* = 10; adrenocortioctrophic hormone [ACTH], *n* = 12) across episodes (postseparation [post-sep], post-neonatal [post-neo], inversion, postinversion [post-invers], postsucrose). Bars represent standard errors. From "Maternal endocrine activation during pregnancy alters neurobehavioral state in primate infants" by E. C. Roughton et al, 1998, *American Journal of Occupational Therapy, 52*(2), pp. 90–98. Copyright 1998. Reprinted with permission.

well (Wasser & Starling, 1988). This experiment also helps establish the generalizability of the results to another nonhuman primate species. The study involved three different pregnancy conditions: (a) midgestation stress (monkeys were moved once), (b) chronic stress (monkeys were moved three times), and (c) undisturbed controls (46 monkeys). The infants remained with their mothers during rearing. However, on day 15 of life they were separated from their mothers briefly for neurobehavioral testing. This particular age point was selected on the basis of previous findings showing that it provides the best and most stable measure of neurobehavior in the primate infant (Schneider & Suomi, 1992).

All squirrel monkey infants were tested under the standardized conditions utilized in our laboratory for assessing early neuromotor capabilities and temperamental characteristics. The infants from the chronic stress condition had shorter attention spans and shorter looking episodes during the administration of the ori-

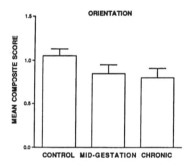
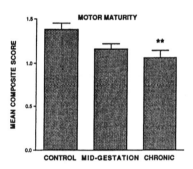

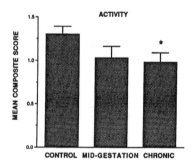
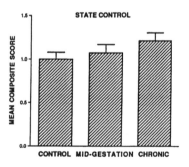

FIG. 6.5.   IBAS scores for infants from three different pregnancy conditions (control $N = 48$; midgestation stress $N = 18$; chronic stress $N = 26$). Bars represent standard errors. $*p < .05$, $**p < .01$. From "Repeated social stress during pregnancy impairs neuromotor development of the primate infant," by M. L. Schneider and C. L. Coe, 1993, *Journal of Developmental and Behavioral Pediatrics, 14*(2), pp. 81–87. Copyright 1993. Reprinted with permission.

entation items, poorer motor abilities, and impaired balance. Figure 6.5 graphs these results. This pattern was strikingly similar to that observed in our study of hand-reared rhesus monkeys born to mothers exposed to a noise stressor for a 6-week period during mid-late gestation. Interestingly, these effects were not evident (compared to the control group) when a single stressful period was imposed on squirrel monkeys during midgestation. Thus, the results suggest that chronic stress may be more deleterious to development than a single stressful event.

In summary, across four separate experiments with two species of nonhuman primates there is evidence that prenatal stress influences the neurobehavioral functioning of the infant. The pattern of results across the four studies is summarized in Table 6.1. We summarize these effects as showing an adverse effect of prenatal stress on motor maturity and attentional functioning. Because the same profile was shown in the offspring of monkeys given ACTH during pregnancy

TABLE 6.1
Summary of Monkey Infant Neurobehavioral Effects

Study (manipulation)	Infant Neurobehavioral Effects
Hand-reared rhesus (noise)	↓ Motor Maturity (tone, response speed, coordination, balance)
	↑ Distractibility
	↑ Passivity
Squirrel monkeys (social relocation)	↓ Motor Maturity (tone, balance, postrotary nystagmus)
	↓ Attention Span
	↓ Activity
Mother-reared rhesus (ACTH-treated)	↓ Motor Maturity (tone, balance, postrotary nystagmus)
	↓ Attention Span
	↓ Active Alert State
	↑ Drowsy State
	↑ Irritability
Mother-reared rhesus (noise-timing) Early gestation stress	↓ Motor Maturity (tone, response speed, coordination, postrotary nystagmus)
	↓ Attention Span
	↓ Motor Activity
Mid-late gestation stress	↓ Motor Maturity (tone, rotation)
	↓ Orientation

Note. ↓ and ↑ denote a decrease or increase, respectively, in the dependent variable as a function of prenatal stress.

(but were not otherwise stressed), this suggests that maternal endocrine activation is one important mechanism of prenatal stress effects.

The mother-reared rhesus monkeys in our second study also allowed the collection of data to examine the potential role of mother–infant interaction in the prenatal stress effects. Mother–infant pairs were observed during the first 27 weeks of life, and the amount of time spent in the species-typical mutual ventral cling was recorded. A typical developmental trend in mutual ventral cling is for it to be close to 100% during the first week or so of life, followed by a decline as the infant gains motor skills and independence. By about 6 months of age, the mothers are beginning to reject their infants' attempts to nurse and cling (approximately 6 months of age is the normal weaning age at the Harlow Primate Laboratory, the time at which infants are separated from their mothers). We thought that the altered motor development shown in the neurobehavioral tests would show up in the amount of mutual-ventral cling. As shown in Fig. 6.6, this was the case. The control monkeys showed a steady decline in the percentage of ventral cling over the first 27 weeks of life. The two groups of prenatally stressed infants showed a more erratic pattern of mutual-ventral clinging, and just before weaning (week 27) both groups were showing higher clinging than the control group.

In addition to recording mutual-ventral cling, the mothers' behavior was coded qualitatively by observers on four dimensions: receptive to needs, nurturance, freedom to explore, hostility to strangers, and a global rating of quality of mothering. A sixth variable, a global rating of infant adjustment, was also rated. There were no effects of condition that approached significance for any of these vari-

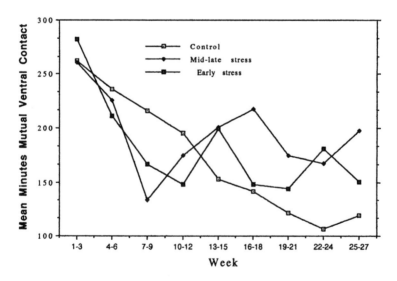

FIG. 6.6.   Mean number of seconds of mutual ventral contact between mother and infant during a 5-minute observation period as a function of prenatal condition (control, early stress, and mid-late gestation stress) across the first 27 weeks of life.

ables (all *ps* > .10). These results suggest that the effects of prenatal stress on early neurobehavior of the offspring are unlikely to be mediated by differential mother–infant interactions (though we are cautious about drawing a conclusion based on nonsignificance, of course, given the modest sample sizes that are a necessity in nonhuman primate research).

Object Permanence Tests

When the infants in our first study were 45-days-old, we began a series of assessments of object permanence to evaluate their early cognitive development (Schneider, 1992b). This is the only study in which we assessed object permanence because these assessments require access to the infant separate from its mother. For our mother-reared samples, it would have been too disruptive to separate the infants from their mothers repeatedly to conduct these tests of infant sensorimotor development. The procedure and apparatus were adapted from the test sequence developed by Burbacher, Grant, and Mottet (1986) that showed sensitivity to neurotoxic effects in monkeys. The infants were tested four times per week on a series of tasks: plain reach, partial and full hiding with a screen and with a well. For plain reach, the infant was shown a stimulus object (plastic toy) baited with a raisin or fruit loop and allowed to pick up the baited object. Once the infant reached a performance criterion on this task, the infant was allowed to watch as the baited object was placed either in full view or partially hidden (partial hiding) or fully concealed (full hiding) behind a screen or in a well. The infant was allowed 15 seconds to retrieve the object. As shown in Fig. 6.7, there were no significant differences across groups for the plain reach task. However, the prenatally stressed infants took more sessions to reach a performance criterion than controls from undisturbed pregnancies, and the prenatally stressed infants were older when they reached the criterion.

Response to Novelty and Social Stress

Thus far, our description has concentrated on sensorimotor behavior, such as required in the infant neurobehavioral testing, and the performance of motor tasks involving retrieval of hidden objects. An important finding is that the prenatally stressed infants were markedly delayed in attaining certain sensorimotor milestones. Because the rodent literature has suggested that prenatally stressed offspring showed heightened behavioral responsivity to stress (Weinstock, 1997), we also examined behavioral characteristics such as exploratory tendencies, as well as disturbance behaviors under mildly stressful conditions.

How would the prenatally stressed infants respond to a novel, challenging situation? Moreover, would the patterns of response to stress observed persist into adulthood? For our first study, the monkeys were tested at several points in their lives for their behavioral reactions to a novel situation. Some of these tests were

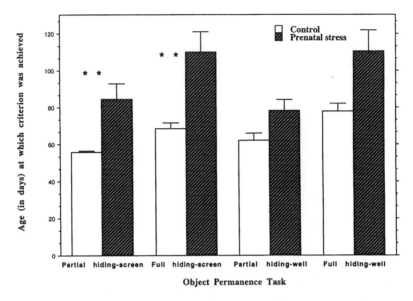

FIG. 6.7.   Mean age at which criterion was reached on object permanence task as a function of prenatal condition (control $N = 12$, mid-late stress $N = 12$).

conducted at important developmental transitions such as weaning (approximately 6 months of age), and at adolescence (approximately 3 years of age).

The first test in this series was undertaken when the monkeys were approximately 6-months-old (Schneider, 1992c). The monkeys were tested for 15-minutes each day for 3 consecutive days in a primate playroom. The playroom is a large room containing a variety of movable and nonmovable wire mesh climbing and sitting platforms. Testers observed the monkeys through a glass observation window and recorded the duration and frequency of well-defined behaviors using a computer-assisted scoring system.

Playroom studies have been employed for decades at the Harlow Primate Laboratory. The typical response for a monkey to show in this situation is initial wariness followed by eventual exploratory behavior. The results are shown in Fig. 6.8. As shown, the typical response is exactly what was observed in the control monkeys; they spent more time in gross motor or exploratory behavior (more locomotion, climbing, and exploring the environment). In contrast, the prenatally stressed monkeys showed high levels of disturbance behavior (clinging to each other and self-directed behaviors). In addition, an unexpected finding emerged as well. Specifically, while observed in the playroom, it was noted that 50% of the prenatally stressed monkeys fell asleep (see the far right-hand bar in Fig. 6.8). This was surprising to us, because we have conducted numerous playroom studies and had yet to observe this unusual phenomenon. We speculate that the heightened state of

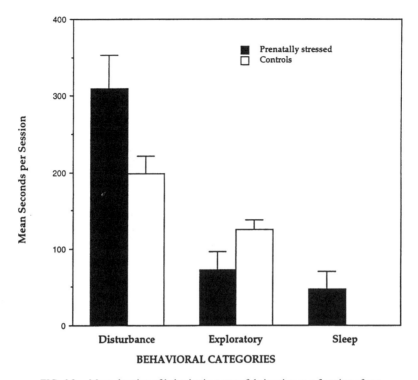

FIG. 6.8. Mean duration of behavior in a stressful situation as a function of prenatal condition (stress, control). Bars represent standard errors. From "Prenatal stress exposure alters postnatal behavioral expression under conditions of novelty challenge in rhesus monkey infants," by M. L. Schneider, 1992, *Developmental Psychobiology, 25*(7), pp. 141–152. Copyright 1992. Reprinted with permission.

distress (evidenced by excessive clinging and self-directed behaviors compared to controls) could have exhausted the stress adaptation resources of the prenatally stressed monkeys, causing them to lapse into drowsiness or a sleep state. As mentioned earlier, analogous findings of sleep in human infants following stress have been reported by Emde and colleagues (1971) and Gunnar et al. (1985).

The second novelty challenge test of the monkeys in our first study was when they were 8-months-old. At this point, the monkeys were separated from their cage mates and housed individually for 3 days. During this 3-day period their behavior was scored three times daily. Blood samples and cerebrospinal fluid samples were collected as well (the physiological measures will be discussed later). The behavioral data indicated that prenatally stressed monkeys exhibited more self-grooming and clinging than controls (these are considered abnormal behaviors), and less locomotion, play, and climbing behaviors (Schneider et al., 1998). Thus, it is evident that there is some developmental continuity in the monkeys' reactions to these novelty challenge episodes (at 6 months in the playroom, and at 8 months during social separation); the prenatally stressed monkeys exhibited more disturbance behavior and less exploratory behavior on both occasions. These findings are strikingly consistent with reports of prenatally stressed rodents, as discussed earlier. Interestingly, these monkeys also react to separation with a behavior profile that may be suggestive of depression. Indeed, it is well documented that dispair or depression in rhesus monkeys is characterized by sharp decreases in play and increases in passive, self-directed behaviors (Harlow & Suomi, 1974; Kaufman & Rosenblum, 1967). This raises the question of whether prenatally stressed monkeys might be more vulnerable to depression.

When the hand-reared monkeys in the first study were 18 months of age, we asked whether the enhanced stress reactivity noted at 6 and 8 months of age would persist. Thus, after collecting baseline data, the monkeys were exposed to four mild stress episodes. These consisted of moving the monkey to a new cage, moving to a new cage with exposure to a noise stressor, separation from cage mates, and separation from cages mates combined with exposure to a noise stressor (employed in a random order across individuals). Videotaped sessions revealed striking differences across groups for social behaviors, with prenatally stressed monkeys engaging in more clinging to peers (a disturbance behavior for rhesus monkeys) and less species-typical social behavior (i.e., proximity and contact) (Clarke & Schneider, 1993).

Because of the shorter life span of the rhesus monkey compared to the human, we were able to follow the monkeys in our first study into adolescence, or 3 to 4 years of age. At 3 to 4 years of age, the monkeys were tested again in the playroom (Clarke, Soto, Bergholz, & Schneider, 1996). The results, provided in Fig. 6.9, show that the control monkeys increased exploration over the 30-minute test period, but the prenatally stressed monkeys did not. Vocalization shows the opposite pattern: control animals show an increase in vocalization over the test time, but the prenatally stressed monkeys show initially high vocalizations followed by a decline. The initially high vocalization of the prenatal stress group, combined with their low exploration, is evidence of a higher arousal level for the prenatally stressed animals compared to the control animals. The experience of just being in the playroom alone leads to a prototypical stress reaction of protest reaction of vocalization in the prenatally stressed group.

Also at 3 to 4 years of age, the monkeys in our first study (hand-reared) were observed after they were separated from their cage mates and placed into a new group. New group formation is a stressful event for rhesus monkeys, in that they must develop new social structures and relationships. Under these socially challenging conditions, prenatally stressed monkeys were found to show more stereotyped behavior, self-clasping, and general disturbance behavior compared to controls. They were also observed to spend significantly less time in play behavior, less time in exploratory behavior, and more time in freezing behavior or inactivity than controls. Prenatally stressed males showed the greatest amount of clinging to cage mates (Clarke et al., 1996).

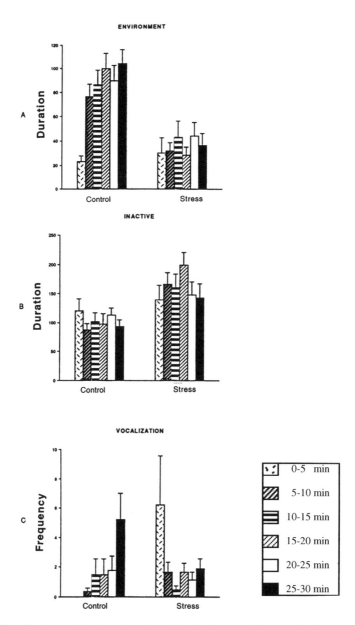

FIG. 6.9. Environmental exploration and vocalizations in prenatally stressed and control monkeys during the 30-minute playroom test. From "Maternal gestational stress alters adaptive and social behavior in adolescent rhesus monkey offspring," A. S. Clarke, A. Soto, T. Bergholz, and M. S. Schneider, 1996, *Infant Behavior and Development, 19*, pp. 453–463. Copyright 1996. Reprinted with permission.

TABLE 6.2
Summary of Novelty Challenge Results for Hand-Reared Monkeys

Novelty Challenge Test	Behavioral Findings
6-month playroom	↑ clinging
	↑ self-directed
	↑ sleep
	↓ exploratory
6-month separation/reunion	↑ clinging
	↑ self-grooming
	↓ locomotion, play, climb
18-month challenge	↑ abnormal (clinging)
	↓ proximity, contact
4-month playroom	↓ exploration
	↑ vocalization (at first)
4-year new group formation	↑ self-clasping
	↑ stereotypes
	↑ general disturbance
	↑ freezing
18-month challenge	↑ exploratory behavior
	↓ play

Note. ↓ and ↑ denote a decrease or increase, respectively, in the dependent variable as a function of prenatal stress.

Table 6.2 summarizes the behavioral responses of the hand-reared prenatally stressed monkeys and controls to the environmental challenges from 6 months of age to adolescence (age 4 years). Taken together, these results from the hand-reared prenatally stressed rhesus monkeys demonstrate that prenatal stress can have long-lasting effects, extending past infancy into adolescence. Interestingly, the prenatally stressed monkeys appear to some extent like inhibited children, in that they showed enhanced disturbance behavior and inactivity under conditions of novelty or challenge, and this was as evident at 4 years of age (adolescence) as at 6 months of age. Moreover, the reduction of exploration at 6 months of age in the playroom, the increased clinging to peers and reduced locomotion during the 8-month social separation, the increased clinging to peers at 18 months, and the self-clasping, freezing, and reduced exploration at 4 years of age all suggest that a small effect early in life can persist and perhaps even become amplified over the course of maturation.

Our second study (mother-reared rhesus monkeys with the timing of prenatal stress varied across groups) provides further evidence for developmental continuity of the effects of prenatal stress. The mother-reared monkeys were separated from their mothers at 6 months of age for 3 days, and housed alone. Behavior was scored, and blood samples were taken (preseparation baseline, 2 hours after separation, and 26 hours after separation) as in our first study. The results showed a significant condition effect in a MANOVA. Univariate analyses showed that there were significant differences between groups in self-grooming, exploration, and marginally significant effects for locomotion. The two prenatally stressed groups showed more self-grooming than the control animals. The results are especially marked for the midgestation-stress animals. The midgestation-stress group showed more exploration than the other two groups. For locomotion, there was a condition by day interaction such that the control and early stress animals both increased their locomotion over days, while the midgestation-stress animals actually decreased their locomotion. Although the nature of the effects of the timing of prenatal stress are not completely clear at this point, it is apparent that the two groups of prenatally stressed animals show more self-grooming (a behavior considered to be an indicator of stress in primates—e.g., the monkey self-grooming behaviors are perhaps analogous to stress-related self-grooming behaviors seen in the human primate such as chewing fingernails, picking at one's cuticles, etc.).

Although we are collecting further data on the cohort of monkeys from our second study, the monkeys are just now reaching adolescence, and so we cannot report additional results at this time. Data on the learning strategies of the animals are being collected using the Wisconsin General Test Apparatus (WGTA). An alcohol challenge test is also being employed using a two-bottle choice paradigm in which the animals are offered alcohol (in a sweetened solution) and vehicle daily for 5 weeks to determine their patterns of alcohol consumption.

Physiological Indicators

It is well documented in rodents that prenatal stress results in HPA dysregulation, which might subserve the neurobehavioral effects associated with prenatal stress. Thus, we used environmental manipulations to determine whether our prenatally stressed monkeys would also show alterations in HPA regulation. We assessed plasma cortisol and ACTH levels under baseline conditions as well as within the context of the environmental challenge or mild stressors described previously. In our first study, because we had access to the 24 monkeys from birth, testing during the neonatal period appeared to be the appropriate place to begin looking for early evidence of HPA-axis functioning. We collected three blood samples during the neonatal period: (a) after maternal separation for testing on postnatal day 2 or 3, (b) after the administration of a 20-minute neurobehavioral assessment scale on postnatal day 22, and (c) 10 minutes after the onset of sleep after the neurobehavioral assessment on day 23.

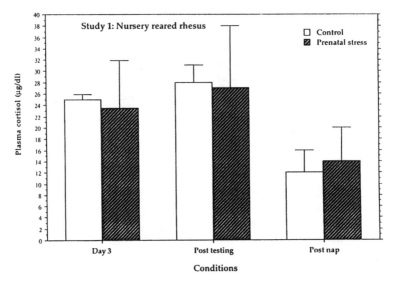

FIG. 6.10.   Mean plasma cortisol levels as a function of prenatal condition (control, mid-late stress), measured after maternal separation, after neurobehavioral testing, and after a 10-minute nap. Bars represent standard errors.

There was no direct evidence that cortisol levels during any of the three sampling times were associated with the prenatal stress condition (see Fig. 6.10). However, we did find significant effects for our testing condition, with lower cortisol values after a period of sleep. Cortisol levels obtained 10 minutes after the onset of sleep averaged 12.6 (1.5) µg/dl, compared to levels following a routine neurobehavioral assessment, averaging 27.5 (2.2) µg/dl, and those on the first few days after birth, averaging 24.3 (1.3) ($p < .001$). These findings are highly consistent with human studies reporting differences in cortisol levels between periods of sleep and nondistressed awake activity in newborns (Anders, Sachar, Kream, Roffwarg, & Hellman, 1970; Tennes & Carter, 1973). We also found a significant effect for sex, with females exhibiting higher cortisol values, averaging 24.8 (2.4) µg/dl compared to 19.2 (1.3) µg/dl for males ($p < .04$). The lack of statistically significant difference in cortisol between the groups is quite common in the neonatal period, as the birth process itself involves a surge in cortisol. During infancy, the HPA axis, including the adrenal gland, undergoes considerable developmental change (Murphy & Branchaud, 1994).

As the animals in our first study matured, we did find that prenatally stressed monkeys showed higher cortisol levels after stressful manipulations. At 8 months of age, levels of plasma cortisol were assayed under baseline and social separation conditions (at this point the monkeys were housed in peer groups of 3 or 4 monkeys). As mentioned earlier, social separation is a powerful psychosocial stressor, and cortisol levels for the entire sample increased approximately three-

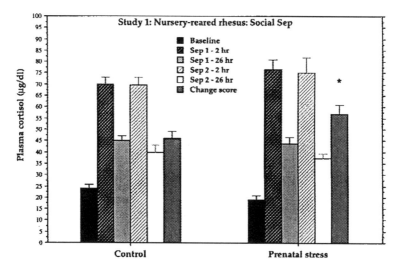

FIG. 6.11.   Adjusted mean plasma ACTH levels with baseline as a covariate as a function of prenatal conditions (early stress, mid-late stress, and control), measured 2 hours and 26 hours after maternal separation. Bars represent standard errors.

fold from an average of 21.5 (1.3) μg/dl at baseline to 73.3 (2.7) μg/dl 2 hours after separation. However, the increase from baseline was significantly larger for the prenatally stressed monkeys ($p < .05$) as shown in Fig. 6.11. The social separation was repeated a second time in order to obtain test–retest reliability for the cortisol data. The intraindividual consistency from the first to the second separation study was $r =. 64, p < .001$, thus indicating good reliability.

In our second experiment (mother-reared rhesus monkeys), when the monkeys were 6 months of age we collected blood samples before (baseline) and twice during the 3-day social separation (2 hours postseparation, and 26 hours postseparation). The samples were assayed for both cortisol and ACTH. Analysis of covariance of the hormonal indices of stress responsivity (with baseline ACTH and cortisol as the covariates, respectively) showed significant effects of prenatal stress condition and time of testing, $F(2,23) = 4.23, p < .03, F(2,23) = 2.84, p < .08$, for ACTH and cortisol, respectively. All the groups showed the highest hormonal levels 2 hours after separation, and levels declined by the time monkeys were tested at 26 hours after separation. The early prenatal stress group showed the largest ACTH response compared to baseline. The adjusted means from the analysis of covariance (with baseline ACTH as the covariate) are shown in Fig. 6.12. Cortisol showed a similar pattern, and the condition and test time effects were also significant in analysis of covariance.

Our next logical question was to ask whether this apparent increase in HPA reactivity in the prenatally stressed monkeys would extend beyond the 6–8 month period. As described previously, when the hand-reared monkeys from our first

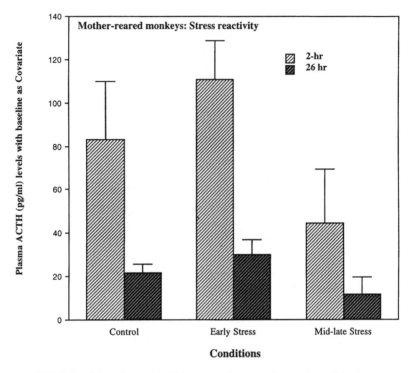

FIG. 6.12.   Mean Plasma ACTH levels as a function of prenatal condition (control, early stress, mid-late gestation stress) measured 2- and 26-hours after maternal separation. Bars represent standard errors.

study were juveniles, or 18-months-old, they were exposed to a series of environmental challenges or stressors over a 6-week period of time (Clarke & Schneider, 1993). (Following a baseline period, they experienced the following episodes, in a random order: (a) placement in a novel cage; (b) placement in a novel cage and exposure to a noise stressor; (c) separation from peers and placement in an individual cage; and (d) placement in an individual cage and exposure to a noise stressor.) After 10-minutes of videotaping of the animals' behaviors during each episode, blood samples were collected for assays of ACTH and cortisol (Clarke, Wittwer, Abbott, & Schneider, 1994), and CSF samples were collected for measures of neurotransmitter activity. The prenatal stress group showed higher ACTH values than controls under all four challenge conditions. Thus, the increased HPA reactivity we had observed in the prenatally stressed monkeys at 8 months of age, compared to controls, persisted into the juvenile period.

The CSF samples from the 8- and 18-month studies of the hand-reared monkeys showed some potentially important differences in neurotransmitter activity. Compared to controls, prenatally stressed monkeys had higher concentrations of MHPG and DOPAC in CSF than controls. These substances are indicators of increased sympathetic nervous system activity (MHPG) and increased activity of dopaminergic neurons (DOPAC). A similar trend toward group differences was found for NE, an indicator of sympathetic nervous system activity, and homovanillic acid (a metabolite of dopamine), although these differences were only marginally significant. Moreover, NE and MHPG responses to stress were consistent from 8 and 18 months of age. There were no group differences under baseline conditions, supporting the idea that because prenatal stress affects the HPA axis, its effects are most likely to appear when the animal encounters stress (Schneider et al., 1998).

For our second study (mother-reared rhesus with the timing of prenatal stress varied), we are examining the relationships among the physiological and behavioral measures of functioning. The results showed that behaviors during separation at 6 months of age were significantly related to ACTH reactivity (the change from baseline to 2 hours postseparation). Both self-grooming and exploration on the first day of separation were significantly negatively related to ACTH reactivity ($r = -.38$, $-.40$, $dfs = 24$, $p < .06$, $.05$ respectively) such that the larger the increase in ACTH, the lower both behaviors were on the first day of separation. This is interesting in light of previous studies showing that increased levels of CRH produced freezing in novel settings (Sutton et al., 1982). Moreover, in hierarchical regression analyses, when prenatal stress condition was entered as a predictor (along with birth weight and sex of animal) before ACTH reactivity, ACTH reactivity no longer was a significant predictor of first day self-grooming, but prenatal stress condition did remain significant when entered after ACTH reactivity (for ACTH reactivity, change in $R^2 = .036$; for Condition, change in $R^2 = .134$).

For first day exploration, a different pattern emerged. ACTH reactivity continued to contribute to prediction of exploration even after condition, sex, and birth weight were entered (change in $R^2 = .114$), but the contribution of condition as a predictor shrank considerably when ACTH reactivity was entered first (change in $R^2 = .063$). Vocalization on the first day of separation was also predicted by ACTH reactivity, but not by condition. These results illustrate both the indirect nature of the relationships between biological indices and behavior, as well as the possibility that prenatal condition has effects that go beyond changes in the HPA-axis indicators of stress. In other words, prenatal stress may be associated directly with increased ACTH reactivity, and, in addition, ACTH hyperresponsivity (resulting from prenatal stress) may contribute to altered behavioral responses under stressful conditions. Because self-grooming and exploration are behaviors with different functions, it is not surprising that they show different relationships to prenatal condition and ACTH reactivity.

CONCLUSIONS AND IMPLICATIONS

The weight of the evidence supports the hypothesis that animals (including humans) that have experienced prenatal stress will have altered functioning of the HPA axis, along with alterations in associated aspects of neuronal functioning especially in the dopaminergic systems of the brain, which are involved in addictions (Blum et al., 1995), among other processes. As mentioned earlier in this chapter, the kinds of alterations that are found are similar to those found in depression in humans. Although the current era is one of rapid emergence of new findings in the field of behavioral neuroscience, the connections between aspects of brain development and functioning with behavior are necessarily indirect. Hopefully, further research will elucidate some of the processes by which prenatal influences (not only stress, but also other events) are carried forward and transformed during the development of the organism.

We began this chapter by posing the question of whether prenatal stress should be considered to be a behavioral teratogen, that is, a prenatal factor that alters behavior deleteriously. What conclusions can be drawn from the data we have presented from our own experimental research with nonhuman primates, along with our review of experiments with other animals and the correlational literature with humans? The pattern of evidence thus far is supportive of the hypothesis that prenatal stress could be a behavioral teratogen; human correlational results show negative effects of prenatal stress, experiments with both nonhuman primates and other animals show significant behavioral and physiological effects of prenatal stress that can extend into adulthood, and the animal research provides evidence regarding the physiological processes that are likely to be altered by prenatal stress. Nevertheless, we are not ready to draw a strong conclusion that prenatal stress is a behavioral teratogen at this point. What we are ready to conclude is that prenatal stress deserves increased research priority. There are some important gaps in the literature that need to be filled. There needs to be further study of the timing of prenatal stress with respect to what neuroendocrine functions are undergoing development and further elucidation of the physiological mechanisms. Research on the effects of the severity of stress, and whether a stressor occurs chronically or in a single short episode, is also important for the future formulation of policy recommendations with respect to prenatal stress.

A comparison of the research on prenatal stress with other research on prenatal effects is helpful. The prenatal effects of teratogens such as lead, mercury, PCBs (polychlorinated biphenyls, a widespread chemical pollutant), tobacco, and alcohol, have received extensive research priority and funding. The research results have formed the background for public policy decisions such as labeling alcoholic beverages as hazardous during pregnancy, restrictions on residency of children in buildings determined to contain lead paint (e.g., in Boston, Massachusetts), and public advisories on the consumption of game fish contaminated by PCBs, especially by pregnant and nursing mothers. Prenatal stress is more difficult to study than these substances for a number of reasons (for example, it is impossible to determine the dosage of stress to which a person or animal has been exposed by assaying samples of body fluids, whereas lead, alcohol, and PCBs can be measured objectively), but based on the research reviewed here, prenatal stress may be just as important as these substances for which research has accumulated a wealth of information.

Based on the evidence available at present, are there any recommendations that should be made to pregnant women with respect to psychosocial stress? Because some degree of uncertainty in making recommendations is unavoidable, the answer to this question depends on how one thinks of the severity of two possible errors (Anastasi, 1976; Hammond, 1996). One error (analogous to Type I error in statistical inference) is to recommend that prenatal stress should be avoided when it may not have serious deleterious effects. The other error (analogous to Type II error) is to fail to recommend that prenatal stress be avoided when it may have serious deleterious effects. Given the evidence at the present time, pregnant women should avoid psychosocial stressors that are perceived to be excessive. This recommendation risks a Type I error and that fact should be kept in mind.

But with prenatal stress, are there costs associated with the Type I error? One potential cost of Type I error could be in job discrimination against pregnant women. There is the possibility that some might use research results on prenatal stress to require that women stay home and out of the workplace during pregnancy. For example, there is evidence that links workplace stress to hypertension during pregnancy, but it is workplace stress and not work per se that has an association with pregnancy-induced hypertension (Landsbergis & Hatch, 1996). Workplace stress is not the only or even the most significant source of psychosocial stress in people's lives, of course. The issue of workplace stress highlights the fact that in humans stress can be highly subjective. The same objective event can have different emotional consequences for different individuals, depending on how the event is viewed (Lazarus & Cohen, 1977). Therefore, how to minimize or avoid workplace stress should be the prerogative of the individual woman.

Reducing other sources of prenatal stress may be more or less controversial than the issue of workplace stress. Are there Type I error costs associated with reducing other potential sources of prenatal stress such as domestic discord and violence, and events associated with poverty in our society such as frequent changes in residence, lack of access to medical care, and residence in high-crime and high-pollution neighborhoods? Children growing up in poverty in our country are disadvantaged in a variety of ways, including higher prenatal and postnatal exposure to lead, as an example (Berney, 1993). Perhaps some of the disadvantages of poverty may begin even before birth in the form of prenatal stress.

Lastly, we want to reemphasize that in humans stress is often correlated with use of alcohol, tobacco, and other drugs. This has three implications. First, pregnant women experiencing psychosocial stress should be made aware of both the increased tendency toward use of substances as a result of stress and the deleterious effects of those substances on the fetus. Perhaps public educational campaigns would be appropriate. A second implication is with respect to the treatment of substance-using pregnant women. In several states (including Wisconsin, our own state of residence), recent legislation intended to protect developing fetuses from maternal substance abuse allows or requires incarceration of a pregnant woman who is using certain substances. Incarceration in cases of substance use could perhaps add further prenatal stress. Some data exist to show poor prenatal care for incarcerated pregnant women (Berry, 1985). Together, this suggests caution in incarcerating pregnant women for substance use.

A third implication of the relation between stress and substance use in humans is with respect to the need for further research. There have been few experimental studies that have tested the effects of prenatal stress in combination with other prenatal exposures. Research in our laboratory that is currently underway is exploring the joint effects of prenatal exposure to alcohol and stress. In the long run, such research should yield evidence that will help the public to make better informed decisions about their own reproductive lives.

As a postscript, what are the implications of research on prenatal stress in laboratory animals for animals in more natural habitats? It is widely acknowledged by both researchers and wildlife managers that events or conditions such as human disturbance, capture, and confinement, raise neuroendocrine indicators of stress such as cortisol in species ranging from possums to endangered cheetahs (Baker, Gemmell, & Gemmell, 1998; Merola, 1994; Saltz, White, & Bartmann, 1992). Furthermore, such events can pose mortality and reproductive problems (Putman, 1995; Reimers, 1991). The exact role of prenatal stress on wildlife offspring and their later production is not known. Combining the laboratory and field research suggests that a Type II error (cf. stressing breeding populations) should be avoided.

ACKNOWLEDGMENTS

We dedicate this chapter to Elizabeth C. Roughton, a former graduate student and treasured friend, who died November 18, 1997, at the age of 39. Her rare spirit will forever inspire those of us who knew and worked with her.

This research was supported in part by grants from the National Institute of Alcohol Abuse and Alcoholism (AA10079), National Institute of Mental Health (MH48417), WT Grant Foundation Faculty Scholars Award, and Maternal & Child Health Bureau (MCJ009102) to MLS.

REFERENCES

Adamsons, K., Mueller-Heubach, E., & Myers, R. E. (1971). Production of fetal asphyxia in the rhesus monkey by administration of catecholamines to the mother. *American Journal of Obstetrics and Gynecology, 109*(2), 248–262.

Anders, T., Sachar, E., Kream, J., Roffwarg, H., & Hellman, L. (1970). Behavioral state and plasma cortisol response in the human newborn. *Pediatrics, 46*, 532–537.

Alonso, S. J., Navarro, E., & Rodriguez, M. (1994). Permanent dopaminergic alterations in the n. accumbens after prenatal stress. *Pharmacology, Biochemistry, and Behavior, 49*, 353–358.

Alonso, S. J., Navarro, E., Santana, C., & Rodriguez, M. (1997). Motor lateralization, behavioral despair and dopaminergic brain asymmetry after prenatal stress. *Pharmacology, Biochemistry, and Behavior, 58*, 443–448.

Anastasi, A. (1976). *Psychological testing* (4th ed.). New York: Macmillan.

Baker, M. L., Gemmell, E., & Gemmell, R. T. (1998). Physiological changes in brushtail possums, Trichosurus vulpecula, transferred from the wild to captivity. *Journal of Experimental Zoology, 280*, 203–212.

Barbazanges, A., Piazza, P. V., Le Moal, M., & Maccari, S. (1996). Maternal glucocorticoid secretion mediates long-term effects of prenatal stress. *Journal of Neuroscience, 16*, 3943–3949.

Berney, B. (1993). Round and round it goes: The epidemiology of childhood lead poisoning 1950–1990. *The Milbank Quarterly, 71*, 3–39.

Berry, E. (1985). Quality of prenatal care for incarcerated women challenged. *Youth Law News, 6*(6), 1–3.

Blum, K., Sheridan, P. J., Wood, R. C., Braverman, E. R., Chen, T. J. H., & Comings, D. E. (1995). Dopamine D2 receptor gene variants: Association and linkage studies in impulsive-addictive-compulsive behaviour. *Pharmacogenetics, 5*, 121–141.

Boyce, W. T., Frank, E., Jensen, P. S., Kessler, R. C., Nelson, C. A., Steinberg, L., & The MacArthur Foundation Research Network on Psychopathology and Development. (1998). Social context in developmental psychopathology: Recommendations for future research from the MacArthur network on psychopathology and development. *Development and Psychopathology, 10*, 143–164.

Brazelton, T. B. (1984). Neonatal Behavioral Assessment Scale (2nd ed.). *Clinics in developmental medicine, 88*. Philadelphia: Lippincott.

Brooke, O. G., Anderson, H. R., Bland, J. M., Peacock, J. L., & Stewart, C. M. (1989). Effects on birth weight of smoking, alcohol, caffeine, socioeconomic factors, and psychosocial stress. *British Medical Journal, 298*, 795–801.

Brown, E. R. (1993). Long-term sequelae of preterm birth. In A. Fuchs, F. Fuchs, & P. G. Stubblefield (Eds.), *Preterm birth: Causes, prevention and management* (2nd ed., pp. 477–492). New York: McGraw-Hill.

Burbacher, T. M., Grant, K. S., & Mottet, N. K. (1986). Retarded object permanence development in methylmercury exposed *Macaca fascicularis* infants. *Developmental Psychology, 22*, 771–776.

Calogero, A. E., Gallucci, W. T., Chrousos, G. P., & Gold, P. W. (1988). Effect of the catecholamines upon rat hypothalamic corticotropin releasing hormone secretion in vitro: Clinical implications. *Journal of Clinical Investigation, 82*, 839–846.

Carmichael, L. (1970). The onset and early development of behavior. In P. H. Mussen (Ed.), *Carmichael's manual of child psychology* (3rd ed., pp. 447–563). New York: Wiley.

Chrousos, G. P., & Gold, P. W. (1992). The concepts of stress and stress system disorders: Overview of physical and behavioral homeostasis. *Journal of the American Medical Association, 267*, 1244–1252.

Cicchetti, D., & Tucker, D. (1994). Development and self-regulatory structures of the mind. *Development and Psychopathology, 6*, 533–549.

Clarke, A. S., Soto, A., Bergholz, T., & Schneider, M. L. (1996). Maternal gestational stress alters adaptive and social behavior in adolescent rhesus monkey offspring. *Infant Behavior and Development, 19*, 453–463.

Clarke, A. S., Wittwer, D. J., Abbott, D. H., & Schneider, M. L. (1994). Long-term effects of prenatal stress on HPA axis activity in juvenile rhesus monkeys. *Developmental Psychobiology, 27*(5), 257–269.

Clarke, A. S., & Schneider, M. L. (1993). Prenatal stress has long-term effects on behavioral responses to stress in juvenile rhesus monkeys. *Developmental Psychobiology, 26*(5), 293–304.

Coe, C. L., Mendoza, S. P., Davidson, J., Smith, E. R., Dallman, M., & Levine, S. (1978). Hormonal response to stress in the squirrel monkey. *Neuroendocrinology, 26*, 356–377.

Coe, C. L., Lubach, G. R., & Karaszewski, J. W. (1999). Prenatal stress and immune recognition of self and non-self in the primate neonate. *Biology of the Neonate, 76*(5), 301–310.

Dawes, R. M. (1988). *Rational choice in an uncertain world*. New York: Harcourt Brace.

Day, J. C., Koehl, M., Deroche, V., Le Moal, M., & Maccari, S. (1998). Prenatal stress enhances stress- and corticotropin-releasing factor-induced stimulation of hippocampal acetylcholine release in adult rats. *The Journal of Neuroscience, 18*(5), 1886–1892.

De Kloet, E. R., & Reul, J. M. H. M. (1987). Feedback action and tonic influence of corticosteroids on brain function: A concept arising from the heterogeneity of brain receptor systems. *Psychoneuroendocrinology, 12*, 83–105.

De Souza, E. B., Insel, T. R., Perrin, M. H., Rivier, J., Vale, W. W., & Kuhar, M. J. (1985). Corticotropin-releasing factor receptors are widely distributed within the rat central nervous system: An autoradiographic study. *Journal of Neuroscience, 5*, 3189–3203.

Emde, R., Harmon, R., Metcalf, D., Koenig, K., & Wagonfeld, S. (1971). Stress and neonatal sleep. *Psychosomatic Medicine, 33*, 491–497.

Evans, G. W., Hygge, S., & Bullinger, M. (1995). Chronic noise and psychological stress. *Psychological Science, 6*, 333–338.

Fameli, M., Kitraki, E., & Stylianopoulou, F. (1994). Effects of hyperactivity of the maternal hypothalamic-pituitary-adrenal (HPA) axis during pregnancy on the development of the HPA axis and brain monoamines of the offspring. *International Journal of Developmental Neuroscience, 12*, 651–659.

File, S. E. (1978). ACTH but not corticosterone impairs habituation and reduces exploration. *Pharmacology, Biochemistry, and Behavior, 9*, 161–166.

Fride, E., Dan, Y., Feldon, J., Halevy, G., & Weinstock, M. (1986). Effects of prenatal stress on vulnerability to stress in prepubertal and adult rats. *Physiology and Behavior, 37*, 681–687.

Fride, E., Dan, Y., Gavish, M., & Weinstock, M. (1985). Prenatal stress impairs maternal behavior in a conflict situation and reduces hippocampal benzodiazepine receptors. *Life Science, 36*, 2103–2109.

Fride, E., & Weinstock, M. (1988). Prenatal stress increases anxiety related behavior and alters cerebral lateralization of dopamine activity. *Life Science, 42*, 1059–1065.

Gipsen, W. H., van der Poel, A., & Wimersma Greidanus, T. B. (1973). Pituitary adrenal influences on behavior: Responses to test situations with or without electric footshock. *Physiology and Behavior, 10*, 345–350.

Goldman-Rakic, P. S., & Brown, R. M. (1982). Postnatal development of monoamine content and syntheses in the cerebral cortex of rhesus monkeys. *Developmental Brain Research, 4*, 339–349.

Gruen, R. J., Folkman, S., & Lazarus, S. (1988). Centrality and individual differences in the meaning of daily hassles. *Journal of Personality, 56*(4), 743–762.

Gunnar, M. R., Malone, S., Vance, G., & Fisch, R. O. (1985). Coping with aversive stimulation in the neonatal period: Quiet sleep and plasma cortisol levels during recovery from circumcision. *Child Development, 56*, 824–834.

Hammond, K. R. (1996). *Human judgment and social policy: Irreducible uncertainty, inevitable error, unavoidable injustice.* New York: Oxford University Press.

Harlow, H. F., & Harlow, M. (1966). Learning to love. *American Scientist, 54*, 244–272.

Harlow, H. F., & Suomi, S. J. (1974). Induced depression in monkeys. *Behavioral Biology, 12*, 273–296.

Henry, C., Guegant, G., Cador, M., Arnauld, E. Arsaut, J., Le Moal, M., & Demotes-Mainard, J. (1995). Prenatal stress in rats facilitates amphetamine-induced sensitization and induces long-lasting changes in dopamine receptors in the nucleus accumbens. *Brain Research, 685*, 179–186.

Henry, C., Kabbaj, M., Simon, H., Le Moal, M., & Maccari, S. (1994). Prenatal stress increases the hypothalamo-pituitary-adrenal axis response in young and adult rats. *Journal of Neuroendocrinology, 6*, 341–345.

Herrenkohl, L. R. (1979). Prenatal stress reduces fertility and fecundity in female offspring. *Science, 206*, 1097–1099.

Huttunen, M. O., & Niskanen, P. (1978). Prenatal loss of father and psychiatric disorders. *Archives of General Psychiatry, 35*, 429–431.

Ising, H., Rebentisch, E., Poustka, F., & Curio, I. (1990). Annoyance and health risk caused by military low-altitude flight noise. *International Archives of Occupational and Environmental Health, 62*, 357–363.

Jacobs, H. S. (1991). The hypothalamus and pituitary gland. In F. Hytten & G. Chamberlain (Eds.), *Clinical Physiology in Obstetrics* (2nd ed., pp. 345–376). London: Blackwell Scientific.

Johnson, E. O., Kamilaris, T. C., Chrousos, G. P., & Gold, P. W. (1992). Mechanisms of stress: A dynamic overview of hormonal and behavioral homeostasis. *Neuroscience and Biobehavioral Reviews, 16*, 115–130.

Kaplan, J. R., Manuck, S. B., & Gatsonis, C. (1990). Heart rate and social status among male cynomolgus monkeys (*Macaca fascicularis*) housed in disrupted social groupings. *American Journal of Primatology, 21*, 175–187.

Kaufman, I. C., & Rosenblum, L. A. (1967). The reaction to separation in infant monkeys: Anaclitic depression and conservation-withdrawal. *Psychosomatic Medicine, 29*, 648–675.

Keller-Wood, M., & Dallman, M. (1984). Corticosteroid inhibition of ACTH secretion. *Endocrinology Review, 5*, 1–24.

Kinsley, C. H., & Bridges, R. S. (1988). Prenatal stress and maternal behavior in intact virgin rats: Response latencies are decreased in males and increased in females. *Hormones and Behavior, 22*, 76–89.

Koehl, M., Barbazanges, A., Le Moal, M., & Maccari, S. (1997). Prenatal stress induces a phase advance of circadian corticosterone rhythm in adult rats which is prevented by postnatal stress. *Brain Research, 759*, 317–320.

Koob, G. F., & Bloom, F. E. (1985). Corticotropin-releasing factor and behavior. *Federation Proceedings, 44*, 259–263.

Kryter, K. D. (1990). Aircraft noise and social factors in psychiatric hospital admission rates: A re-examination of some data. *Psychological Medicine, 20*, 395–411.

Kuo, Z. Y. (1976). *The dynamics of behavior development.* New York: Random House.

Landsbergis, P. A., & Hatch, M. C. (1996). Psychosocial work stess and pregnancy-induced hypertension. *Epidemiology, 7*, 346–351.

Lazarus, R. S., & Cohen, J. B. (1977). Environmental stress. In L. Altman & J. F. Wohlwill (Eds.), *Human behavior and the environment. Current theory and research* (pp. 89–127). New York: Plenum Press.

Lobel, M. (1994). Conceptualizations, measurement, and effects of prenatal maternal stress on birth outcomes. *Journal of Behavioral Medicine, 17*, 225–272.

Maccari, S., Piazza, P. V., Kabbaj, M., Barbazanges, A., Simon, H., & Le Moal, M. (1995). Adoption reverses the long-term impairment in glucocorticoid feedback induced by prenatal stress. *The Journal of Neuroscience, 15*, 110–115.

McCormick, M. C., Brooks-Gunn, J., Shorter, T., Holmes, J. H., Wallace, C. Y., & Heagarty, M. C. (1990). Factors associated with smoking in low-income pregnant women: Relationship to birth weights, stressful life events, social support, health behaviors and mental distress. *Journal of Clinical Epidemiology, 43*(5), 441–448.

McCormick, C. M., Smythe, J. W., Sharma, S., & Meaney, M. J. (1995). Sex-specific effects of prenatal stress on hypothalamic-pituitary-adrenal responses to stress and brain glucocorticoid receptor density in adult rats. *Develomental Brain Research, 84*, 55–61.

McEwen, B. S., De Kloet, E. R., & Rostene, W. (1986). Adrenal steroid receptors and actions in the nervous system. *Physiology Review, 66*, 1121–1188.

McIntosh, D. E., Mulkins, R. S., & Dean, R. S. (1995). Utilization of maternal perinatal risk indicators in the differential diagnosis of ADHD and UADD children. *International Journal of Neuroscience, 81*, 35–46.

Meijer, A. (1985). Child psychiatric sequelae of maternal war stress. *Acta Psychiatrica Scandinavica, 72*, 505–511.

Mendoza, S., Coe, C. L., & Levine, S. (1979). Physiological response to group formation in the squirrel monkey. *Psychoendocrinology, 3*, 221–229.

Merola, M. (1994). A reassessment of homozygosity and the case for inbreeding depression on the cheetah, *Acinonyx jubatus*: Implications for conservation. *Conservation Biology, 8*, 961–971.

Myers, R. E. (1975). Maternal psychological stress and fetal asphyxia: A study in the monkey. *American Journal of Obstetrics and Gynecology, 122*, 47–59.

Morishima, H. O., Pedersen, H., & Finster, M. (1978). The influence of maternal psychological stress on the fetus. *American Journal of Obstetrics and Gynecology, 131*, 286–290.

Murphy, B. E., & Branchaud, C. L. (1994). The fetal adrenal. In D. Tulchinsky & A. B. Little (Eds.), *Maternal-fetal endocrinology* (2nd ed., pp. 275–295). Philadelphia: Saunders.

Murphy, B. E. (1991). Steroids and depression. *Journal of Steroid Biochemical Molecular Biology, 38*, 537–559.

Newell-Morris, L., & Fahrenbruch, C. E. (1985). Practical and evolutionary considerations for use of the nonhuman primate model in prenatal research. In E. S. Watts (Eds.), *Nonhuman primate models for human growth and development* (pp. 9–40). New York: Liss.

Newell-Morris, L., Fahrenbruch, C. E., & Sackett, G. P. (1989). Prenatal psychological stress, der-matoglyphic asymmetry, and pregnancy outcome in the pigtailed macaque (*Macaca nemestrina*). *Biology of the Neonate, 56,* 61–75.

Oyemade, U. J., Cole, O. J., Johnson, A. A., Knight, E. M., Westney, O. E., Laryea, H., Hill, G., Cannon, E., Fomufod, A., Westney, L. S., Jones, S., & Edwards, C. H. (1994). Prenatal predictors of per-formance on the Brazelton neonatal behavioral assessment scale. *Journal of Nutrition, 124*(Suppl. 6), 1000S–1005S.

Paarlberg, K. M., Vingerhoets, J. P., Dekker, G. A., & Van Geijn, H. P. (1995). Psychosocial factors and pregnancy outcome: A review with emphasis on methodological issues. *Journal of Psychoso-matic Research, 39,* 563–595.

Peters, D. A. (1982). Prenatal stress effects of brain biogenic amine and plasma corticosterone levels. *Pharmacology, Biochemistry & Behavior, 17,* 721–725.

Peters, D. A. V. (1986). Prenatal stress increases the behavioral response to serotonin agonists and al-ters open field behavior in the rat. *Pharmacology, Biochemistry & Behavior, 25,* 873–877.

Peters, D. A. V. (1988). Both prenatal and postnatal factors contribute to the effects of maternal stress on offspring behavior and central 5-hydroxytryptamine receptors in the rat. *Pharmacology, Bio-chemistry & Behavior, 30,* 669–673.

Peters, D. A. V. (1990). Maternal stress increases fetal brain and neonatal cerebral cortex 5-hydroxy-tryptamine synthesis in rats: A possible mechanism by which stress influences brain development. *Pharmacology, Biochemistry & Behavior, 35,* 943–947.

Plotsky, P. M., & Meaney, M. J. (1993). Early postnatal experience alters hypothalamic corticotropin releasing factor (CRF), mRNA, median eminence CRF content and stress-induced release in adult rats. *Molecular Brain Research, 18,* 195–200.

Putman, R. J. (1995). Ethical considerations and animal welfare in ecological field studies. *Biodiver-sity and Conservation, 4,* 903–915.

Reimers, E. (1991). Ecological effects of snowmachine traffic: A literature survey. *Fauna, 44,* 255–268.

Roughton, E. C., Schneider, M. L., Bromley, L. J., & Coe, C. L. (1998). Maternal endocrine activa-tion during pregnancy alters neurobehavioral state in primate infants. *American Journal of Occu-pational Therapy, 52,* 90–98.

Sackett, G. P. (1981). A nonhuman primate model for studying causes and effects of poor pregnancy outcomes. In S. Friedman & M. Sigman (Eds.), *Preterm birth and psychological development* (pp. 41–63). New York: Academic Press.

Saltz, D., White, G. C., & Bartmann, R. M. (1992). Urinary cortisol, urea nitrogen excretion, and win-ter survival in male deer fawns. *Journal of Wildlife Management, 56,* 640–644.

Sapolsky, R. (1992). *Stress, the aging brain, and the mechanisms of neuron death.* Cambridge, MA: MIT Press.

Sapolsky, R., Krey, L., & McEwen, B. (1985). Prolonged glucocorticoid exposure reduces hippocam-pal neural number: Implications for aging. *Journal of Neuroscience, 5,* 1221–1224.

Schneider, M. L. (1992a). The effect of mild stress during pregnancy on birth weight and neuromotor mat-uration in rhesus monkey infants (*Macaca mulatta*). *Infant Behavior and Development, 15,* 389–403.

Schneider, M. L. (1992b). Delayed object permanence development in prenatally stressed rhesus mon-key infants (*Macaca mulatta*). *Occupational Therapy Journal of Research, 12*(2), 96–110.

Schneider, M. L. (1992c). Prenatal stress exposure alters postnatal behavioral expression under condi-tions of novelty challenge in rhesus monkey infants. *Developmental Psychobiology, 25*(7), 141–152.

Schneider, M. L., Clarke, A. S., Kraemer, G. W., Roughton, E. C., Lubach, G. R., Rimm-Kaufman, S. E., Schmidt, D., & Ebert, M. (1998). Prenatal stress alters brain biogenic amine levels in pri-mates. *Development and Psychopathology, 10,* 427–440.

Schneider, M. L., & Coe, C. L. (1993). Repeated social stress during pregnancy impairs neuromotor de-velopment of the primate infant. *Journal of Developmental and Behavioral Pediatrics, 14*(2), 81–87.

Schneider, M. L., Coe, C. L., & Lubach, G. R. (1992). Endocrine activation mimics the adverse ef-fects of prenatal stress on the neuromotor development of the infant primate. *Developmental Psy-chobiology, 25*(6), 427–439.

Schneider, M. L., Moore, C., Suomi, S. J., & Champoux, M. (1991). Laboratory assessment of temperament and environmental enrichment in rhesus monkey infants (*Macaca mulatta*). *American Journal of Primatology, 25*, 137–155.

Schneider, M. L., Roughton, E. C., Koehler, A., & Lubach, G. R. (1999). Growth and development following prenatal stress in primates: An examination of ontogenetic vulnerability. *Child Development, 70*(2), 263–274.

Schneider, M. L., & Suomi, S. J. (1992). Neurobehavioral assessment in rhesus monkey neonates (*Macaca mulatta*): Developmental changes, behavioral stability, and early experience. *Infant Behavior and Development, 15*(2), 155–177.

Selye, H. (1936). A syndrome produced by severe noxious agents. *Nature (London), 138*, 32–41.

Suchecki, D., & Neto, J. P. (1991). Prenatal stress and emotional response of adult offspring. *Physiology & Behavior, 49*, 423–426.

Suomi, S. J. (1997). Early determinants of behavior: Evidence from primate studies. *British Medical Bulletin, 53*, 170–184.

Sutton, R. E., Koob, G. F., Le Moal, M., Rivier, J., & Vale, W. (1982). Corticotropin releasing factor (CRF) produces behavioral activation in rats. *Nature, 297*, 331–333.

Takahashi, L. K., & Kalin, N. H. (1991). Early developmental and temporal characteristics of stress-induced secretion of pituitary-adrenal hormones in prenatally stressed pups. *Brain Research, 558*, 75–78.

Takahashi, L. K., Turner, J. G., & Kalin, N. H. (1992). Prenatal stress alters brain catecholaminergic activity and potentiates stress-induced behavior in adult rats. *Brain Research, 574*, 131–137.

Tennes, K., & Carter, D. (1973). Plasma cortisol levels and behavioral states in early infancy. *Psychosomatic Medicine, 35*, 121–128.

Thompson, W. R. (1957). Influence of prenatal maternal anxiety on emotionality in young rats. *Science, 15*, 698–699.

Valentino, R. J., Cha, C. I., & Foote, S. L. (1986). Anatomic and physiologic evidence for innervation of noradrenergic locus coeruleus by neuronal corticotropin-releasing factor. *Society of Neuroscience Abstract, 12*, 1003.

Van Praag, H. M. (1982). Neurotransmitters and CNS disease: Depression. *Lancet, 1*, 1259–1264.

Wadhwa, P. D. (1998). Prenatal stress and life-span development. *Encyclopedia of mental health* (Vol. 3, pp. 265–280). Orlando, FL: Academic Press.

Wadhwa, P. D., Dunkel-Schetter, C., Chicz-DeMet, A., Porto, M., & Sandman, C. A. (1996). Prenatal psychosocial factors and the neuroendocrine axis in human pregnancy. *Psychosomatic Medicine, 58*, 432–446.

Ward, A. J. (1990). A comparison and analysis of the presence of family problems during pregnancy of mothers of "autistic" children and mothers of normal children. *Child Psychiatry and Human Development, 20*, 279–288.

Ward, A. J. (1991). Prenatal stress and childhood psychopathology. *Child Psychiatry and Human Development, 22*, 97–110.

Ward, I. L. (1972). Prenatal stress feminizes and demasculinizes the behavior of males. *Science, 175*, 82–84.

Ward, I. L., & Ward, O. B. (1985). Sexual behavior differentiation: Effects of prenatal manipulation in rats. In N. Adler, D. Pfaff, & R. W. Goy (Eds.), *Handbook of behavioral neurobiology* (pp. 77–98). New York: Plenum Press.

Wasser, S., & Starling, A. K. (1988). Proximate and ultimate causes of reproductive suppression among female yellow baboons at Mikumi National Park, Tanzania. *American Journal of Primatology, 16*, 97–121.

Weinstock, M. (1997). Does prenatal stress impair coping and regulation of hypothalamic-pituitary-adrenal axis? *Neuroscience Biobehavioral Reviews, 21*, 1–10.

Weinstock, M., Matlina, E., Maor, E., Rosen, G. I., & McEwen, B. S. (1992). Prenatal stress selectively alters the reactivity of the hypothalamic-pituitary-adrenal system in the female rat. *Brain Research, 595*, 195–200.

Weir, R. J., Paintin, D. B., Brown, J. J., Fraser, R., Lever, A. F., Robertson, J. I. S., & Young, J. (1971). A serial study in pregnancy of the plasma concentration of renin, corticosteroids, electrolytes and proteins and of haematocrit and plasma volume. *Journal of Obstetrics and Gynaecology of the British Commonwealth, 78,* 590–602.

Williams, M. T., Hennessy, M. B., & Davis, H. N. (1995). CRF administered to pregnant rats alters offspring behavior and morphology. *Pharmacology Biochemistry & Behavior, 52,* 161–167.

7

▼▼▼▼▼▼▼▼▼

On the Origins of a Vulnerability to Depression: The Influence of the Early Social Environment on the Development of Psychobiological Systems Related to Risk for Affective Disorder

Geraldine Dawson
Sharon B. Ashman
Department of Psychology and the Center on Human Development and Disability University of Washington

It is well-established that having a parent who suffers from depression places children at higher risk for developing depression, themselves. Children with a clinically depressed parent are six times more likely than other children to develop major depression (Downey & Coyne, 1990). Furthermore, such children are at higher risk for problems in self-control, aggression, poor peer relationships, behavioral problems, academic difficulties, and attentional problems (Coghill, Caplan, Alexandra, Robson, & Kumar, 1986; Downey & Walker, 1992; Erickson, Sroufe, & Egeland, 1985; Ghodsian, Zajicek, & Wolkind, 1984; Grunebaum, Cohler, Kaufman, & Gallant, 1978; Orvaschel, Welsh-Allis, & Weijai, 1988; Panak & Garber, 1992; Redding, Harmon, & Morgan, 1990). A number of family risk factors associated with parental depression have been identified, including course and severity of parental depression, exposure to parental depression, marital conflict, maltreatment, and adverse living conditions (Downey & Walker, 1992). Child risk factors include early developmental difficulties, gender, age, low self-esteem, aggressive behavior, perceived rejection, and social-cognitive deficits (Downey & Walker, 1992; Hammon, 1988; Panak & Garber, 1992).

In this chapter, we focus on the potential influences of maternal depression on early developing psychobiological systems that we hypothesize to be related to risk for later depression and other behavioral problems. Specifically, we examine the influences of maternal depression on the development of psychobiological systems related to emotional expression, emotion regulation, and stress responses. We explore how the parent–child relationship acts as a facilitator and regulator in the development of such systems, how maternal depression may interfere with the parent's ability to adaptively carry out this critical role, and its consequences for the development and functioning of psychobiological systems that are involved in mental health. We provide beginning evidence in support of these hypotheses from studies of infants of depressed mothers and from a longitudinal study of approximately 160 mother–child pairs for whom we have examined the associations between maternal depression and children's behavior, brain activity, and stress responses. Our goal is to demonstrate not only how the early social environment influences children's behavior, attitudes, beliefs, and thoughts, but also how it influences the neural processes that underlie them. We believe this endeavor is important because an appreciation of potential postnatal effects of the social environment on the development of neural processes related to emotional well-being may expand our current conception of the biological variables in stress-diathesis models of psychopathology and may yield new perspectives and insights regarding the question of biologically related sensitive periods in early development. Furthermore, it is well known that adult depression involves significant disruptions of biological systems (Heuser, 1998; Nemeroff, 1988; Plotsky, Owens, & Nemeroff, 1998). Thus, by studying the early emergence of such systems and how they might be perturbed by the social environment, we hope to learn more about the etiology of depression.

We focus on two interrelated psychobiological systems, both of which are influenced by early social development: Emotional expression and regulation, and responses to stress. For each system, we discuss aspects of its neuroanatomical basis and how the parent–child relationship may facilitate or disrupt its development. We then provide empirical evidence supporting these ideas based on studies that have examined both the parent–child relationship and the child's behavior and psychophysiology.

EMOTIONAL EXPRESSION AND REGULATION: NEUROANATOMICAL AND DEVELOPMENTAL CONSIDERATIONS

During the first part of the 20th century, the notion of a system of interrelated brain regions that mediate emotions, referred to as the limbic system, was introduced. Building on earlier ideas introduced by Cannon (1927), Papez (1937) attempted one of the first models of emotion that was anchored in neuroanatomy. He postulated that the hypothalamus in interaction with the thalamus, cingulate gyrus, and hippocampus, mediates emotional expression whereas the neocortex mediates emotional experience. Eventually, the limbic system was thought to be comprised of several cortical (orbital frontal, anterior temporal, cingulate gyrus, and hippocampus) and subcortical (amygdala, hypothalamus, and brain-stem reticular formation) regions (MacLean, 1952). Although current evidence casts some doubt on the existence of the limbic system as originally conceived, the notion that there are specific brain regions that are specialized for the processing of social and emotional stimuli continues to be viable.

For example, evidence suggests that it is likely that arousal and alerting responses are mediated by the ascending influences on the cortex of the reticular formation (Fuster, 1989; Heilman, Watson, Valenstein, & Goldberg, 1987; Nauta, 1971; Tucker, 1992). This reciprocol frontal-cortical-thalamic-reticular system prepares the individual to meaningfully respond to emotionally salient stimuli. The amygdala, on the other hand, is hypothesized to code the biological or affective significance of stimuli, whereas the neocortex is believed to mediate conscious awareness and interpretation of emotional stimuli (LeDoux, 1987). Thus, rapid processing of primitive emotional responses representing hard-wired, species-typical behaviors related to survival, is believed to occur at the level of the amygdala, whereas, the interpretation of and behavioral responses to more complex emotional information require the capacities of the neocortex. Such complex behaviors involve reciprocal cortical-subcortical interaction, as shown in Fig. 7.1.

At the neocortical level, research suggests that the frontal lobe plays an important role in both the expression and regulation of emotion. Studies of humans

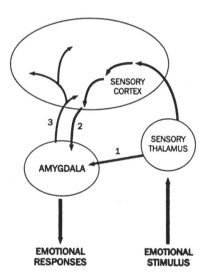

FIG. 7.1.   Thalamo-amygdala and thalamo-cortico-amygdala emotion-processing pathways. According to LeDoux, the emotional significance of sensory stimuli is processed by multiple input systems to the amygdala. From "Emotion and the brain," by J. E. LeDoux, 1991, *Journal of NIH Research, 3*, pp. 49–51. Copyright 1991. Reprinted with permission.

and animals with lesions to the frontal lobe have demonstrated differences both in the type of emotion expressed and in the ability to inhibit inappropriate emotional responses. Interestingly, the left and right frontal regions appear to mediate different types of emotions. Lesions of the right frontal region tend to result in apathy or euphoria, where lesions of the left frontal region tend to result in depression and catastrophic reactions (Gainotti, 1969, 1972; Robinson & Benson, 1981; Robinson, Kubos, Starr, Reo, & Price, 1984; Robinson & Stetela, 1981). Furthermore, frontal brain damage often impairs the individual's ability to regulate their emotional responses (Fuster, 1989).

The notion that the left versus right frontal regions differentially mediate expression of specific emotions rests on evidence garnered from a wide range of methods, including studies of the effects of left- versus right-sided electroconvulsive treatment, the effects of unilateral injection of sodium amytal, and frontal EEG activity during the expression of specific emotions in adults, children, and infants (Davidson, Ekman, Saron, Senulis, & Friesen, 1990; Davidson & Fox, 1988, 1989; Dawson, Panagiotides, Grofer Klinger, & Hill, 1992; Finman, Davidson, Colton, Strauss, & Kagan, 1989). The studies of frontal electroencephalogram (EEG) activity have demonstrated that during the expression of *approach* emotions, such as joy and interest, the left frontal region shows relative activation, whereas during the expression of *withdrawal* emotions, such as distress and fear, the right frontal region shows relative activation. Figure 7.2 illustrates the hypothesized range of approach and withdrawal emotions.

Furthermore, individual differences in patterns of emotional expression have been found to be related to such frontal EEG asymmetries. Davidson and Fox (1989) found that infants with relative right frontal activation were more likely to

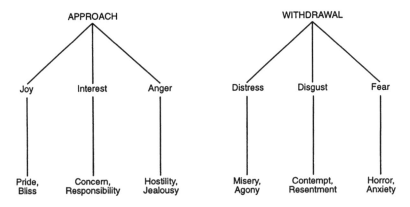

FIG. 7.2. Fox's proposed model for the differentiation of emotions from the approach-withdrawal continuum. From "If it's not left, it's right: Electroencephalograph asymmetry and the development of emotion," by N. A. Fox, 1991, *American Psychologist, 46*, p. 864. Copyright 1991 by the American Psychological Association. Reprinted with permission.

cry when separated from their mothers. Finman et al. (1989) found that behaviorally inhibited children displayed greater resting right frontal asymmetry, compared to uninhibited children. Davidson (1987) found relations between individual differences in resting frontal EEG asymmetry and negative responses to emotional films in adults.

It has been hypothesized that frontal activation asymmetries index individual differences in a propensity to experience approach versus withdrawal emotions (Davidson & Fox, 1988; Fox, 1991). For example, persons with relative right frontal asymmetry are hypothesized to have a lower threshold for the experience of withdrawal emotions such as distress and irritability. Others have hypothesized that frontal activation asymmetries index different emotion-regulatory strategies with right frontal activation being associated with disruption in ongoing activity and withdrawal from the environment, and left frontal activation being associated with engagement in ongoing activity and approach behavior (Dawson, 1994; Dawson, Panagiotides, et al., 1992; Kinsbourne & Bemporad, 1984; Tucker & Williamson, 1984). This latter view is in keeping with a perspective on emotion proposed by Campos and colleagues (Campos, Campos, & Barrett, 1989). Campos described emotions as "processes of establishing, maintaining, and/or disrupting the relations between the person and the internal or external environment" (Campos et al., 1989). In this view, behaviors involved in emotion regulation are considered as components of the emotions rather than responses to them. For example, the emotion of happiness involves monitoring and initiating progress toward a goal, whereas the emotion of sadness may involve relinquishing the strive toward a desired goal or object. This view is consistent with the evidence we are now gathering on the relation between frontal lobe activity and the mother–infant relationship that will be discussed later in this chapter.

As mentioned before, the frontal lobe also plays an important role in regulating behavior, a fact that is evident from the effects of frontal brain damage on emotion regulation (Fuster, 1989). Frontal lobe lesions result in distractibility (Hecaen, 1964), perseverative behavior and thinking (Fuster, 1989), difficulties in directing and sustaining attention (Luria, 1966/1980), and in monitoring of temporal sequences (Milner, Petrides, & Smith, 1985). The frontal lobe is specialized for numerous functions that are necessary for emotion regulation including the ability to inhibit prepotent responses (Diamond, 1990), to guide one's behavior on the basis of internal representations (Goldman-Rakic, 1987), to monitor complex temporal sequences, and to form generalizable mental representations related to expectancies for reward and punishment (Goldman-Rakic, 1987; Jones & Mishkin, 1972).

Frontal lobe abilities are acquired over a person's lifetime and, most likely, are influenced by experience. During the first few years of life, when the frontal lobe begins a rapid period of growth and development, important achievements in emotion regulation occur. During the first 6 months of postnatal life, these achievements include learning to selectively attend to relevant stimuli, and perceiving temporal contingent sequences between their own actions and external stimuli (Aslin, Pisoni, & Jusczyk, 1983; Watson, 1979). The infant becomes able to signal to his or her caretaker when emotionally aroused, for example. The second half of the 1st year is marked by a substantial expansion of emotion regulatory abilities as the infant's behavior becomes more intentional and planful. Newly acquired skills, such as means-end schemas, anticipatory responses, and more complex sequences of gaze (such as required for shared attention and social referencing) allow the infant to better regulate his or her emotional states (Bruner, 1977; Campos, Barrett, Lamb, Goldsmith, & Sternberg, 1983; Klinnert, Campos, Sorce, Emde, & Svejda, 1983; Piaget, 1954; Scaife & Bruner, 1975; Stern, 1985). These newly acquired skills require the ability of the infant to inhibit prepotent responses, to guide behavior by stored representations, and to engage in planful temporal sequences of behavior. All of these abilities are believed to be hallmarks of frontal lobe function as typified by the classic frontal lobe task, the delayed response task (Goldman-Rakic, 1987; Fuster, 1989). The delayed response task, which is akin to Piaget's A not B task, is successfully mastered during this period of development. As Goldman-Rakic (1987) remarked, it is noteworthy that the time period of highest synaptic density in the frontal region coincides in time with the period of acquisition of the delayed response task (about 2–4 months in the monkey and about 12 months in the human infant) (Huttenlocher, 1979, 1994). At about the same time, a rise in brain activity (as indexed by glucose metabolism) in the frontal cortex is evident (Chugani & Phelps, 1986; Chugani, Phelps, & Mazziotta, 1987). Importantly, the successful acquisition of such frontal lobe abilities may be facilitated by a caretaker who is able to respond quickly and sensitively to the infant's emotional and other behavioral cues and to scaffold the environment in such a way that the infant is likely to succeed when practicing self-regulatory behaviors. The role of the environment in facilitating or hampering the development of emotion regulatory behavior is discussed in the next section.

Environmental Influences on the Development of Patterns of Emotion Expression and Regulation

Research has demonstrated that caretakers play an important role in shaping the infant's developing abilities to express and regulate emotions (e.g., Cicchetti, Ganiban, & Barnett, 1991; Malatesta & Haviland, 1982; Tronick & Gianino, 1986). Individual differences in patterns of emotional expression and regulation are influenced by the ways in which parents imitate and reinforce specific emotions (Malatesta & Haviland, 1982) and by the strategies they use to calm and soothe an infant or toddler who is emotionally aroused (Tronick, 1989).

Parental psychopathology can interfere with the parent's ability to optimally provide positive models of emotional expression and to facilitate emotion regulation through sensitive scaffolding and contingent responding. For example, when a mother is depressed, her interactions with the infant typically involve reduced expression and sharing of positive affect, and increased expression and sharing of negative affect (Cohn, Matias, Tronick, Connell, & Lyons-Ruth, 1986; Cohn & Tronick, 1989; Field, 1986; Field et al., 1988). A depressed mother is also more likely to have an intrusive style of interaction with her infant, and less likely to respond contingently to her infant's emotional responses. The infant, in turn, tends to display less positive affect and increased negative affect, irritability, gaze aversion, and passivity (Cohn et al., 1986; Field, 1986; Field et al., 1985). Field and colleagues (Field et al., 1988) found that the depressed behavior of these infants generalized to interactions with a stranger.

Field (1986) hypothesized that the infant mimics the mother's depressed behavior, and that this learned pattern of emotional expression becomes stable across different social partners. Tronick and Gianino (1986) emphasized the impact of the mother's depression on the infant's developing regulatory style. They have proposed that the depressed mother's failure to respond appropriately to her infant's emotional signals results in a poorly coordinated interaction and negative affect on the infant's part. For a time, the infant may persist in attempting to repair the interaction but, with repeated unsuccessful attempts, may turn to other self-regulation strategies in order to cope with negative arousal. They hypothesize that the infant turns inward, adopting an overly self-directed style of emotion regulation. Another way of characterizing this is that, when distressed or sad, the infant is less likely to adopt approach strategies such as signaling to mother and initiating active, planful, coping behaviors directed toward the external environment, and is instead more likely to adopt withdrawal strategies such as engaging in self-directed behavior (e.g., thumb-sucking and rocking), turning away from the external environment (e.g., gaze aversion), and passivity. These behaviors, on the surface, seem to parallel what is seen in adult depression when the individual responds to periods of high emotional distress, loss, and sadness by withdrawing from others and adopting a passive, hopeless orientation toward the external environment.

Interestingly, adult depression has been linked to reduced activity in the left frontal region that mediates approach behaviors. Robinson and colleagues found that left-hemisphere lesions were related to depressive symptoms in patients with brain damage (Robinson & Benson, 1981; Robinson et al., 1984; Robinson & Stetela, 1981). Based on measures of brain glucose metabolism, Baxter et al. (1989) found reduced left frontal activity in depressed adults. Drevets and coworkers (Drevets et al., 1991) found increased activity in the left prefrontal cortex in depressed adults. However, examination of individual differences revealed that higher levels of depressive symptoms were associated with decreased activity in the left prefrontal cortex and increased activity of the left amygdala. Schaffer and coworkers (Schaffer, Davidson, & Saron, 1983) found reduced left frontal EEG activity in depressed adults. Thus, several studies have reported an association between adult depression and reduced activation of the left frontal brain region.

Social Influences on Patterns of Brain Activity Related to Emotional Expression and Regulation

Interactions between the child and his or her parents, such as the ones described previously, influence not only the infant's behavior but also developing patterns of neural systems that mediate emotional and social behavior. In fact, the first several years of life represent a key period in the establishment of neural networks underlying such behaviors. Synapses during this period are selectively eliminated or amplified in large part as a result of experience, a process that has been referred to as ontogenetic sculpting of neural networks (Kolb, 1989). The individual variability that is seen in neural pattern is remarkable (Edelman, 1987, 1989). Selective amplification of specific neural groups is hypothesized to occur as a result of the frequency and intensity of environmental stimulation (Edelman, 1987; Hebb, 1949). Edelman (1989) argued that these emerging neural patterns become stabilized and less susceptible to change over time. Once a specific pattern of neuronal groups is selected in a mapped area, exposure to the same or similar stimuli is likely to preferentially activate previously selected neuronal groups. Such maps are believed to involve cortical sensory and motor maps as well as the brain regions with which these cortical areas interact, such as subcortical limbic regions in the case of emotional processing.

Returning to the example of maternal depression to illustrate this point, the infant exposed to maternal depression is likely to receive less-than-normal amplification of neural networks related to approach behaviors and more-than-normal amplification of neural networks related to withdrawal behaviors during a period when such networks are undergoing rapid development and stabilization. Thus, it is not unreasonable to hypothesize that one might find atypical patterns of frontal brain activity in such infants that may reflect the impact of the social environment on developing brain systems.

In 1992, Dawson and colleagues reported that infants of teenaged mothers who endorsed clinically high levels of depressive symptoms displayed different patterns of frontal EEG activity, when compared to a group of teenaged mothers who were experiencing no or relatively few depressive symptoms (Dawson, Grofer Klinger, Panagiotides, Hill, and Spieker, 1992). Infants' frontal and parietal EEG activity (6–9 Hz) was recorded during three conditions: a baseline condition, playing peek-a-boo with mother, and separation from mother. Compared with infants of nondepressed mothers, infants of depressed mothers exhibited reduced left frontal brain activity during playful interactions with their mothers and failed to exhibit the typical pattern of greater right frontal activity during a condition designed to elicit distress (maternal separation). These data, which are expressed as frontal asymmetry scores (log [right EEG power] minus log [left EEG power]) are shown in Fig. 7.3. Note that reduced EEG power represents increased brain activation (Steriade, 1981) such that higher asymmetry scores reflect greater relative left hemisphere activation and lower asymmetry scores reflect greater relative right hemisphere activation.

Infants of depressed mother also displayed lower levels of distress during maternal separation, consistent with Tronick and Gianino's (1986) prediction that such infants are less likely to adopt other-directed regulatory strategies when distressed. No group differences in affective behavior were found during the playful condition, however, suggesting that the psychophysiological measures were more sensitive in detecting differences than were the behavioral measures in this con-

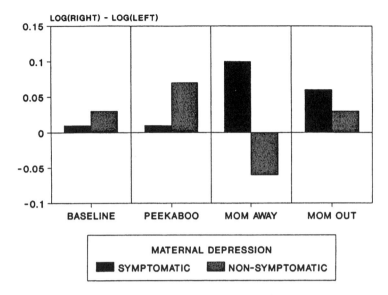

FIG. 7.3.   Frontal EEG asymmetry scores from infants of symptomatic and non-symptomatic mothers during baseline and maternal interaction. Conditions: Note that positive asymmetry scores indicated greater left than right hemisphere activation and vice versa. From "Frontal lobe activity and affective behavior of infants of mothers with depressive symptoms," by G. Dawson, L. Grofer Klinger, H. Panagiotides, D. Hill, & S. Spieker, 1992, *Child Development*, 1963, pp. 725–737. Reprinted with permission.

dition. Importantly, group differences were found only in the frontal region, and not in the parietal region.

We later coded from videotapes the same infants' emotional displays during the baseline, mother play, and maternal separation conditions using Ekman's Facial Action Coding System (FACS) (Dawson, Panagiotides, Grofer Klinger, & Spieker, 1997). Even with this fine-grained behavioral coding system, no differences in the frequency or types of emotional displays between infants of depressed and nondepressed mothers were observed. This is not particularly surprising given that the behavior was observed in a highly structured and relatively brief experimental situation. Infants' EEG activity was then examined during those periods when infants were displaying prototypic emotions, as defined by FACS. It was found that, compared to infants of nondepressed mothers, infants of depressed mothers exhibited increased EEG activity in the frontal but not the parietal region, specifically when the infants were expressing negative emotions (unfelt smiles and anger) (see Fig. 7.4). This evidence suggested that, when the infants of depressed mothers were experiencing negative emotions, the brain systems that mediate such emotions were more highly activated than normal.

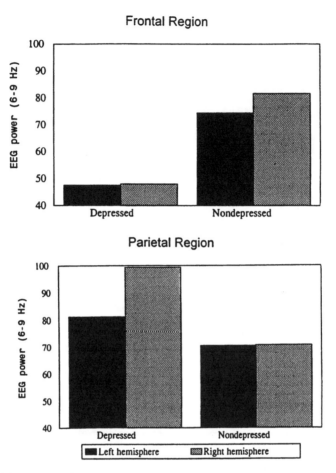

FIG. 7.4. Frontal and parietal EEG power during the expression of anger by infants of depressed versus nondepressed mothers. Note that lower EEG power indicates greater brain activation. From "Infants of depressed and nondepressed mothers exhibit differences in frontal brain electrical activity during the expression of negative emotions," by G. Dawson, H. Panagiotides, L. Grofer Klinger, and S. Spieker, 1997, *Developmental Psychology, 33*, pp. 650–656. Copyright 1997 by the American Psychological Association. Reprinted with permission.

These initial findings raised several questions. Were these findings specific of teenaged mothers who were experiencing depression, or would similar patterns of frontal EEG be found in adult mothers with depression? Were these findings specifically related to maternal depression or would atypical patterns of frontal EEG be exhibited by infants of mothers with other forms of psychopathology, for example, anxiety? Were the atypical patterns of infant frontal EEG only evident during situations involving direct interactions with mother (i.e., the mother play condition), or would they generalize to other conditions such as play with an experimenter and baseline conditions? Are variations in patterns of frontal EEG predictive of individual differences in infant behavior? And finally, what evidence do we have that the atypical patterns of infant frontal EEG are specifically related to the depressed mother's behavior with her infant?

To address these questions, we launched a longitudinal study of approximately 160 mother–infant pairs. In this study, we collected other psychobiological measures in addition to electrical brain activity. Table 7.1 displays the psychophysiological measures taken at each of two time points: Time 1 when the infant was 13–15 months of age, and Time 2 when the child was 42 months of age. Data collection is ongoing; we have recently completed a comprehensive assessment of the sample at Time 3 when the children were $6^1/_2$ years of age. In this chapter, we will review some of the results that have emerged at Time 1 and briefly discuss some of the preliminary analyses from Time 2. We will report what we have learned up to this point regarding the effects of maternal depression on children's brain activity and stress responses, as reflected in both autonomic responses (heart rate) and salivary cortisol. Note that whereas EEG and heart rate were collected for this sample at Times 1, 2, and 3, salivary cortisol was measured only at Times 2 and 3. Before reporting these data, however, a discussion of how maternal depression plays a role in the development of stress responses is in order.

CHILDREN'S STRESS RESPONSES: DEVELOPMENTAL AND EXPERIENTIAL CONSIDERATIONS

Why study stress responses in children of depressed mothers? To begin, it is well established that major depression in adulthood involves dysregulation of the body's physiological response to stress (Heuser, 1998; Nemeroff, 1988; Plotsky et al., 1998). Furthermore, evidence supports the notion that stressful life events and lifetime traumas often precede the onset of major depression (Kendler et al., 1993; Plotsky et al., 1998). These findings are consistent with a stress-diathesis model of major depression, in which multiple factors, including genetic liabilities, early adverse life events, and additional stressors, contribute to the etiology of depression. Genetic factors and early life stress may interact to sensitize the neural pathways mediating the stress response, thus increasing vulnerability to

TABLE 7.1
Physiological Measures Collected During Longitudinal Study

Time 1 (13–15 months)	Time 2 (42 months)
Electrical brain activity (EEG)	Electrical brain activity (EEG)
Heart rate	Heart rate
Vagal tone	Vagal tone
	Salivary cortisol

major depression (Plotsky et al., 1998). In this model, maternal depression may represent both a genetic and environmental risk factor for the development of major depression. Infants may experience the behaviors of a depressed mother as unpredictable and stressful, and this experience may negatively impact the development of the child's physiological responses to stress.

In this section, we endeavor to explain how maternal depression influences the development of children's stress responses and how those influences may increase children's vulnerability to develop depression, themselves. First, we briefly review the biological systems that mediate stress responses (also see Gunnar, chapt. 5, this volume). Then, we examine animal and clinical literature that demonstrates the important influence of the early social environment on children's stress responses. Finally, we discuss previous research on the effects of maternal depression on children's stress responses as reflected in autonomic and cortisol activity.

The Role of the HPA Axis in the Stress Response

The principle of homeostasis underlies our current understanding of physiological and behavioral responses to stress. Under typical (nonstressful) conditions, the body exists in a state of equilibrium; however, when exposed to a stressful event, our bodies respond with adaptive changes designed to restore balance. These adaptive changes are known as the stress response. The stress response has multiple components, including the hypothalamic pituitary adrenal (HPA) axis and the locus coeruleus-norepinephrine (LC/NE) system. These two systems appear to function in a positive feedback loop, in which one system activates the other. We focus here on the HPA axis.

The neuroendocrine responses mediated by the HPA axis represent a primary component of the body's physiological response to stress. Seyle (1936, 1946) first articulated the concept of a nonspecific stress response centered on the pituitary-adrenocortical system and called this response the general adaptation syndrome. According to Seyle (1946), the general adaptation syndrome consists of three stages: the general alarm reaction, the stage of resistance, and the stage of exhaustion. The first stage occurs in acute response to a damaging agent (i.e. shock, exercise, infectious disease, hemorrhage, and exposure to cold) and the latter stages occur only after continuous exposure. Seyle (1946) hypothesized that the general alarm reaction was mediated by the discharge of adrenotropic hormones from the anterior lobe of the pituitary and the subsequent stimulation of the adrenal cortex, which caused the production of corticoid hormones. This theory developed into what we now know about the stress response.

Building on Seyle's theory, subsequent research elucidated the specific neuroendocrine responses resulting from activation of the HPA axis. Initially, stress causes the paraventricular nucleus (PVN) of the hypothalamus to release corticotropin-releasing hormone (CRH). CRH then travels to the anterior lobe of the pituitary, where it stimulates the release of adrenocorticotropin (ACTH) and generates the precursors of beta-endorphin and melanin-stimulating hormone (alpha MSH). ACTH then activates the adrenal cortex, initiating the release of cortisol, the primary peripheral stress hormone (Michelson, Licinio, & Gold, 1995).

The activity of the HPA axis serves to combat perceived threat and restore homeostasis. Behaviorally, HPA-axis activity promotes increased vigilance, focused attention, and alertness. On a physiological level, the stress response induces changes that make energy available where it is needed most. These changes include suppression of reproductive and growth systems, and increases in: (a) central nervous system concentrations of oxygen and nutrients, (b) cardiovascular tone, (c) respiratory rate, (d) glucose production, and (e) lipolysis (Michelson et al., 1995).

Glucocorticoids, such as cortisol, also serve to restore equilibrium in the stress response system through a negative feedback loop. Thus, elevations in plasma cortisol actually reduce activity of the HPA axis. This restraint on the system counteracts the potentially harmful effects of stress-activated responses. Current research suggests that glucocorticoid receptors mediate this feedback loop by inhibiting hypothalamic CRH secretion (Michelson et al., 1995). Psychological mechanisms, such as control, predictability, and feedback, can also regulate HPA-axis activity. When an animal can control a stressor (by pressing a lever to terminate a loud noise, for example), the animal will show plasma cortisol levels similar to those of unstressed animals (see Levine, Coe, & Wiener, 1989 for a review).

Under conditions of chronic stress, the stress-response system fails to return to equilibrium and remains activated. Current research suggests that this prolonged activation during chronic stress may result from increased arginine vasopressin (AVP) release as opposed to increased CRH. Although weaker than CRH, AVP also stimulates the anterior pituitary to secrete ACTH (Michelson et al., 1995).

Sustained high levels of glucocorticoids can have deleterious effects on brain regions that contain high concentrations of glucocorticoid receptors, including the hippocampus, cingulate gyrus, amygdala, and frontal brain regions (Gunnar, 1998). Among these brain regions, the most research exists on the effects of high glucocorticoid levels on the hippocampus, a brain structure involved in learning and memory. In the rat, a few days of overexposure to stress can compromise the ability of hippocampal neurons to survive seizures or ischemia. Increasingly longer exposures can cause atrophy of hippocampal dendrites and, ultimately, permanent loss of hippocampal neurons (Sapolsky, 1996).

In humans, HPA-axis hyperactivity has been associated with psychopathology, especially major depression. Specifically, adults with major depression have been observed to have elevated ACTH and plasma cortisol concentrations, possibly mediated by increased release of CRH (Heuser, 1998; Nemeroff, 1988; Plotsky et al., 1998). Little research documents the effects of elevated glucocorticoid levels on the human brain. However, Sapolsky (1996) reviewed studies indicating relations between duration of depression and hippocampal atrophy and, in veterans, duration of combat exposure and hippocampal atrophy. For both these groups, longer durations were associated with increased atrophy. Because both depression and combat exposure are associated with elevated glucocorticoid levels, we can speculate that glucocorticoids might be responsible for the damage; however, these studies are correlational in nature and cannot definitively establish causality. In infants, Gunnar and Nelson (1994) found a negative correlation between cortisol levels and event-related potentials hypothesized to be related to hippocampal activity.

Because high levels of glucocorticoids may have harmful effects on the developing brain, biological mechanisms have developed to maintain glucocorticoids at low levels during early development. In rats, research has documented a developmental stage from postnatal days 4 to 14 when the HPA axis is relatively insensitive to stressors (Suchecki, Rosenfeld, & Levine, 1993). Researchers have named this stage the Stress Hyporesponsive Period (SHRP). During the SHRP, rats secrete decreased amounts of baseline and stress-induced corticosterone, ACTH, corticotropin-releasing factor (CRF), and AVP (Rosenfeld, Suchecki, & Levine, 1992). Researchers have hypothesized several different mechanisms that regulate the HPA axis during the SHRP. These include immaturity of underlying structures, increased negative feedback, and adrenal hyporesponsiveness (Rosenfeld et al., 1992).

Social Influences on the Development of the Stress Response

A great deal of research points to the role of mother–infant interactions in the development and regulation of HPA-axis activity. In addition to the innate mechanisms controlling the SHRP, evidence now indicates that maternal behavior plays a role in maintaining downregulation of the stress response. In rats, prolonged maternal separation (3 hours or longer) stimulates HPA-axis activity and leads to elevated corticosterone levels as well as changes in CRF concentrations and receptor number (Kuhn, Pauk, & Schanberg, 1990; Kuhn & Schanberg, 1998; Pihoker, Owens, Kuhn, Schanberg, & Nemeroff, 1993). Specific maternal behaviors, such as feeding and stroking, can weaken this adrenocortical response to maternal deprivation. Suchecki et al. (1993) demonstrated that, in maternally deprived rat pups, feeding inhibits corticosterone secretion, while stroking suppresses ACTH secretion. In addition, the attenuating effects of tactile stimulation appear to be specific to the presence of maternal stimuli, as opposed to nonspecific social stimuli (Stanton & Levine, 1990).

Similar research with nonhuman primates (squirrel monkeys and rhesus macaques) demonstrated increases in plasma cortisol following maternal separation (Levine & Wiener, 1988). These cortisol elevations increase as a function of the duration of maternal separation. Unlike rats, however, for the nonhuman primates, the presence of a familiar social group can buffer the endocrine effects of maternal separation. In addition, when permitted to remain with the social group, squirrel monkeys demonstrated a lower adrenal response to maternal separation and a more rapid return to baseline following reunion. Monkeys who were separated and isolated displayed a more profound increase in plasma cortisol levels and a slower return to baseline. Levine and Wiener (1988) posited that the attenuated stress response in the presence of familiar conspecifics reflects the continued availability of a stable, predictable social environment as opposed to the uncertainty of isolation.

Longitudinal studies of both rodents and nonhuman primates indicate that the effects of maternal separation can persist into adulthood (Anisman, Zaharia, Meaney, & Merali, 1998; Ladd, Owens, & Nemeroff, 1996; Plotsky & Meaney, 1993). Ladd et al. (1996) found that adult rats who had been maternally deprived during the SHRP exhibited increased baseline and stress-induced plasma ACTH concentrations as well as changes in CRF neural systems. Similarly, Plotsky and Meaney (1993) observed that daily maternal separation during the first 2 weeks of life resulted in elevated stress responses in adult rats. Compared to briefly handled and nonhandled peers, maternally deprived rats exhibited increased CRF mRNA expression, median eminence CRF content, and plasma ACTH and corticosterone levels in response to stress.

Research with nonhuman primates demonstrated similar long-term consequences of early life stress (Capitanio, Rasmussen, Snyder, Laudenslager, & Reite, 1986; Coplan et al., 1996). Coplan et al. (1996) exposed bonnet macaques to either predictable or unpredictable rearing conditions by varying the amount and predictability of foraging that mothers needed to do to acquire food. Years later, compared to primates exposed to predictable high foraging or predictable low foraging conditions, primates exposed to variable foraging conditions displayed elevated cerebrospinal fluid concentrations of CRF. Capitanio et al. (1986) observed that monkeys who had experienced maternal separations as infants displayed more disturbed behavior as adults.

If the social environment can influence the development of the stress response in animals, does the environment have similar effects on human infant development? In human infants, researchers have explored the relationship between attachment security and cortisol reactivity as a means of investigating how the mother–infant relationship affects cortisol levels. For example, Nachmias, Gunnar, Mangelsdorf, Parritz, and Buss (1996) found that secure attachment relationships buffer the cortisol responses of behaviorally inhibited 18-month-olds to a novel situation. Only the inhibited toddlers who were also insecurely attached to their mothers displayed significant elevations in salivary cortisol. In a similar study, Gunnar, Brodersen, Nachmias, Buss, and Rigatuso (1996) found that attachment security moderates the cortisol response of 15-month-olds to inoculation distress. Fearful toddlers who were also insecurely attached displayed elevated cortisol levels. These data suggest the importance of sensitive, responsive caretaking in the development of the HPA axis, especially for tempermentally inhibited or fearful children.

In human infants, the most profound, long-term naturalistic study of early deprivation has occurred with the tragic case of Romanian orphanage children. These children underwent significant deprivation until their adoption into homes in Europe, Canada, and the United States. Approximately 6 years postadoption, Gunnar and Chisholm (1999) conducted a follow-up study to examine the effects of early institutional rearing on cortisol levels and attachment quality. They found that children who had experienced 8 or more months of institutional rearing displayed significantly higher salivary cortisol compared to sex, age, and socioeconomic status (SES) matched controls and compared to children who had experienced 4 or fewer months of institutional life. In addition, there was a significant positive correlation between evening cortisol levels and time in institution, suggesting that the longer exposure to deprivation is associated with more pronounced effects on the HPA axis. Finally, more securely attached institutionalized children displayed more normative cortisol levels.

There exist very few data on the effects of maternal depression on children's stress responses. One study conducted by Field and colleagues (Field et al., 1988) found that infants of depressed mothers had higher salivary cortisol levels than infants of nondepressed mothers during face-to-face interactions. Interestingly, during the interactions, the infants of depressed mothers showed lower frequencies of gaze, facial expression, and physical activity, as compared to nondepressed dyads. Thus, as in adult depression, the physiological arousal was associated with depressed behavior in the infants.

LONGITUDINAL STUDY OF THE EFFECTS OF MATERNAL DEPRESSION ON CHILDREN'S PSYCHOBIOLOGICAL AND BEHAVIORAL DEVELOPMENT: ANALYSES OF DATA FROM TIME 1 (13–15-MONTH-OLD INFANTS)

In this section, we review findings from our current longitudinal study of the effects of maternal depression on children's psychobiological and behavioral development based on analyses of data from Time 1 when the infants were 13–15 months of age. We begin by examining questions posed earlier in the chapter regarding the nature and interpretation of the finding that infants of depressed mothers exhibit atypical frontal brain activity. We then discuss emerging findings from our laboratory regarding the effects of maternal depression on infant's stress response, as measured by autonomic activity (heart rate).

Does the Finding of Atypical Frontal EEG in Infants of Teenaged Depressed Mothers Generalize to Adult Mothers? Is the Finding of Atypical Infant Frontal EEG Specific to Maternal Depression?

The current longitudinal study involves 159 adult mothers (mean age around 30 years) with and without depression who are primarily married, middle income level, and European American. Mothers were carefully screened for a range of other difficulties that could potentially affect their infants, including other major psychiatric disorders (e.g., psychosis and bipolar affective disorder), substance abuse, contact with Child Protective Services, and prenatal and birth difficulties. The assessment of depression included both a questionnaire-based self-report of depressive symptoms (Center for Epidemiological Studies – Depression Questionnaire; CES-D) and a standardized psychiatric interview (Structured Clinical Interview of the DSM-III-R; SCID). Mother's course of depression has been chronicled on a month-to-month basis from the point of the infant's conception. Based on this comprehensive assessment, 90 of the 159 mothers were considered depressed at Time 1. Mothers were also assessed for presence of anxiety and hostility via the Brief Symptom Inventory (Deragotis & Melisaratos, 1983).

Results based on this sample of adult mothers replicated previous findings with teenaged depressed mothers (Dawson, Frey, Panagiotides, Osterling, & Hessl, 1997). Again, infants of depressed mothers showed reduced left frontal EEG activity. Figure 7.5 displays mean frontal and parietal EEG asymmetry scores (log [right] minus log [left] EEG power) taken during an alert baseline condition for 13–15-month-old infants of mothers with and without depression. Infants of depressed mothers showed significantly lower frontal asymmetry scores compared to infants of nondepressed mothers. In contrast, the two groups did not differ in terms of their parietal EEG activity. Examination of individual differences in infant frontal EEG activity revealed that infants of depressed mothers

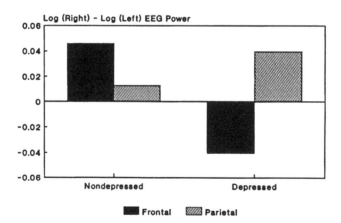

FIG. 7.5.   Mean frontal and parietal EEG asymmetry scores based on EEG recording taken from 13–15-month-old infants of mothers with and without clinical depression. Lower asymmetry scores indicate relative right hemisphere activation and higher scores indicate relative left hemisphere activation. From "Infants of depressed mothers exhibit atypical frontal brain activity: A replication and extension of previous findings," by G. Dawson, K. Frey, H. Panagiotides, J. Osterling, and D. Hessl, 1997, *Journal of Child Psychology and Psychiatry, 38*, pp. 179–186. Reprinted with permission.

were underrepresented in the subgroup of infants with highly positive frontal EEG asymmetry scores (one standard deviation above the mean) and overrepresented in the subgroup of infants with highly negative frontal EEG asymmetry scores (one standard deviation below the mean). These individual differences are illustrated in Fig. 7.6. Only 10% (1 out of 10) of the infants with highly positive scores were infants of depressed mothers, whereas 75% (21 out of 28) of the infants with highly negative scores were infants of depressed mothers.

Infant frontal EEG patterns also were found to be related to the severity of maternal depression (Dawson, Frey, et al., 1997). As can be see in Fig. 7.7, infants of mothers with more severe depression showed more extreme negative asymmetry scores. Furthermore, infant frontal EEG patterns were not found to be related to mothers' levels of anxiety or hostility, as reported on the Brief Symptom Inventory, even though depressed mothers reported significantly higher levels of symptoms in each of these domains compared to nondepressed mothers (Dawson, Frey, et al., 1997). These findings suggest that reduced left frontal EEG activity may be specifically related to maternal depression, rather than more generally to maternal psychopathology or other symptoms associated with depression.

Do Patterns of Atypical Frontal EEG Activity Generalize to Conditions Other Than Those Directly Involving Interactions With Mother?

In the original 1992 study, atypical patterns of frontal EEG in infants of depressed mothers were found primarily in the mother play condition. Thus, it is possible that the atypical frontal EEG activity was due to the proximal effects of the depressed mother's behavior with her infant during EEG recording. In the 1992 study, mean differences in infant frontal EEG activity during the baseline condition were only marginally significant. However, as reported earlier, in the larger study of mother–infant pairs, significant differences were found in frontal brain activity between infants of depressed and nondepressed mothers during the baseline condition (Dawson, Frey, et al., 1997). Furthermore, similar differences were found in a standardized playful condition carried out with a familiar experimenter (Dawson, Frey, Panagiotides, Yamada, Hessl, & Osterling, 1999).

In fact, infant frontal brain activity was examined in five different experimental conditions designed to elicit a range of infant emotions. These conditions consisted of: (a) baseline condition that was designed to induce a state of relaxed alertness; (b) mother play during which she played peek-a-boo without using speech; (c) experimenter play during which a familiar female experimenter silently played peek-a-boo in a highly animated fashion using a pom-pom, funny hats, and a squeaky toy while smiling broadly at the infant; (d) stranger approach during which an unfamiliar person with a neutral expression silently approached the infant; and (e) maternal separation during which the mother briefly left the room.

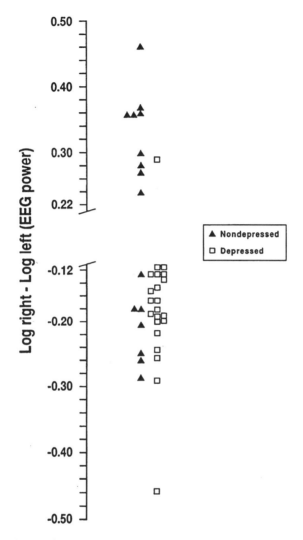

FIG. 7.6.   Individual infants' frontal EEG asymmetry scores falling one standard deviation above or below the mean. Ten percent of the infants with highly positive scores are infants of depressed mothers, whereas 75% of the infants with highly negative scores are infants of depressed mothers. Lower asymmetry scores indicate relative right hemisphere activation and higher scores indicate relative left hemisphere activation. From "Infants of depressed mothers exhibit atypical frontal brain activity: A replication and extension of previous findings," by G. Dawson, K. Frey, H. Panagiotides, J. Osterling, and D. Hessl, 1997, *Journal of Child Psychology and Psychiatry, 38*, pp. 179–186. Reprinted with permission.

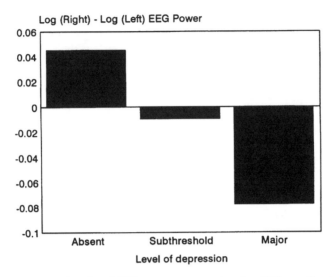

FIG. 7.7.   Mean frontal EEG asymmetry scores based on EEG recordings taken
from 13–15-month-old infants of mothers with varying levels of depression: (1) No
or few depressive symptoms; (2) Subthreshold depression or depression in partial
remission; and (3) Major depression. Lower asymmetry scores indicate relative
right hemisphere activation and higher scores indicate relative left hemisphere activation. From "Infants of depressed mothers exhibit atypical frontal brain activity:
A replication and extension of previous findings," by G. Dawson, K. Frey, H. Panagiotides, J. Osterling, and D. Hessl, 1997, *Journal of Child Psychology and Psychiatry, 38*, pp. 179–186. Reprinted with permission.

Infants' and mothers' affective behavior was coded from videotapes by raters
blind to mothers' diagnostic status. Although infants' affective behavior for both
groups varied significantly as a function of experimental condition, infants of depressed and nondepressed mothers did not significantly differ from each other in
their affective responses. Similarly, depressed and nondepressed mothers did not
differ in their affective behavior in this relatively brief and highly structured period of play interaction.

Across all conditions except the stranger approach condition, infants of depressed mothers displayed significantly lower frontal EEG asymmetry scores indicating relatively lower levels of left frontal activity. These results are shown in
Fig. 7.8. Subsequent analyses that separately examined infants' frontal EEG
asymmetry scores during the positive affect conditions (baseline, mother play,
and experimenter play) and the negative affect conditions (stranger approach and
maternal separation) revealed that group differences in frontal brain activity were
primarily present in the positive affect conditions. These situations all involve approach behaviors (interest, happiness, and engagement with external environment) mediated by the left frontal region. This suggests that maternal depression

may have a more specific effect on altering left frontal brain activity that has been associated with approach behavior. To further explore this question, in the next section, we report on the results of analyses that examined the relation between infant frontal brain activity and variations in infant behavior.

Are Variations in Patterns of Frontal EEG Related to Individual Differences in Infant Behavior?

A critical question is whether or not individual differences in patterns of frontal brain activity are related to variations in behavior. If so, measures of brain activity might allow us to identify children at risk for depression early in life, provide clues to the etiology of affective disorder, and provide insights into possible preventative interventions. In order to begin to address this question, the relation between individual differences in frontal brain activity and infant behavior as observed in naturalistic situations outside the psychophysiology laboratory was

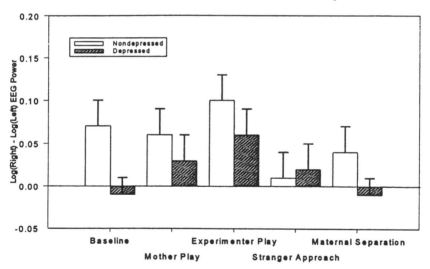

FIG. 7.8. Mean frontal and parietal brain electrical activity, expressed as log (right EEG power) - log (left EEG power) in microvolts squared, recorded from infants of depressed and nondepressed mothers during baseline and four experimental conditions. Note the EEG is expressed as an asymmetry score, such as lower scores indicate reduced relative left hemisphere power. From "Infants of depressed mothers exhibit reduced left frontal brain activity during interactions with mother and a familiar nondepressed adult," by G. Dawson, K. Frey, H. Panagiotides, E. Yamada, D. Hessl, and J. Osterling, 1999, *Child Development*. Reprinted with permission.

examined. It was reasoned that if measures of brain activity are to potentially serve as an indicator of future risk for child psychopathology, a contemporaneous relation between brain activity and behavior should exist. We were interested not only in the strength of this relation, should it exist, but also whether or not certain patterns of EEG activity were associated with specific behaviors of interest. Drawing upon previous theoretical and experimental work linking the left frontal region with approach behaviors and the right frontal region with withdrawal behaviors (Davidson et al., 1990; Fox, 1991) and our own findings that differences in brain activity between infants of depressed and nondepressed mothers are primarily evident in approach situations (e.g., mother and experimenter play), it was predicted that reduced left frontal activity would be related to reduced levels of positive approach behaviors in the infants.

It was also of interest whether individual differences in generalized frontal activation would be associated with variations in infant behavior. This interest came from a previous finding from our laboratory that infants of depressed mothers showed increased generalized frontal activation during the expression of negative emotions, discussed previously (Dawson, Panagiotides, et al., 1997). Thus, it was hypothesized that increased levels of generalized frontal activation would be related to increased levels of intense negative affect, such as might be expected to occur during aggression.

Finally, it was also of interest whether or not variations in infant frontal brain activity would be related to measures of infant temperament. Some investigators have hypothesized that individual differences in frontal EEG asymmetry are linked to specific temperamental dimensions, such as shyness and inhibition (Calkins, Fox, & Marshall, 1996). Mothers were asked to complete the Adapted Colorado Infant Temperament Inventory (Goldman & Mitchell, 1990). Relations between infant brain activity and language as reflected in the MacArthur Communicative Development Inventory were also examined (Fenson et al., 1993).

Observations of infant behavior were made on a separate day from psychophysiological testing. Observations were made during (a) 15 minutes of mother–infant free play, (b) a divided attention situation during which the mother was asked to complete a questionnaire while her infant entertained herself with only a few toys with which the infant was already familiar, and (c) a mastery motivation task. The mastery motivation task was conducted with an experimenter and involved a procedure developed at the National Institute of Child Health and Human Development (NICHD) (Morgan, Maslin, & Harmon, 1988) designed to assess the infant's ability to persist in the face of cognitive challenge. Several infant behaviors were coded by raters blind to maternal diagnosis. Behaviors tapped the domains of affection and positive affect, negative affect, hostility, aggression and tantrums, and types of bids used by the infant to gain mother's attention (both positive and negative) during the divided attention situation.

It was found that infants of depressed mothers were less likely to be affectionate and to touch their mothers during free play (Dawson, Frey, Self, Panagiotides,

Hessl, Yamada, & Rinaldi, 1999). These infants also had the most difficulty quietly occupying themselves during the divided attention situation, a situation that required self-regulatory capabilities on the part of the infant. In this challenging situation, infants of depressed mothers were more likely than infants of nondepressed mothers to visually monitor their mothers, gesture and vocalize to get attention, sit on mother's lap, and eventually become aggressive toward their mothers while their mother attempted to complete the questionnaire. Based on mother's report on the temperament questionnaire, infants of depressed mothers also were found to have higher levels of emotionality, reaction to food, and lower levels of attention.

Significant relations between frontal EEG asymmetry scores and infant behavior were primarily found for infants of depressed mothers (Dawson, Frey, Self, Panagiotides, Hessl, Yamada, & Rinaldi, 1999). For these infants, reduced left frontal activity was correlated with lower levels of positive approach behaviors (affection toward mother during free play) and higher frequencies of negative bids for attention (grabbing mother's clipboard or pen while she attempted to fill out questionnaire).

Relations between infant brain activity and behavior also were found when patterns of generalized frontal brain activation were examined. Such relations existed only for the infants of depressed mothers. Increased generalized frontal brain activity was associated with higher levels of negative affect, hostility, tantrums, and aggression. No relations between patterns of parietal activity and infant behavior were found. Moreover, for infants of depressed mothers, no relation between infant brain activity and language ability or temperament were found.

Thus, consistent with previous theoretical and empirical work, reduced left frontal activity was associated with reduced levels of infant positive affiliative–approach behavior, and increased generalized frontal activation was associated with increased levels of behaviors indicative of intensive negative affect, such as aggression, hostility, and tantrums. Relations between infant brain activity and behavior were specific to the frontal brain region. Furthermore, the behaviors that were found to be associated with frontal brain activity reflect the dimensions of positive approach–affiliative behaviors and regulation of negative emotions. These findings, taken together with the results of our previous studies and analyses, suggest that the alterations in infant brain activity that are associated with maternal depression are linked both to lower levels of approach behaviors and increased intensity of negative affect or difficulties in regulating negative affect.

What Evidence Do We Have That the Atypical Patterns of EEG Are Specifically Related to Mother's Behavior?

The evidence reviewed in this chapter indicates that parental depression may affect a young child's emotional well-being and patterns of early brain activity. The mechanisms underlying these effects are poorly understood. Possible mechanisms include genetic factors, prenatal exposure to maternal depression, and postnatal effects of parental behavior on child development. Depression during pregnancy could potentially expose the fetus to an altered physiological environment and perhaps to other associated risk factors such as poor nutrition, maternal anxiety, and so on. Evidence supporting prenatal effects of maternal depression comes from studies of neonates born to depressed mothers. These infants have been found to be less active, less socially responsive, and fussier than those born to nondepressed mothers (Field et al., 1985; Whiffen & Gotlib, 1989; Zuckerman, Als, Bauchner, Parker, & Cabral, 1990).

What evidence do we have that maternal depression during the infant's postnatal life influences not only infant behavior, but also infant brain activity? At this point, our evidence is not definitive because we cannot control for genetic effects (this would require something like a twin adoption study); rather, the data are highly suggestive that such postnatal effects exist. It is important that studies have shown that maternal depression does indeed have an influence on mother's behavior toward her infant (Cohn et al., 1986; Cohn & Tronick, 1989; Field, 1986; Field et al., 1988). The question is whether or not mother's behavior mediates, fully or in part, the relation between maternal depression and infant frontal EEG activity. Subsequently, we discuss two ways in which we have attempted to address this question based on data collected at Time 1 from the longitudinal study of maternal depression.

Prenatal Versus Postnatal Effects.   Recall that, in the longitudinal study, we chronicled the mother's course of depression since the infant's conception. Mothers were administered an adapted version of the Longitudinal Interval Follow-up Evaluation (LIFE; Keller, Shapiro, Lavori, & Wolfe, 1982; Keller et al., 1987) that was designed to assess, on a month-to-month basis, the longitudinal history of the mother's depression. Of the group of mothers who met criteria for depression on the Structured Clinical Interview of the *DSM-III-R* ($N = 54$), 23 mothers experienced depression only after their child was born (postnatal only group), whereas 31 mothers experienced depression during both the prenatal and postnatal periods (prenatal and postnatal group). When these two groups were compared to the group of nondepressed mothers in terms of their infants' frontal asymmetry scores, significant group differences were found (mean frontal asymmetry scores for the three groups were .05, −.02, −.05 for the nondepressed, postnatal only, and prenatal plus postnatal groups, respectively (Dawson, Frey, et al., 1997). Two points are important with respect to the question being addressed here: First, the postnatal only group did, in fact, show the atypical infant frontal asymmetry pattern indicating that exposure during the prenatal period is not necessary for this effect. Second, both groups of infants of depressed mothers (postnatal only and prenatal plus postnatal) differed from the nondepressed groups in terms of infant brain activity, but they did not differ from each other. Furthermore, a multiple regression analysis demonstrated that, after accounting for the effect of the number of postpartum months of depression, the number of prepartum months of maternal depression was not predictive of infant frontal EEG patterns. When the order of these two variables was reversed, the number of prenatal months was marginally predictive of infant frontal EEG and the number of postnatal months of maternal depression remained a significant predictor of infant frontal brain activity (Dawson, Frey, et al., 1997). These results showed that the number of postpartum months of depression was clearly the stronger predictor of patterns of infant frontal brain activity.

Relations Between Mother's Behavior and Infant Brain Activity

One way of examining the question of whether or not alteration of frontal brain activity in infants of depressed mothers is related to the mother–child relationship after birth is to examine whether variations in observed mother–infant interaction mediate the relation between maternal depression and infant frontal brain activity. Based on this approach, results from our study suggest that the mother's behavior during the postnatal period does influence infant frontal brain activity.

In the longitudinal study, we used this approach at Time 1 when the infants were 13–15 months of age by observing the mother's behavior with her infant outside the psychophysiology laboratory on a separate day from that on which the psychophysiological measures were taken. Previous studies have indicated that mothers experiencing depression vary substantially in terms of their patterns of behavior with their infants. Maternal styles can range from normal positive interaction to withdrawn, disengaged patterns to an intrusive, irritable style of interaction (Field, 1992). Thus, we anticipated that there would, in fact, be significant variability in the mothers' behavior toward their infants that would allow us to examine whether or not such variability was associated with variability in infant frontal brain activity.

We examined mother's behavior with her infant during 15 minutes of mother–infant free play and a divided attention situation during which the mother was asked to complete a questionnaire while her infant entertained herself or himself with only a few toys with which the infant was already familiar. Consistent with previous findings in the literature on mother–infant interaction and maternal depression, differences between depressed and nondepressed mothers emerged on the factor of maternal insensitivity, which was comprised of the following types of maternal behaviors: frequent noncontingent initiation by the mother of physical contact, responding to infant's bid for attention by either simply physically holding the infant or by dismissing the infant (withdrawing, moving the infant away, or by terminating or rejecting contact), and intrusive behaviors (Dawson, Frey, Self, Panagiotides, Ashman, & Embry, in preparation). Depressed mothers showed higher frequencies of insensitive behavior as compared to nondepressed mothers.

We next used path analysis to examine whether mother's insensitive behavior mediated the relation between maternal depression and infant frontal EEG. The results suggested that the relation between depression and EEG is not fully mediated by mother's behavior. However, a partial mediation hypothesis was supported by these analyses. That is, both maternal depression, per se, and the mother's behavior were found to be contributors to infant brain activity.

Prenatal Versus Postnatal Depression.   The analysis discussed earlier concerning the relation between maternal depression, mothers' behavior, and infant frontal EEG included mothers with depression during the prenatal as well as the postnatal period. In order to more specifically evaluate the effects of mother's behavior on infant frontal EEG activity, we next decided to repeat the path analyses utilizing only that subsample of mothers who had only experienced depression during the infant's postnatal life, excluding those mothers who experienced depression during both the prenatal and postnatal period (there were no mothers in this study who had experienced depression only during the prenatal period). Interestingly, using only those mothers with postnatal depression in the analyses, it was found that mother's insensitivity with her infant mediated the relation between maternal depression and infant frontal EEG activity. The direct path between maternal depression and infant frontal EEG activity was no longer found to be significant. These results provide support for the hypothesis that the behavior of a depressed mother toward her infant, in particular, the degree of maternal insensitivity, can influence patterns of infant frontal brain activity. Specifically, high levels of maternal insensitivity appear to be associated with lower levels of infant left frontal brain activity.

Preliminary Analyses of Autonomic Activity in Infants of Depressed Mothers

As described earlier in this chapter, studies of young infants (4–6 months of age) have shown that infants of depressed mothers tend to exhibit elevated heart rates when interacting with their mothers (Field et al., 1988). Such evidence has been interpreted as indicating that infants of depressed mothers are more highly aroused during mother–infant interaction, perhaps because the interaction is experienced as stressful.

In our longitudinal study, we also examined autonomic activity in infants of depressed mothers, who were 13–15 months of age. We measured electrocardiac activity (heart rate) in the infants during a baseline condition, and during two social conditions, one in which mother played peek-a-boo with her infant and a second in which a familiar female experimenter played peek-a-boo with the infants. An interesting pattern of results emerged. On average, the infants of nondepressed mothers showed stable or decreased heart rates during the social interaction conditions as compared to the baseline condition. Since the baseline condition occurred before the social interaction conditions, this pattern could indicate that either the infants were become familiarized with the testing situation over time or that they found the social conditions to be generally equal or less arousing than the baseline condition. Both would result in a pattern of decreased heart rate over time.

In contrast, infants of depressed mothers tended to show increased heart rates during the social interaction conditions as compared to the baseline condition, suggesting that either they were not becoming more comfortable with the testing situation over time, or that there was something about the interaction conditions that was arousing to them. Regardless, these results indicate that, similar to past studies of younger infants of depressed mothers, toddlers of depressed mothers also tend to exhibit higher arousal levels during social interactions.

LONGITUDINAL STUDY OF THE EFFECTS OF MATERNAL DEPRESSION: PRELIMINARY ANALYSES OF DATA FROM TIME 2 (42-MONTH-OLD CHILDREN)

We end this chapter by briefly discussing some preliminary findings from analyses conducted at Time 2. These findings should be considered preliminary since only part of the entire sample was included in these analyses. They serve to highlight, however, the power of conducting longitudinal research of this kind and underscore the need to examine issues related to the effects of the timing of social influences on the child's behavioral and psychobiological development. The question we were interested in addressing was whether the timing of mother's depression differentially influenced different psychobiological systems. Specifically, as reviewed previously, animal research (e.g., Ladd et al., 1996; Plotsky & Meaney, 1993) suggests that exposure to stress very early in life predisposes an individual to abnormal stress responses by causing long-term overproduction of hormones such as cortisol in the HPA system. We have hypothesized that maternal depression acts as a type of stressor for the young infant in at least three ways: first, the mother's irritability and insensitive style may be experienced as stressful by the infant. Evidence for this comes from research, including our own which was discussed earlier, showing that, during interactions with mothers, infants of depressed mothers showed higher than normal heart rates and cortisol levels. Second, the mother's failure to provide regulatory assistance for her infant in the form of modeling positive affect, calming, soothing, and other regulatory strategies may add to the infant's stress levels. Third, because of the episodic nature of depression, the mother's behavior may be less predictable and stable. It is plausible that periods of depression in the mother may be experienced as a type of loss by the infant who may have previously experienced the mother as more affectionate and available. For all of these reasons, it is reasonable to hypothesize that maternal depression may act as a potent environmental stressor for the young infant.

Furthermore, animal research indicates that exposure to such stressors very early in life has long-term effects on the development of the HPA axis. Thus, one might predict that maternal depression that occurred during the first year of the infant's life would affect cortisol levels measured later in childhood.

What would one predict in terms of the effects of the timing of maternal depression on infant frontal EEG? Based on studies of brain development (e.g., Chugani & Phelps, 1986; Chugani et al., 1987), it appears that the period beginning at about 12 months of age and ending in late preschool age is a period of very rapid development of the frontal lobe. Furthermore, it is a period of very rapid development of self-regulation, particularly regulation of emotions (Kopp, 1982, 1989). Thus, one might predict that maternal depression would have its greatest effect on both infant frontal EEG and self-regulatory behavior if it occurred during the 2nd through 4th years of the infant's life.

One way of beginning to test some of these hypotheses is to examine separately the effects of maternal depression during specific years of the child's life on the development of different psychobiological measures. In preliminary analyses of data from the longitudinal study examining child's frontal EEG patterns and salivary cortisol levels at age $3^{1}/_{2}$ years, we found that maternal depression during the child's 1st year of life was the best predictor of elevations in cortisol at $3^{1}/_{2}$ years of age. In contrast, maternal depression during the child's 2nd and 3rd years of life were the best predictors of patterns of frontal brain activity at 3 years of age (Hessl et al., 1998). Although these results are tentative and require replication using the larger sample, they suggest that different psychobiological systems may have specific sensitive periods in terms of the influences of the social environment on their development.

CONCLUSIONS

Our findings suggest that, by 1 year of age, maternal depression is associated with disruptions in both infant behavior and psychobiolology. Behaviorally, these disruptions are characterized by less affection toward mother and more frequent displays of problematic negative behaviors, such as aggression and hostility. Psychophysiologically, these disruptions are characterized by reduced activity in a brain region that mediates positive approach behavior (left frontal region) and increased autonomic arousal during social interactions. Although not definitive, evidence is suggestive that these effects are partially mediated by the mother's behavior toward her infant during the postnatal period.

Thus, at both behavioral and physiological levels, we have evidence that maternal depression is associated with both a reduction in approach behavior and difficulties in regulating negative emotions and arousal. This double-edged sword may represent an early risk factor for the development of depression (Dawson, Frey, Self, Panagiotides, Hessl, Yamada, & Rinaldi, 1999). That is, children of depressed mothers not only appear to experience negative affect and arousal more easily and intensely, but also have failed to develop adaptive regulatory strategies to cope with these emotions. When distressed, sad, or angry, such a child may be less likely to reach out to others for comfort and assistance and less likely to have internalized regulatory strategies that have been derived from social contexts, and more likely to withdraw from social interaction or to resort to aggressive and hostile behavior.

Future longitudinal analyses will be needed to address the question of whether or not there, in fact, exist sensitive periods in terms of the effects of the social environment on psychobiological development. Furthermore, the question of whether or not alterations in psychobiology that occur early in life are stable and predictive of future psychopathology needs to be addressed. It is possible that, if such alterations persist over time, they may become a more stable characteristic of the nervous system and predispose an individual to psychopathology later in life. On a more positive note, in light of the remarkable plasticity of the nervous system throughout the lifespan, one can remain optimistic that, if a parent's mental illness is treated or if the child is exposed to other healthy caretakers, be it another parent or relative, teacher, or therapist, positive and lasting changes in both psychobiology and behavior can occur. Importantly, depression responds well to both psychopharmacological and behavioral treatment. In any case, the findings discussed in this chapter underscore the need to identify and treat maternal depression as soon as possible so that we can maximize children's potential for emotional well-being.

ACKNOWLEDGMENTS

The writing of this chapter and much of the research reported in it was supported by a grant from the National Institute of Mental Health (#MH47117). We wish to express our appreciation to the mothers, fathers, and children who have volunteered for the studies reported in this chapter.

REFERENCES

Anisman, H., Zaharia, M. D., Meaney, M. J., & Merali, Z. (1998). Do early-life events permanently alter behavioral and hormonal responses to stressors? *International Journal of Developmental Neuroscience, 16*(3/4), 149–164.

Aslin, R. M., Pisoni, D. B., & Jusczyk, P. W. (1983). Auditory development and speech perception in infancy. In P. H. Mussen (Series Ed.) & M. M. Haith & J. J. Campos (Vol. Eds.), *Handbook of child psychology: Infancy and developmental psychobiology* (4th ed., Vol. 2). New York: Wiley.

Baxter, L. R., Schwartz, J. M., Phelps, M. E., Mazziotta, J. C., Guze, B. H., Selin, C. E., Gerner, R. H., & Sumida, R. M. (1989). Reduction in prefrontal cortex glucose metabolism common to three types of depression. *Archives of General Psychiatry, 46*, 243–250.

Bruner, J. S. (1977). Early social interaction and language acquisition. In H. R. Schaffer (Ed.), *Studies in mother-infant interaction*. London: Academic Press.

Calkins, S. D., Fox, N. A., & Marshall, T. R. (1996). Behavioral and physiological antecedents of inhibition in infancy. *Child Development, 67*, 523–540.

Campos, J. J., Barrett, K. C., Lamb, M. E., Goldsmith, H. H., & Stinberg, C. R. (1983). Socioemotional development. In M. M. Haith & J. J. Campos (Eds.), P. H. Mussen (Series Ed.), *Handbook of child psychology: Vol 2. Infancy and developmental psychobiology*. New York: Wiley.

Campos, J. J., Campos, R. G., & Barrett, K. C. (1989). Emergent themes in the study of emotional development and emotion regulation. *Developmental Psychology, 25*, 394–402.

Cannon, W. B. (1927). The James-Lange theory of emotions: A critical examination and an alternative theory. *American Journal of Psychology, 39*, 106–124.

Capitanio, J. P., Rasmussen, K. L. R., Snyder, D. S., Laudenslager, M., & Reite, M. (1986). Long-term follow-up of previously separated pigtail macaques: Group and individual differences in response to novel situations. *Journal of Child Psychology and Psychiatry, 27*(4), 531–538.

Chugani, H. T., & Phelps, M. E. (1986). Maturational changes in cerebral function in infants determined by 18FDG positron emission tomography. *Science, 231*, 840–843.

Chugani, H. T., Phelps, M. E., & Mazziotta, J. C. (1987). Positron emission tomography study of human brain functional development. *Annals of Neurology, 22*, 487–497.

Cicchetti, D., Ganiban, J., & Barnett, D. (1991). Contributions from the study of high risk populations to understanding the development of emotion regulation. In K. Dodge & J. Garber (Eds.), *The development of emotion regulation* (pp. 15–48). New York: Cambridge University Press.

Coghill, S. R., Caplan, H. L., Alexandra, H., Robson, K., & Kumar. R. (1986). Impact of maternal postnatal depression on cognitive development of young children. *British Medical Journal, 292*, 1165–1167.

Cohn, J. F., Matias, R., Tronick, E. Z., Connell, D., & Lyons-Ruth, D. (1986). Face-to face interactions of depressed mothers and their infants. In E. Z. Tronick & T. Field (Eds.), *Maternal depression and infant disturbance* (pp. 31–45). San Francisco: Jossey-Bass.

Cohn, J. F., & Tronick, E. Z. (1989). Specificity of infants' response to mothers' affective behavior. *Journal of the American Academy of Child and Adolescent Psychiatry, 28*, 242–248.

Coplan, J. D., Andrews, M. W., Rosenblum, L. A., Owens, M. J., Friedman, S., Gorman, J. M., & Nemeroff, C. B. (1996). Persistent elevations of cerebrospinal fluid concentrations of corticotropin-releasing factor in adult nonhuman primates exposed to early-life stressors: Implications for the pathophysiology of mood and anxiety disorders. *Proceedings of the National Academy of Sciences, USA, 93*, 1619–1623.

Davidson, R. J. (1987). Cerebral asymmetry and the nature of emotion: Implications for the study of individual differences and psychopathology. In R. Takahashi, P. Flor-Henry, J. Gruzelier, & S. Niwa (Eds.), *Cerebral dynamics, laterality, and psychopathology* (pp. 71–83). New York: Elsevier.

Davidson, R. J., Ekman, P., Saron, C., Senulis, R., & Friesen, W. V. (1990). Approach-withdrawal and cerebral asymmetry: Emotional expression and brain physiology I. *Journal of Personality and Social Psychology, 58*, 330–341.

Davidson, R. J., & Fox, N. A. (1988). Cerebral asymmetry and emotion: Development and individual differences. In S. Segalowitz & D. Molfese (Eds.), *Developmental implications of brain lateralization* (pp. 191–206). New York: Guilford.

Davidson, R. J., & Fox, N. A. (1989). Frontal brain asymmetry predicts infants' response to maternal separation. *Journal of Abnormal Psychology, 98*, 127–131.

Dawson, G. (1994). Frontal electroencephalographic correlates of individual differences in emotional expression in infants: A brain systems perspective on emotion. In N. A. Fox (Ed.), Emotion regulation: Behavioral and biological considerations. *Society for Research in Child Development Monographs, 59*, Nos. 2–3, 135–151.

Dawson, G., Frey, K., Panagiotides, H., Osterling, J., & Hessl, D. (1997). Infants of depressed mothers exhibit atypical frontal brain activity: A replication and extension of previous findings. *Journal of Child Psychology and Psychiatry, 38*, 179–186.

Dawson, G., Frey, K., Panagiotides, H., Yamada, E., Hessl, D., & Osterling, J. (1999). Infants of depressed mothers exhibit atypical frontal brain activity during interactions with mother and with a familiar nondepressed adult. *Child Development, 70*, 1058–1066.

Dawson, G., Frey, K., Self, J., Panagiotides, H., Ashman, S., & Embry, L. (1999). *Mothers' behavior mediates the relation between maternal depression and infant frontal brain activity.* Manuscript in preparation.

Dawson, G., Frey, K., Self, J., Panagiotides, H., Hessl, D., Yamada, E., & Rinaldi, J. (1999). Frontal brain electrical activity in infants of depressed and nondepressed mothers: Relation to variations in infant behavior. *Development and Psychopathology, 11*(3), 589–605.

Dawson, G., Grofer Klinger, L., Panagiotides, H., Hill, D., & Spieker, S. (1992). Frontal lobe activity and affective behavior of infants of mothers with depressive symptoms. *Child Development, 63*, 725–737.

Dawson, G., Panagiotides, H., Grofer Klinger, L., & Hill, D. (1992). The role of frontal lobe functioning in the development of self-regulatory behavior in infancy. *Brain and Cognition, 20*, 152–175.

Dawson, G., Panagiotides, H., Grofer Klinger, L., & Spieker, S. (1997). Infants of depressed and nondepressed mothers exhibit differences in frontal brain electrical activity during the expression of negative emotions. *Developmental Psychology, 33*, 650–656.

Diamond, A. (1990). Developmental time course in human infants and infant monkeys, and the neural bases of, inhibitory control in reaching. In A. Diamond (Ed.), *The development of and neural bases of high cognitive functions. Annals of the New York Academy of Sciences, Vol. 608.*

Deragotis, L. R., & Melisaratos, N. (1983). The Brief Symptom Inventory: An introductory report. *Psychological Medicine, 13*, 595–605.

Downey, G., & Coyne, J. (1990). Children of depressed parents: An integrative review. *Psychological Bulletin, 108*, 50–76.

Downey, G., & Walker, E. (1992). Distinguishing family-level and child-level influences on the development of depression and aggression in children at risk. *Development and Psychopathology, 4*, 81–95.

Drevets, W. C., Videen, T. O., Price, J. L., Preskorn, S. H., Carmichael, S. T., & Raichle, M. E. (1991). A functional anatomical study of unipolar depression. *The Journal of Neuroscience, 12*, 3628–3641.

Edelman, G. M. (1987). *Neural Darwinism: The theory of neuronal group selection.* New York: Basic Books.

Edelman, G. M. (1989). *The remembered present: A biological theory of consciousness.* New York: Basic Books.

Erickson, M., Sroufe, L. A., & Egeland, B. (1985). The relationship between quality of attachment and behavior problems in preschool in a high-risk sample. In I. Bretherton & E. Waters (Eds.), *Growing points of attachment theory and research. Society for Research in Child Development Monographs, 50*, Nos. 1–2, 147–166.

Fenson, L., Dale, P. S., Reznick, J. S., Thal., D., Bates, E., Hartung, J. P., Pethick, S., & Reilly, J. S. (1993). *MacArthur communicative development inventory user guide and technical manual.* San Diego, CA: Singular Publishing Group.

Field, T. (1986). Models for reactive and chronic depression in infancy. In E. Z. Tronick & T. Field (Eds.), *Maternal depression and infant disturbance* (No. 34, pp. 47–60). San Francisco: Jossey-Bass.

Field, T. (1992). Infants of depressed mothers. *Development and Psychopathology, 4*, 49–66.

Field, T., Healy, B., Goldstein, S., Perry, S., Bendall, D., Schanberg, S., Zimmerman, E., & Kuhn, C. (1988). Infants of depressed mothers show "depressed" behavior even with non-depressed adults. *Child Development, 59*, 1569–1579.

Field, T., Sandberg, D., Garcia, R., Vega-Lahr, N., Goldstein, S., & Guy, L. (1985). Prenatal problems, postpartum depression, and early mother–infant interactions, *Developmental Psychology, 12*, 1152–1156.

Finman, R., Davidson, R. J., Colton, M. B., Straus, A. M., & Kagan, J. (1989). Psychophysiological correlates of inhibition to the unfamiliar in children [Abstract]. *Psychophysiology, 26*, No. 4A, S24.

Fox, N. A. (1991). If it's not left, it's right: Electroencephalograph asymmetry and the development of emotion. *American Psychologist, 46*, 863–872.

Fuster, J. M. (1989). *The prefrontal cortex: Anatomy, physiology, and neuropsychology of the frontal lobe.* New York: Raven Press.

Gainotti, G. (1969). Reactions "Catastrophiques" et manifestations 3 d'indifference au cours des atteintes cerebrais. *Neuropsychologia, 7*, 195–204.

Gainotti, G. (1972). Emotional behavior and hemispheric side of lesion. *Cortex, 8*, 41–55.

Ghodsian, M., Zajicek, E., & Wolkind, S. (1984). A longitudinal study of maternal depression and child behavior problems. *Journal of Child Psychology and Psychiatry, 25*, 91–109.

Goldman, B. A., & Mitchell, D. (1990). *Directory of unpublished experimental measures* (Vol. 5). New York: W. C. Brown.

Goldman-Rakic, P. S. (1987). Circuitry of primate prefrontal cortex and regulation of behavior by representational memory. *Handbook of physiology. Section 1: The nervous system. Volume. V. Higher functions of the brain* (pp. 373–417). Bethesda, MD: American Physiological Society.

Grunebaum, H. U., Cohler, B. J., Kaufman, C., & Gallant, D. H. (1978). Children of depressed and schizophrenic mothers. *Child Psychiatry and Human Development, 8*, 219–228.

Gunnar, M. R. (1998). Quality of early care and the buffering of neuroendocrine stress reactions: Potential effects on the developing human brain. *Preventive Medicine, 27*, 208–211.

Gunnar, M. R., Broderson, L., Buss, K., & Rigatuso, J. (1996). Stress reactivity and attachment security. *Developmental Psychobiology, 29*(3), 191–204.

Gunnar, M. R., & Chisholm, K. C. (1999, April). *Effects of early institutional rearing and attachment quality on salivary cortisol levels in adopted Romanian children.* Poster session presented at the biennial meeting of the Society for Research in Child Development, Albuquerque, NM.

Gunnar, M. R., & Nelson, C. A. (1994). Event-related potentials in year-old infants: Relations with emotionality and cortisol. *Child Development, 65*, 80–94.

Hammon, C. (1988). Self-cognition, stressful events, and the prediction of depression in children of depressed mothers. *Journal of Abnormal Child Psychology, 16*, 347–360.

Hebb, D. O. (1949). *The organization of behavior: A neuropsychological theory.* New York: Wiley.

Hecaen, H. (1964). Mental symptoms associated with tumors of the frontal lobe. In J. M. Warren & K. Akert (Eds.), *The frontal granular cortex and behavior.* New York: McGraw-Hill.

Heilman, K. M., Watson, R. T., Valenstein, E., & Goldberg, M. E. (1987). Attention: Behavior and neural mechanisms. *Handbook of physiology: Sec. 1. The nervous system: Vol 5. Higher functions of the brain.* Bethesda, MD: American Physiological Society.

Hessl, D., Dawson, G., Frey, K., Panagiotides, H., Self, J., Yamada, E., and Osterling, J. (1998). A longitudinal study of children of depressed mothers: Psychobiological findings related to stress. In D. M. Hann, L. C. Huffman, K. K. Lederhendler, & D. Meinecke (Eds.), *Advancing research on developmental plasticity: Integrating the behavioral science and the neuroscience of mental health* (p. 256). Bethesda, MD: National Institute of Mental Health.

Heuser, I. (1998). The hypothalamic-pituitary-adrenal system in depression. *Pharmacopsychiatry, 31*, 10–13.

Huttenlocher, P. R. (1979). Synaptic density in human frontal cortex – developmental changes and effects of aging. *Brain Research, 163*, 195–205.

Huttenlocher, P. R. (1994). Synaptogenesis in human cerebral cortex. In G. Dawson & K. Fischer (Eds.), *Human Behavior and the Developing Brain* (pp. 137–152). New York: Guilford.

Jones, B. M., & Mishkin, M. (1972). Limbic lesions and the problem of stimulus reinforcement association. *Experimental Neurology, 36*, 362–377.

Keller, M. B., Lavori, P., Friedman, B., Nielsen, E., Endicott, J., McDonald-Scott, P., & Andreasen, N. C. (1987). The longitudinal interval follow-up evaluation: A comprehensive method for assessing outcome in prospective longitudinal studies. *Archives of General Psychiatry, 44*, 540–548.

Keller, M. B., Shapiro, R. W., Lavori, P. W., & Wolfe, N. (1982). Recovery in major depressive disorder: Analysis with the life table and regression models. *Archives of General Psychiatry, 39*(8), 905–915.

Kendler, K. S., Kessler, R. C., Neale, M. C., Heath, A. C., Phil, D., & Eaves, L. J. (1993). The prediction of major depression in women: Toward an integrated etiological model. *American Journal of Psychiatry, 150*(8), 1139–1148.

Kinsbourne, M., & Bemporad, B. (1984). Lateralization of emotion: A model and the evidence. In N. A. Fox & R. J. Davidson (Eds.), *The psychobiology of affective development*. Hillsdale, NJ: Lawrence Erlbaum Associates.

Klinnert, M. D., Campos, J., Sorce, J., Emde, R. N., & Svejda, J. (1983). Emotions as behavior regulators: The development of social referencing. In R. Plutchik & H. Kellerman (Eds.), *Emotions in early development*. New York: Academic Press.

Kolb, B. (1989). Brain development, plasticity, and behavior. *American Psychologist, 44*, 1203–1212.

Kopp, C. B. (1982). Antecedents of self-regulation: A developmental perspective. *Developmental Psychology, 18*, 199–214.

Kopp, C. B. (1989). Regulation of distress and negative emotions: A developmental view. *Developmental Psychology, 25*, 343–354.

Kuhn, C. M., Pauk, J., & Schanberg, S. M. (1990). Endocrine responses to mother–infant separation in developing rats. *Developmental Psychobiology, 23*(5), 395–410.

Kuhn, C. M., & Schanberg, S. M. (1998). Responses to maternal separation: Mechanisms and mediators. *International Journal of Developmental Neuroscience, 16*(3/4), 261–270.

Ladd, C. O., Owens, M. J., & Nemeroff, C. B. (1996). Persistent changes in corticotropin-releasing factor neuronal systems induced by maternal deprivation. *Endocrinology, 137*(4), 1212–1218.

LeDoux, J. E. (1987). Emotion. In F. Plum (Ed.), *Handbook of physiology: I. The nervous system. Vol. V. Higher functions of the brain* (pp. 419–460). Bethesda, MD: American Physiological Society.

LeDoux, J. E. (1991). Emotion and the brain. *Journal of NIH Research, 3*, 49–51.

Levine, S., Coe, C., & Wiener, S. G. (1989). Psychoneuroendocrinology of stress: A psychobiological perspective. In F. R. Brush & S. Levine (Eds.), *Psychoneuroendocrinology* (pp. 341–377). San Diego: Academic Press.

Levine, S., & Wiener, S. G. (1988). Psychoendocrine aspects of mother–infant relationships in nonhuman primates. *Psychoneuroendocrinology, 13*(1/2), 143–154.

Luria, A. R. (1966/1980). *Higher Cortical Functions in Man*. New York: Basic Books.

MacLean, P. D. (1952). Some psychiatric implications of physiological studies on frontotemporal portion of limbic system (visceral brain). *Electroencephalography and Clinical Neurophysiology, 4*, 407–418.

Malatesta, C. Z., & Haviland, J. M. (1982). Learning display rules: The socialization of emotion expression in infancy. *Child Development, 53*, 991–1003.

Michelson, D., Licinio, J., & Gold, P. W. (1995). Mediation of the stress response by the hypothalamic-pituitary-adrenal axis. In M. J. Friedman, D. S. Charney, & A. Y. Deutch (Eds). *Neurobiological and clinical consequences of stress: From normal adaptation to post-traumatic stress disorder* (pp. 225–238). Philadelphia: Lippincott.

Milner, B., Petrides, M., & Smith, M. L. (1985). Frontal lobes and the temporal organization of memory. *Human Neurobiology, 4*, 137–142.

Morgan, G. A., Maslin, C. A., & Harmon, R. J. (1988). *Mastery motivation tasks: Manual for 15 to 36 month old children*. Unpublished manuscript.

Nachmias, M., Gunnar, M., Mangelsdorf, S., Parritz, R. H., & Buss, K. (1996). Behavioral inhibition and stress reactivity: The moderating role of attachment security. *Child Development, 67*, 508–522.

Nauta, W. J. H. (1971). The problem of the frontal lobes: A reinterpretation. *Journal of Psychiatric Research, 8*, 167–187.

Nemeroff, C. B. (1988). The role of corticotropin-releasing factor in the pathogenesis of major depression. *Pharmacopsychiatry, 21,* 76–82.

Orvaschel, H., Welsh-Allis, G., & Weijai, Y. (1988). Psychopathology in children of parents with recurrent depression. *Journal of Abnormal Child Psychology, 16,* 17–28.

Panak, W. F., & Garber, J. (1992). Role of aggression, rejection, and attributions in the prediction of depression in children, *Development and Psychopathology, 4,* 145–165.

Papez, J. W. (1937). A proposed mechanism of emotion. *Archives of Neurology and Psychiatry, 38,* 725–743.

Piaget, J. (1954). *The construction of reality in the child.* New York: International Universities Press.

Pihoker, C., Owens, M. J., Kuhn, C. M., Schanberg, S. M., & Nemeroff, C. B. (1993). Maternal separation in neonatal rats elicits activation of the hypothalamic-pituitary-adrenocortical axis: A putative role for corticotropin-releasing factor. *Psychoneuroendocrinology, 18*(7), 485–493.

Plotsky, P. M., & Meaney, M. J. (1993). Early, postnatal experience alters hypothalamic corticotropin-releasing factor (CRF) mRNA, median eminence CRF content and stress-induced release in adult rats. *Molecular Brain Research, 18,* 195–200.

Plotsky, P. M., Owens, M. J., & Nemeroff, C. B. (1998). Psychoneuroendocrinology of depression. *The Psychiatric Clinics of North America, 21*(2), 293–307.

Redding, R. E., Harmon, R. J., & Morgan, G. A. (1990). Relationships between maternal depression and infants' mastery behaviors. *Infant Behavior and Development, 13,* 391–395.

Robinson, R. G., & Benson, D. F. (1981). Depression in aphasic patients: Frequency, severity, and clinical-pathological correlations. *Brain and Language, 14,* 282–291.

Robinson, R. G., Kubos, K. L., Starr, L. B., Reo, K., & Price, T. R. (1984). Mood disorders in stroke patients: Importance of location of lesion. *Brain, 107,* 81–93.

Robinson, R. G., & Stetela, B. (1981). Mood change following left hemispheric brain injury. *Annals of Neurology, 9,* 447–453.

Rosenfeld, P., Suchecki, D., & Levine, S. (1992). Multifactorial regulation of the hypothalamic-pituitary-adrenal axis during development. *Neuroscience and Biobehavioral Reviews, 16,* 553–568.

Sapolsky, R. M. (1996). Why stress is bad for your brain. *Science, 273,* 749–750.

Schaffer, C. E., Davidson, R. V., & Saron, C. (1983). Frontal and parietal electroencephalogram asymmetry in depressed and non-depressed subjects. *Biological Psychiatry, 18,* 753–762.

Scaife, M., & Bruner, J. S. (1975). The capacity for joint visual attention in the infant. *Nature, 253,* 265–266.

Selye, H. (1936). A syndrome produced by diverse noxious agents. *Nature (London), 138,* 32.

Selye, H. (1946). General adaptation syndrome and diseases of adaptation. *Journal of Clinical Endocrinology and Metabolism, 6,* 117–230.

Stanton, M. E., & Levine, S. (1990). Inhibition of infant glucocorticoid stress response: Specific role of maternal cues. *Developmental Psychobiology, 23*(5), 411–426.

Steriade, M. (1981). EEG desynchronization is associated with cellular events that are prerequisites for active behavioral states. Commentary on "Reticulo-cortical activity and behavior: A critique of the arousal theory and a new synthesis" by C. H. Vanderwolf & T. E. Robinson. *The Behavioral and Brain Sciences, 4,* 489–492.

Stern, D. (1985). *The interpersonal world of the infant.* New York: Basic Books.

Suchecki, D., Rosenfeld, P., & Levine, S. (1993). Maternal regulation of the hypothalamic-pituitary-adrenal axis in the infant rat: The roles of feeding and stroking. *Developmental Brain Research, 75,* 185–192.

Tronick, E. Z. (1989). Emotions and emotional communication in infants. *American Psychologist, 44,* 112–119.

Tronick, E. Z., & Gianino, A. F. (1986). The transmission of maternal disturbances to the infant. In E. Z. Tronick & T. Field (Eds.), *Maternal depression and infant disturbance* (pp. 5–11). San Francisco: Jossey-Bass.

Tucker, D. (1992). Developing emotions and cortical networks. In M. Gunnar and C. A. Nelson (Eds.), *Developmental Behavioral Neuroscience: Minnesota Symposium on Child Psychology, Vol. 24* (pp. 75–128). Hillsdale, NJ: Lawrence Erlbaum Associates.

Tucker, D. M., & Williamson, P. A. (1984). Asymmetric neural control systems in human self-regulation. *Psychological Review, 91*, 185–215.

Watson, J. F. (1979). Perception of contingency as a determinant of social responsiveness. In E. B. Thoman (Ed.), *The origins of social responsiveness*. Hillsdale, NJ: Lawrence Erlbaum Associates.

Whiffen, V. E., & Gotlib, I. M. (1989). Infants of postpartum depressed mothers: Temperament and cognitive status. *Journal of Abnormal Psychology, 98*, 274–279.

Zuckerman, B., Als, H., Bauchner, H., Parker, S., & Cabral, H. (1990). Maternal depressive symptoms during pregnancy and newborn irritability. *Developmental and Behavioral Pediatrics, 11*, 190–194.

8

▼▼▼▼▼▼▼▼▼

Familial and Genetic Factors and Psychopathology

Kathleen Ries Merikangas
Departments of Epidemiology and Public Health, and Psychiatry
Yale University School of Medicine

The Human Genome Project has enhanced dramatically our potential in genetic information (Watson, 1990). Of the estimated 100,000 human genes, more than 9,000 have been discovered, and more than 5,000 have been mapped to specific chromosomes (Guyer & Collins, 1995). Genetic testing for about 500 genes is now available in clinical practice. Gene variants have been identified that affect the risks of diseases of major public health importance, ranging from adult chronic diseases, such as cancer and diabetes, to infectious and immunologic disorders, to diseases affecting the health of infants and children (Khoury, 1997).

How can this information be applied to enhance our understanding of childhood psychopathology? Despite the advances in unraveling the genetic basis of several human diseases, there has been far less success than originally anticipated in identifying genes for complex disorders, or common diseases without simple Mendelian modes of inheritance such as diabetes, heart disease, and the psychiatric disorders. Failure to identify genes for these conditions can be attributed to the lack of validity of phenotypic definitions, complex modes of inheritance characterized by genetic heterogeneity, phenotypic heterogeneity, or both; strong environmental inputs; and gene-environment interaction, polygenic inheritance, or both.

This chapter will demonstrate how the application of the methods of the discipline of genetic epidemiology is ideally suited to address sources of complexity of chronic human diseases, particularly the psychiatric disorders. Evidence that a family history of psychopathology is one of the most potent and consistent risk factors warrants the use of the family study method to: (a) examine the validity of the classification (or phenotypic definitions) of psychopathology; (b) identify vulnerability factors particularly those that are premorbid; and (c) enhance understanding of the genetic and environmental mechanisms for familial aggregation using the strategies described in the next section. The goals of this chapter are: (a) to provide background on principles of genetic epidemiology with respect to its role in identifying the role of genetic factors in the development of psychopathology; (b) to review the evidence from family studies of offspring of parents with anxiety disorders and substance abuse; and (c) to present illustrative data from a family–high-risk study of comorbidity of anxiety disorders and substance abuse.

BACKGROUND: GENETIC EPIDEMIOLOGY

Epidemiology is defined as the study of the distribution and determinants of diseases in human populations. Epidemiologic studies are concerned with the extent and types of illnesses in groups of people and with the factors that influence their distribution (Mausner & Kramer, 1985). Researchers in this domain are concerned with the role of both intrinsic and extrinsic factors, consisting of interactions that may occur between the host, the agent, and the environment (the classic triangle of epidemiology) to produce a disease state. In chronic disease epidemiology, the host is the individual, the agent is the specific causal factor (e.g., virus, drug, bacteria, etc.), and the environment is the background that links the host and the agent. The ultimate goal of epidemiologic studies is to identify the etiology of a disease and thereby prevent or intervene in the progression of the disorder. In order to achieve this goal, epidemiologic studies generally proceed from descriptive studies that specify the amount and distribution of a disease within a population by person, place, and time (that is, descriptive epidemiology), to more focused studies of the determinants of disease in specific groups (that is, analytic epidemiology (Mausner & Kramer, 1985).

One problem with the risk factor-based approach in contemporary epidemiology is the lack of integration of host factors, particularly genetic vulnerability. Although the goal of epidemiology is to study the interaction between the host, agent, and environment, epidemiologists have tended to neglect host characteristics other than demographics, and geneticists consider environmental factors as noise (Kuller, 1979). Despite their history of independence, the fields of epidemiology and genetics share much common ground. Both are interested in determining the etiology of complex human disorders and in predicting familial recurrence risks for such disorders. The advent of the field of genetic epidemiology has served to bridge the gap between the two fields (Morton, 1982). As Morton noted, the "synthesis of genetics and epidemiology is necessary before diseases of complex etiology can be understood and ultimately controlled" (p. 4). The application of the methods of genetic epidemiology (the study of risk factors and etiology of familial diseases) appears to be one of the most promising avenues to unravel the complex mechanisms through which genes may exert their influence (Robins, 1992). Although there is substantial overlap in the goals and methods of the fields of genetic epidemiology and behavior genetics, the two fields can be distinguished by the focus of genetic epidemiology on diseases rather than normal traits, and its chief goal of identifying specific genetic and environmental risk factors and their mutual influences on disease etiology as opposed to the focus of behavior genetics on identifying the genetic and environmental components of variance.

The most common misconception regarding the role of genetic factors in the manifestation of a particular trait or disease is that the term genetic implies determinism by innate factors with a subsequently immutable course. Nothing has impeded progress in knowledge of the development of human traits and disorders more than the nature versus nurture discussion. This concept was originally introduced by Galton (1894) more appropriately as the nature and nurture debate. Increasing evidence reveals that environmental risk factors may either potentiate or protect against expression of underlying genetic and biological vulnerability factors. Studies of familial aggregation suggest that the most compelling model for complex disorders involves susceptibility genes that may enhance vulnerability, but only lead to disease in the presence of additional environmental, genetic, or biologic factors. The major types of studies that yield evidence on the role of genetic factors in the etiology of diseases are family studies, twin studies, and adoption studies.

Study Designs in Genetic Epidemiology

Family Studies. The observation that some disorders aggregate in families is the primary source of evidence suggesting a possible genetic component in the etiology of a disease or trait. The basic family study approach involves identifying individuals with a particular psychiatric disorder (the proband) and then determining the rates of disorder in the proband's relatives. These morbidity statistics can then be compared to the rates of disorder in families of unaffected individuals (controls). Although family studies cannot distinguish between genetic and cultural transmission, there are a number of applications of family study data that may provide indices of genetic and environmental factors underlying familial aggregation. These include: familial specificity of the subtype or trait of focus; a dose-response relationship between the magnitude of familial loading in prior generations for the risk of the disease among unaffected individuals; and specificity of vulnerability markers for the disease in offspring.

The major advantage of studying diseases within families is that the assumption of etiologic homogeneity of the underlying causal factors minimizes the effects of heterogeneity that are present in most between-family comparisons. Family studies can therefore be employed to examine the validity of diagnostic categories by assessing the specificity of familial aggregation of discrete disorders and subtypes (Tsuang et al., 1996). Data from family studies may also provide evidence regarding etiologic or phenotypic heterogeneity. Phenotypic heterogeneity is suggested by variable expressivity of symptoms of the same etiologic factors, whereas etiologic heterogeneity is demonstrated by homotypic expression of different etiologic factors within families. The family study method also permits assessment of associations between disorders by evaluating specific patterns of associations of two or more disorders within families. Controlled family studies have been employed to examine sources of comorbidity and sex differences for complex disorders such as pyloric stenosis (Carter, 1961), as well as several psychiatric disorders including anxiety and depression (Merikangas, 1990), panic disorder and depression (Maier, Buller, & Hallmayer, 1988), alcoholism and depression (Merikangas, Leckman, Prusoff, Pauls, & Weissman, 1985), and simultaneous familial associations between anxiety, affective disorders, and alcoholism (Maier & Merikangas, 1992; Merikangas, Risch, & Weissman, 1994; Merikangas et al., 1998c).

Twin Studies. The twin study method compares concordance rates for monozygotic twins (who share the same genotype) with those of dizygotic twins (who share an average of 50 percent of their genes in common). To support a genetic etiology, the concordance rates for monozygotic twins should be significantly greater than dizygotic twins. Consistent with the concept of familial aggregation, the degree of concordance between co-twins of either type can also be used to provide information about the magnitude of genetic or environmental effects. However, the problem of confounding between genes and shared environment has also been raised against twin study paradigms. The possibility of environmental factors that may covary with zygosity is therefore an important consideration.

Although the traditional application of the twin design focuses on the estimation of the heritability (i.e., proportion of variance attributable to genetic factors) of a trait, there are several other research questions for which the twin study may be of value. Differences in concordance rates between monozygotic and dizygotic twins may be investigated at the level of symptoms or symptom clusters in order to study the validity of symptom complexes. Varying forms or degrees of expression of a particular disease in monozygotic twins may be an important source of evidence of the validity of the construct or disease entity. For example, Kendler, Neale, Kessler, Heath, and Eaves (1992) employed the twin study design to investigate the validity of the diagnostic categories of schizophrenia and depression, respectively. In addition, Kendler et al. (1996) showed that monozygotic twins were not only more often concordant for depression than dizygotic twins, but that they were concordant for specific depression subtypes, underscoring the heterogeneity of these disorders and need for nosology that reflects these entities.

Adoption Studies. Family and twin studies are genetically informative because they hold the environment constant while examining the rates of disorder across different levels of genetic relationship. An alternative approach is to vary the environment while comparing individuals across degrees of genetic similarity. Adoption studies are part of this latter approach in that psychiatric similarity between an adoptee and his or her biological versus adoptive relatives is examined. An alternative design compares the biological relatives of affected adoptees with those of unaffected or control adoptees. This approach is the most powerful for identifying genetic factors by minimizing the degree of familial aggregation that can be explained by same-environment confounds. However, adoption studies are also characterized by certain characteristics that may bias results. Biological parents of adopted children are known to have higher rates of psychopathology, alcoholism, or criminality than other parents, and adopted children may themselves be at greater risk for psychiatric disorders (e.g. Bohman, 1978; Lipman, Offord, & Boyle, 1993). Although such criticisms may be valid reasons to carefully interpret the rates of disorder found in these studies, they do not negate the value of adoption studies to clarify genetic and environmental effects (in particular for disorders showing specificity of transmission).

Study Designs for Investigating Links Between the Genotype and Phenotype

After familial aggregation has been established, genetic epidemiologic study designs examine both cultural and genetic mechanisms for familial clustering. Human genetics concepts for describing the complex links between genotype and phenotype include: epistasis (interaction between genes); variable expressivity (extent to which a particular trait is manifest); penetrance (proportion of persons with a susceptibility genotype who actually express the phenotype); and gene-environment interaction. Until recently, the role of environmental factors in modifying gene expression has been dramatically underestimated. In some cases, the specific environmental exposure involved in gene-environment interactions has actually been identified. For example, a recent case-control study revealed that oral clefts were increased only among offspring of women with a vulnerability gene (i.e., the TaqI polymorphism of the transforming growth factor gene) who also smoked during pregnancy (Hwang et al., 1995).

Genetic epidemiologic studies attempt to identify gene-environment interactions by employing study designs that hold environmental factors constant while allowing genetic factors to vary (or the converse), employing paradigms such as comparisons between discordant monozygotic twins, and cross-fostering studies. In general, genetic-epidemiologic studies differ from traditional genetic study paradigms by including control groups; assessing factors involved in sampling bias among treated populations; incorporating measurement of the environment such as diet, stress, and the social environment; studying the effects of cohabitation; and examining time-space clustering. Such studies are ideally suited to study the mutual influence of genetic and environmental factors on disease etiology. For example, multiple sclerosis was always believed to have a strong environmental component due to the geographic gradient in risk. However, evidence from studies of extended families of probands with multiple sclerosis is also consistent with strong genetic influences: the risk of multiple sclerosis among first degree relatives is 10-times that of population controls; there is a 50% decrement in risk between first and second degree relatives; and the risk to first degree relatives reared together versus apart is nearly identical (Sadovnik, 1997).

GENETIC EPIDEMIOLOGY OF PSYCHIATRIC DISORDERS

One of the major barriers to establishing the prevalence of psychiatric disorders in the general population has been the lack of validity of the diagnostic nomenclature in psychiatry (Kendell, 1989). Although universal communication has been facilitated by the development of explicit operational definitions for the major categories of psychiatric diagnosis, there are still no pathognomonic markers by which a disease may be diagnosed with certainty. Epidemiologic data are key to examining the reliability and validity of these operationalized diagnostic entities in the general population.

Despite these formidable challenges to applying genetic epidemiology to psychopathology, progress continues to be made in each of the four paradigms described previously. A comprehensive review of the genetic epidemiology of all of the major psychiatric disorders is beyond the scope of this chapter. However, the familial clustering of the major forms of psychopathology has now been well-established. The recurrence risks among adult relatives of individuals with the major classes of psychiatric disorders are summarized in Table 8.1. The rate ratio represents the prevalence of a particular disorder among the relatives of affected probands compared to those of unaffected probands. With the exception of obsessive–compulsive disorder, all of the major psychiatric disorders exhibit a significant degree of familial aggregation. Inspection of the range of rate ratios reveals little difference in the extent to which these disorders cluster in families. A more detailed summary of the genetic epidemiology of the anxiety disorders and substance use disorders is discussed later.

Studies of familial aggregation of psychiatric disorders suggest that the most compelling model involves susceptibility genes that convey increased disease risk but only in the presence of additional environmental, genetic, or biologic factors. The most notable example is schizophrenia for which there is emerging evidence for gene-environment interaction (Tienari et al., 1994) and oligogenic inheritance (i.e., small number of genes; Risch, 1990). It now seems likely that many, or most, mental problems involve a complex mixture of multiple genetic and environmen-

TABLE 8.1
Familial Factors and Psychiatric Disorders

Disorder	Average Rate Ratio	Ratio Range
Alcohol Abuse/Dependence	7.0	2.5–20.1
Anxiety		
Panic	9.4	3.0–3.2
Social Phobia	3.1	4.2–17.8
Obsessive–Compulsive	1.0	1.0–1.1
Mood		
Bipolar	10.8	3.7–17.7
Unipolar	5.0	1.5–18.9
Schizophrenia	8.9	2.7–18.5

tal influences, interacting in a nonlinear and nonadditive fashion. This complex web of interacting factors will be understood only with careful choice of genetically informative samples, as well as carefully selected measures of the environment. Environmental influences may include so-called biologic factors such as obstetric complications, infections, and exposure to toxins, as well as the social and psychological environment.

SUBSTANCE USE DISORDERS

The genetic epidemiologic approach provides an excellent model for examining risk factors for the development of substance use disorders. Figure 8.1 shows the epidemiologic triangle linking the three domains of risk factors including the host, the agent, and the environmental context that underlie the development of substance use disorders. The drug can be clearly identified as the agent, the environmental contextual factors determine exposure to the drug, and the individual characteristics of the host determine susceptibility to exposure and continued use of drugs. Although the majority of work on the familial aggregation of substance use disorders has focused on alcoholism, research on other substance use disorders is growing at a fast pace. Controlled family studies reveal that drug use disorders are familial (Bierut et al., 1998; Merikangas et al., 1998c); in fact, a family history of substance use disorders is the most potent and consistent risk factor for the development of substance use disorders in offspring. Factors associated with increased familial aggregation of substance use disorders include male gender, parental concordance for drug use disorders, and comorbid psychopathology,

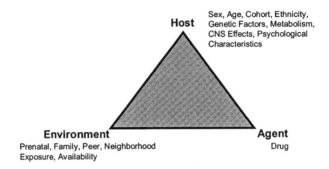

FIG. 8.1.   Epidemiology of drug abuse.

particularly alcoholism and antisocial behavior. Drug dependence is far more her-
itable than either drug use or abuse, and genetic factors appear to be more important in the transmission of drug problems among males. Adoption studies have
demonstrated that both genetic and environmental factors are important in the development of drug use disorders (Cadoret, Yates, Troughton, Woodworth, &
Stewart, 1995). Recent work from family studies and twin studies (Tsuang et al.,
1998) of specific drugs of abuse have confirmed the observation that drug abuse
in general is highly familial, and that there is some specificity of familial patterns
of expression of abuse or dependence on particular drugs. These findings are particularly compelling when the aggregrate evidence from sources of genetic evidence suggests two independent pathways to drug use disorders; one in which
shared etiologic factors influence the development of antisocial personlity and
drug use; and another that appears to underlie the development of drug dependence. However, there is a striking lack of controlled family studies of drug use
disorders. These studies are critical for elucidating the role of genetic and environmental factors in the transmission of substance use disorders, validating phenotypic definitions of substance use–abuse dependence, and identifying sources
of heterogeneity in their etiology, particularly with respect to the role of comorbid psychiatric disorders and polysubstance abuse.

ANXIETY DISORDERS

At present, relatively few studies have examined anxiety disorders from the perspective of genetic epidemiology, and there are virtually no data from certain paradigms (such as adoption studies). However, the existing research indicates that
most anxiety disorders aggregate in families, and several investigations have offered specific support for genetic etiology. Perhaps the most consistent support
for the role of genetic factors has been found for panic disorder. A review of six
controlled family studies using direct interviews provides an average relative risk
of 9.4 (Weissman, 1993), and new investigations continue to report high levels of

aggregation (e.g. Battaglis et al., 1995). Although there has been some inconsistency reported by twin studies of panic disorder (see McGuffin, Asherson, Owen, & Farmer, 1994), two recent studies applying modern diagnostic criteria demonstrated considerably higher rates for monozygotic compared to dizygotic twins (Kendler, Neale, Kessler, Heath, & Eaves, 1993a; Skre, Onstad, Torgersen, Lygren, & Kringlen, 1993). Furthermore, current estimates derived from the Virginia Twin Registry show panic disorder to have the highest heritability of all anxiety disorders at 44% (Kendler et al., 1995).

Genetic factors are implicated in other anxiety disorders, although comparatively few investigations have been completed. For example, social phobia aggregates in families and twin studies show a higher concordance for monozygotic twins (see Table 8.1). Other phobias (i.e. specific phobia and agoraphobia) have also been shown to be familial, with the three phobia subtypes having similar relative risks and specificity of transmission (for reviews, see Merikangas & Angst, 1995; Woodman & Crowe, 1996). More recent data from the Virginia Twin Study report the estimated total heritability for phobias to be 35% (Kendler et al., 1995). The application of genetic epidemiologic studies to other anxiety disorders has been limited chiefly by uncertainty about the appropriateness of phenotypic descriptions.

Concerning marker studies of anxiety disorders, the high heritability rates seen for panic disorder have made them the natural focus of research in this area, and many clinical and neurobiological challenge studies have served as a guide by implicating the adrenergic system (for a review see Goddard, Woods, & Charney, 1996). However, recent linkage studies have excluded the possibility that panic disorder was due to mutations in adrenergic receptor loci on chromosomes 4, 5, or 10 (Wang, Crowe, & Noyes, 1992), and other work has similarly excluded linkage with γ-aminobutyric acid (GABA)-A receptor genes (Schmidt, Zoega, & Crowe, 1993). Recent reports from a genomic survey of panic disorder using 600 markers have not yielded evidence of linkage (Nurnberger & Byerley, 1995). While the status of current biologic marker studies of panic disorder are still in their infancy, there is reason to be optimistic as the Human Genome Project (and the identification of numerous highly polymorphic markers) will soon lead to major increases in the precision of the human genome map (Crowe, 1994).

HIGH-RISK STUDIES

The high-risk design, a subset of the family study approach, is one of the most powerful strategies for identifying premorbid vulnerability factors for a particular disease. By focusing on individuals with the greatest probability of developing specific disorders, the high-risk design maximizes the potential case yield, increases the power within a particular sample to observe hypothesized risk factor associations, minimizes the heterogeneity that is likely to characterize unrelated samples of youth enrolled in prospective studies, increases the likelihood of observing the effects of mediating and moderating variables on the primary risk factor of interest (e.g., children of alcoholics with or without accompanying risk factors), and identifies early patterns of disease given the exposure (e.g. parental psychopathology).

Limitations of the high-risk design include: the inability to identify the offspring who are truly at risk since on average, only 50% will possess the genetic vulnerability factors; the wide age range and developmental level represented in the sample often preclude common assessment methods for the entire sample both cross-sectionally and longitudinally; and the relatively low number of actual cases, despite maximizing potential caseness based on family history. Perhaps the most important limitation of high-risk studies is the inability to employ the wide range of tools to probe susceptibility in unaffected individuals, particularly in children, because of the potential for triggering onset of the disorder and ethical concerns. In addition, the disadvantages of all prospective longitudinal research also apply to the high-risk study design; namely, the high expense and effort devoted to tracking and assessing samples, high attrition rates, and long duration before conclusive findings may be generated. Despite these limitations, the high-risk design remains one of the most valuable tools for studying premorbid risk factors.

High-Risk Studies of Psychiatric Disorders

The role of a family history of psychiatric disorders as one of the most potent risk factors for the development of psychopathology in offspring has generated a substantial body of research on offspring of parents with schizophrenia, alcoholism, anxiety, and affective disorders (Downey & Coyne, 1990; Erlenmeyer-Kimling, Cornblatt, & Golden, 1983; Johnson & Lydiard, 1995; Last, Hersen, Kazdin, Orvaschel, & Perrin, 1991). These studies have attempted to identify the correlates and consequences of parental psychopathology and to map the complex developmental course of psychopathology during relevant periods of risk. Few of the high-risk studies to date, however, have studied the specificity of associations between vulnerability markers due to a lack of adequate controls. Such studies enable investigation of the specificity of familial factors as opposed to the impact of psychopathology in general (Laucht, Esser, & Schmidt, 1994).

There are several design issues that preclude aggregation across studies. First, the majority of high-risk studies have failed to consider either the characteristics or information provided by fathers, despite their important genetic and environmental contribution to their offspring; second, the control groups are selected via diverse methods that often differ from the sampling of the probands; third, the control group is often devoid of any psychopathology, thereby limiting the ability of the study to examine specificity; fourth, siblings of the high-risk sample are often not assessed despite the important information they provide on familial transmission; and fifth, many studies examine only the diagnostic entities of interest rather than a wide range of potential risk and protective factors.

High-Risk Studies of Anxiety Disorders

There are fewer high-risk studies of anxiety than of schizophrenia, alcoholism, or depression, and most of these have focused on parental panic disorder. A summary of controlled high-risk studies of anxiety disorders is presented in Table 8.2.

There are seven controlled studies of anxiety disorders among offspring of parents (primarily mothers) with anxiety disorders (Beidel, 1988; Capps, Sigman, Sena, & Henker, 1996; Merikangas, Dierker, & Szatmari, 1998a; Sylvester, Hyde, & Reichler, 1987; Turner, Beidel, & Costello, 1987; Unnewehr, Schneider, Florin, & Margraf, 1998; Warner, Kessler, Hughes, Anthony, & Nelson, 1995a). The risk of anxiety disorders among offspring of parents with anxiety disorders compared to controls averages 3.5 (range 1.3–13.3), suggesting specificity of parent–child concordance within broad subtypes of anxiety disorders. The wide range of estimates is chiefly attributable to the diagnostic methods and sampling of the individual studies. For example, Sylvester et al. (1987) excluded coparents with any other psychiatric disorder, whereas many of the other studies did not evaluate the nonproband parent. The age composition of the samples was also quite different and the diagnostic methods were quite variable.

However, similar to studies of adults that show common familial and genetic risk factors for anxiety and depression (Kendler, Neale, Kessler, Heath, & Eaves, 1993b; Merikangas, 1990; Stavrakaki & Vargo, 1986), these studies have also revealed that there is a lack of specificity with respect to depression (Beidel & Turner, 1997; Sylvester et al., 1987; Turner et al., 1987; Warner et al., 1995a). Studies that employed a comparison group of parent probands with depressive disorders have shown that rates of anxiety disorders are also increased among the offspring of these parents (Beidel & Turner, 1997; Sylvester, Hyde, & Reichler, 1988; Turner et al., 1987; Warner, Mufson, & Weissman, 1995b). Conversely, offspring of parents with anxiety disorders and depression have elevated rates of depression when compared to those of controls (Sylvester et al., 1988) or to offspring of anxiety disordered parents without depression (Biederman, Rosenbaum, Bolduc, Faraone, & Hirshfeld, 1991). Similar findings emerged from the family study by Last et al. (1991) who found an increase in rates of major depression among the adult relatives of children with anxiety. These findings are usually interpreted as providing evidence for age-specific expression of common risk factors for anxiety in childhood and depression with or without comorbid anxiety in adulthood.

The high rates of anxiety disorders among offspring of parents with anxiety suggest that there may be underlying psychological or biological vulnerability factors for anxiety disorders in general that may already manifest themselves in children prior to puberty. Previous research has shown that children at risk for anxiety disorders are characterized by behavioral inhibition (Rosenbaum, Biederman, & Gersten, 1988), autonomic reactivity (Beidel, 1988), somatic symptoms (Reichler, Sylvester, & Hyde, 1988; Turner et al., 1987), and social fears (Sylvester et al., 1988; Turner et al., 1987). Fears involving social evaluation have been shown to be far more stable than other childhood fears that may be self-limited (Achenbach, 1985).

TABLE 8.2
Controlled High-Risk Studies of Anxiety

Study	Sample					Offspring		Relative Risk
	Proband							
Author (year)	Anxiety	Other	Other	Controls	Spouse	N	Age	
Sylvester et al. (1987)	Panic Disorder	Major Depressive Disorder	—	No Diagnosis	No Diagnosis	91	7-17	13.3
Turner et al. (1987)	Agoraphobia/OCD	Dysthymia	—	—	Not Evaluated	43	7-12	4.8
Capps et al. (1996)	Agoraphobia	Agoraphobia/ Panic	—	—	Not Evaluated	43	8-24	—
Warner, V. et al. (1995)	Panic/Major Depressive Disorder	Panic Disorder	Early onset Major Depressive Disorder	No Diagnosis	Diagnosis	145	6-29	1.3
Beidel et al. (1997)	Anxiety + Depression	Anxiety	Major Depressive Disorder	No Diagnosis	No Diagnosis	129	7-12	4.0
Merikangas et al. (1998)	Panic/Social Phobia	Alcohol or drugs	Substance + Anxiety	No Diagnosis	Diagnosis	192	7-17	2.0
Unnewehr et al. (1998)	Panic Disorder	Simple Phobia	—	—	Not Evaluated	87	5-15	9.2

Several studies have also suggested that there is an association between childhood medical conditions and the subsequent development of anxiety. Kagan, Reznick, Clarke, Snidman, and Garcia-Coll (1984) reported an association between allergic symptoms, particularly hay fever, and inhibited temperament in young children. In a retrospective review of prenatal and perinatal, and early childhood risk factors for different forms of psychiatric disorders in adolescence and early adulthood, Allen, Lewinsohn, and Seeley (1998) found that anxiety disorders in adolescents were associated specifically with illness during the first year of life, particularly high fever. Taylor, Sandberg, Thorley, and Giles (1991) reported that immunologic diseases and infections were specifically associated with emotional disorders since children with developmental or behavioral disorders had no elevation in infections or allergic diseases. These findings suggest that it may be fruitful to examine links between immunologic function and the development of anxiety disorders.

High-Risk Studies of Substance Use Disorders

Aside from preexisting emotional and behavior disorders, a family history of alcoholism has been shown to be the most consistent risk factor for the development of alcoholism in vulnerable youth (Sher, Walitzer, Woods, & Brent, 1991). Among high-risk studies that have focused on the young offspring of alcoholic parents, findings have generally supported an increase in risk for the development of alcohol use, drug use, and related problems (West & Prinz, 1987). For example, Chassin, Rogosch, and Barrera (1991) found that parental alcoholism is a significant risk factor for child symptomatology and substance use among 10- to 15-year-old offspring, with the risk found to be stronger among those offspring of parents with current rather than remitted alcoholism. Similarly, several investigators (Hill, Steinhauer, & Zubin, 1992; Johnson, Leonard, & Jacob, 1989; Merikangas et al., 1998a; Reich, Earls, Frankel, & Shayka, 1993) have reported an increased risk of substance-related problems among the offspring of alcoholic parents. Aside from genetic factors, there are numerous other mechanisms through which parents may convey an increased risk of substance abuse to their offspring including serving as negative role models for the use–abuse of drugs, as well as using drugs as a coping mechanisms (Brook, Whiteman, Gordon, & Cohen, 1986). Moreover, adolescents with a family history of substance abuse are more likely to associate with deviant peers than those without familial loading (Kandel & Andrews, 1987). Despite abundant research seeking to identify premorbid vulnerability markers for alcoholism (especially in youth), however, there are to date no confirmed markers aside from family history that specifically predict its development. One major reason for the problems in developing successful models for alcoholism is that there are multiple pathways to the development of this disorder, with varying degrees of environmental and genetic contributions.

There is now substantial evidence that different risk factors may be involved in the different stages of development of alcoholism. Whereas individual demographic characteristics and peer influences strongly influence exposure and initial patterns of use of alcohol and drugs, family history of substance abuse and both familial and personal psychopathology play a more salient role in the transition to problematic alcohol use and dependence. For example, the adoption studies of Cadoret et al. (1995) revealed that drug disorders in the biologic parent are associated far more strongly with drug abuse than with initial use of drugs. Likewise, twin (Pickens et al., 1991) and family study data (Merikangas et al., 1998b) confirm the greater impact of genetic and familial risk factors on the later stages of the alcohol trajectory.

There are fewer controlled studies of offspring of drug abusers than of alcoholics. Moss, Majumder, and Vanyukov (1994) reported that the preadolescent sons of fathers with substance abuse had elevated rates of externalizing problems and socialization, increased rates of conduct problems, depression, anxiety disorders, and substance use (Clark et al., 1997; Clark, Kinsci, & Moss, 1998; Moss, Mezzich, Yao, Gavaler, & Martin, 1995), and higher levels of aggressivity, inattention, and impulsivity (Martin et al., 1994) than offspring of nonsubstance abusers. Similarly, Gabel and Shindledecker (1992) reported that sons of substance abusing parents had more conduct disorder in association with severe aggressive–destructive behavior than sons of nonsubstance abusing parents, while daughters of substance abusing parents were more likely to receive a diagnosis of attention-deficit hyperactivity disorder, and conduct disorder than the female offspring of nonsubstance abusing parents. Wilens, Biederman, Kiely, Bredin, and Spencer (1994) likewise reported significantly elevated scores on a dimensional symptom rating scale of psychopathology among the children of opioid-dependent parents.

In summary, the family study provides a powerful method for investigating not only the extent of familial aggregation of psychopathology, but also may yield valuable information regarding the diagnostic definitions, the range of expression of particular syndromes, mechanisms for comorbidity, sources of sex differences in disease prevalence, and the extent to which familial patterns adhere to traditional Mendelian patterns of genetic transmission. The high-risk study design, particularly when prospective, is an important source of information on premorbid risk and protective factors, early forms of expression, specificity of expression, and early sequelae of psychopathology. In order to demonstrate the utility of the family–high-risk study designs, the goals and major findings from the Yale Family Study of Comorbidity of Substance Use Disorders and Anxiety are presented in the next section.

YALE FAMILY STUDY OF COMORBIDITY OF ANXIETY DISORDERS AND SUBSTANCE ABUSE

Adult Family Study

The chief goals of the Yale Family Study are: (a) investigate the familial aggregation of substance abuse and anxiety disorders; (b) identify mechanisms for comorbidity between anxiety disorders and substance use disorders; and (c) examine pathways to substance use disorders among high-risk offspring.

Sample. A total of 260 adult probands with anxiety disorders, substance use, or both, were recruited from outpatient clinics and the community via a random-digit dialing procedure. All probands in the present study were White; separate family studies of similar diagnostic groups of African American and Hispanic probands are now underway. Probands and relatives were directly interviewed with the semi-structured Schedule for Affective Disorders and Schizophrenia (SADS), current and lifetime versions (Endicott & Spitzer, 1978), extensively modified to obtain DSM-III and DSM-III-R criteria (American Psychiatric Association, 1987). Adult first-degree relatives and spouses were directly interviewed by experienced clinical interviewers who were blind to the diagnostic status of the proband. There were a total of 1218 adult first-degree relatives of the adult probands. A comprehensive summary of these findings is presented in Merikangas et al. (1998b) and Merikangas et al. (1998c).

Chief Findings: Adult Family Study. With respect to familial transmission of substance use disorders, the family study data revealed that substance use disorders were highly familial and that there was specificity of familial aggregation of predominant drug abuse among adult first-degree relatives of probands with substance abuse. Cannabis and opioids exhibited the greatest specificity. Data from this study also revealed independence of familial aggregation of alcoholism and drug dependence, suggesting some unique risk factors for the two classes of substances (Merikangas et al., 1998c).

Investigation of patterns of comorbidity showed that most disorders (including major depression, bipolar depression, social phobia, and antisocial personality disorder) were transmitted independently of substance use disorders in families, despite the large magnitude of comorbidity between them. In contrast, panic disorder, alcoholism, and major depression appeared to result from shared underlying familial risk factors (Merikangas et al., 1998b).

High-Risk Study

Sample. In order to be eligible for the high-risk study, the potential probands (cases and controls) were required to have offspring between the ages of 7 and 17 and to provide consent for their offspring to be interviewed. The families included in this subset of the larger family study consisted of 123 probands, 3 of whom had offspring with two different spouses, for a total of 126 couples. There was approximately equal distribution of male and female probands, with an average age of 39.

Parent probands consisted of 52 probands diagnosed with alcoholism or drug use disorders (or both) including anxiolytic, sedative, benzodiazepine abuse, marijuana abuse, or dependence (substance abuse–dependence group); 36 probands diagnosed with anxiety disorders including panic with or without agoraphobia, social phobia, or both generalized anxiety disorder (anxiety group); and 35 proband controls having no lifetime history of psychiatric disorder (control group). Probands with comorbid affective disorders, antisocial personality disorder (ASP), or other nonpsychotic Axis I disorders were not excluded from the study.

There are a total of 192 children who were assessed at the time of the original study. Thirty-eight were children of probands diagnosed with alcoholism, drug use disorders, or both; 39 were children of probands diagnosed with both an anxiety disorder and a substance disorder; 58 were children of probands diagnosed with anxiety; and 57 were children of proband controls. Probands were recontacted at approximately 2-year intervals to obtain permission for follow-up of the offspring (Dierker, Merikangas, & Szatmari, 1999; Merikangas et al., 1998a; Merikangas et al., 1999). Approximately 80% of the original sample participated at Wave 2 of data collection, and 72% of those who participated at Wave 2 were again interviewed at Wave 3. Ninety-one percent of the original sample participated in at least one subsequent assessment. In addition, younger siblings were interviewed at subsequent data collection points. Analyses of the follow-up data are currently in progress. There were approximately equal proportions of males and females with an average age of 12 (range 7–17) at study entry and 18 (range 13–23) at follow-up. The distribution of socioeconomic status was similar for children of probands with anxiety disorders and children of controls; however, these groups differ from children of probands with substance disorder who tended to come from families of lower social and economic status.

Measures

Psychiatric Assessment.   A modified version of the Kiddie-Schedule for Affective Disorders and Schizophrenia (K-SADS) was used for diagnostic assessment of the offspring (Orvaschel, Thompson, Belanger, Prusoff, & Kidd, 1982), modified for DSM-III-R (Chambers, Puig-Antich, Tabrizi, & Davies, 1985; Gammon et al., 1983; Orvaschel et al., 1982). The diagnostic interview was administered independently by experienced clinical interviewers, primarily clinical psychologists, with the offspring and with the mother about the offspring. Diagnoses were derived by an independent child psychiatrist. The psychiatrist was blind to the diagnostic status of the parents and was not involved in direct interviews, after review of all available information, including the diagnostic interview, family history reports on the offspring, teachers' reports, and medical records. Diagnoses were coded on a four-point scale reflecting the level of certainty of diagnosis (i.e., none, possible, probable, and definite).

Other Assessments.   Other assessment domains include: familial factors, developmental and medical history, temperamental factors, indirect indices of central nervous system functioning including neurologic and neuropsychologic evaluations, and psychophysiologic function.

Major Findings

Offspring Diagnoses By Parent Proband Group.   The links between disorders in parent probands and offspring at Wave 1 are shown in Table 8.3. Offspring of probands with anxiety disorders had marginally ($p < .10$) elevated rates of anx-

TABLE 8.3
Disorders in Offspring by Parent Proband Group

	Proband Parent Group			
Disorders in Offspring	Substance Disorders	Anxiety Disorders	Controls	p
	N = 77	N = 58	N = 57	
Anxiety Disorders[a]	10.4	22.4	10.5	+
Affective Disorders	13.0	12.1	3.5	n.s.
Conduct Disorder	15.6	5.2	0	*
Oppositional-Deviant Disorder	11.7	13.8	3.5	n.s.
Attention-Deficit/Hyperactivity Disorder	13.0	13.8	15.8	n.s.
Alcohol Abuse/Dependence	18.0	11.1	0	+
Drug Abuse/Dependence	10.3	11.1	0	n.s.

Note. [a]Except specific phobia. +p < .10. *p < .05.

iety disorders compared to those of parents with substance use disorders. In contrast, the offspring of parents with substance use disorders had an elevated rate of conduct disorder compared to those of parents with anxiety disorders or controls. In contrast, rates of composite affective disorders and attention deficit hyperactivity disorder did not differ by proband parent group.

To assess drug use among offspring, drug types were collapsed and a single dichotomous variable was used to characterize drug experimentation. Similar to patterns of alcohol use, drug use was most common in offspring of substance use disorder probands, lower in those of anxiety disorder, and least common in the offspring of control probands according to both parent and child report.

Since many offspring in this sample had not yet entered the age of risk for alcohol or drug use disorders, analyses conducted on substance abuse and dependence were subset to adolescents age 12 and above. Elevated rates of substance abuse, dependence, or both, were evaluated among the offspring of probands with substance use disorders compared to the offspring of controls. In fact, none of the offspring of the controls reported problematic drug or alcohol use.

Disorders In Offspring By Parental Mating Type.   Although the high-risk design involves selection of one parent, for common disorders it is also essential to characterize the other parent who contributes 50% of his or her genes as well to the familial environment. Disorders in offspring were then evaluated according to disorders in parental couples rather than to the index parent proband. The rates of disorders in offspring by parental mating types are presented in Table 8.4. There was evidence for specificity of transmission of anxiety disorders. The proportion of offspring of dually affected parents with anxiety, affective disorders, or both, was significantly greater than that of the offspring from each comparison group, with the exception of the offspring of couples in which one parent was affected with anxiety, affective disorders, or both. There was also a dose-response relationship between the number of parents with anxiety disorders and the rates of anxiety among offspring.

Elevated rates of conduct disorder emerged only among offspring of couples in which both parents were affected (Table 8.4). These rates were significantly different from those among offspring of parents of controls and those of parents in which only one parent was affected with anxiety or affective disorders. The lack of specificity of parental disorder suggests the importance of the role of the family environment on the development of conduct problems.

Domains of Assessment

As described previously, aside from examining specificity of familial aggregation of psychopathology, the high-risk study design may also be employed to examine premorbid vulnerability factors, and correlates and sequelae of psychopathology, particularly when the design includes a prospective follow-up of the cohort of offspring. Preliminary findings based on a priori hypotheses regarding each of the

TABLE 8.4
Disorders in Offspring by Parental Mating Type

Disorders in Offspring	Both			One		Neither	p value $(X^2, 5\ df)$
	Substance	Substance + Anxiety/ Affective	Anxiety/ Affective	Substance	Anxiety/ Affective	Normal	
	$N = 18$	$N = 54$	$N = 23$	$N = 19$	$N = 48$	$N = 26$	
	%	%	%	%	%	%	
Anxiety Disorders[a]	0.0	14.8	39.1	5.3	16.7	3.9	**
Affective Disorders	5.6	14.8	21.7	15.8	4.2	0.0	n.s.
Conduct Disorder	16.7	16.7	8.7	0.0	0.0	0.0	**
Oppositional Disorder	16.7	11.1	21.7	0.0	8.3	3.9	n.s.
Substance Use Disorders[b]	12.5	22.2	16.7	10.0	0.0	--	n.s.

Note. [a]Without specific phobia. [b]Over age 12. *$p < .01$.

domains of vulnerability for anxiety disorders are summarized in Fig. 8.2. A comprehensive summary of these findings is presented in Merikangas et al. (1998b) and Merikangas et al. (1998c).

Family Functioning. Family and parental functioning were measured by several instruments administered to the entire family including the Family Adaptability and Cohesion Scale III (FACES; Olson, Sprenkle, & Russell, 1979; Olson, Portner, & Bell, 1985a; Olson, Portner, & Lavee, 1985b), the McMaster Family Assessment Device (FAD; Epstein, Baldwin, & Bishop, 1983), and the Parental Bonding Inventory (PBI; Parker, Tupling, & Brown, 1979) to assess maternal and paternal care and protection. The results of family adaptability and cohesion measures, general familial functioning, and parental care and protection indicate that offspring of parents with anxiety disorders alone were not exposed to greater family disruption or poorer parenting than those of normal parents. In fact, anxious fathers actually exhibited more care than nonanxious fathers. In contrast, offspring of parents with substance use disorders tended to experience significantly poorer family cohesion than either those of anxiety parents or controls.

Developmental And Medical Disorders In Childhood. The second major domain of inquiry in the present study involved the early developmental factors, prenatal and perinatal exposure to drugs, alcohol, or major illness or trauma, as well as childhood diseases, injuries, and major stressful life events. No differences were found between offspring of parents with anxiety disorders compared to normals in any of the prenatal and perinatal factors including drug or alcohol exposure, birth complications, or developmental anomalies as well as developmental milestones. However, offspring of parents with anxiety had more sleep ter-

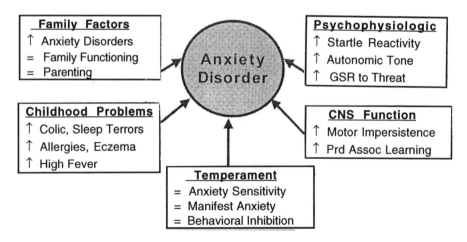

FIG. 8.2   Vulnerability factors for anxiety disorders in offspring.

rors. In terms of childhood illnesses, a greater proportion of offspring of parents with anxiety had allergies, eczema, and high fever than those of normals. As noted earlier, only those disorders that had been previously suggested as associated with anxiety were included in these analyses.

Temperamental Factors. The third major area of investigation as a risk domain for the development of anxiety involves temperamental factors, such as behavioral inhibition, anxiety sensitivity, and fearfulness, believed to predispose individuals to the subsequent development of anxiety in adolescence and adulthood. Because the age composition of this sample was well beyond that in which temperament can be truly assessed, the retrospective measures employed herein are necessarily limited in their utility for examining links between temperament and anxiety. Nevertheless, some self-reported scales were employed as well as parental and teacher reports to examine shy and inhibited temperament in this sample, as described previously. The offspring of parents with anxiety did not differ from those of the other proband groups with respect to any of the measures. However, there were significant differences between children with anxiety disorders and others on all of these scales after controlling for sex and age. Thus, these measures tended to characterize children with anxiety states rather than those with vulnerability for the development of anxiety.

Neurologic And Neuropsychologic Function. The evaluation of neurologic function was undertaken to identify specific signs that may indicate central or motor disturbances associated with anxiety disorders. Results indicate that offspring of probands with anxiety exhibited greater motor impersistence and brisker patellar reflex than offspring of other proband groups. There were no differences in neurologic hard signs or left–right anomalies among those at risk for anxiety disorders compared to those at risk for substance use disorders or normals.

The Peabody Picture Vocabulary Test (PPVT) was used to assess auditory comprehension of picture names. A full battery of traditional neuropsychological tests, including the Wechsler Intelligence Scale for Children (WISC), was also administered. The Cambridge Neuropsychological Test Automated Batteries (CANTAB, Downes, 1994) is a system of computerized neuropsychological tests developed at the University of Cambridge. To assess cognitive function, six different tests are used to examine three main components: visual memory, attention, and spatial working memory and planning. The tests provide separate assessments of the relative integrity of different neurophysiological and neuroanatomical subsystems.

In general, there were few differences between those at risk for anxiety and normals on most of the neuropsychological tests. In fact, the offspring of parents with anxiety tended to have somewhat higher functioning in several domains compared to those of the substance abuse groups, particularly in verbal intelligence. The main difference among those with vulnerability to anxiety when compared to normals emerged in the Paired Associative Learning Subtest of the CANTAB on which they performed more poorly on the memory task and made more errors than normals.

Psychophysiologic Function. Autonomic function assessment at baseline did not differ between the at-risk groups. However, there was higher autonomic tone (i.e., background homeostatic regulation of the central and peripheral vascular systems against which reactivity to the environment occurs), lower sensitivity to orthostatic change, and greater galvanic skin response (GSR) among offspring of parents with anxiety compared to those of the other proband groups. Although the high-risk anxiety group had higher baseline GSR, the difference was far more pronounced under the threat condition. Similar to the other domains, those off-spring with anxiety states exhibited greater differences on all of these measures than those without anxiety. The results of the anticipatory anxiety experiment of this cohort were described in Grillon, Dierker, and Merikangas (1998) and Grillon, Pellowski, Merikangas, and Davis (1997). The high-risk group exhibited gender-specific abnormal startle reactivity; high-risk females showed enhanced baseline startle, whereas high-risk males exhibited elevated potentiated startle to the threat signal. High-risk females also had increased baseline startle in the dark–light experiment, whereas males did not.

Significance of Findings

Anxiety. These findings reveal a strong degree of specificity of expression of anxiety disorders among offspring of parents with anxiety. Similar to previous studies, the findings of the present study also yielded elevated rates of depression among the offspring of parents with anxiety. However, depression was more strongly associated with parental depression than with anxiety. The specificity of expression of anxiety and the direct relationship between the number of parents with anxiety and increased rates of anxiety disorders in offspring are consistent with the expectations of increased genetic propensity to anxiety. Biologic and genetic explanations are further supported by the lack of evidence for impairment in either parenting or family function associated with either parental or offspring anxiety. In fact, fathers with anxiety disorders were reported as having greater levels of care than those without. The lack of evidence for familial environmental factors, when taken together with the strong degree of specificity of transmission of anxiety disorders and dose-response relationship between parental and child anxiety disorders, suggest that there may be temperamental or other biological vulnerability factors for anxiety disorders (in general) that may already manifest in children prior to puberty. In contrast, both depression and substance abuse in parents were strongly associated with severe disruption in parental and family functioning leading to increased behavioral disorders and depression in exposed youth.

Findings from the Yale Family Study confirm those of the growing evidence that women have higher rates of anxiety disorders and symptoms than men across the age span. None of the possible artifactual explanations including sampling, demographic, or social risk factors appear to convincingly explain the preponderance of anxiety in women. However, there is some evidence that males are less likely to report anxiety symptoms and to suffer from a lower magnitude of impairment and distress as women, with the possible exception of social phobia.

In a review of the multiple possible explanations for the higher rates of anxiety in women by Merikangas and Pollock (2000), the most compelling explanation is that women are more likely to have higher levels of arousal, psychophysiologic response to stress, and somatic symptoms, as well as greater awareness of somatic anxiety than men. Increased social sensitivity may also lead to increased awareness of anxiety symptoms in women. There is also substantial evidence that the oscillation of female reproductive hormones across the life cycle may be associated with greater levels of expression of underlying vulnerability for anxiety in women, as well as increased severity and frequency of anxiety symptoms among ongoing cases.

With respect to vulnerability factors, the lack of prenatal and perinatal risk factors for the development of anxiety disorders confirms the findings of Allen et al. (1998), who found no difference in prenatal risk factors among adolescents and young adults with anxiety disorders. In contrast, children who suffered from a variety of exposures ranging from prenatal substance use to postnatal injuries were more likely to develop behavior disorders, particularly attention deficit disorder and conduct problems.

The link between childhood allergies and eczema, and behavioral inhibition was discussed by Kagan (1994), who proposed that the high levels of cortisol associated with anxiety may lead to immunologic sensitivity to environmental stimuli. Likewise, Allen and Matthews (1997) reported that adolescents and young adults with anxiety disorders were more likely to have suffered from infections during early childhood than others. Confirmation of this finding from the perspective of a sample of high-risk youth provides more compelling evidence for an association between enhanced vigilance of these children to environmental stimuli. In the present study, the prevalence of high fevers in childhood along with diseases associated with the immune system suggest future inquiry into the possible role of the immune system in anxiety states.

Clues regarding the neural pathways underlying anxiety were provided by all of the indirect assessments of central nervous system function including the neurologic examination, the nonverbal computerized neuropsychological evaluation and the psychophysiologic studies. Motor impersistence, which is a test of motor-cortical pathways, reflects an inability to suppress the motor system that is an important component of anxiety (Joynt, 1990). In the present study, nearly half of the high-risk subjects exhibited motor impersistence of tongue protrusion, which has most often been reported from lesions of the dorsolateral prefrontal cortex (Joynt, Benton, & Fogel, 1962).

Although no direct biochemical or brain functioning measures were employed, the findings from these indirect measures may provide clues for future studies employing tools of neuroimaging or neurochemistry. Possible serotonergic mechanisms for vulnerability to anxiety in the present study were suggested by the pattern of performance of the high-risk offspring on the neuropsychological testing. Based on prior studies of specific deficits in paired associate learning, but not other subtests of the CANTAB sensitive to frontal lobe dysfunction, after reduction of serotonin by tryptophan depletion in normal subjects, Park et al. (1994) concluded that the serotonergic system may have a specific role in the processes of memory and learning not directly implicated in frontal lobe function. The role of serotonergic mechanisms in anxiety states has been reviewed by Goddard et al. (1996). However, whether disturbance in serotonergic function was perturbed by the acute stressful circumstances rather than representing trait related dysregulation was not determined, suggesting a potentially exciting direction for future research.

The disturbances in autonomic and psychophysiologic function confirm the abundant research on both clinical samples of anxiety disorders as well as induced anxiety in experimental studies. However, this is the first study to our knowledge that begins to yield indicators from a variety of tests tapping different aspects of fear, vigilance, and arousal in a high-risk sample. The increased patellar reflex when taken together with far lower orthostatic changes in pulse and blood pressure may signify increased autonomic tone, another potential indicator of hypervigiliance of the autonomic nervous system to environmental stimuli.

Our results suggest that high risk for anxiety disorders involves a gender-specific differential sensitivity of the neural pathways underlying fear. Whereas male offspring of anxiety disordered parents exhibited increased potentiated startle, female offspring could be differentiated by increased baseline startle. When taken together with the results of the adult family study that revealed a higher threshold for expression of anxiety disorders among male compared to female relatives, these findings suggest that males may develop anxiety in the face of environmental triggers, whereas females may be more prone to develop anxiety without provocation.

Assessment of the prognostic significance of these study measures within and across domains will be the ultimate test of the extent to which they serve as premorbid markers of vulnerability for anxiety. This suggests that studies of biologic, genetic, and environmental factors underlying anxiety in these families may be fruitful. Future analyses of the predictive significance of these findings, and their specificity with respect to anxiety states may elucidate the involvement of these systems in the development of anxiety. If confirmed, these preliminary findings may provide leads regarding specific hypotheses that may be examined using the tools of neuroimaging and pharmacological challenges that may lead to the discovery of the biologic factors conveying vulnerability to the development of anxiety disorders and the environmental contexts that potentiate or suppress their expression.

Substance Use Disorders.   The findings of the Yale High Risk Study revealed a strong association between parental and child substance use disorders. The high rates of drug disorders in the relatively young sample (mean age 15) in the present study were striking; approximately one fifth of the adolescent offspring of substance abusing parents already met criteria for alcohol abuse or dependence, and one fourth of the child and adolescent offspring were already smoking regularly. Parental anxiety was also associated with increased rates of substance abuse, but the magnitude was one half of that of the offspring of substance abusers. Most notable was the lack of a single case of any type of alcohol or drug abuse as well as the absence of regular smokers among the offspring of normal parents.

Evidence from the present study as well as previous research reveals that parental substance disorders are more common in lower social classes and are associated with increased rates of disrupted family structure (Merikangas et al., 1998a). Further inspection of the data revealed that comorbid depression was a key mediator of familial disruption associated with substance use disorders. Evidence for the latter has been suggested by a strong association between depression and environmental adversity (Rutter, 1986), increased incidence of depression in youth after acute stress (Reinherz et al., 1993), and increased rates of conduct disorder among offspring of parents concordant for psychiatric disorders in general (Dierker et al., 1999).

Possible mechanisms for the associations between parental substance use disorders and behavioral disorders in offspring have been examined extensively in studies using a variety of research designs including family, high risk, longitudinal cohort, twin, and adoption methods. When taken together, the results suggest that there is no direct link between behavior disorders in children and parental alcoholism (Robins, 1980). Rather, the increased rates of behavior disorders may stem directly from parental antisocial personality disorder or indirectly from the disrupted and stressful family environment associated with alcoholism, particularly in the presence of psychopathology in the coparent (Chassin et al., 1991, 1993; Rubio-Stipec, Bravo, & Canino, 1991). In the latter study, it was found that decreased parental monitoring among alcoholics and negative emotionality both contributed to the development of substance use among adolescent offspring. The results of recent adoption studies of males (Cadoret et al., 1995) and females (Cadoret, Yates, Troughton, Woodworth, & Stewart, 1996) reveal clear evidence for gene-environment interactions between biologic vulnerability to alcoholism or drug abuse and antisocial behavior and disturbed rearing family environment. In fact, family stress may have the greatest impact on those youngsters with the greatest vulnerability to substance abuse and behavior disorders.

In addition to biologic risk factors for substance disorders, there are several environmental mechanisms through which parents may convey an increased risk of substance abuse and externalizing disorders to their offspring including serving as negative role models for the use–abuse of drugs as well as using drugs as a coping mechanism (Brook et al., 1986). Moreover, adolescents with a family history of substance abuse are more likely to associate with deviant peers than those without familial loading (Kandel & Andrews, 1987). Patterns of family functioning in the present study will be presented in future reports.

Despite the evidence from several previous studies (Earls, 1988; Gabel & Shindledecker, 1992; Martin et al., 1994; Reich et al., 1993) describing the link between parental substance abuse and behavior problems in offspring, the results of this study did not reveal a direct association between parental substance disorders and child conduct disorder. Moreover, the proportion of offspring with conduct disorder was elevated only among dually affected couples, irrespective of the specific parental diagnoses. This finding suggests that concordance for psychopathology in general is a more potent indicator of behavior disorders than the specific diagnostic category of either parent.

Family environmental influences, such as poor relationships and lack of involvement between parents and offspring, have been shown to be related to early substance use and behavior problems in adolescents (Brook, Whiteman, Nomura, Gordon, & Cohen, 1988). This interpretation was supported by the finding of the present study that specific family environment indicators were found to differ according to the number of parents affected with psychopathology. Future analyses based on this sample will attempt to more clearly characterize the family environment constructs that may act as mediators in the relationship between parent and child psychopathology as a means of establishing an overall model of risk specific to individual psychiatric outcomes as well as to general dysfunction.

IMPLICATIONS FOR FUTURE RESEARCH

Study Designs

Though preliminary, these findings demonstrate the relevance of the high-risk design to studying the etiologic pathways not only to anxiety disorders, but also to other psychiatric and nonpsychiatric disorders. The small number of studies employing this design, particularly the absence of a biological conceptualization of potential risk factors, suggests this as an extremely important future area of research. Such research will be critical to reducing the heterogeneity that underlies the development of the psychiatric disorders as well as to defining more precise phenotypes that may be amenable to etiologic investigation using the powerful tools of genetics and neuroscience. The differential link between family functioning with substance abuse and anxiety disorders suggests two different sets of etiologic factors underlying these disorders. Whereas adverse environmental familial factors are strongly associated with behavior problems among exposed offspring, the aggregate evidence revealing specificity, a dose-response relationship, and low familial dysfunction among the families of probands with anxiety disorders are consistent with underlying biologic vulnerability factors. Differential etiologic mechanisms would also imply distinct treatment and prevention strategies for anxiety and substance use disorders. Finally, the widespread lack of consideration of sex differences in anxiety despite intriguing clues regarding differential thresholds and perhaps risk factors for the development of anxiety disorders in males and females indicates the need for research that systematically examines sex differences in vulnerability, manifestation, causes, and consequences of anxiety disorders.

The results of this paper reveal that a family history of substance abuse is one of the most potent risk factors for the development of substance abuse among exposed offspring. Both specific and nonspecific factors in the family contribute to the increased risk of drug abuse. Future research should seek an understanding of the mechanisms through which the family conveys an increased risk of drug abuse to offspring since a family history of substance abuse is the most potent predictor of vulnerability to its development. Study designs that incorporate the complexity of factors involved in familial transmission including genetic factors, transmitted biologic factors, social and cultural factors, and nontransmitted biologic and social factors are critical to gaining an understanding of these processes. The genetic epidemiologic approach is one of the most powerful to understanding the mechanisms through which families exert their influence on the transmission of drug abuse across generations to incorporate the components of the host vulnerability, factors associated with exposure to drugs, and the contribution of the family, peer neighborhood, and larger cultural environment conducive to its development.

IMPACT OF HUMAN GENOME PROJECT

The Human Genome Project will spawn new understandings of human physiology, and new chemical therapies for diseases, and there undoubtedly will be important spin-off results for psychiatry (Watson, 1990). Advances in genetics and neuroscience will gradually inform classification and assist in identifying sources of heterogeneity at both the genotypic and phenotypic level. Designing research to elucidate these multiple influences will require changes in the (mostly genetic) paradigm that has generated the question itself. New research will incorporate many causal factors, from many disciplines, into longitudinal designs that allow for relatively long latencies of causal effect. The new research will take advantage of developments of DNA and bioassays that facilitate use under field conditions (Steinberg et al., 1997), as well as independent advances in statistical techniques for analysis of genetic linkage and association (Risch & Merikangas, 1996), gene-environment interactions (Khoury, 1997; Khoury, Beaty, & Cohen, 1993; Ottman, 1995), and longitudinal data (Diggle, Liang, & Zeger, 1994). In addition, the identification of susceptibility genes solely on the basis of high-density families will require population studies that examine the extent to which these genetic markers are associated with disease risk in the general population. Likewise, population data will be critical for determining the health policy implications of newly discovered human gene variants.

Interest in social factors as causes of mental disorders has waned as the biologic revolution got underway, culminating recently in the Human Genome Project.
Paradoxically, however, new understandings of animal and human physiology, and
new capabilities in measurement, may reassert the importance of social factors. Recent research in animal populations has shown that changes in basic dimensions of
social structure, such as social stratification (Jones, Stoddart, & Mallick, 1995), or
social integration (Uchino, Capioppo, & Kiecolt-Glaser, 1996) (the dual thrusts of
the second generation of psychiatric epidemiology), produce strong changes in
physiology that are arguably quite close to changes occurring in humans during
episodes of psychopathology. Human examples include interactive influences of
soft neurologic signs and low social class in the development of behavior disorders
(Lunsing, Hadders-Algra, Touwen, & Huisjes, 1991) and the protective effect of behavioral inhibition in the development of conduct disorders (Kagan, 1992). The ca-
pability for understanding the effects of social interaction is greatly potentiated by
the development of statistical approaches that model group-level effects, as well as
individual risk for disorder (Bryk & Raudenbush, 1992).

The lack of replication and inconsistent findings that have plagued psychiatric
genetics suggest a cautious approach to gaining understanding of the role of
genes. The use of family and twin study paradigms to examine the specificity of
transmission of the components of psychiatric disorders, comorbid disorders, and
putative markers is a critical step before attempting to employ linkage analyses.
Large-scale controlled family studies of extended pedigrees of systematically selected probands should also be conducted using phenotypic definitions to clarify
the modes of transmission of migraine. Simulation studies indicate a very large
number of families is necessary to detect Quantitative Trait Loci (QTL) in the
presence of oligogenic inheritance and to replicate linkage claims in order to
avoid false positive findings. The large number of families necessary to detect the
underlying genetic mechanisms in the presence of genetic heterogeneity, gene-
environment interactions, epistasis, or polygenic inheritance would best be obtained through collaborative research with standardized methodology.

Although caution is warranted in the investigation of the etiology of complex
disorders, this does not imply that discovery of the role of genes is a phenomenon
in the distant future. Investigations have established in recent years the strength
of the combined approach of genetic epidemiology and molecular genetics to
gain understanding of the gene-environment interactions involved in the pathogenesis of complex diseases (e.g., Hall et al., 1990). In fact, the magnitude of ethnic–geographic heterogeneity that has been demonstrated for the BRCA gene and
breast cancer underscores the importance of epidemiologic data on the distribution of these polymorphisms in the general population (Szabo & King, 1997). An
integration of population genetics and epidemiology will be critical in determining the attributable risk of particular DNA markers for disease, the environmental conditions that potentiate or suppress expression of genetic vulnerability, and
the implications of biologic and genetic markers for public health.

Once these genes are identified for some of the major psychiatric disorders, genetic markers can be employed to gain understanding of this pathogenesis. Knowledge of trait markers will elucidate the role of environmental factors, reduce the heterogeneity of the clinical phenotypes, inform psychiatric nosology, and permit more specific approaches to prevention and treatment.

IMPLICATIONS FOR PREVENTION

Evidence presented herein strongly supports the critical importance of family-based prevention programs for reducing substance abuse (Kumpfer, Molgaard, & Spoth, 1996). Targeted prevention programs should be geared towards offspring of substance abusers, even those who have not been identified in treatment settings. These findings also have important implications for both primary and secondary prevention efforts. Primary prevention programs should identify those youth at increased risk for the development of substance abuse based not only on their own characteristics but also parental and family risk. More intensive effort may then be devoted to risk reduction among such youth and their families. The risk of substance abuse secondary to psychopathology may also be reduced through treatment of such primary disorders as conduct disorder, anxiety, or depression (Kessler & Price, 1993). The finding of the superiority of Lithium over placebo in reducing symptoms of both depression and alcoholism in a recent randomized clinical trial of adolescents with comorbid bipolar disorder and alcohol abuse or dependence is particularly promising (Geller et al., 1998). In summary, a combination of individual and family treatment in conjunction with broader efforts towards education and primary prevention at the community level are likely to provide the optimal approach to reduce substance abuse.

ACKNOWLEDGMENTS

Research supported in part by grants AA07080, DA05348, MH30929, from Alcohol, Drug Abuse, and Mental Health Administration of the United States Public Health Service, and a Research Scientist Development Award K02-DA 00293.

REFERENCES

Achenbach, T. M. (1985). Assessment of anxiety in children. In A. H. Tuma & J. Maser (Eds.), *Anxiety and the anxiety disorders* (pp. 707–734). Hillsdale, NJ: Lawrence Erlbaum Associates.

Allen, N. B., Lewinsohn, P. M., & Seeley, J. R. (1998). Prenatal and perinatal influences on risk for psychopathology in childhood and adolescence. *Development and Psychopathology, 10*, 513–529.

Allen, M., & Matthews, K. (1997). Hemodynamic responses to laboratory stressors in children and adolescents: The influences of age, race, and gender. *Psychophysiology, 34*, 329–339.

American Psychiatric Association. (1987). *Diagnostic and statistical manual of mental disorders* (3rd ed.). Washington, DC: American Psychiatric Association Press.

Battaglis, M., Bertella, S., Politi, E., Bernardeschi, L., Perna, G., Gabriele, A., & Bellodi, L. (1995). Age at onset of panic disorder: Influence of familial liability to the disease and of childhood separation anxiety disorder. *American Journal of Psychiatry, 152*(9), 1362–1364.

Beidel, D., & Turner, S. (1997). At risk for anxiety: I. Psychopathology in the offspring of anxious parents. *Journal of the American Academy of Child and Adolescent Psychiatry, 36*, 918–924.

Beidel, D. C. (1988). Psychophysiological assessment of anxious emotional states in children. *Journal of Abnormal Psychology, 97*, 80–82.

Biederman, J., Rosenbaum, J. F., Bolduc, E. A., Faraone, S. V., & Hirshfeld, D. R. (1991). A high risk study of young children of parents with panic disorders and agoraphobia with and without comorbid major depression. *Psychiatry Research, 37*, 333–348.

Bierut, L. J., Dinwiddie, S. H., Begleiter, H., Crowe, R. R., Hesselbrock, V., Nurnberger, J. I., Jr., Porjesz, B., Schuckit, M. A., & Reich, T. (1998). Familial transmission of substance dependence: Alcohol, marijuana, cocaine, and habitual smoking: A report from the Collaborative Study on the Genetics of Alcoholism. *Archives of General Psychiatry, 55*, 982–988.

Bohman, M. (1978). Some genetic aspects of alcoholism and criminality: A population of adoptees. *Archives of General Psychiatry, 35*, 269–276.

Brook, J. S., Whiteman, M., Gordon, A. S., & Cohen, P. (1986). Some model mechanisms for explaining the impact of maternal and adolescent characteristics on adolescent stage of drug use. *Developmental Psychology, 22*, 460–467.

Brook, J. S., Whiteman, M., Nomura, C., Gordon, A. S., & Cohen, P. (1988). Personality, family, and ecological influences on adolescent drug use: A developmental analysis. *Journal of Chemical Dependency Treatment, 1*(2), 123–161.

Bryk, A., & Raudenbush, S. (1992). *Hierarchical linear models.* Newbury Park, CA: Sage.

Cadoret, R. J., Yates, W. R., Troughton, E., Woodworth, G., & Stewart, M. A. (1995). Adoption study demonstrating two genetic pathways to drug abuse. *Archives of General Psychiatry, 52*(1), 42–52.

Cadoret, R. J., Yates, W. R., Troughton, E., Woodworth, G., & Stewart, M. A. (1996). An adoption study of drug abuse/dependency in females. *Comprehensive Psychiatry, 37*(2), 88–94.

Capps, L., Sigman, M., Sena, R., & Henker, B. (1996). Fear, anxiety and perceived control in children of agoraphobic parents. *Journal of Child Psychology and Psychiatry and Allied Disciplines, 37*(4), 445–452.

Carter, C. O. (1961). The inheritance of congenital pyloric stenosis. *British Medical Bulletin, 17*, 251–254.

Chambers, W., Puig-Antich, J., Tabrizi, M., & Davies, M. (1985). The assessment of affective disorders in children and adolescents by semi-structured interview: Test-retest reliability of the Schedule for Affective Disorders and Schizophrenia for school age children, present episode version. *Archives of General Psychiatry, 42*, 696–697.

Chassin, L., Pillow, D. R., Curran, P. J., Brooke, S., Molina, G., & Barrera, M. (1993). Relation of parental alcoholism to early adolescent substance use: A test of three mediating mechanisms. *Journal of Abnormal Psychology, 102*(1), 3–19.

Chassin, L., Rogosch, F., & Barrera, M. (1991). Substance use and symptomatology among adolescent children of alcoholics. *Journal of Abnormal Psychology, 100*(4), 449–463.

Clark, D. B., Kirisci, L., & Moss, H. B. (1998). Early adolescent gateway drug use in sons of fathers with substance use disorders. *Addictive Behaviors, 23*, 561–566.

Clark, D. B., Moss, H. B., Kirisci, L., Mezzich, A. C., Miles, R., & Ott, P. (1997). Psychopathology in preadolescent sons of fathers with substance use disorders. *Journal of the American Academy of Child and Adolescent Psychiatry, 36*, 495–502.

Crowe, R. R. (1994). The Iowa linkage study of panic disorder. In E. S. Gershon & C. R. Clinger (Eds.), *Genetic approaches to mental disorders.* Washington, DC: American Psychiatric Press.

Dierker, L. C., Merikangas, K. R., & Szatmari, P. (1999). Influence of parental concordance for psychiatric disorders on psychopathology in offspring. *Journal of the American Academy of Child & Adolescent Psychiatry, 38*(3), 280–288.

Diggle, P. J., Liang, K., & Zeger, S. L. (1994). *Analysis of longitudinal data*. Oxford: Clarendon Press.

Downes, J., Evenden, J., Morris, R., Owen, A., Robbins, T., Roberts, A., & Sahakian, B. (1994). *Cambridge Neurological Test Automated Battery (CANTAB): Instruction manual*. Waterbeach, Cambridge: Paul Fray.

Downey, G., & Coyne, J. C. (1990). Children of depressed parents: An integrative review. *Psychological Bulletin, 108*(1), 50–76.

Earls, F., Reich, W., Kenneth, G., Jung, M. A., & Cloninger, R. (1988). Psychopathology in children of alcoholic and anti-social parents. *Alcoholism: Clinical and Experimental Research, 12*, 481–487.

Endicott, J., & Spitzer, R. L. (1978). A diagnostic interview: The Schedule for Affective Disorders and Schizophrenia—Lifetime version. *Archives of General Psychiatry, 35*, 837–844.

Epstein, N. B., Baldwin, L. M., & Bishop, D. S. (1983). The McMaster Family Assessment Device. *Journal of Marital and Family Therapy, 9*, 171–180.

Erlenmeyer-Kimling, L., Cornblatt, B., & Golden, R. R. (1983). Early indicators of vulnerability to schizophrenia in children at high genetic risk. In S. B. Guze, F. J. Earls, & J. E. Barrett (Eds.), *Childhood psychopathology and development* (pp. 247–264). New York: Raven.

Gabel, S., & Shindledecker, R. (1992). Behavior problems in sons and daughters of substance abusing parents. *Child Psychiatry and Human Development, 23*(2), 99–115.

Galton, F. (1894). *Natural inheritance*. New York: MacMillan.

Gammon, G. D., John, K., Rothblum, E. D., Mullen, K., Tischler, G. L., & Weissman, M. M. (1983). Use of a structured diagnostic interview to identify bipolar disorder in adolescent inpatients: Frequency and manifestations of the disorder. *American Journal of Psychiatry, 140*, 543–547.

Geller, B., Cooper, T., Sun, K., Zimermann, B., Frazier, J., Williams, M., & Heath, J. (1998). Double-blind and placebo-controlled study of lithium for adolescent bipolar disorders with secondary substance dependency. *Journal of the American Academy of Child and Adolescent Psychiatry, 37*(2), 171–178.

Goddard, A. W., Woods, S. C., & Charney, D. S. (1996). A critical review of the role of norepinephrine in panic disorder: Focus on its interaction with serotonin. In H. G. M. Westenberg, J. A. Den Boer, & D. L. Murphy (Eds.), *Advances in the neurobiology of anxiety disorders* (pp. 107–137). New York: Wiley.

Grillon, C., Dierker, L., & Merikangas, K. R. (1998). Fear-potentiated startle in adolescent offspring of parents with anxiety disorders. *Biological Psychiatry, 44*, 990–997.

Grillon, C., Pellowski, M., Merikangas, K. R., & Davis, M. (1997). Darkness facilitates the acoustic startle in humans. *Biological Psychiatry, 42*, 453–460.

Guyer, M. S., & Collins, F. S. (1995). How is the Human Genome Project doing, and what have we learned so far? *Proceedings of the National Academy of Sciences of the United States of America, 92*(24), 10841–10848.

Hall, J. M., Lee, M. K., Morrow, J., Newman, B., Anderson, L., Huey, B., & King, M. C. (1990). Linkage analysis of early onset familial breast cancer to chromosome 17q21. *Science, 259*, 1684–1689.

Hill, S. Y., Steinhauer, S. R., & Zubin, J. (1992). Cardiac responsivity in individuals at high risk for alcoholism. *Journal of Studies on Alcohol, 53*(4), 378–388.

Hwang, S. J., Beaty, T. H., Panny, S. R., Street, N. A., Joseph, J. M., Gordon, S., McIntosh, I., & Francomano, C. A. (1995). Association study of Transforming Growth Factor Alpha (TGFα) TaqI polymorphism and oral clefts: Indication of gene-environment interaction in a population-based sample of infants with birth defects. *American Journal of Epidemiology, 141*(7), 629–636.

Johnson, M. R., & Lydiard, R. B. (1995). The neurobiology of anxiety disorders. *The Psychiatric Clinics of North America, 18*(4), 681–725.

Johnson, S., Leonard, K. E., & Jacob, T. (1989). Drinking, drinking styles and drug use in children of alcoholics, depressives and controls. *Journal of Studies on Alcohol, 50*(5), 427–431.

Jones, I. H., Stoddart, D. M., & Mallick, J. (1995). Towards a sociobiological model of depression: A marsupial model (petaurus breviceps). *British Journal of Psychiatry, 166*, 475–479.

Joynt, R. J. (1990). *Behavioral aspects of neurological disease* (Vol. 2). Philadelphia: Lippincott.

Joynt, R. J., Benton, A. L., & Fogel, M. (1962). Behavioral and pathological correlates of motor impersistence. *Neurology, 12*, 876–881.

Kagan, J. (1992). Behavior, biology, and the meanings of temperamental constructs. *Pediatrics, 90*(3), 510–513.

Kagan, J. (1994). *Galen's prophecy: Temperament in human nature*. New York: Basic Books.

Kagan, J., Reznick, J., Clarke, C., Snidman, N., & Garcia-Coll, C. (1984). Behavioral inhibition to the unfamiliar. *Child Development, 55*, 2212–2225.

Kandel, D. B., & Andrews, K. (1987). Processes of adolescent socialization by parents and peers. *International Journal of the Addictions, 22*(4), 319–42.

Kendell, R. E. (1989). Clinical validity. *Psychological Medicine, 19*, 45–55.

Kendler, K. S., Eaves, L. J., Walters, E. E., Neale, M. C., Heath, A. C., & Kessler, R. C. (1996). The identification and validation of distinct depressive syndromes in a population-based sample of female twins. *Archives of General Psychiatry, 53*(5), 391–399.

Kendler, K., Neale, M., Kessler, R., Heath, A., & Eaves, L. (1992). A population-based twin study of major depression in women: The impact of varying definitions of illness. *Archives of General Psychiatry, 49*, 257–266.

Kendler, K., Neale, M., Kessler, R., Heath, A. C., & Eaves, L. J. (1993a). Panic disorder in women: A population-based twin study. *Psychological Medicine, 23*, 397–406.

Kendler, K. S., Neale, M. C., Kessler, R. C., Heath, A. C., & Eaves, L. J. (1993b). Major depression and phobias: The genetic and environmental sources of comorbidity. *Psychological Medicine, 23*, 361–371.

Kendler, K. S., Walters, E. E., Neale, M. C., Kessler, R. C., Heath, A. C., & Eaves, L. J. (1995). The structure of the genetic and environmental risk factors for six major psychiatric disorders in women. *Archives of General Psychiatry, 52*, 374–383.

Kessler, R. C., & Price, R. (1993). Primary prevention of secondary disorders: A proposal and agenda. *American Journal of Community Psychology, 21*(5), 607–631.

Khoury, M. J. (1997). Genetic epidemiology and the future of disease prevention and public health. *Epidemiologic Reviews, 19*, 175–180.

Khoury, M. J., Beaty, T. H., & Cohen, B. H. (1993). *Fundamentals of Genetic Epidemiology*. New York: Oxford University Press.

Kuller, L. H. (1979). The role of population genetics in the study of the epidemiology of cardiovascular risk factors. In D. C. Rao, R. Elston, L. H. Kuller, M. Feinleib, C. Carter, & R. Havlick (Eds.), *Genetic analysis of common disease: Application to predictive factors in coronary disease* (pp. 489–495). New York: Alan R. Liss.

Kumpfer, K., Molgaard, V., & Spoth, R. (Eds.). (1996). *The strengthening families program for the prevention of delinquency and drug use*. Thousand Oaks, CA: Sage.

Last, C., Hersen, M., Kazdin, A., Orvaschel, H., & Perrin, S. (1991). Anxiety disorders in children and their families. *Archives of General Psychiatry, 48*, 928–934.

Laucht, M., Esser, G., & Schmidt, M. H. (1994). Parental mental disorder and early child development. *European Child and Adolescent Psychiatry, 3*(3), 125–137.

Lipman, E. L., Offord, D. R., & Boyle, M. H. (1993). Follow-up of psychiatric and educational morbidity among adopted children. *Journal of the American Academy of Child and Adolescent Psychiatry, 32*, 1007–1012.

Lunsing, R. J., Hadders-Algra, M., Touwen, B. C., & Huisjes, H. J. (1991). Nocturnal enuresis and minor neurological dysfunction at 12 years: A follow-up study. *Developmental Medicine and Child Neurology, 33*, 439–445.

Maier, W., Buller, R., & Hallmayer, J. (1988). Comorbidity of panic disorder and major depression: Results from a family study. In I. Hand & H. U. Wittchen (Eds.), *Panic and phobias: Treatments and variables affecting course and outcome* (pp. 180–185). Berlin: Springer-Verlag.

Maier, W., & Merikangas, K. R. (1992). *Co- transmission and comorbidity of affective disorders, anxiety disorders and alcoholism in families*. New York: Springer-Verlag.

Martin, C. S., Earleywine, M., Blackson, T. C., Vanyukov, M. M., Moss, H. B., & Tarter, R. E. (1994). Aggressivity, inattention, hyperactivity, and impulsivity in boys at high and low risk for substance abuse. *Journal of Abnormal Child Psychology, 22*(2), 177–203.

Mausner, J. S., & Kramer, S. (1985). *Mausner and Bahn Epidemiology: An introductory text* (2nd ed.). Philadelphia: W. B. Saunders.

McGuffin, P., Asherson, P., Owen, M., & Farmer, A. (1994). The strength of the genetic effect. Is there room for an environmental influence in the etiology of schizophrenia? *British Journal of Psychiatry, 164*(5), 593–599.

Merikangas, K. R. (1990). Co-morbidity for anxiety and depression: Review of family and genetic studies. In J. D. Maser & C. R. Cloninger (Eds.), *Comorbidity of mood and anxiety disorders* (pp. 331–348). Washington, DC: American Psychiatric Press.

Merikangas, K., & Angst, J. (1995). Comorbidity and social phobia: Evidence from clinical, epidemiologic and genetic studies. *European Archives of Psychiatry and Clinical Neuroscience, 244*, 297–303.

Merikangas, K., Dierker, L., Avenevoli, L., & Grillon, D. (1999). Vulnerability factors among children at risk for anxiety disorders. *Biological Psychiatry, 46*, 1523–1535.

Merikangas, K., Dierker, L., & Szatmari, P. (1998a). Psychopathology among offspring of parents with substance abuse and/or anxiety: A high risk study. *Journal of Child Psychology and Psychiatry, 39*(5), 711–720.

Merikangas, K. R., Leckman, J. F., Prusoff, B. A., Pauls, D. L., & Weissman, M. M. (1985). Familial transmission of depression and alcoholism. *Archives of General Psychiatry, 42*, 367–372.

Merikangas, K. R., & Pollock, R. (2000). Anxiety in women. In M. Goldman & M. Hatch (Eds.), *Women and health* (pp. 1010–1023). San Diego: Academic Press.

Merikangas, K. R., Risch, N. J., & Weissman, M. M. (1994). Comorbidity and co-transmission of alcoholism, anxiety, and depression. *Psychological Medicine, 24*, 69–80.

Merikangas, K. R., Stevens, D. E., Fenton, B., O'Malley, S., Woods, S., Stolar, M., & Risch, N. (1998b). Co-morbidity and familial aggregation of alcoholism and anxiety disorders. *Psychological Medicine, 28*, 773–788.

Merikangas, K. R., Stolar, M., Stevens, D. E., Goulet, J., Preisig, M., Fenton, B., O'Malley, S., & Rounsaville, B. J. (1998c). Familial transmission of substance use disorders. *Archives of General Psychiatry, 55*, 973–979.

Morton, N. (1982). *Outline of genetic epidemiology*. Basel, Switzerland: Karger.

Moss, H. B., Majumder, P. P., & Vanyukov, M. (1994). Familial resemblance for psychoactive substance use disorders: Behavioral profile of high-risk boys. *Addictive Behaviors, 19*(2), 199–208.

Moss, H. B., Mezzich, A., Yao, J. K., Gavaler, J., & Martin, C. S. (1995). Aggressivity among sons of substance-abusing fathers: Association with psychiatric disorder in the father and son, paternal personality, pubertal development, and socioeconomic status. *American Journal of Drug and Alcohol Abuse, 21*(2), 195–208.

Nurnberger, J., & Byerley, W. (1995). Molecular genetics of anxiety disorders. *Psychiatric Genetics, 5*, 5–7.

Olson, D. H., Portner, J., & Bell, R. (1985a). *Family Adaptability and Cohesion Evaluation Scales (FACES II)*. St. Paul: University of Minnesota.

Olson, D. H., Portner, J., & Lavee, Y. (1985b). *FACES III. Family Social Science*. St. Paul: University of Minnesota.

Olson, D. H., Sprenkle, D. H., & Russell, C. S. (1979). Circumflex model of marital and family systems. 1: Cohesion and adaptability dimensions, family types and clinical applications. *Family Process, 18*, 3–78.

Orvaschel, H., Thompson, W. D., Belanger, A., Prusoff, B. A., & Kidd, K. K. (1982). Comparison of the family history method to direct interview: Factors affecting the diagnosis of depression. *Journal of Affective Disorders, 4*, 49–59.

Ottman, R. (1995). Gene-environment interaction and public health. *American Journal of Human Genetics, 56*, 821–823.

Park, S. B., Coull, R. H., Young, A. H., Sahakian, B. J., Robbins, T. W., & Cowen, P. J. (1994). Tryptophan depletion in normal volunteers produces selective impairments in learning and memory. *Neuropharmacology, 33*, 575–588.

Parker, G., Tupling, H., & Brown, L. B. (1979). A parental bonding instrument. *British Journal of Medical Psychology, 52*, 1–10.

Pickens, R., Svikis, D., McGue, M., Lykken, D., Heston, L., & Clayton, P. (1991). Heterogeneity in the inheritance of alcoholism: A study of male and female twins. *Archives of General Psychology, 48*, 19–28.

Reich, W., Earls, F., Frankel, O., & Shayka, J. J. (1993). Psychopathology in children of alcoholics. *Journal of the American Academy of Child and Adolescent Psychiatry, 32*(5), 955–1002.

Reichler, R. J., Sylvester, C. E., & Hyde, T. S. (1988). Biological studies on offspring of panic disorder probands. In David L. Dunner, E. S. Gershon, & J. E. Barrett (Eds.), *Relatives at risk for mental disorder*. New York: Raven Press.

Reinherz, H. Z., Giaconia, R. M., Pakiz, B., Silverman, A. B., Frost, A. K., & Lefkowitz, E. S. (1993). Psychosocial risks for major depression in late adolescence: A longitudinal community study. *Journal of the American Academy of Child and Adolescent Psychiatry, 32*, 1155–1163.

Risch, N. (1990). Linkage strategies for genetically complex traits. I. Multilocus models. *American Journal of Human Genetics, 46*, 222–228.

Risch, N., & Merikangas, K. (1996). The future of genetic studies of complex human diseases. *Science, 273*, 1516–1517.

Robins, L. (1992). The future of psychiatric epidemiology. *International Journal of Methods in Psychiatric Research, 2*, 1–3.

Robins, L. N. (1980). The natural history of drug abuse. *Acta Psychiatrica Scandinavica, 62*(Suppl. 284), 7–20.

Rosenbaum, J., Biederman, J., & Gersten, M. (1988). Behavioral inhibition in children of parents with panic disorder and agoraphobia: A controlled study. *Archives of General Psychiatry, 45*, 463–470.

Rubio-Stipec, M., Bird, H., Canino, G., Bravo, M., & Alegria, M. (1991). Children of alcoholic parents in the community. *Journal of Studies on Alcohol, 52*, 78–87.

Rutter, M. (1986). *The developmental psychopathology of depression: Issues and perspectives*. New York: Guilford Press.

Sadovnick, A. D., Dyment, D., & Ebers, G. C. (1997). Genetic epidemiology of multiple sclerosis. *Epidemiologic Reviews, 19*, 99–106.

Schmidt, S. M., Zoega, T., & Crowe, R. R. (1993). Excluding linkage between panic disorder and the gamma-aminobutyric acid beta I reactor locus in five Icelandic pedigrees. *Acta Psychiatrica Scandinavica, 88*, 225–228.

Sher, K. J., Walizter, K. S., Wood, P. K., & Brent, E. E. (1991). Characteristics of children of alcoholics: Putative risk factors, substance use and abuse, and psychopathology. *Journal of Abnormal Psychology, 100*(4), 427–448.

Skre, I., Onstad, S., Torgersen, S., Lygren, S., & Kringlen, E. (1993). A twin study of DSM-III-R anxiety disorders. *Acta Psychiatrica Scandinavica, 88*, 85–92.

Stavrakaki, C., & Vargo, B. (1986). The relationship of anxiety and depression: A review of literature. *British Journal of Psychiatry, 149*, 7–16.

Steinberg, K. K., Sanderlin, K. C., Ou, C. Y., Hannon, W. H., McQuillan, G. M., & Sampson, E. J. (1997). DNA Banking in Epidemiologic studies. *Epidemiologic Reviews, 19*(1), 156–162.

Sylvester, C., Hyde, T., & Reichler, R. (1988). Clinical psychopathology among children of adults with panic disorder. In D. Dunner, E. Gershon, & J. Barrett (Eds.), *Relatives at risk for mental disorder* (pp. 87–102). New York: Raven Press.

Sylvester, C. E., Hyde, T. S., & Reichler, R. J. (1987). Clinical psychopathology among children of adults with panic disorder. *Journal of the American Academy of Child and Adolescent Psychiatry, 26*, 668–675.

Szabo, C. I., & King, M. C. (1997). Population genetics of BRCA1 and BRCA2. *American Journal of Human Genetics, 60*(5), 1013–1020.

Taylor, E. A., Sandberg, S. J., Thorley, G., & Gilles, S. (1991). *The epidemiology of childhood hyperactivity*. New York: Oxford University Press.

Tienari, P., Wynne, L. C., Moring, J., Lahti, I., Naarala, M., Sorri, A., Wahlberg, K. E., Saarento, O., Seitamaa, M., & Kaleva, M. (1994). The Finish adoptive family study of schizophrenia: Implications for family research. *British Journal of Psychiatry, 23*, 20–26.

Tsuang, M. T., Lyons, M. J., Eisen, S. A., Goldberg, J., True, W., Nong, L., Meyer, J. M., & Eaves, L. (1996). Genetic influences on abuse of illicit drugs: A study of 3372 twin pairs. *American Journal of Medical Genetics (Neuropsychiatric Genetics), 5*, 473–477.

Tsuang, M. T., Lyons, M. J., Meyer, J. M., Doyle, T., Eisen, S. A., Goldberg, J., True, W., Lin, N., Toomey, R., & Eaves, L. (1998). Co-occurrence of abuse of different drugs in men: The role of drug-specifics of General Psychiatry. *Archives of General Psychiatry, 55*(11), 967–972.

Turner, S. M., Beidel, D. C., & Costello, A. (1987). Psychopathology in the offspring of anxiety disorder patients. *Journal of Consulting and Clinical Psychology, 55*(2), 229–235.

Uchino, B. N., Capioppo, J. T., & Kiecolt-Glaser, J. K. (1996). The relationship between social support and physiological processes: A review with emphasis on underlying mechanisms and implications for health. *Psychological Bulletin, 119*(3), 488–531.

Unnewehr, S., Schneider, S., Florin, I., & Margraf, J. (1998). Psychopathology in children of patients with panic disorder or animal phobia. *Psychopathology, 31*, 69–84.

Wang, Z. W., Crowe, R. R., & Noyes, R. J. (1992). Adrenergic receptor genes as candidate genes for panic disorder: A linkage study. *American Journal of Psychiatry, 149*, 470–474.

Warner, L., Kessler, R., Hughes, M., Anthony, J., & Nelson, C. (1995). Prevalence and correlates of drug use and dependence in the United States. *Archives of General Psychiatry, 52*, 219–29.

Warner, V., Mufson, L., & Weissman, M. (1995). Offspring at high risk for depression and anxiety: Mechanisms of psychiatric disorder. *Journal of the American Academy of Child and Adolescent Psychiatry, 34*(6), 786–797.

Watson, J. D. (1990). The human genome project: Past, present, and future. *Science, 248*(6), 44–49.

Weissman, M. M. (1993). Family genetic studies of panic disorder. *Journal of Psychiatric Research, 27*, 69–78.

West, M. O., & Prinz, R. J. (1987). Parental alcoholism and childhood psychopathology. *Psychological Bulletin, 102*(2), 204–218.

Wilens, T., Biederman, J., Kiely, K., Bredin, E., & Spencer, T. (1994). Pilot study of behavioral and emotional disturbances in the high-risk children of parents with opioid dependence. *Journal of the American Academy of Child and Adolescent Psychiatry, 34*(6), 779–785.

Woodman, C., & Crowe, R. (1996). The genetics of the anxiety disorders. *Bailliere's Clinical Psychiatry, 2*(1), 47–57.

Author Index

Subject Index